LIFE UNDER THE BAOBAB TREE

TRANSDISCIPLINARY THEOLOGICAL COLLOQUIA

Theology has hovered for two millennia between scriptural metaphor and philosophical thinking; it takes flesh in its symbolic, communal, and ethical practices. With the gift of this history and in the spirit of its unrealized potential, the Transdisciplinary Theological Colloquia intensify movement between and beyond the fields of religion. A multivocal discourse of theology takes place in the interstices, at once self-deconstructive in its pluralism and constructive in its affirmations.

Hosted annually by Drew University's Theological School, the colloquia provide a matrix for such conversations, while Fordham University Press serves as the midwife for their publication. Committed to the slow transformation of religio-cultural symbolism, the colloquia continue Drew's long history of engaging historical, biblical, and philosophical hermeneutics, practices of social justice, and experiments in theopoetics.

Catherine Keller, *Director*

LIFE UNDER THE BAOBAB TREE

Africana Studies and Religion in a Transitional Age

KENNETH N. NGWA,
ALIOU CISSÉ NIANG, AND
ARTHUR PRESSLEY, EDITORS

FORDHAM UNIVERSITY PRESS ❦ NEW YORK ❦ 2023

Copyright © 2023 Fordham University Press

All rights reserved. No part of this publication may be reproduced, stored in a retrieval system, or transmitted in any form or by any means—electronic, mechanical, photocopy, recording, or any other—except for brief quotations in printed reviews, without the prior permission of the publisher.

Fordham University Press has no responsibility for the persistence or accuracy of URLs for external or third-party Internet websites referred to in this publication and does not guarantee that any content on such websites is, or will remain, accurate or appropriate.

Fordham University Press also publishes its books in a variety of electronic formats. Some content that appears in print may not be available in electronic books.

Visit us online at www.fordhampress.com.

Library of Congress Cataloging-in-Publication Data available online at https://catalog.loc.gov.

Printed in the United States of America
25 24 23   5 4 3 2 1
First edition

CONTENTS

Introduction. Life Under the Baobab Tree:
            Africana Studies and Religion in a Transitional Age |
            Kenneth N. Ngwa, Aliou Cissé Niang, and Arthur Pressley   1

  PART I: UN/FOLDING IDENTITIES
            Archangel Gabriel Speaks to Mary |
            Pamela Mordecai   23
  1. Nella Larsen's *Quicksand*: Mourning through
     Biracial Identities | Arthur Pressley   29
  2. Body as Praxis: Disarticulating the Human
     from Ownership and Property | An Yountae   57
  3. What It's Like to Be a Blackened Body, and
     Why It's Like That: A Preliminary Exploration |
     Desmond Coleman   75
  4. The Rhizome and/as the Tree of Life:
     The Relational Poetics of Wisdom and
     Decolonizing Biblical Studies | A. Paige Rawson   92
  5. Senghorian Négritude and Postcolonial Biblical
     Criticism | Aliou Cissé Niang   126

PART II: AFRICANA ACTIVISM

Litany on the Line |
Pamela Mordecai — 171

6. God Killed! God Interrupted, Long Live the People!: Political Theory in Religious Act | Nimi Wariboko — 173

7. "Doing the Will of God" as Loving God Whose Way Is Peace | Aliou Cissé Niang — 195

8. Mysticism and Mothering in Black Women's Social Justice Activism: Brazil/USA | Rachel Elizabeth Harding — 223

9. A Theopoetics of Exodus and the Africana Spirit in Music | Sharon Kimberly Williams — 235

10. Must We Burn Isaac?: A Four-Part Hermeneutical Fantasy for Africana Epistemology | Minenhle Nomalungelo Khumalo — 250

PART III: AFRICANA HISTORIOGRAPHIES AND MEMORIES

Temitope Temitope |
Pamela Mordecai — 273

11. From White Man's Magic to Black Folks' Wisdom | Althea Spencer Miller — 275

12. Solidarity by Sharing Power: An Inculturated Organic Storytelling of Jonah and Mami Wata | 'Shola D. Adegbite — 307

13. Envisioning Africana Religions: Seeking a Distinctive Voice for the Study of Religions in Africa and the African Diaspora | Salim Faraji — 328

14. Interpreting from the Back/Black-Side: Exodus through the Shawl of Memory | Kenneth N. Ngwa — 355

15. Conjuring Lost Books: (Re-)membering
    Fragmented Litanies at the Intersection
    of Africana and Biblical Studies |
    (The Rev. Canon) Hugh R. Page Jr.   400

Afterword. *Catherine Keller*   409

List of Contributors   413
Index of Modern Authors   419
Index of Ancient Documents   427

LIFE UNDER THE BAOBAB TREE

❧ Introduction: Life Under the Baobab Tree: Africana Studies and Religion in a Transitional Age

KENNETH N. NGWA, ALIOU CISSÉ NIANG, AND ARTHUR PRESSLEY

Life Under the Baobab Tree: Africana Studies and Religion in a Transitional Age is a twenty-first century conversation of and by diaspora voices. These voices are in conversations about the meanings of our variegated experiences emerging from traditions that are complex and prophetic, religious and intellectual, artistic and revolutionary. These voices arise from specific contexts that ask questions about health care disparities, gender violence, and prison systems that reintroduce new forms of slavery. Some of these problems have continued since the middle passage, and the colonial exploitation of Africa. Some of the problems are shaped by current conditions such as gentrification and the resulting new migrations that reinscribe historical feelings of erasure, invisibility, and lack of community. These variegated voices seek new strategies and hermeneutics that are reflected in the dialectics of afropesssimism and afrofuturism. These voices/conversations on the nature of Blackness, Caribbeanness, gender identity, and other Afro-cultural traditions, examine the processes of becoming, meaning making, identity formation, significations, and political movements in the face of historic and psychological erasures.

The intellectual substance and structure of these conversations is—in important ways—quintessentially "Africana" in its centering of multiplicity: methodological, theoretical, epistemological, and hermeneutical complexity that assumes nonlinear and dialectic approaches to developing liberating epistemologies. This volume emerged from papers presented at the 2017 annual Transdisciplinary Theological Colloquium (TTC) at Drew Theological School. The TTC is "committed to the long-range transformation of religio-cultural symbolism," and the books in its series engage "historical, biblical and cultural hermeneutics, current philosophy, practices of social justice and experiments in theopoetics."[1] The chapters in this volume reflect the central commitments of the TTC.

Several important events have visited the world since 2017: especially a global health pandemic (COVID-19) and its exacerbation of racial and health inequities; the multiracial uprising in the wake of the killing of George Floyd; and an insurrection in the United States. Africana scholars of religion have continued to labor to put forth credible and compelling analyses of these events for the purposes of engendering and enhancing justice and liberation for humankind and the ecosystems we all share.[2]

This book can be understood as an interlocutor—an articulation of Africana experiences and responses to material realities of the world of Africana/Black subjects; and creative enunciations of the theological and political imaginaries that infuse Africana lives with purpose and meaning and productivity. This "conversation" is the essence of what Gilroy considers a critical dynamic of Blackness/Africana thought that assumes that what is most essential is the gathering of diasporic voices whose body, subjectivity, and identity must always be created in the midst of psychological, political, and social struggle. This struggle, which includes questions of the nature of identity formation and community across time and space, necessarily involves some discussion of what Paul Zeleza has identified as constituent pieces to diaspora scholarship: "the continuous processes by which a diaspora is made, unmade and remade, the changing conditions in which it lives and expresses itself, the places where it is moulded and imagined, and the contentious ways in which it is studied and discussed."[3]

The use of the word "religion" in this volume, as a loanword from antiquity, is heuristic and captures much of its intended meaning in Cicero's *Natura deorum* 1.1, 2.71–72. As a construct deployed by colonial Christian missionary supersessionism, the locution "religion" would have been foreign to precolonial sub-Saharan people of African descent who practiced African spirituality. They would not have named their corporate lived experiences of the divine as "religion" but Lived Experiential Spirituality; thus, they signal that "religion" is intimately connected to social realities of communal health, economics, culture, politics, environment, violence, and war, and so on. For most Diola of Senegal, West Africa, this phenomenon is called *Butin bat' èmit*, "divine path,"[4] a locution that enshrines or conceptualizes ontological experience as in "What We Do" collectively that permeates all dimensions of life—a symbiotic divine-nature relationship. As Jacob Olupona has argued, this integrated understanding and study of religion has been rigorously engaged by scholars interested in African and African Diaspora engagement with racism, colonialism, and African cosmologies.[5] Such work continues around issues of methodology as well as hermeneutics around precolonial "religious" traditions, encounters between African religions and Christianity and Islam, and with the modern world. Such work continues to unfold with individual scholars as well as within Pan-African organizations such as the African Association for the Study of Religion (AASR); and it continues in the work of African Diaspora religions, including the works of Tracey Hucks and Yvonne Chireau, among others.[6]

Within this discussion, form and content of scholarship intersect in transdisciplinary and hopefully transformative ways. Poems by Pamela Mordecai frame the three sections of this manuscript. Yet those three poems also function as windows (pathways) into unlocking and extending the variegated dimensions of Africana studies. Echoing liberative Hebrew poems and Second Testament angelic visitations, they enshrine resilient hopes and reimage life beyond crushing lived experiences of peoples of African descent—the distasteful and inhumane forms of dehumanization—slavery, colonization, gender objectification, and racism. Tenacious as the Baobab tree, they deploy daring voices of violent and nonviolent resistance to all forms of oppression, and proclaim a promissory phoenix-like resurrection to conscientize and incubate lasting freedoms. Readers with an eye for detail may perceive the genius in the poems of Mordecai and the essays that frame and spearhead a defiant voice beyond the so-called "Door of No Return" to a creative *return* inspired by *living memory*—memory that is also generative.

This compendium has many parents, not just as a matter of course, but with a predisposition toward community and the largess of generative generosity. In other words, the compendium is intentionally structured and entrenched in the notion that Black lives are legion—and what Michelle Wright in her groundbreaking book, *Physics of Blackness: Beyond the Middle Passage Epistemology*,[7] argues —that the time, place, and gender of Blackness matter. This conversation is critical since the focus on any one context, or time and place, tends to re-create existing hegemonic structures and ideology. Consequently, this compendium sought to be as global as possible and attempted to lean on the four Pan-African conferences,[8] the Harlem Renaissance,[9] and conferences held with a view to unify African independent states and relate to diasporic communities in the Americas.[10] In and through those gatherings and movements, Black subjects gradually moved forward against the odds—pushing back on multifarious colonial, neocolonial, imperial, geopolitical discourses that objectified us as less than human beings and perpetually moved us to liminal spaces. These antecedent strivings foreground this volume and bind all the essays therein; they provide the interpretive framework for the core concerns in this volume; and they provide the conceptual rationale for our deployment of the towering and complex image of *the Baobab Tree* as its working metaphor.

Why the Baobab Tree? Nicknamed the upside-down tree, the Baobab Tree represents sturdiness and variation. First, it is a tree naturally endowed with the capacity to thrive in wilderness spaces. Second, its foliage manifests the living rhythm of dry and rainy seasons. Its roots conquer the toughest, rockiest, and most arid soils one can imagine. This makes the Baobab Tree a suitable image that in many ways manifests the complex lived experience of the peoples of African descent. As such, the metaphor resists reductionist, essentialist, and assured conclusions on the nature of diasporic lived experiences. In a world in profound transition in which identity is in constant construction, resisting othering, adjusting to resurging nationalism, *Life Under the Baobab Tree* offers an alternative way of making sense of these times by anchoring, affirming, contextualizing, and recontextualizing Africanness either at home (continental Africa) or home away from home (diaspora) to deliberate on what it means to be persons of African descent. Speaking from lived experiences away and still connected to their roots in many ways, each contributor—as a living Baobab worthy of that name, reflects their resilience to weather seasonal diasporic and diasporizing storms.

When this Africana Conference was being formed, it was instructive that the image that united scholar/practitioners was that of a tree. Trees are wonderful since in form, size, and structure, they are always similar and different. For example, the palm tree represents multipurpose existence: the stem is resourced for palm wine, the red palm nuts produce oil and kernels (for snack or for oil/lotion), the nut shells are used for fire fuel, the branches are used for making brooms and storage huts. Beyond their nutritional, social, and cosmetic utility, palm trees are wonderful because of the relational poetics of their spatial form: They simultaneously grow in three dimensions— downward, as they are rooted and grounded; outward, as they become wider and expansive; and upward, as they become taller and "transcendent." Thus, even differently, trees of different sizes, shapes, and species all represent vivid illustrations of the simultaneity of geospatial and communal dimensions of life: They interact with, and contribute to, the production, quality, and security of the ground, water, and air. The poetics of trees is relationality of simultaneous multiplicity; in musical terms (applicable to literary and Africana postcolonial theory), they represent simultaneous polyphony, intersubjectivity, and creativity. As their roots navigate the subterranean world (interacting with and drawing from the wells of watery memory), trees also prevent surface erosion of the ground, and their leaves contribute to the regulation and production of quality air/wind. In desert spaces, trees are the potent visual and material signs of life—of harmonious interaction of water, land, and air. In tropical regions, trees offer cooling shade and help to slow down rushing winds; that is, they regulate the ecosystem. No wonder large trees attract human attention and social gathering. They represent the poetics of transdisciplinarity as communal. The image of the poetics and tree-ness of Africana and Blackness is reflected in this text as it was in our conference. Those at the conference included poets, musicians, and drummers, along with biblical, theological, and ethics scholars, with social scientists and historians from a range of social and political contexts, all with the aim of acknowledging and repairing the rupture that has taken place with diasporic people. The repair is no longer searching for a place—a return to our place—but we have concluded that our new home is in the conversation, in these compendiums. This compendium is now a form of Baobab Tree that has multiple functions.

In her captivating book, *A Map to the Door of No Return*, Dionne Brand remembers, as a thirteen-year-old, trying to help her grandfather remember "what people we came from." They worked through a few possible African ethnic names, but settled on none. That unresolved search and conversation, on this side of the Atlantic, opened a small space in Brand and, over time, came to "reveal a tear in the world." We quote Brand:

> I would have proceeded happily with a simple name. I may have played with it for a few days and then stored it away. Forgotten. But

the rupture this exchange with my grandfather revealed was greater than the need for familial bonds. It was a rupture in history, a rupture in the quality of being. It was also a physical rupture, a rupture of geography.[11]

More than physical spaces across several countries along the coast of the Atlantic Ocean, the doors of no return have become a powerful symbol of ruptured identity in African Diasporic studies—not just for those who were forcefully removed from their homes and placed on slave ships, but also for those who remained—for whom the doors they never physically entered nevertheless represent a gateway to unclaimed and unclaimable loss of familial kin and community, captured and taken. Identity is forever fractured. And the fracturing is coded in bodies and stories—official and unofficial—but also in the structures that hold the doors. And its institutional embodiment in the constructed slave castle's architecture performs the story of fracture and its layers of nightmare premised on political, religious, and racial patronage: the governor's residence at the very top, a chapel at the middle level, and dungeons at the bottom, all designed to compel the captured mind and body to bend and even break (cf. Exod. 6:9).

As an "upside-down" tree, the Baobab is also a metaphor for non-unilinear thinking and belonging. That is how this compendium also draws on the legacy of Pan-Africanism, Blackness, Négritude, neo-Négritude, and the intellectual and political traditions and movements galvanizing global Africana work. In and around the Baobab, the questions of diaspora and return are present, immanent, and urgent. As depicted, for example, in the epic of Sundiata of Old Mali, the Baobab immediately conjures diaspora-home discourse: Can the diasporic subject make a return? Should it attempt to make a return? What does return look like? Does the "home" space and subject have the intellectual, cultural, political, and religious resources to receive and host the returning self and subject? The multidimensionality of the Baobab becomes both a planetary metaphor and a communal metaphor for precisely those sorts of questions. These questions about home, the space for community, identity, and subjectivity, are developed in some depth in the chapter by Arthur Pressley, who examines a novel by Nella Larsen, a "biracial" (read African American Woman) searching for home, identity, repair of personal and family ruptures, who does so in part by criticizing how various Black communities have attempted to find home and identity.

The movement of humans, animals, and plants within and beyond the continent has a long history, as has been been theorized in relation to the economic realities and systems that have developed in and beyond the continent for thousands of years.[12] Thus, in the edited volume, *African Migrations: Patterns and Perspectives*, authors examine modern realities and theories about African migrants, moving beyond the push-pull economic theories to include psychosocial, cultural, and political factors; identify and assess intra- and inter-regional migrations; examine gender dynamics of postcolonial African migrations, and so on.[13] The rhythmic character of migration—especially when explored in relation to the rhythms of seasonal changes and the geography of land itself—also provides an entry point into the generative and contested character of migration. African migration has thus been studied and theorized around a musical perspective—how music occupies a position of pride in African diaspora imaginary, but also attends to the contestations that define local and global audiences, gender categorizing, culture, and politics.[14]

The rhythmic—and musical—character of migration is vividly embodied in the sounds of flowing water, especially as it navigates uneven terrain and rocks. The creation story in Genesis puts the reader in the face of water, with the priestly writer's transformation of that watery space into a rhythmic narrative around day and night. The creating deity is hovering over the face of the water, as if to signal that water itself is the space of reflection about beginnings, but also the subject of beginnings. In fact, in the second creation story, the water becomes four heads—four beginnings. This requires not just thinking about water but also thinking with water and its ability to engender multiple genealogies—genealogies that escape ethnonationalism.

In the opening chapters of Zora Neale Hurston's *Moses, Man of the Mountain*, the oppressed Hebrews struggle to survive the standing law authorizing the killing of sons at birth. The Hebrews rely on the compassion of midwives but also learn (?) how not to cry out loud at childbirth ("Ah, it is awful when a woman cannot even cry out in childbirth"),[15] a recurring act that also transitions into a secretive lifestyle of debating and hiding from the menacing threats of a governing structure bent on erasing Hebrew life. During one of these moments of debate between the Hebrews and Pharaoh, Hurston theorizes on memory, citizenship, creativity, and unrelenting demands for freedom to be and create new homes:

> "Give us a chance, Great Pharaoh. We proved ourselves builders and generally constructive under the last regime. We love Egypt. It is the only home we know. Trust us and see if we are good citizens or not."
>
> "Why should I trust people without monuments and memories? It looks bad to me—a people who honor nobody. It is a sign that you forget your benefactors as soon as possible after the need is past."
>
> "We don't build monuments, but we do have memories."
>
> "How is anyone to know that? Take for instance your great man Joseph. As long as you have been in Egypt you have not raised one stone to his memory."
>
> "Look at it another way. Perhaps we do not need stones to remind us. It could be that some folks need stones to remind them. It could be that memorial stones are signs of bad memories. We just don't trust our memories to stones."
>
> Pharaoh's face darkened at this. He laughed in a harsh way.[16]

For Africana, the crisis of the diaspora-home struggle is the crisis of a world/space where home becomes somehow uninhabitable because its resources are extracted to feed an insatiable beast of violent global landscaping. The cosmology of travel and its multidirectional character not only affords a fuller understanding of human experience but also provides a useful cognitive map for hermeneutics. That is, "global" mapping is not just the aggregate of different forms of travel and their associated phenomena; nor is it simply an aggregate of disparate places and stories. Rather, this global mapping from the back/black-side is the phenomenon of study and analysis that gathers around broken spaces, broken bodies, and broken stories. It is hermeneutics that examines the "trans" of transatlantic and trans-Sahara as a form of narrative and spatial lacunae, not narrative and spatial transition. Here, return is possible as a form of hindsight hermeneutic, a form of self-positioning that ensures and explains survival but also propels accountable inquiry.

In Black Diasporic texts, transatlantic travel prioritizes (for good reasons and for bad) east-west movement, and immediately associates that movement with the quest for something superior. It fits into eighteenth- and nineteenth-century European celebration of exploration as heroic acts of self-affirmation and the discovery/conquest of the "unknown" world. Because travel, by definition, dislocates, a certain form of narrative "beginning" and chronicling is unavoidable—that is, if history is understood as something that happens when things move. And then to also assume, almost in the spirit of Newtonian laws of thermodynamics, that things will remain in their state of rest or uniform motion unless something else causes them to act otherwise. But there is also another form of history, experienced and defined not by change and movement, but by stagnation; it is a history of permanence, and for those who are marginalized, that is a history of unchanging reality; it is a history that does not go away, and that is best understood by the metaphor of depth than horizon, a history best accessed and challenged through excavation rather than exploration. Only upon such returns and only in the wake of such engagements with returns do the narratives in the backside of history and their political force begin to participate in the transformation of erasure into life-forms.

In the colonial travel model, with each European passing—which partially and temporally eclipsed Africa and Africans, and left them watching and seeing mostly from the backsides—Africa was not only blackened, but blackness was deployed as an ideological and embodied subsidy for preserving the exclusivity of the white face, the extraterritorial face, that could not be encountered face-to-face without leaving a trail of death. Because colonial passing included intentional eclipsing of the African body and space, postcolonial preservation of Africa also manifests itself as a form of resistance to linear chronicling in which Africa is not in front; it is a probing and exploration of Africana that did not simply pass into the oblivion of an unknown future. For the Africana hermeneut, colonized and diaspora Africa was both restrained and displaced: It saw something pass in front of it, and it experienced something that displaced it. Having survived both violent episodes, it could deploy memory—of its preexistent self and its surviving self—to forge new futures.

In his writing on history and memory, the French historian Pierre Nora speaks of *les lieux de memoire* (sites of memory), *les milieux de memoire* (environments of memory) in relation to history. For Nora, part of modern Western understandings and studies of history and memory have included reflections on methodologies of the study of the history of memory and even the history of history. This ability to "step back," organize, and structure the memory of a highly forgetful community has contributed to a deep fracture between memory and history. Thus, Nora argues that "the remnants of experience [that] still lived in the warmth of tradition, the silence of custom, in the repetition of the ancestral, have been displaced under the pressure of a fundamentally historical sensibility. . . . We speak so much of memory because there is so little of it left."[17] A form of doing history mounts an assault on memory: "On the one hand," writes Nora, "we find an integrated dictatorial memory—unself-conscious, commanding, all-powerful, spontaneously actualizing, a memory without a past that ceaselessly reinvents tradition, linking the history of its ancestors to the undifferentiated time of heroes, origins, and myth—and on the other hand, our memory, nothing more in fact than sifted and sorted historical facts."[18] With the introduction of a trace or separation, the community on the other side of that trace is no longer in the realm of actual memory but rather in the realm of history. History and memory perform different functions. Memory creates a bond with that which appears eternal, perpetual; history severs that bond; memory links the act of remembering to the sacred; history releases that sacredness and introduces criticism and analyses. In the end, "history is perpetually suspicious of memory, and its true mission is to suppress and destroy it."[19]

Set in his analyses of the political crisis in France in the 1930s—a crisis moment that, for Aimé Césaire, Leon Damas, and Léopold Senghor, led to the creation of Négritude—Nora argued that history, which had become a tradition of memory, was transformed into a self-knowledge of society, and thus was able to highlight "many kinds of memory" and even transform itself into "a laboratory of past mentalities." Nora situates his *lieux de memoire* at the intersection of historiographical work, a kind of "self-reflexive turning of history upon itself," and proper historical movement, which constitutes the end of a tradition of memory. These moments of crisis and ensuing movements cause people to go both to the library and museum and dictionary, as well as to commemoration ceremonies and ritual activities and celebrations.[20]

Remembering has a political and social function, particularly for marginalized communities:

> The defense, by certain minorities, of a privileged memory that has retreated to jealously protected enclaves . . . illuminates the truth of

lieux de memoires—that without commemorative vigilance, history would soon sweep them away. We buttress our identities upon such bastions but if what they defended were not threatened, there would be no need to build them. Conversely, if the memories that they enclosed were to be set free they would be useless; if history did not besiege memory, deforming and transforming it, penetrating and petrifying it, there would be no *lieux de memoire*. Indeed, it is this very push and pull that produces *lieux de memoire*—moments of history torn away from the movement of history, then returned; no longer quite life, not yet death, like shells on the shore when the sea of living memory has receded.[21]

Whether Nora's reference to "certain minorities" includes the founders of the Négritude movement in Paris in the early 1930s is unclear. But what it highlights is the ethical and political functions and forms of memory studies over time and space, and the deployment of memory for the purpose of survival of colonial erasure and diasporic alienation, the double impetus for the creation of Négritude.

At the intersection of race and gender, bell hooks's stimulating book *Yearning: Race, Gender and Cultural Politics* speaks of language as a place of struggle. Because struggle takes place in space and location, bell hooks remembers the recurring phrase in the Freedom Charter for the struggle against apartheid in South Africa: "Our struggle is also a struggle of memory against forgetting." This statement, bell hooks argues, is "a politicization of memory that distinguishes nostalgia, that longing for something to be as once it was, a kind of useless act, from that remembering that serves to illuminate and transform the present."[22] This is memory work of spatial construction, one that continuously navigates the institutional and cultural barriers that threaten to alienate or even destroy what is considered unfamiliar, strange. The pressures that accompany the act of moving from one place to another often compel people to indulge in loneliness or nihilism and despair. But to survive these tight spaces requires the ability to "invent spaces of radical openness" because "our living depends on our ability to conceptualize alternatives, often improvised." For bell hooks, "this radical space of openness is a margin—a profound edge. Locating oneself there is difficult yet necessary. It is not a 'safe' place. One is always at risk. One needs a community of resistance."[23] Marginality—the space and lived experience that create oppositional thinking for the oppressed and marginalized—is not something that one wants to abandon for the center, or when one gets to the center. Instead, marginality functions as the impetus for continuing radical openness. Marginality is the space and the process of returning to the place of deprivation or commodification created and legislatively enshrined by the center. Yet, ironically, the move to the center does not result in a desire to abandon or flee marginality; instead, marginality is "a site one stays in, clings to even, because it nourishes one's capacity to resist. It offers to one the possibility of radical perspective from which to see and create, to imagine alternatives, new worlds."[24]

Yes, it is possible to have conversations across the material and proverbial door of no return. This compendium, and the essays therein, are an attempt to forge just such conversations. It is structured in three parts.

Part I, "Un/Folding Identities," consists of five chapters. In chapter 1, Arthur Pressley examines Nella Larsen's novel *Quicksand* and her use of the trope of mulatto. A critical feature of this biomythography is how the trope of a mulatto is used to suggest new possibilities for Black subjectivity. This chapter illustrates how the figure of a mulatto demonstrates how creoleness, colorism, and Pan-Africanism are crucial in the healing of colonial oppression and creating complex identities. In Nella Larsen's protagonist, Helga Craine, she foreshadows and extends the racial dynamics analyzed by Frantz Fanon's *Black Skin, White Masks*. Larsen reveals that mulattos do not merely live between Black and white worlds, but express the racial melancholia later examined by theorists such as Paul Gilroy and Anne Cheng. This racial melancholia, a dread of self and others, a fear of both loss and gain, a denial of life, death, and resurrection, continues to direct intraracial and interracial dynamics that never entirely become (post) colonial. Last, the subjectivity of the mulatto always challenges and destabilizes traditional Africana tropes of home, mother/daughter, middle passage, and racial identity in a manner that makes each of these more of an ethical, rather than psychological, social, or political commitment. Although Nella Larsen's book moves through several times and places, Africana hermeneutics used in this study would suggest that a more compelling understanding of this work assumes that sequencing and linear understanding of the text hides the richness of the work. This article approaches the multiple events and places of the novel as representing the creoleness of all racial, ethnic, and gender identities.

In chapter 2, "Body as Praxis: Disarticulating the Human from Ownership and Property," An Yountae argues that Western intellectual and religious history, and consequently that of European humanity, is developed on the negation of the full humanity of non-Europeans. An's thesis is that posthuman scholarship, as well as that of J. Butler and F. Fanon, does not go far enough to emphasize the importance of the body in rethinking the human. This chapter points out how abstract concepts of the human obscure the processes by which necropolitics affirms some bodies as rational subjects and relegates other bodies for labor and death. In this work An proposes, much like Sylvia Wynter, that we understand being human as a praxis that moves toward liberation. The praxis of humanity offered by An breaks the double binds of the Hegelian master-slave dialect and essentialist definitions of the relationship of humanness to the body.

Desmond Coleman's "What It's Like to Be a Blackened Body, and *Why* It's Like That: A Preliminary Exploration" addresses a major focus in Africana scholarship, which gives increased attention to understanding the interconnectedness between identity, the body, and how these are located within a historical, social, and religious process. The sociogenic process unfolded by Coleman is essential to understanding (in ways similar to those of Wynter, Fanon, and Vasquez) how exterior material-socio-historic conditions become the interiority of the Black body/self. The exterior-interiority of Black identity as a sociogenic process is a praxis and parasensory. The term "parasensory" describes how even material artifacts and environment shape neurological and cognitive processes. This is an exciting article that moves between alchemy, neuroscience, and contemporary film analyses, and expands what it means to be an embodied self and the transmuting process of blackening.

Paige Rawson's chapter "The Rhizome and/as the Tree of Life" gives a creative and engaging analysis of the Genesis passage on the Tree of Life and the discussion of Wisdom in the book of Proverbs. Rawson's creation of an original biblical hermeneutic presents Wisdom, the (Baobab) Tree of Life, as affect, relational, and a vital component that unifies our archipelagic state of existence. In this chapter, Rawson interprets Wisdom through the lens of Creoleness and views Wisdom as a relational and unfolding possibility for an identity that is affective, justice-seeking, diverse, and seeks to tear down old boundaries even as it builds new revolutionary ways of existence. From this perspective, Rawson's work fits squarely within the context of "Un/Folding Identities." Like most Africana, postcolonial, and critical thought, Rawson's thought crosses several disciplinary and discursive boundaries critiquing and exploding traditional scholarly parameters. Rawson's engagement with Rhizome and/as the Tree of Life unfolds a relational poetics of wisdom for decolonizing biblical studies. It builds on the work of Édouard Glissant and Dorothy Akoto-Abutiate to develop a biblical hermeneutic and theopoetics she defines as Bibliorality. Rawson's Bibliorality uses Africana, Afro-Caribbean, and Queer philosophical traditions anchored around the Baobab Tree.

Aliou Cissé Niang writes another fascinating chapter, similar to that of Paige Rawson's, on the poetics of biblical hermeneutics and interpretation. Niang presents Léopold Sédar Senghor as an intellectual Baobab Tree who developed a proto-postcolonial theory as a forerunner to those of Gayatri Chakravorty Spivak, Edward Said, and Homi Bhabha. Niang creatively demonstrates that the Négritude of Senghor as a poetic of biblical hermeneutics adopts and then destabilizes and subverts colonial epistemology. What is more important, Senghor's proto-postcolonial theory engages the entirety of African culture and its vital life force to liberate and rehabilitate the oppressed. Niang suggests that Senghor's postcolonial theory offers a direction forward, although it does not provide answers. After delivering a fresh and innovative analysis of Senghor, Niang then illustrates the liberating conscientization that emerges with his proto-postcolonial theory.

The essays in Part II, "Africana Activism," present that activism as partly nebulous, partly concrete, partly theoretical and epistemological, and even partly fantastical. It is political as it is religious; it reads and unfolds from readings of sacred texts as well as narrative lacunae. To that work of reading alternatively, perhaps even noncanonically, yet communally and rationally, the essays in this part constitute, as a cluster, a form of Africana activism that is deconstructive and creative in its engagement with history, religious experience, interpretation of texts (written and aural). In short, it is activism that not only moves but seeks to create meaningful movement and progress and then reexamine that movement and its underside, for the purposes of more fully embodying worldviews of creative and productive lives.

Nimi Wariboko's "God Killed! God Interrupted, Long Live the People!: Political Theory in Religious Act" reads the historical act of deicide effected by the Kalabari people (Izon, Niger Delta, Nigeria) on September 27,

1857, as a disruptive event that also signaled the role of a community in determining questions of divine self-autonomy, the movement of the Spirit, and the political identity formation around the notion of peoplehood. For Wariboko, this revolutionary act, when read alongside national epic narratives (such as the *Ozidi Saga* of the Ijo people), offers fruitful diagnostic entry points into analyzing the political systems and structures in Africa, with an eye toward democratic forms of accountability and resistance against autocratic rule. Precisely, argues Wariboko, the killing of the deity represents a form of "disincarnation of power," meaning that political leadership cannot claim either external or internal mandates (divine, political) to justify the use of power without the consent of the community. This "disincarnation of power" creates a void that creates space for Indigenous forms of freedom, which reside in the capacity to act in ways that affect divine-human relations. If a god becomes too violent, the people can cause it to cease to exist and, with it, the political and religious systems that oppress. The people create something new, the very essence and process of democracy. This transition, Wariboko argues, is not without its own risks of becoming imperial and totalitarian.

Aliou Cissé Niang's "'Doing the Will of God' as Loving God Whose Way Is Peace" is an ethical epistemology on what he calls the ability for a Christian to "embrace healthy ethical values exercised by Muslim and African Traditionalists." It comes out of his experience of missionary Christianity in Senegal; but mostly, it unfolds as a reflection on his formative religious praxis, rooted as much in the influence of his parents as in the philosophical and epistemological writings of Léopold Senghor on Négritude and the reality of his political leadership of Senegal after official colonization. The ethos of love, variously articulated in the Abrahamic traditions as well as in African Traditional Religion, provides the impetus for "resilient hope for a healthier action-oriented future." In this way, Niang argues that the religious texts are part of how one gets to recognize Jesus as potentially the Good Samaritan in the New Testament parable, the Samaritan as "God *incognito*, extending mercy to the needy." With this epistemological framing, Niang explores concrete ways/actions by which the world can be transformed into a hospitable place. These include peace building, interreligious dialogue for the divine and the human, and an illustration of interreligious dialogue in the history and politics of Senegal. The work is also a hermeneutical display of the scholarly rigor that is necessary to unmask the ethnocentrisms and ethnonationalisms, terrorism, corruption, and ecological exploitation that ravage our world. For Niang, a historiography of religious thought and biblical interpretation is necessary to harness the deep cultural and religious values and praxis of peace and love, which are fragile, but invaluable for a healthy world.

Drawing on the role of spectral guides in Stephan Palmié's work, *Wizards and Scientists*, Rachel Elizabeth Harding's chapter, "Mysticism and Mothering in Black Women's Social Justice Activism: Brazil/USA," examines the moral and ethical universe of Black women's involvement in creating and nurturing social activism in the United States and in Brazil. Rooted in a history of religions approach to Afro-Brazilian religious thought and life, Harding's essay combines critical theory and praxis around womanism, mysticism, and mothering to understand history differently, or, as Harding puts it, to "find ways to disocclude what lies hidden, muted in the interstices of conventional understandings of how the world we live in came to be and at what sacrifice it continues." What unfolds is a disocclusion and a recovery of "some other kinds of intelligence about the New World." To illustrate this theory, Harding examine and profiles four women from the USA and Brazil, whose work represents the intersections of womanism, mysticism, and mothering—all in the service of social transformation.

In "A Theopoetics of Exodus and the Africana Spirit in Music," Sharon Kimberly Williams proposes to explore the diasporic movement of Africans to the West as a disruptive and traumatic movement that nevertheless becomes stitched and gathered together into a rhythm that effects and affects a liberation ethos, exodus. As Williams articulates, "Exodus movement allows the African Diaspora to animate itself as Spirit for the sake of its own survival and the survival of the world." The cost is enormous and compels engagement with the divine, and even with divine purpose. It is this repurposing that makes exodus possible, and hopeful; it is this kind of exodus narrative and narration that "moves the African Diaspora from an offbeat rhythm of despair to a soaring song of hope bound together by one transcendent, ancestral spirit." This move, this flow, continues to wrestle with entrenched systems, whether they be colonialism, patriarchy, imperialism, or environmental subjugation. These are the "Way Down" places that are captured in *Negro Spiritual* songs, but also the *Sunken Places* of science fiction out of which liberation is forged. The rhythm between lament and praise is constantly attempting to go from the offbeat of trauma to new breath. For Williams, the Spirit of Africana music gives voice, theory, energy, and life to this relation between lament and liberation.

Minenhle Nomalungelo Khumalo's essay, "Must We Burn Isaac?: A Four-Part Hermeneutical Fantasy for Africana Epistemology," locates itself not so much in the tension between canonical and noncanonical modes of interpretation and episteme, but rather in counter-reading that is activated as much in the centers of power as in the marginal and marginalized spaces. Khumalo locates this work in conversation with notions of gaze as developed by bell hooks, interpretive excavation and resistance advocated by Vincent Wimbush, and the vitality of Black experience. All of this to activate her own agency, and that of others, seeking to create what she calls livable lives. Khumalo's question, "Must we burn Isaac?" is an epistemological and a hermeneutical question that asks about "the costs we are willing to pay for solidarity among Black folk and the kinds of (potentially violent) demands our struggles make of each other" but also about whether we are to "burn bridges with (dominant) white epistemological perspectives, lest we crash and *burn* under the weight of trying to serve Black communities through writing and thinking that takes place within and is even curated by/for predominantly white institutions." With this epistemological and hermeneutical framing, Khumalo presents an oppositional gaze reading (or retelling) of the Hagar and Ishmael story that resists singular narration, resists finality, and instead irrupts into fantasy about the communal, where the work of self-definition, survival, and perhaps even flourishing may yet be a fantastical possibility for livable Africana lives.

The closing essays in Part III, "Africana Historiographies and Memories," are anchored by an *embodied memory*, symbolized by the Baobab Tree, that gives birth to transgressive hopes for life against life-domineering and negating forces. These negating forces are often constructed as normative by productions of knowledge and philosophical investigative methods that the marginalized and people of African descent must adopt if they were to be counted as humans. These closing essays call for alternative modes of inquiry—binding transcultural conversations and dialogues that embrace a diverse unity by a people acquainted with suffering and objectifications of all kinds simply because they are *othered bodies*.

Althea Spencer Miller initiates this part by guiding readers through a complex and yet fascinating conversation with Vincent Wimbush's *Theorizing*

Scriptures. Spencer Miller offers a dense argument about heroic ancestral negotiations of life in diaspora spaces. Just as the roots of the baobab tree transcend arid wilderness spaces, creolization, as a creative literary trope, rhythms and vitalizes diasporic life in such a way that it embeds African roots and living memory. In the end, Spencer Miller rightly and persistently calls for a genuine and broader "Africana conversation" without which Africana self-actualization cannot survive the insidious, schismatic, and alienating anti-pluralism wiles of Western imperialism ever tilted toward the negation of otherness. Such a conversation might incubate equity, namely "an intratelluric shout for kinship and recognition, erupting with the heat of magmatic hope for the igneous strength of an amphictyony plurality—completely its own indigene."

'Shola D. Adegbite's "Solidarity by Sharing Power" offers insights into sub-Saharan African orature. Introducing her argument with the too familiar story of American police brutality she feels is inspired by racialized injustice that leads to the murder of numerous people of African descent and is epitomized by the public lynching of George Floyd, Adegbite delves into the power of storytelling that incarnates and conveys practical and spiritual truths that cannot be told in any other way except through truth-telling myths. Inculturation is inspiringly corrective of imperial missionary hermeneutics in that "Jonah's story can be read as an encounter with Mami Wata." Adegbite astutely hears the voice of Jonah in Wata and proceeds to craft a contextual hermeneutics worthy of African sensibility manifested in the practice of solidarity. Using a psychoanalytic investigative approach defined as a "multi-method Africa-centric" that builds on key African thinkers such as David T. Adamo, Justin Ukpong, Alphaeus Masonga, and Gerald O. West, Adegbite rejects the imperial construction of Wata as inimical, cunning, and satanic and portrays Wata as a "complex" figure who is anything but inimical. Inspired by a new locution, "marine power," a term arising from vernacular hermeneutics, Adegbite argues that the role of the fish in rescuing Jonah the prophet from "marine power" echoes Wata's unfailing role to assist humans to adapt and negotiate life in various contexts. In other words, Wata shapes humans into baobab trees to weather harsh spaces.

"Envisioning Africana Religions" is Salim Faraji's intriguing autobiographical journey and determination to document the inception, development, and contribution of Africana Religious Studies. Faraji is clear about the influences that key thinkers of African descent in America and Africa made in shaping life and thought. Faraji's aim is broad but builds on his education—an experience that equipped him with a unique lens that enables him to unearth what is lacking as well as what is needed to ensure a lasting future for the burgeoning field of Africana studies. His call for a clear interdisciplinary methodology is indispensable if Africana studies are to survive and guide people of African descent. This is quintessential by virtue of the fact that the innovative nature of African Traditional Religion and its worldview as he sees it is a function of its flowering adaptability in new contexts—a multivalence the baobab embodies.

Kenneth N. Ngwa conceptualizes a fascinating picture of God's journey with Israel and people of African descent as "Interpreting from the Back/Black-Side: Exodus through the Shawl of Memory." Israel and people of African descent struggle while safely positioned on God's hindered back—a metaphor daily performed by many childbearing African mothers. To Ngwa, this is a collective identity story of survival being created out of "chirographic text about the future" reimaged as "embodied" that lives on through the creative arts of its telling and retelling in and above the fray of the liminal at home as well as in diasporic spaces. "Back/Black-Side Hermeneutics" draws the works of concerned hermeneuts to reposition Africana hermeneutics above the threat of oppressive erasure and exercise "exile-exodus modes of seeing," namely to see, hear, remember, and move to deliberative practical actions. Ngwa's Cameroonian postcolonial optic informs his fascinating argument—a rereading of the exodus story that insightfully delves into the creative side of trauma and yields "trauma-hope" and ultimately "exodus" that transcends and resists identity annihilation.

Hugh R. Page's "Conjuring Lost Books, (Re-) membering Fragmented Litanies at the Intersection of Africana and Biblical Studies" speaks of a biblical autobiography in which the metaphor of "the open door" functions as a resilient work of trailblazing against oddities of identity erasure and paves the way for others. Page guides readers in how "helping to ensure that people of color and others marginalized in the academy are guaranteed access" might be achieved—a form of farming baobab trees that would not only continue to resist but also change what Page terms the "arid terrain of biblical and theological studies." Echoing the Jewish Haggadah, Page shows how his autobiographical theological story is programmatic for diasporic would-be baobabs. Introspective journeys into the depths of our academic journeys might yield some actionable insights to form, sharpen, and reimage our variegated Africana studies methodologies.

Catherine Keller's Afterword provides a summative and reflective analysis of the volume but also locates the volume within the ongoing work of the Transdisciplinary Theological Colloquium. As Keller notes, the critical work of Africana religious studies continues to unfold at the intersections of memory and future-making, transgressing multiple temporal and spatial demarcations.

NOTES

1. Transdisciplinary Theological Colloquium, https://depts.drew.edu/tsfac/colloquium/index.html (accessed April 12, 2022).
2. See, for example, Stacy M. Floyd-Thomas, ed., *Religion, Race and Covid-19: Confronting White Supremacy in the Pandemic* (New York: NYU Press, 2022).
3. Paul Tiyambe Zeleza, "Rewriting the African Diaspora: Beyond the Black Atlantic," *African Affairs* 104, no. 414 (2005): 41.
4. Le R. P. Edouard Wintz, *Dictionnaire Français-Dyola et Dyola-Français* (Paris : Mission Catholique, 1909), 94, 128.
5. Jacob K. Olupona, *African Religions: A Very Short Introduction* (New York: Oxford University Press, 2014), xxii–xxiv. See also Afe Adogame and Jim Spickard, *Religion Crossing Boundaries: Transnational Religious and Social Dynamics in Africa and the New African Diaspora* (Leiden: Brill, 2010); J. Lorand Matory, *Black Atlantic Religion: Tradition* (Princeton, NJ: Princeton University Press, 2009). The dynamic nature of religion, as conceptualized and described in these volumes, emerges in what these works frame as translocal and transnational phenomena and practices.
6. Tracey E. Hucks, *Yoruba Traditions and African American Religious Nationalism* (Albuquerque: University of New Mexico Press, 2012); Yvonne Patricia Chireau, *Black Magic: Religion and the African American Conjuring Tradition* (Berkeley: University of California Press, 2003).
7. Michelle Wright, *Physics of Blackness: Beyond the Middle Passage Epistemology* (Minneapolis: University of Minnesota Press, 2015).
8. Colin Legun, *Pan-Africanism: A Short Political Guide* (London: Pall Mall Press, 1962, 1965), 24–37.
9. Legun, *Pan-Africanism*, 93-111; 128–30; Aimé Césaire, *Cahier d'un retour au pay natal,* 2nd ed., ed. Abiola Irele (Columbus: Ohio State University Press, 2000); U. O. Umozurike, *International Law and Colonialism in Africa* (Enugu, Nigeria: Nwamife Publishers, 1979).

10. Legun, *Pan-Africanism*.
11. Dionne Brand, *A Map to the Door of No Return: Notes to Belonging* (Toronto: Vintage, 2001), 4–5.
12. Patrick Manning, *The African Diaspora: A History through Culture* (New York: Columbia University Press, 2009).
13. Abdoulaye Kane and Todd H. Leedy, eds., *African Migrations: Patterns and Perspectives* (Bloomington: Indiana University Press, 2013).
14. Ingrid Monson, *African Diaspora: A Musical Perspective* (London: Routledge, 2004), 2–3.
15. Zora Neale Hurston, *Moses, Man of the Mountain* (New York: HarperCollins, 1991), 9.
16. Neale Huston, *Moses, Man of the Mountain*, 22.
17. Pierre Nora, "Between Memory and History: les Lieux de Mémoire," *Representations* 26 (1989), 7.
18. Nora, "Between Memory and History," 8.
19. Nora, "Between Memory and History," 8–9.
20. Nora, "Between Memory and History," 11–12.
21. Nora, "Between Memory and History," 12.
22. bell hooks, *Yearning: Race, Gender and Cultural Politics* (Boston: South End Press, 1990), 205.
23. hooks, *Yearning*, 206.
24. hooks, *Yearning*, 207.

PART I

◆ Un/Folding Identities

ARCHANGEL GABRIEL SPEAKS TO MARY

PAMELA MORDECAI

"Howdy do, holy one!" A voice sound
all around like it come from deep down
in de womb, in de tomb of a drum.
Cold sweat wash my whole body, same time
big fraid ketch me. I frighten
and shake, hold my breath as I wait
for de far-up-far-down-all-round
speaker to speak. "Child, you fill up de eye
of de great El Shaddai! Out of all
womankind, de plain good
of you quicken him heart. It look like
you same one is to have a star part
in a mystery play him write a script for.
So him send me across de deep black of sky,
a few billion cubits to ask you to be
so good as to grant him urgent plea.
When him talk him voice beat
like a hummingbird wing!
Jah-Jah know is not any small thing him require of you.
Dat is why I am asking you down
on my knees. He say make.

sure to ask so, and ask, 'If you please . . .'
So sweet lady, speaking for Elohim, Most High,
I fly over to ask dat you make a small fry,
fingerling, a pikni dat will wring
every joy from de earth, every ache
from your heart. Your belly
going swell wid Yeshua, Godsend
of de world. But is your choice to make,
is your amen to say.
I am Archangel asking, no mind
dem insist I am Gabriel announcing. Dese earth
creature too love to take
tings and twist to dem suit!
Am-Who-Am-Over-All, De Great One-Who-
Run-Tings, say is choose
you must choose. But for sure he would glad
if you grant him behest and send
me back home wid a 'Yes.'"

Second chorus of male and female voices
(Lights up. Women are already in their places; the men are shuffling in.)
Male voices
(To audience) Look like Mary story
turn into skit, so might as well
play we part, do we likl bit.
Female voices
(To audience.) Cho, don't pay dem no mind.
Dem don't have too much sense.
Dem think since dem say so,
de whole Jesus-Jah-son story is
pretense. Dem admit him was here
and him preach and baptize
and de Roman dem crucify him:
but dem say de Messiah
and Jah-my-pa part is lies.
Male voices
So how far we did reach in dis tall tale again?
Ah yes! Push come to shub! Mary just

tell Joseph she making a baby. (*They laugh loudly.*)
Better Joseph than any of we!
You would think a man quick
wid him carpentry hand
would have intelligence in him head!
One thing all-o-we done decide:
no way we would married to any woman
wid a next man pikni big
in her belly. Nobody want no
jacket in dem family!
Female voices
How you know is jacket? Is one of you grandpa
put de child in her womb? For how else
you could know is not Joseph pikni?
Male voices
But don't every soul dere in dat Nazareth town
know de girl come to him wid her belly weigh down?
Dat she breed wid another man seed?
Female voices
(*The women laugh raucously.*) Well we must beg pardon for dis
big buss-out laugh
for de lot of you say is woman love talk,
and is we put we nose into people affairs.
So it well amuse all-o-we gossiping hags
dat de su-su bout Mary did spread like disease
from one bad-mouth-man to a next.
Male voices
You can go right ahead and confuse reasoning
wid su-su if you choose. From long time we response
for good morals just like we response for good sense.
What a thing when any young woman can excuse
fornication and adultery wid de news
is Jah-Jah offspring dem carrying!
Is we have to save you from gullibility,
faith in nothing more than a pikni poppyshow.
Same thing now, just as two generation ago.
Female voices

Good morals and good sense? You must be
making fun. You best remember who
all-a-you talking to.
Nobody here forget Nazareth history.
Nobody here forget who twist
which one story.
Nobody here forget is de high.
and mighty who choose how things go.
"Same thing now, just as two generation ago."
Male Voices
All-o-you making joke! It could never be we
dat you calling mighty? You all look carefully?
You see anybody look like Roman to you?
Female Voices
You name man. Dat is all and dat is everyting.
You is judge and jury. You could stone
anyone of we till we dead anytime.
Take dat child, Esther—my gran say
she spend all day everyday
in Miss Ann yard playing wid Mary
and a next girl from on de same road.
De elders in de town did stone
de young girl down like a harlot.
You lot not no better. You all love violence.
Dem cut your navel string
on disruption and war.
Male voices
(*Interrupting the women.*) Best you damp your lip shut for
enough is enough.
If you keep talking so, you will find dat many
a woman lose dem head to dem tongue.
Female Voices
(*Women turn away, kissing their teeth.*) How you all come so
smart? You proving
what we say! Make we open we mouth likl way
and you gallop to chop off we head!
Come let we go long, yah!

Leave dese sages to see which of us
dem going charge wid what breach of which decree.
Jesus long come and gone. Him did bring
a New Law. It say de likes of you
do not own none of we.
(*Women flounce off.*)

1. Nella Larsen's *Quicksand*: Mourning through Biracial Identities

ARTHUR PRESSLEY

Mama, What Color Am I: Mulatto, Jamaican Yellow, High Yeller, Red Bone, Crispy, Quadroon, Milk Dud, Lilly White?

And some there be, which have no memorial; who are perished, as though they had never been; and are become as though they had never been born; and their children after them."

Only the Black Woman can say "when and where I enter, in the quiet undisputed dignity of my womanhood, without violence and without suing of special patronage, and then the whole Negro race enters with me."

This essay seeks to expand the epistemology of Blackness through a psychoanalytic and Africana engagement with the novel *Quicksand*, by Nella Larsen, written in 1926 during the overlapping periods of the Harlem Renaissance and the Great Migration. This historical moment sees African Americans moving to escape structural and political violence in the South and needing to create new identities and communities in Northern refugee centers. Larsen's *Quicksand* is a narrative about that migration and the social and political identities forged to survive and grow during this moment that reflect essential aspects of contemporary struggles of African Americans. Mary Helen Washington described Larsen as the invisible woman of the Harlem Renaissance.[1] Hazel Carby states that Larsen's main character in *Quicksand*, a mulatto, is the first fully sexual Black woman shown within the context of American Capitalism.[2] The protagonist of *Quicksand* is a fully sexualized, mulatto, Black woman, born in the United

States and with international roots. This biomythography is an interesting novel with which to analyze strategies to develop a more inclusive Africana epistemology. A more inclusive epistemology is needed with the political and social demands on African Americans causing more questions and fostering more divisions and segregations between Blacks internally, as well as splinters among social, religious, and political efforts to confront the growing racism of neoliberalism. This critique of Larsen analyzes the impact of colorism, the polyphonic voices of each person, and the givenness of acts of resistance in all oppressed persons. The significance of using the novel about and by a woman of color who is mulatto, is that she is the ultimate outsider/insider/outsider. The interstitiality of her life highlights the ongoing mourning of diasporic peoples, the social, cultural and institutional barriers that invite and reject participation, the struggles to find a place that feels like home, and like Zora Neal Hurston the complexities and dynamics of the relationship with mothers and other women of color. Interstitiality of Black women's lives demonstrates alternate strategies for creating identity and community.[3]

Quicksand, as novel and biomythography, requires an understanding of the writer. In biomythography the writer is examining their own life as a portal for their community to understand its development, identity, and how it lives in community. Biomythography is almost a social and cultural example of recapitulation theory that assumes the history of a community or given population can be observed in the developmental history of a single individual.[4] This means that the study of a single person, whether Malcolm X, Angela Davis, Michael Brown, Tawana Brawley, or Anna Julia Cooper, is to gain new insights about their race—their community. The hidden and clearly seen aspects of Blackness, conscious and unconscious, the admired and feared dynamics of Blackness, are seen in many respects in the life of Larsen, even with the millions of variations within a community.

George Hutchinson has written perhaps the most detailed biography of Larsen, including her relationship with her parents and locating her work within the Harlem Renaissance.[5] Larsen's mother was a white Danish immigrant and her father was Black and from the Danish West Indies. Her father died when she was young, and her mother remarried a white Danish immigrant whom Larsen felt strongly disliked her. Although it is never stated explicitly, it is suggested that Larsen felt rejected by her stepfather because of her mixed heritage, that is, that he was comfortable marrying a white woman, but not her Black child. Soon after the marriage, Larsen was sent to live with a Black family and felt as uncomfortable and unwelcomed there, as she was in the home of her mother and stepfather. Early in her childhood, she spent time in Denmark and lived in Chicago and New York, never discovering a place that she could call home.

Larsen was a student at both Fisk University and Tuskegee University, and she felt bruised and unappreciated at both Black institutions. The struggles with Black institutions and Black communities are themes that would haunt Larsen throughout her life. She was expelled from Fisk after her participation in a student protest against the university's dress code. After the dismissal from Fisk, Larsen returned to Denmark for three years where she wrote children's books. While in Denmark, Larsen felt invisible and alienated, as she did in the United States, but for different reasons. In Denmark, Larsen felt that others saw her as an exotic object to be gazed upon. After returning to the United States, Larsen won a Guggenheim fellowship to study the African Diaspora in the Americas, Europe, and the Caribbean. Later in life she married a Black physicist and felt as alienated and invisible as she did with parents and religious and civic societies, both Black and white. After her marriage failed, she attended nursing school and lived in obscurity in lower Manhattan, refusing contact with anyone from her past. Her novels revolve around the dynamics of Black female subjectivity within an international and diasporic and capitalist context.

The characters that come alive in Larsen's work testify to her almost Marxist and diasporic understanding of the frequent alienation people feel within themselves, their families, and their communities. Hazel Carby argues that Larsen's work demonstrates how this alienation is intensified within empires that exist on ideologies of consumerism, capitalism, and racial and sexual polarization.[6] Larsen, much like her protagonists, has experienced numerous personal traumas and social rejections. Soon after the "rediscovery" of Zora Neale Hurston's work, contemporary Black feminist critics began using Larsen's work as an alternate model of Black women's fiction. Larsen's life resembled many of the characters who were invisible and existed between communities. The invisibility of Larsen's characters is always the result of the moral, political, and imaginative failures endemic to American life.

QUICKSAND

Quicksand centers on Helga Crane, a biracial woman and teacher at Naxos, a Black school in the southern United States, which is described in a way that resembles Fisk or Tuskegee. In Naxos, Larsen is critiquing what she saw as a tradition of some Black colleges that sought primarily to be a showplace for whites and Blacks—to demonstrate to whites the appreciation of Blacks for their generosity, and to demonstrate to Blacks that they could eventually meet white expectations. Helga is dissatisfied with the repression and stunting of Black intellectual growth by white charity and Black submissiveness to gain the recognition of whites. It is the passive response to white denigration that forces Helga to resign her job after a conversation with the university president, Dr. Anderson. Dr. Anderson attempts to have Helga remain at the school by telling her that with her breeding, her white blood, and her middle-class values, she is a valuable asset to the college. Anderson tells Helga that at Naxos she would be an exemplar for Black students to emulate and for whites to know the possibilities for the Black race. The example that he refers to is not her scholarship, superior teaching, or intellect, but her light skin color that is almost white. When she leaves Naxos, Helga returns to Chicago where she had grown up in an all-white neighborhood, and she is unable to find the home she is searching for or memories of her childhood.

Helga eventually journeys to Harlem as secretary to a "famous spokeswoman for the race." In Harlem, she lived with a woman called Anne Grey, worked in a Black insurance company, and observed the Black intelligentsia. Helga was disdainful of the ideology of racial uplift and of Anne's continual preoccupation with the problems of the race and disparaging of the hypocrisy of the emerging Black middle class. This class, she felt, condemned white racism while imitating white middle-class behavior and adopting their values and moral codes. Feeling that she was again being stifled, Helga was determined to leave Harlem and used money from her white uncle to visit her Danish family in Copenhagen. Helga lived in Europe for two years, where the appreciation she had so desired seems to be available, but Helga realized that she was being treated like an exotic object, admired only as a representative of the primitive and sensual. Experiencing a desperate need to be again among Black people, she sailed to Harlem for the wedding of Anne and Dr. Anderson, intending to make only a temporary visit but staying long after the wedding. Helga recognized a long-repressed sexual attraction for Anderson, and in response to his encouragement determines to sleep with him. In the midst of their affair, Anderson rejects the sexual encounter with Helga, which propels her into a confused state. Running from her failed sexual encounter, Helga meets a hedonistic Southern preacher in a storefront church and feels empowered by seducing him. She returned to the South as the wife of Rev. Mr. Pleasant Green, blind to all except the sensual aspect of their relationship. Helga planned to uplift the women and instruct the children of this community of Southern folk, but instead repeated childbirths degraded and oppressed her. She nearly dies giving birth to her fourth child, and the novel ends with her fifth pregnancy, which means her certain death, which she seems almost unable to resist.

The narrative of *Quicksand* can be more deeply understood in relationship to Larsen's second novel *Passing*. *Passing* is about two light-skinned women, one passing for white throughout the entirety of her life and living with a racist husband; the other woman, while committed to Black progress, occasionally passes when separated from people she knows. Both biomythographic novels argue for the fluidity of racial identity and how identity is a matter of performance and performativity. The performance of racial identity is understood as capacity to destabilize and subvert racial categories through how an individual lives out their racial/ethnic identity. Performativity likewise can either reinforce or subvert racial identity or prescribed norms.

Quicksand was written during the height of the Harlem Renaissance with all its concern for developing and articulating concepts of Black identity. The Harlem Renaissance was a moment in history when millions of diasporic Black bodies arrived in Northern cities, and traditional social roles, personal identities, and spiritual traditions were unable to provide grounding for Black souls and bodies. This was a historical moment when it was unclear what was being signified by "Black community" and Black identity since this was part of what was lost during the great migration, when thousands of African Americans escaping the lynching, poverty, and harsh segregation of the South encountered the race riots, police brutality, housing discrimination, and structural oppression of the North. The Harlem Renaissance was a time of phenomenal intellectual and artistic production, and there were growing efforts to produce standards to model

Black personal and artistic life. These models were designed to "uplift" the Black masses and to demonstrate to whites that Blacks had similar social and economic goals for their lives. This period had diverse leadership and intellectuals such as W. E. B. Du Bois, Marcus Garvey, James Weldon Johnson, Alain Lock, and A. Philip Randolph, and each had different ideas about the meaning of Blackness and who was to provide leadership or be the spokesperson for this diverse and complex community claiming the arrival of a New Negro.

Quicksand is a counter-discourse to the counter-discourse of Du Bois, Washington, and other Black male leaders of that day who began defining the character and identity of the "New Negro." Larsen represented an overlooked womanist perspective in the Harlem Renaissance, and this included a critique of Black attempts to develop Black marital arrangements and lifestyles that resembled those of white domestic relations. Larsen's ideas and intellectual development are influenced by other Black women of the period such as Anne Cooper Smith, Ida B. Wells, Paula Hopkins, and Jessie Redman Faust. Larsen and other Black women who were novelists, intellectuals, and activists established a different aesthetic approach to that of their male counterparts. The Black women who were activists and intellectuals saw the need for Black cultural productions that not only presented a "New Negro" equal or superior to whites but also intimately explored the fabric of a rapidly changing and challenged Black community that was more than a combination of African heritage and Euro-American social values.

There are multiple reasons for choosing Larsen's *Quicksand* for this discussion of Blackness and diasporic identity. The protagonist in *Quicksand*, Helga, is a biracial woman, and Carby argues that her sexuality and race amplify the extent that she is both a consumer and a consumable object. Helga is obsessed with the acquisition of commercial products and consumer goods. At one point in the narrative, even though homeless and jobless, she goes to the shopping district to have a fancy meal and window shop at expensive stores. As a woman, she is at the center of a complex process of exchange. Money was crucial to Larsen's narrative, structuring power relations, controlling social movement, and defining the boundaries and replacing kinship as the prime mediator of social relations. Helga, a mulatto, is the penultimate insider/outsider to both Black and white communities. She is emotionally, socially, and historically connected to, and outside of, both Black and white communities. She is not so much an expression of double consciousness, or a synthesis of Black and white communities, but a person who is alienated from the accommodations communities make to their existential, political, and economic conditions. This novel takes place in several locations: two in the South, Chicago, as well as Copenhagen. There is almost a transatlantic or migratory quality to the story. I would argue that the travels of the protagonist do not indicate a journey narrative, but that these are sites of memory where the repetition illuminates particular tropes or themes.

BIOMYTHOGRAPHY AND DEVELOPING A MORE INCLUSIVE AFRICANA EPISTEMOLOGY

This diasporic novel, located amid powerful historical, political, and cultural movements, mirrors much of our current political, cultural, and economic landscape. The Harlem Renaissance and the Great Migration witnessed tremendous economic and cultural growth in many areas for some Blacks. These periods also witnessed waves of violence and repression against almost all efforts toward Black self-determination as if the colonial masters were attempting to put down a slave rebellion. African Americans fleeing lynching and poor economic conditions in the South became immigrants in the Northern states encountering similar but different conditions in the form of riots, housing segregation, poor schools, and inadequate health care. Blacks comparing their experience of the North with that of the South were forced to acknowledge that time and place mattered as to how they lived out Blackness.

Larsen's novel expands the epistemology of Blackness, by addressing the significance of skin color and the performance of Blackness, as well as the importance of the time and place when Blackness is performed and reacted to within and outside of Black communities. In *Quicksand*, Larsen makes Black epistemology more inclusive in presenting Black experience as polyphonic by including gender, economic, and international lenses. Last, and most critically, Larsen, like Zora Neale Hurston, Toni Morrison, and other Black women novelists, develops a central character who reflects agency, critical awareness, and creative subjectivity. This heroic figure is significant, not because she changed communities, performed public miracles, or led political movements, but because of the ordinariness of her activities.

The biomythography of Larsen/Helga challenges traditional framing of complex and creative human existence by how she presents the heroic. This framing of complex subjectivity was reflected forty years after her writing by a debate between Bruno Bettelheim and Terrence Des Pres about what constituted heroic life in situations of severe repression. Bettelheim argued that to be heroic in oppressive situations an individual needed to display a significant act of courage in the face of adversity. Countering this argument, Des Pres posited that in a world where overwhelming forces are attempting to destroy you, simply surviving is a heroic act. Larsen views the achievement and heroic actions as evident in the survival and the work of witnessing of a community. Her view is similar to that expressed in many of the novels of Toni Morrison as well as in the spiritual directions of Howard Thurman, Alexander Weheliye, and others. Protest and heroic actions alone point to the meritocracy of the individual. Larsen explodes traditional notions of subjectivity and agency that heretofore were reserved for whites, and begins with an ontological assumption, later developed by Hannah Arendt, of the givenness of resistance, complex subjectivity, creativity, and heroic action in response to institutional and personal degradation. This inherent desire for subjectivity with the accompanied need to resist domination is reflected in a diversity of forms and expressions. A sharecropper who gets up early regardless of how tired, a single parent who works two jobs and cannot think beyond the next paycheck, or the person who organizes a strike against unfair wages are all to be considered as displaying subjectivity. In a conversation with his daughter, Howard Thurman suggested that the heart of a person is not always determined by the size of an individual's actions, but by the size of the forces that are thrown against them. For Helga, the forces thrown against her were the economic and political repression of European and American cultures, the dehumanizing and terrorizing structural violence of racism and sexism that denied adequate housing, education, and health care systems, and the backlash of African Americans who reacted as violently as whites against a Black woman who did not fit neatly into reified social categories.

Larsen's biomythographic novels *Quicksand* and *Passing* suggest multiple selves that are essential parts of each self. Consequently, although there are different themes and stories in *Passing* and *Quicksand*, there are significant similarities in the two novels. Each person could write a different autobiography of her life, or multiple biographies could be written about them with profound points of overlap, contradictions, and varying perspectives. The perspective that all persons have multiple selves, which are not always integrated, which speak to diverse social, political, and spiritual[7] contexts, is a reality of human life. The problem arises only when we assume that there must be a single unified self that is consistent and that contradictions must be overcome or eliminated. Recent and traditional Africana theories of identity and intersubjective psychoanalytic theories of the self by theorists such as Pam Cooper-White, Heather Russell, Zora Neal Hurston, W. E. B. Du Bois, Michelle Wright, and numerous others point out that a self evolves over time, but also shifts depending on social location. This way appreciates the creoleness, the complexity of the self that shifts along with sociogenic, historical, and environmental factors that even include orientation to the future. This creoleness is a self that is always interpreting, responding to, and creating new possibilities of being.

The biomythography by Larsen explores a protean self that only discovers "home" when it resourcefully adapts and re-creates itself and at times is created by the economic, social, racial, and gender forces of the day. *Quicksand* points to the significance of environmental forces that make identity feel unstable even if the desire is to have a singular, integrated self that has stable values, ideas, and beliefs regardless of environment. Instead of reading the novel as a pilgrimage, or coming of age story, where the order and stage of life and place are essential for understanding the narrative, an Africana and intrasubjective psychoanalytic reading of the story suggests that all the places and times should be read as all at once. This Africana and psychoanalytic reading suggests that the various places are the backstory and context for the multiple selves of the protagonist who are in dialogue and in process of reflecting and creating. As a result, the story is ever unfolding before the reader who must internalize and hold each time/place/movement as it engages, rather than leads to or from the previous time/place/movement. This Africana reading is grounded in multiple times/places/movements where multiple selves speak among themselves and then knowingly as a polyphony of voices to the multipersonas of the reader.

Some novels, like Toni Morrison's *Beloved*, and biomythographies are similar in that they fuse history, truths, social meanings, and aesthetics with either polyphony or polyglossia. Biomythography is close to psychohistory, and such novels as *Roots*, *Native Son*, *The Color Purple*, and *Soledad Brothers* intermingle autobiography, history, and mythology. They go beyond recounting past events to uncover deeper meanings of identity, culture, and social truths. There is an area of play between the person and society where the reader enters as a character in the novel—a third space where the reader anticipates an unfolding beyond the ending of the text. This space in novels is created in the intersection of myth, biography, episodic memory, and social history (semantic memory), which creates a space even as it is written where the reader interprets the unspoken, unconscious meaning between the words and motion of the novel. This space, where the novel reads the reader, even as they read the text, the space between literary production, social project, and autobiography, presents a story with indeterminate endings. It is different from most novels because of the still unfolding nature of the narrative. In the narrative, the protagonist is frequently a trickster (like the signifying monkey of Henry Louis Gates and the trickster of Zora Neal Hurston) that turns meaning around and sideways. This is not a meaning that is turned upside down for the simplicity of a new meaning, but one that argues that the meanings of the oppressed, the subaltern, and people on the margins expand the meaning of contemporary events, especially when the repressed meanings of race keep erupting into consciousness and force us to see the hidden, the significant, and the impossible.

Biomythography, more than autobiography, assumes that narratives on race and gender are more than affirming selfhood, but these develop a creative, liminal, tightly bounded space that is political and psychological and that challenge, interrogate, and reconfigure new possibilities. Biomythographies challenge extant realities and offer new definitions with a subjectivity that offers alternative ways of viewing choices. Biomythographies, like *Quicksand* and *Passing*, are acts of resistance to hegemonic discourses that are more than semantic memory, the long-term memory of community and family, which is important to those for whom racial identity is fluid, flexible, and remains a daily commitment to a creoleness that is always historical and mythic. A key feature of Larsen's work is a reworking and recovery of traumatic memories that is essential for healing, identity formation, creative productions, problem solving, and community building. From this perspective, creoleness is not limited to viewing one's self as have multiple ethnic origins. The biomythography of *Quicksand* seems to suggest that the deeper meaning of creoleness is that of a liminal period, where creative, potential space is created and there is a reworking of individual and community.

The working through of traumatic memory has particular significance for African Americans. Trauma has a significant impact on semantic memory that allows people to make sense of their present because of its access to constructive memory. The past is complex for people of color since the past is not a place of security or an ordered universe. Past traumas, the draft riots in New York that scattered most of the Black population out of New York City, the riots of Tulsa where 10,000 Blacks were left homeless, and the Great Migrations suggest that memory is unable to heal the traumas of the past when it has limited access to memories of home, community, or family. Without the capacity to make meaning or have access to historical memory then a community is left only with the interpretation of others about the meaning of past events and the implication of these events for identity and community, making it harder to attain complex subjectivity.

Without access to memory, deciding for one's self and one's community are nearly impossible tasks. In 1964 three civil rights workers went missing in Mississippi while they were investigating the burning of a Black church. Federal law enforcement was brought in to find the missing civil rights workers. While they were searching for these bodies, authorities also begun dredging the Mississippi River where almost each day there were additional bodies discovered. When two of the bodies were discovered, authorities ceased dredging the Mississippi River. There was no attempt to identify the other bodies found in the Mississippi River. Delany Lloyd suggests that trauma includes the difficulty of making meaning of actions, recalling, and naming what is significant. This assumes that the discovery of the other bodies, while horrifying, was a denial of the significance of the loss.[8] In another way, not naming the dead, is a re-creation of the countless souls lost during the middle passage, and during slavery. Not naming the dead is simultaneously an act of avoidance and an act of resistance. Part of trauma includes lack of semantic memory. Although the country has some deaths that are raised to the level of meaning—Emmett Till, Eric Garner, George Floyd—for every one individual, there are hundreds, perhaps thousands who die each year. The dynamic of trauma is significant not primarily in the distortions of desires and wishes; trauma is more than the interlocking pathogenic process, and its impact and meaning cannot be fully experienced at the time but later possesses the mind and body of the person who has experienced the event. The person becomes a living, breathing representation of the traumatic event. The image of the Black body, its gender, race, and age all become signifiers of the event. The person, in their identity and very self, is an embodiment. There is a re-enactment of the event that now "possesses" the individual. Cathy Caruth argues that the person carries an impossible history within them or they become the symptom that they cannot entirely process.[9] Trauma must be understood in terms of how it possesses the body and its reoccurrence in the life of the person. Trauma is a truth that must be articulated and is a demand for justice.

Novels were critical to the development of Africana Theory in imagining futures not primarily dependent on places of origins, or current historical and political conditions such as Afrofuturism. Novels are places where Blacks have been able to perceive and recognize the unconscious, hidden, and contradictory events that have been experienced. In *Quicksand*, Larsen theorizes and signifies about becoming and defining Blackness by centering her work on a mulatto woman. In placing herself, her mulatto character center stage, Larsen's novel, similar to those of many Black women novelists, becomes part of a sacred canon of Black women's literature. Black women's "fiction" must be understood as scripturalization, as an aesthetic, a cultural and political critique, a creative expression, and an art form that opens new possibilities for the process of becoming Black.

Novels of the Black canon are always exploring the dynamic between the political and the individual and the meaning of this interplay for interior life and social relationships. Novels allow us to recapture and reexamine those parts of ourselves that have been repressed and forgotten. If we are able to be careful readers, novels enable us to remember and recover memories that maybe on this occasion can be healing and allow new insights that provide a place to stand in the quicksand between identities torn between hyperindividualism and hypercollectivity. The structure of novels is the same as the mental and cognitive process. Stories, like the workings of the human mind, attempt to hide and reveal those things that are most in the human heart, those things that we most desire and fear. Skip Gates reminds us in *Signifying Monkey* that there is always displacement, condensation, and elaboration in our stories, and that like quicksand the ground beneath us is always unstable and nothing is as it might seem.[10] The stories will tell us they are being deceptive about one thing and then confuse us about how we should unravel this deception.

COLORISM: TEAM LIGHT SKIN VERSUS TEAM DARK SKIN

It's been said that African Americans have as many words for shades of skin color as Eskimos have for snow. Perhaps in each case there is minute attention for what some might consider minor variances when these differences have significant meanings for an individual's life. For those whose lives are shaped not only by race but by the lightness or darkness of their pigmentation, the amount of melanin in their skin will establish where they fit within their racial group, and to lesser or greater degrees within other racial ethnic groups. The lightness or darkness of skin for Blacks has impact within families where children observe that siblings of lighter shades get preferential treatment from parents. It was not only a historical artifact that skin color mattered, such as when some social clubs, churches, and other Black groups used skin color along with other social factors to determine membership, but currently it is also an issue, with the growing phenomena of #teamlightskin vs. #teamdarkskin, and projections that by 2026 skin lightening products will reach sales of over $8 billion. Most would easily conclude that there would be some preference for lighter skin colors in a universe where there are three categories of people—human, partial human, and nonhuman—that people simply wanted to mimic the appearance of a human being. Fanon in *Black Skins, White Masks* would suggest that an intraracial version of this, dark skin/light mask is a much more complex, melancholic meaning that points to and re-creates past and present interracial traumas and is suggestive of future healings and acts of resistance. In the interactions of light-skinned and dark-skinned Blacks it is curious that this area of Black life receives only tangential treatment. This chapter next examines a number of issues related to colorism, the performance of Blackness, time and place and polyphony, and creoleness as liminality in order to develop a more inclusive Africana epistemology. Larsen brings to center stage an aspect of Black life seldom discussed when formally considering race, and that is the role of color in facilitating and maintaining racial and engendered racial categories in the United States, Europe, and the Caribbean.

In addition to the attention given to the range of categories for skin color, there are as many terms for how individuals perform their racial identity. Terms such as Oreo, banana, coconut, Twinkie, Jezebel, ghetto, uppity, house nigga, and Uncle Tom are critiques of the performance of sexual and racial identity. Racial identity is formed, in part, at the nexus of colorization, the performance of racial identity, and how these locate persons within their gender/racial group, based on a number of factors, including skin color. The performance of racial identity is constantly evaluated in terms of its meaning within one's racial group and the meaning within opposing racial/ethnic groups. There are occasions in which an individual's recognition by white groups will significantly determine, either positively or negatively, their social or political capital among African American groups. This may be determined by professional identity, social class, personal attributes, or numerous other factors. The tension is at times how closely the individual is thought to prize Black cultural values and attributes, in contrast to how they are perceived to be committed to Euro-American values.

Other significant factors in understanding and interpreting racial identity are the time and place in which the person's racial identity is lived and experienced. Attending to the time and place of this lived identity then adds texture and complexity to the identity and adds multiple voices to the identity. This polyphony of Black identity that is located in various places creates a creoleness that is more than a cultural, racial, and gender mixture. The concept of creoleness must be understood as liminality, a potential space, a spirituality, a creativity in which new identity can be developed. The significance of creoleness and its liminal space is that the other aspect of Black identity is the place of subjectivity. Complex subjectivity was used by early early Western philosophers, such as Hegel and Jefferson, to argue against the humanity of Blacks. In response to this approach, early African American theorists, artists, and educators worked to demonstrate the subjectivity of Blacks to argue that whites need to see Blacks as having a similar humanity. More contemporary Black theorists have suggested that subjectivity should be understood as a given, and have argued that subjectivity includes the capacity to perceive, interpret, and respond to the environment. This subjectivity is always evidenced in communal attachment to family and community, and this approach to subjectivity and consciousness is a more universal understanding of humanity as more communal than the Euro-American understanding of subjectivity that was based on individual meritocracy. The survivorship existed when the inner core of a person remained intact regardless of the demonic and mistaken ideology that racist and capitalist systems thought of themselves as having ultimate power.

This discussion on the importance of all the shades of Blackness and its performance are central aspects of understanding Blackness, which is more than biology, shared history, common tropes, or shared aesthetics. Jamaica Kincaid argues that Blackness is found in the in-betweenness and contradictions of life. Kincaid argues that Blackness, which began with legal definitions of chattel slavery, the "one-drop-rule," and Jim Crow and consequently develops into the complexity of any cultural or national or racial group. Kincaid also argues that Blackness is never bound by national borders or tropes but is a methodology that tears down repressive cultural ways of knowing and being.[11]

A more inclusive epistemology for Africana Studies and Black life is needed for multiple reasons. There are generally strong feelings of unity that are refreshing when it appears that diverse segments of Black communities are working in concert. Events like the Million Man March, the Black Lives Matter movement, and the Black Women's March all feel like they enrich the soul. In contrast, there are walls that seem to separate folks touched by the sun, whose origin was Africa, and the colonial exploitation of Africa. This is evidenced as Black people react with the same kind of abjection to other Blacks who do not meet their criteria of Blackness: The personal shame bordering on rage some Blacks have for other Blacks who ignore the split verb rule; the conversations around Barack Obama, with comments that he did not experience the "same Black experience as other Blacks"; the assumption that people needed to choose between Malcolm and Martin, or that the authentic Black experience was either on farms or in urban projects; the billions spent in Africa, and around the Diasporic communities on skin-bleaching agents; and the current versions of team light and team dark. The fixedness of colorism is as much a dimension of Black life today as it was for Black social clubs, churches, and intimate relationships in the past. Larsen pulls back the layers of complex, institutional, and intergenerational colorism that are overlapping and yet distinct between Black and white communities.

Africana epistemology is related to the interpretation and hermeneutics for understanding Black life, desires, and political strivings. Africana epistemology needs to become more inclusive; as the work of Dwayne

Tunstall, Heather Russell, and other scholars point out, Africana epistemology tends to be reductionist as it seeks to find common factors among the Black Atlantic communities. Next, there is a similarity between postcolonial West African religious traditions and much of the philosophical traditions of African American, Caribbean, and Africana philosophies of existence and religious traditions. But even with the similarities of various diasporic Africana communities, there remains a tendency for many in Africana thought to emphasize their distinctive characteristics. This suggests that even with a strong orientation toward communal identity, there remain multiple forces on Africana religious and philosophical thought that create different forms of othering and pseudospeciation that increase the likelihood of viewing other Africans in the diasporic community as different, a potential threat, and as competing for scarce resources. Because of this possible human tendency, and the effects of colonialization, orientations toward multiplicity and communal understandings of self and community are buried in singular notions of identity, community, sexuality, and subjectivity. A more inclusive epistemology creates more diversity in Africana's understanding of modes of knowledge production, the political, aesthetics, and acts of resistance.

In the work of developing a more inclusive epistemology there are a number of questions that will be addressed along the way. In her opening remarks for a symposium honoring Hazel Carby titled "A Future Beyond Empire," Saidiya Hartman offers a number of useful questions related to studying the lives of Black women.[12]

1. Who patrols the boundaries of race, and what are the institutions and instruments used in the maintenance of these boundaries?
2. How does one reconstruct the lives of the anonymous, the disposables, and the forgotten and the relationship of this reconstruction to the healing of community?
3. How does one describe the social life of objects, are these objects gendered, and if so how?
4. How does one tell the story of the life of those who are dead and retrieve the remains that are dormant?
5. What is the purchase of those stories on our lives and work?
6. How does one create a story from the locus of impossible speech and resurrect lives from the ruins?[13]

The framing and discussions of these questions that are never answered become almost hermeneutics for exploring every new racialized, engendered, and class interaction. The purpose is to explore each question with a curiosity that moves beyond reaction formation, or reified ways of responding to life that do not simply reestablish archaic and repressive ways of being in the world. Larsen presents Helga as being like a young mulatto girl who comes home from school one day and simply asks, "What color am I?" The question was raised by a five-year-old biracial girl with blond hair and skin color that was somewhere between an olive tan, high yella, or what others would call Jamaica White. As a psychologist, I held group marital counseling for interracial couples. That year there were seven couples, most married an average of ten years, all with preadolescent children. The couples were in counseling not primarily because they were interracial, but because they had biracial children asking disturbing questions about race, racial classification, and the meaning of their racial identity, and I think, whether the chosen racial identity might foreclose a relationship with the parent identified as the "opposing" racial group. The children were like a Greek Chorus, or in psychological terms, the return of the repressed that articulates and dramatizes the unspoken and the emotional ghosts of their parents and culture. One spunky eight-year-old boy, when told "no" by his dark-skinned African American mother, would walk out of the room and in a stage whisper say, "When I get older, I'm going to marry a white woman." The enraged mother chose counseling over killing the boy, though feeling that the latter was always the right of every Black mother.

It was surprising how much anxiety, bordering on shame and terror, was generated in parents when their children asked questions about their racial identity. This was surprising because the intensity of the parents' response was close to expressing the feeling that the day they had feared most had come and they now must face what they had worked to repress. It was evident that for both Black and white partners these were questions about race they were unable to confront. This is not the simple question of whether to put Black or white on a census form. It is the set of questions of what kind of Black person they will be in relation to the diversity of Blacks and whites; how this will differ depending on context and location; how will they anticipate how others will respond to how they decide to perform their racial identity. More important, how will they manage the shaming and intergenerational trauma that families, schools, and institutions use to teach racial identity? Thandeka, in *Learning to Be White*, outlines the shaming and trauma that almost always accompany whites learning a racial identity.[14] There is a similar shaming that is related to the racial melancholia: mourning of the middle passage and the millions lost, mourning the subjugation of slavery, mourning the trauma of racial apartheid, all of which frequently seem to be more in the actions and values of others rather than in one's self. The response of Blacks and whites to Helga/Larsen can be most accurately understood as racial melancholia; the Blackness and whiteness of mulattos, biracial, mixed, and creole persons are a living testimony, symbols of an intense and horrific racialized history that continues to replicate itself in each succeeding generation. *Quicksand* traces this history and is always suggesting strategies for breaking out of this obsessive, self-reproducing history upon which empires are dependent.

The question by the young girl caused profound anxiety and grief in her parents, which likely matched the anxiety and grief in the young child. Feeling powerless in the face of essentialist definitions of race, there are numerous other unspoken and unacknowledged experiences that have already become foundational to her identity. What was most interesting was the anxiety and grief of the parents as they sought to respond to their biracial child and what this would mean for their future relationship to the child. Does choosing one identity mean that she would lose the other side of her identity? Larsen seemed intent that African Americans were Black and they were also American—not more or less than other communities, but they had a unique identity that was fully their own, a complex interiority that was both universal and peculiar to just them. The Black literary canon, especially works by Black women, more often displayed this combination of being at home nowhere and yet the whole world was their home. This sense of complete alienation and at home-ness was and is a critical aspect of an identity that mourned what is lost in choices and yet creates an identity beyond empire.

For Larsen, Helga Crane, and the young girl from my parents' group, the question "What color am I?" in multiple ways is asked by each person every day of their life. This question is asked repeatedly by *Quicksand* depending on a variety of factors. This question has different meanings when she is unemployed, teaching in a college, the impoverished wife rejected by her community, or living in Europe. Even more critical is whether there is a centering creolized identity that frees Helga to reflect on the significance of the questions within each context. The biomythography migrates along places of injury throughout Larsen's life. The critical difference in the novel is that now she is able to reflect on the meanings of the interactions and the motives of the people she encounters. The creolization provides a liminal space to decide on her identity and the meaning this has for her. The core of trauma is that the event is inscribed on the body and the victim is unable to give meaning to the events. Regardless of the outcome of Helga's travels and encounters, Larsen always presents her as reflective, interpreting, deciding, gaining new insights about herself and the people around her. This empowering and transcending capacity to interpret the narrative of her life makes Helga a powerful protagonist. She is very different from the characters of many Black novels who appear to be unable to understand the racial and economic forces that are driving them.

Helga provides keen insight into the socialization process that inscribes racialized social categories onto her mulatto body. This social, political, and cultural inscription on bodies is racialized and gendered and has historical, social, and cultural reinforcements. These reinforcements attempt to block memories of how this inscription occurs; blocking the memories then leads to an avoidance of persons viewed as being like us—and of persons seen as other. The question "What color am I?" highlights the inherent instability of racial categories not only because the questioner is biracial. Rather, this essay points out that all racial identities require, insist on, and demand a daily decision about lifestyles, political actions, religious sentiments, choices about food, and sexual partners. The conscious, unconscious, and subconscious personal and cultural decisions that each person asks of themselves and of each other ("what color am I/are you") are perpetual and determined by a confluence of forces that are responding and readjusting to the facets of one's ethnic identity, both within one's ethnic group and with a range of other ethnic groups.

Larsen—like the little girl who asks, "What color am I?"—is not only asking about the Black-white binary, but is asking about which Black community should I attempt to identity with, to call my people. Who is my tribe? What would it mean to associate with Blacks who are just "folks"—those down-home folks who are uneducated, poor, and living in tenements? What would it mean to situate herself with the blue-collar working-class folks or the Black intelligentsia? Larsen theorizes that the efforts of African Americans are in the emotions and create a psychic culture of repair from the trauma of slavery and its aftermath. She also argues that these reparative efforts often become pathogenic and what is is often celebrated as Black culture are conditions that may be as problematic as the diseases of racism and capitalism. The obsession with regaining lost objects seen in consumerism; the fixation on the shape, coloring, and adornment of the body; the intensity by which people are desperate for recognition and approval from others, and experience no identification with those who are different—all suggest dynamics of mourning and melancholia. Mourning and melancholia are conditions in which persons are unable to grieve, to move beyond the traumas of the past, and then move to create identities and communities that are beyond empire. Like the protagonist in her novels, Larsen seeks to find a place where women feel vital in a social, cultural, and psychological economy that routinely inscribes mothers in general, and Black mothers, specifically, in terms of a paradox of omnipotence and lack.

Much of the recent scholarship and aesthetics of Blackness have allowed the humanity of Blackness to break through the boundaries that re-create the dehumanizing templates of Euro-American colonial capitalism. *Quicksand* by Larsen playfully examines the intersection of skin color and the performance and performativity of racial and gender identity, which are frequently taken to be reflective of how individuals view themselves in comparison with other people of color, whether in the United States or around the world, and in relationships to whites. This interaction is interpreted as a display of allegiance to and pride in Black cultural values or a choice to be submissive to Euro-American culture.[15] This aspect of the performativity of Black identity is also considered to signify a diversity of meaning including the phantasmagoric legacy of slavery, and how the repressed memories of this past horror are evoked with every interracial, gendered, and familiar encounter. As James Baldwin points out, this legacy, remaining largely unconscious, determines whether we play pool, checkers or chess, who we love or fail to love, as well as our performance in the bedroom. What is called the legacy of slavery in other places is referred to as intergenerational cultural trauma, that is re-created and relived in subsequent generations. These tragic encounters would be relived in the psyches and in individuals, but would also emerge in the cultures and institutions of Blacks and whites.

Helga Crane foreshadows and extends our understanding of the desires, rage, and envy analyzed by Frantz Fanon, Paul Gilroy, and Anne Cheng. Larsen reveals that mulattos do not live merely between Black and white worlds, but are instead powerful tricksters who instead express racial melancholia. This racial melancholia, a dread of self and others, a fear of both loss and gain, a denial of life, death, and resurrection, continues to direct intraracial and interracial dynamics that never entirely become (post)colonial. Last, the subjectivity of the mulatto always challenges and destabilizes traditional diasporic themes of home, mother/daughter, middle passage, and racial identity in a manner that makes each of these more of an ethical, rather than psychological, social or political commitment. Although Larsen's character moves through several times and places, Africana hermeneutics used in this study would suggest that a more compelling understanding of this work assumes that sequencing and linear understanding of the text hides the richness of the work. This essay approaches the multiple events and places of the novel as representing various dynamics of the individual. This approach then reveals the creoleness of all racial, ethnic, and gender identity.

Michelle Wright refers to this shifting, ever-changing dynamics of ethnic identity as the "physics of Blackness." Her argument is that the diversity of a community makes it impossible to make general statements about Black identity and history. The life of a sharecropper is different in innumerous ways from that of an African American lawyer on Wall Street. There is not only the difference of experience between sharecropper and Wall Street lawyer, but we must also consider additional differences such as disabilities, gender, biraciality, immigration, and how these variations relate within groups and with the diverse members of other racial and ethnic groups. The question "What color am I?" suggests that these differences are also shaped by time and place. This looks different in New York during the Harlem Renaissance than in the civil rights movement or the riots in Detroit. When Blacks are assessing how they perform their ethnic identity, biracial and light-skinned persons are a critical point of comparison. The social, cultural, and political exchanges between these groups are pivotal in assessing how people judge the normative and how they embody and perform their racial identity.

Interracial couples and biracial children frame many of the fundamental issues related to Diasporic consciousness, racial identity formation, and the expressions of mourning and the drive toward complex subjectivity. Interracial families perform their own enactments of racial melancholia that include fears of the significance of racial identity and the extent this identity is dependent on the actions of racial others. The son's taunts to his mother and the girl asking the question are the living embodiment of Fanon's *Black Skins, White Masks* and the complexity of Black/white relationships. An aspect of Black-white relationships is the pseudoscientific binary that is used as a taunt to a Black mother as a less desirable object. In one deft move, the son denigrates the mother as undesirable, either as a love object or one to pass on cultural heritage and values. In his denigration of his mother, he also critiques his father's failure for not having chosen a more desirable object.

On the evening the parents were distressed by a question from their young daughter who came home from school and asked, "What color am I?," the mother gave the typical answer of many interracial parents: that she was all the colors of the rainbow, that she was a bright, articulate, amazing young lady who could accomplish anything she wanted in life. The daughter, hands on hips, feet planted firmly, said to her mother, "You're Black, your mother is Black, and your whole family is Black." The little girl went on to say that dad was white, his parents were white, and all the rest of his family were all white. The parents were more upset by the question of racial and ethnic identity than ones like: Where do babies come from, why are mommy and daddy fighting, or what's the funny smelling stuff dad smokes in the backyard. Of all the statements that caused discomfort between and within these interracial couples it was the question about the child's racial identity that clearly caused the most anxiety, an anxiety that was somewhere between mourning and grief. Anne Cheng, reflecting Fanon's treatise in *Black Skins, White Mask*, and Thandeka in *Learning to Be White*, argue that the initial conscious and social awareness of racial identity and its subsequent development is a process of shaming and melancholia. The parents' distress is most likely not an awareness of the various and complex implications of the daughter's question about her life, but a reminder of their own experience of racial trauma.

The young biracial girl and boy embody and signify the focal concern outlined by Fanon and other diasporic Africana theorists about the construction of Black identity. The identity formation of Blackness is not only about the time and space in which Blackness was created by the dynamics between Blacks and whites. This is a dynamic in which all racialized and gendered bodies develop a racial identity in a lived narrative in relationship with members of their ethnic group. The psycho-social-political theories of Fanon, Du Bois, Michelle Wright, and others argue that the relationship is intersubjective, not one of object and subject. Biraciality is the result of interracial encounters. Interracial encounters that produce the construct of Blackness and whiteness assume a homogeneity among ethnic groups and confront fantasies of Jefferson, Hegel, and others, especially those that assume the American Myth of founding fathers that construct a nation as originally white, which simultaneously denies past and previous racial mixture. This interracial mixture suggests contradictions in the construct of race. Diasporic people possess an array of different cultural, national, ethnic, religious, and ancestral origins. Black identity and Black subjectivity consider that the contradictions in the Africana Diaspora are negotiated between extremes—hypercollectivity and postcolonial hyperindividuality.

Historical and contemporary scholars, artists, and activists of Diasporic expressions in one way or another seem to be focused on the same question of the young girl, asking "What color am I?" This question has layers of complexity and eddies beyond whether the individual or group is asking if they should call themselves Black or white. To ask the question "What color am I?" is the question of identity and subjectivity. The other and more central question is the implication of the daughter's question. The mother's response that suggests creolization or hybridity has the intriguing quality of feeling that the mother has both avoided answering the question and spoken a deeper reality. The young girl is aware that most persons identify with one particular ethnic group, regardless of how mixed their cultural heritage. Even when a parent or grandparent generally reflects a vast array of ethnic and social complexity, most individuals choose to live with the racial/ethnic identity that reflects a number of factors such as language, parental decisions, skin color, early social environment, and what may be most important, how their social world defines them.

Quicksand clearly outlines the process of the construction and deconstruction of race as a given of diasporic lives. The approach used in this essay assumes that the performed mask of biraciality is used as a trope to maintain and destabilize the binary of Black and white identities. The social construct of biraciality, since all persons are biracial, seems to affirm the fantasy that some people have a pure ethnic identity and enables the hierarchical ranking of races. The trope of biraciality is also an embodied memorial to a legacy of the transatlantic slave trade, and the economic, social, and political discrimination against persons of color. The trope of biraciality is also an embodied and psychological memorial to the legacy of the transatlantic slave, and the economic, social, and political discrimination against persons of color.

The question that day, "What color am I?" arose because of its immediate relevance for the young child who had just started school. Much of a child's life is organized around the issue of race, fitting into one racial group or the other, and deciding how to treat other racial groups. Typical questions about race emerge in children soon after they learn to talk. This is the likely result of their processing so much information, so many feelings, and so many images of race before the acquisition of language. This process is aided and heightened by images from television, in cartoons, at family gatherings, in church, and between their parents. The development of the racial identity for children at such an early stage in their life suggests that feelings and thoughts of racial identity would be embodied and reside predominantly in unconscious processes. Beverly Tatum's *Why Are All the Black Kids Sitting Together in the Cafeteria: And Other Conversations about Race*,[16] and Debra Van Ausdale's *The First R: How Children Learn Race and Racism*[17] give strong arguments for the enormous psychic and emotional energy children use in forming their racial and gender identity that is embodied and unconscious, and later they have only fragmented memories of how they have come to feel and think of themselves as racial objects. Since this early narrative on race is internalized before the acquisition of language, and is done in conjunction with rituals of shaming, dynamics of power and affection, privileging and social ranking and intense social anxiety, the process of racial identity is often a shaming and traumatic process.[18] Just imagine the inner life of a two-year-old child, who has the processing capacity of a computer observing the last presidential election, with all the stark images of walls, migration, and social conflict about color and then also watching the fear that often accompanies mom and dad negotiating issues of color and race.

In most cases the children have little conscious memory or later awareness of these early racial transactions, and these images become entombed and memorialized in a sociomatic process that is epigenetic, emotional, and determines social interactions and culture productions. It will influence whether they play basketball or hockey, their choice to be a good student or avoid school, whom they love or fail to love, and as Baldwin stated, their comfort in the bedroom and the bathroom.[19] Since the foundations of gender, racial, and contextual identity are shaped by processes that are out of awareness and embodied, most of our insight into this process comes through our stories. Stories are where the hidden and secret places of our hearts emerge. The desires and fears of the heart are hidden in the depths of our stories and narratives. Stories are by definition unfaithful. Reality can't be told or reported. The only thing that can be done with reality is to make it again. We tell the analysis of our stories in connection with what is embodied, and this can add significant insights into how persons are theorizing and experiencing their Blackness.

A possible way of understanding the significance of the little girl's question, "What color am I?" and why it stirred such deep and powerful emotions in her parents is by closely examining stories and narratives about race and how they get memorialized in the body. The analysis of stories, particularly what is signified by bodies in these stories, may be productive in interpreting new or different aspects of diasporic identity and how Blacks experience their own subjectivity. It is evident in the growing attention to literary criticism within diasporic communities, among womanists and queer theorists, that stories—both written and oral—and novels and other artistic productions and representations are crucial sites of counterdiscourse and creative narratives for developing complex interiority.

BIRACIALITY: EMBODIMENT AND PERFORMANCE OF RACIAL IDENTITY

Biraciality is the performance of masks that destabilize Western binaries of race. Biraciality performs the traditional Western understanding of racial identity that understands racial identity as being worn on the skin and that this marker of identity signifies the interior and social life of the individual. Biraciality might stir anxiety for some in pointing to the social reality that parents have broken social taboos against the mixing of races. Biraciality though also opens the door that biracial identity and creolization is a possibility for everyone. Biraciality is an act of resistance as well as a space for creativity. Masking signals the simultaneous emergence of a Black subject by denial of the idealistic dialectic. Masking is a strategy to deconstruct Western logos, allowing one to analyze the relationship of

Black consciousness within the context of Western racist discourse. Biraciality as a form of masking explores the subjectivity of Black consciousness by refusing to give authority over one's life to any particular group or ideology. Masking has the role of providing a home for the exploration and analysis of the Black self, a home that can never be totally provided for by father or mother, or any religious or political organization. The home is something that is made, found, and created individually and collectively. The mask of biraciality has a double function. It creates colonial discourse and expresses the counterclaim of the Black and racialized subject. It is a speech act of logos, and it is a performance of subversion. It is mimicry and hybridity. It is Africana diasporic counterdiscourse that is inscribed on the body, and a performed act of subversion of neocolonial discourse and much of Black counterdiscourse that replicates and articulates the space for a Black complex interiority.

Larsen's particular use of the mulatto figure allowed her protagonist to be both inside and outside contemporary race issues. Helga was critical of what she regarded as an all-pervasive concern with race problems and simultaneously she herself was subject to racism. The section of the novel set in Copenhagen confronted directly the question of the representation of Blacks by whites in contrast with how Blacks represented themselves to each other and to whites. Biraciality exists between the the abstract, the ideal, the social and the material. It is abstract in that it is a category that reaffirms the Western ideological construct of whiteness, since anyone who is not white is Black. From another perspective, biraciality—instead of bridging expanding notions of race, if not understood from the space of creolization—makes the categories of race more rigid and bounded. Biraciality is an identity that is produced in the contradictions and ambivalences of postcolonial life. Larsen presents a view of Black and White racial identities in which all subjectivity exists in the in-between space, the visible and invisible that is now home. Larsen is contending that life is always that thing, the way of being and becoming and can only be known indirectly, can never be accurately named, and which confounds each of us. Biraciality represents the way that each racial group remembers, recollecting lost selves and relationships, and memorializing metanarratives of suffering and erasure. Naming someone as biracial challenges the myths of racial purity, and racial othering. Biraciality is an expression of the body as a text that calls for new ways for people to connect to the past and orient themselves to the future. Biraciality as a performativity and as a mask is a two-edged sword that challenges traditional discourses on race and poses new directions and goals for diasporic identity that are not fixed in melancholic strategies of existence. Wearing or embodying a mask, or multiple masks in the case of Helga Crane, suggests that the struggle and process of identity formation takes place neither underneath or behind the demands for justice and a desire for a safe, ethical place that facilitates stable communal process. This is a sociomatic process where the social is inscribed on the body, and a process that leans toward the epigenetic, shapes the identity, body, and emotions of the subject, and also changes and alters the social, the economic, and the political. Larsen critiques the discourse on race in the United States, and reveals dynamics of this discourse that remain hidden and yet determines so much of our social, political, and intimate lives. This critique displays not only the problems of the past, but also points to possible hope for the future.

NOTES

1. Mary Helen Washington, "Nella Larsen: Mystery Woman of the Harlem Renaissance," *Ms Magazine*, December 1980, 45.
2. Hazel Carby, *Restructuring Womanhood: The Emergence of the Afro-American Woman Novelist* (New York: Oxford University Press, 1987).
3. Falguni A. Sheth, "Interstitiality: Making Space for Migration, Diaspora, and Racial Complexity," *Hypatia* 29, no. 1 (2014): 75–93.
4. Heather Russell, *Legba's Crossing: Narratology in the African Atlantic* (Athens: University of Georgia Press, 2009).
5. George Hutchinson, *In Search of Nella Larsen: A Biography of the Color Line* (Cambridge, MA: Belknap Press of Harvard University Press, 2006).
6. Hazel V. Carby, "'On the Threshold of Woman's Era': Lynching, Empire, and Sexuality in Black Feminist Theory," *Critical Inquiry* 12, no. 1 (1985): 262–77.
7. Pamela Cooper-White, *Many Voices: Pastoral Psychotherapy in Relational Theological Perspective* (Minneapolis: Fortress Press, 2011), 51–61.
8. Lloyd T. Delany, "The Other Bodies in the River," in Reginald L. Jones, ed., *Black Psychology*, (California: Cobb & Henry Publishers, 1991), 597–607.
9. Cathy Caruth, *Unclaimed Experience: Trauma, Narration and History* (Baltimore: John Hopkins University Press, 1996), 115–18.
10. Skip Gates, *The Signifying Monkey* (New York: Oxford University Press, 1988).
11. Jamaica Kincaid, *At the Bottom of the River* (New York: Farrar, Straus and Giroux, 1983).

12. Saidiya Hartman, "A Future Beyond Empire," in honor of Hazel Carby, conference "Reconstructing Womanhood: A Future Beyond Empire," Barnard College, New York, December 12, 2007.
13. Ibid.
14. Thandeka, *Learning to Be White* (New York: Continuum Books, 2000).
15. Michelle M. Wallace, *The Physics of Blackness: Beyond the Middle Passage Epistemology* (Minneapolis: University of Minnesota Press, 2015).
16. Beverly Tatum, *Why Are All the Black Kids Sitting Together in the Cafeteria* (New York: Basic Books, 1999).
17. Debra Van Ausdale, *The First R: How Children Learn Race and Racism* (Lanham, MD: Rowman & Littlefield, 2001).
18. Anne Anlin Cheng, *The Melancholy of Race: Psychoanalysis, Assimilation, and Hidden Grief* (Oxford: Oxford University Press, 2001).
19. James Baldwin, *Evidence of Things Not Seen* (New York: Henry Holt, 1985).

2. Body as Praxis: Disarticulating the Human from Ownership and Property

AN YOUNTAE

I want to propose here that this uprising is directed
not only at our present order of discourse . . .
but also at the tradition of discourse to which
its specific discourse of man belongs:
that is, at the tradition on whose basis, from 1512 onward,
Western Europe was to effect the first stage
in the secularization of human existence
in the context of its own global expansion
and to lay the basis of plantation structure . . .
—SYLVIA WYNTER, *Beyond the Word of Man*

Decolonization is truly the Creation of New Men.
—FRANTZ FANON, *The Wretched of the Earth*

The body bears witness to a complex history of signification. Through time, it has constantly been a contested battlefield of social signification. Straddling both the public and the private, the body is an active social text through which the production of subjects and power takes place. But the normativity of particular bodies entails foreclosure of certain others. Certain bodies are deemed worthy of life over others who are constantly exposed to the threat of being crushed to death; certain bodies embody the quality of full humanity while others do not.

The body as the site for the inscription of power takes the place of modern political subject. Giorgio Agamben traces the birth of this biopolitical subject back to the inception of modern democracy as found in *habeas corpus*, the legal writ that orders release of the detainee, which translates as "you shall have the body."[1] *Habeas corpus* puts the body subject to both freedom and sovereign power at the same time. It marks the production of what he calls "the bare life," a life articulated in terms of *zoe* (biological life) stripped of *bios* (political life).[2] However, as Alexander Weheliye has pointed out, Agamben's bare life is blind to the deep and complex structure of racialization that constitutes "the human." Although all bodies are subject to sovereign power, only particular bodies are deemed human over others who are not. Biopower and biopolitics are not color-blind. Some bodies are subject to sovereign power but not to freedom. One's humanity is defined only by the non-humanness of others who are incapable of transcending the finitude of their bodily lives.

The modern Western subject has constantly denied its association with body. White Christian bodies transcend corpus, the carnal weaknesses and desires. The notion of the human grounding modern liberal humanism parallels the long history of the denial of humanity of colonized and racialized bodies. Sylvia Wynter challenges modern-liberal humanism by calling it the overrepresentation of Man, which means that the Western liberal ideal of secular-rational human has taken the place of universal humanity.[3] However, Black and brown bodies are indispensable for the survival of white bodies. The colonial other *must be the body* for the European subject who represents reason. The master's livability depends on the body and the labor of the slave.

Hegel's well-known section on Lordship and Bondsman, otherwise known as the master-slave dialectic, offers important insights when read through the American philosopher Judith Butler who suggests that the Hegelian dialectic presents the imperative of being a body for the master. The master, Butler writes, commands the slave to *be* the body: "You be my body for me."[4] What does it mean that the body, as bare life, is not only subject to sovereign violence but also to the command to be the body for the bodiless Man? What happens to the body between the double transactions of transfer (of body) and suspension (of humanness)? What do these injunctions reveal about the meaning of being a human? Are contemporary philosophical discussions of the human—which have their roots in Renaissance and modern humanism—capable of accommodating critical analyses of violence inflicted on those bodies that are unqualified for the category of the human? The notion of the human conditions to a certain extent the understanding of the self's relation to its body. Conversely, rethinking our relation to body may open a new perspective for resignifying the notion of the human. Might the recent turn to flesh allow us to think differently as well as explore new sites, possibilities, and orientations in the ways we conceive our humanity in relation to body, the other, and the sacred?

The emerging discourse of posthumanism has compellingly contributed to the resituating of "the human," which has been hitherto heavily constructed by the conceptual apparatus of Enlightenment humanism. Despite its close examination of regulatory social categories that produce the normative notion of the human such as technology, animals and non-human life forms, gender and sexuality, other key constitutive elements of the human, such as race and coloniality, have been largely ignored.

The question of the human is also central to many Africana critical theorists. In their work, the "post" predicating human is often met with strong skepticism. As Lewis Gordon has put it, humanism cannot be easily discarded in Africana tradition as "dominant groups can 'give up' humanism for the simple fact that *their humanity* is presumed, while other communities have struggled too long for the humanistic prize."[5] This does not mean that Black critical thinkers have strived to be included in the Enlightenment humanist idea of the human. Rather, it indicates, they have for a long time strived to rethink and challenge the notion of the human itself. The works of thinkers such as Aimé Césaire, Frantz Fanon, and Sylvia Wynter are some of the many examples that attempt to rethink the notion of the human and its relationship to the constitution of racial and colonial power relations. In particular, Sylvia Wynter has been insistent in pressing the question of the human.

Wynter reads the colonial expansion of Europe in the Americas as a secularist-humanist reinvention of itself as the rational political subject over the religious other of the New World. The insight Wynter offers carries profound implications for both the study of colonialism (or coloniality) and the study of religion. By reading modernity/coloniality as essentially a project of secularization, Wynter questions the fundamental categories of religion and the secular—and, even more importantly, how such notions have informed the construction of modern humanism.

This chapter seeks to rethink the question of the human as a theological problem. Following Sylvia Wynter who views modern/colonial reinvention of the human as a secularist project, I trace the political theology behind the modern/colonial notion of the human back to the sixteenth-century Valladolid debate. I pay close attention to the notion of the body understood in terms of possession and property. The denial of full humanity of non-European others relied on the reduction of their being to body. By looking at both the Hegelian master-slave dialectic and Africana critical theorists' (especially Hortense Spillers and Alexander Weheliye) use of the flesh, I search for possibilities to undo the colonial political theology's construction of the human.

As David Scott remarks in his interview with Sylvia Wynter, the story of humanism as "a kind of European-coming-of-age-story" obscures the connection between humanism and dehumanization. In this sense, the birth of Renaissance humanism is "simultaneously the moment of initiation of Europe's colonial project."[6] Therefore, rethinking the terms of Eurocentric humanism is the first step for constructing an anti-colonial or anti-necropolitical theology. The self-generative capacity of life and its unbreakable bind to the other displaces the self-possessed subject of the modern liberal-political tradition. Caught in between double injunctions, between prescription and suspension, the body as flesh offers new forms of thinking about political subjectivity, labor, and of being human as a praxis.

THE HUMAN: MAN AND THE DEHUMANIZATION OF THE COLONIAL OTHER

Posthumanism has advanced important theoretical and conceptual frameworks for probing the limits of modern humanist discourse. By deconstructing the normative attributes of the human established by Renaissance-modern humanism, it displaces the strong sovereignty of human agency. In doing so, posthumanism "studies cultural representations and power relations that have situated humans above other life forms."[7] But despite acknowledging the connection between speciesist humanism and discriminatory practices,[8] posthumanist discourse has not been able to move beyond the narrow boundary of its West-centric focus. The large absence of interest in non-Western thought as well as the problem of race and colonialism in posthumanist discourse indicates its limits as a theoretical tool caught within the confines of liberalism. This tendency is shared by many contemporary postmodern theories that view race and coloniality as a mere addendum to the vast web of social oppression. Such approaches to modernity fall regrettably short as they are unable to locate the power mechanism of coloniality organizing the basic principles of modern-liberalism. Posthumanism questions the normative category of the human by following Foucault's claims that "man is a recent invention."[9] But despite viewing the human as a contestable political category, posthumanism fails to examine how colonial production of racialized subjects has informed the modern notion of the human.

Although rarely invoked by most Eurocentric theorists of posthumanism, the Jamaican essayist and critical theorist Sylvia Wynter makes crucial contributions to posthumanist discourse. Wynter challenges the fundamental foundations of Renaissance and modern humanism by disarticulating the gendered and racialized elements that constitute the idea of Man within the historical and epistemological framework of modernity/coloniality. Religion's significant role in this process often goes unnoticed. But in Wynter's reading, the colonization of the Americas cannot be separated from the invention of religion and "the secular." The driving ethos behind the colonial enterprise was the continuing endeavor of Europe's self-transformation in which the reinvention of its selfhood as secularist-humanist-based political subject against the theocratic hegemony of the Church was at stake.[10] Thus begins the invention of "Man" with Renaissance humanism's reformulation of the "Judeo-Christian genre of the human," culminating in the encounter with colonial others.[11] As the other of the secular-rational self, the Native/Black became the repository of original lack (sin), the lack of being:[12]

> Ontological Lack [is] therefore the signifier of symbolic "death.". . .
> At the end of the eighteenth and during the nineteenth century the construct of an atavistic, genetically dysselected Lack of normal human nature took the now purely secular place of both Original Sin and of the earlier hybridly religio-secular construct of Sensory-Nature. The new Lack was now conceptualized as that of racial "normalcy" and was embodied in the recently freed Black/Africoid population, who now took the place of the prebaptismal Laity as conceptual Other, as the embodiment, that is, of the "dysgenic human subject" in place of the "fallen natural man" of the feudal-Christian schema.[13]

The Western history of secularization cannot be separated from the history of racialization of colonial others in which original lack was translated into racial lack, the space of otherness. The Indio and the Negro were the symbolic other of the Rational Man. The question of who is the human, therefore, emerges as a colonial-theological project. The human in this sense is a theological question, a question of political theology.

The transition from the theocratic order to the modern secular state does not indicate that theological sovereignty is displaced from the power of theopolitical governance and biopolitical management. In Carl Schmitt's classical thesis, the essence of sovereignty is defined by the decision on the state of exception. Achille Mbembe refines the politico-theological notion of sovereignty advanced by Carl Schmitt. Drawing on Michel Foucault's notion of biopower and Giorgio Agamben's idea of sovereign exception, Mbembe defines sovereignty as "the capacity to dictate who may live and who must die."[14] The modern (and colonial) state's biopolitical production of subjects consists of managing bodies that are regulated by normative notions of reason and freedom, while sovereignty is determined not by "the struggle for autonomy" as modern political philosophers would argue, but by the right to kill.[15] Colonies exemplify the site in which such necropolitical states of exception and suspension of judicial right are enacted, par excellence. The extra-judicial rule is enabled for Mbembe by "the racial denial of any common bond between the conqueror and the native." The notion of the human facilitates the break of such a tie as savages are deemed to lack human quality.[16]

The *de*humanization of colonial others was a juridical conclusion that overshadowed the theology lying underneath it: a colonial political theology with the imperial sovereign deciding who is human and who is not, life over death. Such political theology was already budding in the thoughts of the sixteenth-century Renaissance humanists whose ideas had a significant influence on the Valladolid debate, which consisted of a series of exchanges between juridical scholars and theologians over the Indigenous question.

Part of my goal in this essay is to demonstrate that the modern-secularist and necropolitical invention of Man was made possible by the reduction of colonial other into body and how the notion of property and ownership played a key role in the process. At stake was the incorporation of Native/Black bodies into a labor force and the control (delegation and exploitation) of their labor. Referring to the 1512 Spanish laws of Burgos, Wynter demonstrates how coloniality in the Americas was enacted through biopolitical governance and organization of Indigenous bodies aimed at cultivating a rational, disenchanted, yet malleable labor force.[17] Thus, anti-colonial struggles aim at challenging the biopolitical manifestation of power and rethinking the particular genre of human imposed by Europe. The universalizing notion of the human is provincialized in the works of Wynter, who politicizes the term by uncovering the politico-theological meaning inscribed in its fabric. The hegemonic installation of the West's monohumanist Man first took place with the Renaissance humanists' conceptualization of the human as a rational political subject (secular oriented) and later by modern humanists who gave rise to the bourgeois mode of being a human (science and biocentric).[18]

The history of the Antilles is a living testimony to the struggle against the hegemonic monopoly of humanity by Europe. The intellectual genealogy of the Black Caribbean tradition signals an upheaval against not only colonialism, but also Europe's project of secularization of human existence.[19] The modernization of colonies cannot be separated from the project of disenchanting the Natives from their beliefs in "magic" and "superstitious cosmology." The role that the Western academic discipline of religious studies played in Europe's imperialist expansion through modernity cannot be emphasized enough. Modern comparative religion's definition of religion necessitated its other, namely, the non-Western others whose beliefs in "primitive myths" and "irrational cosmology" put the nature of their humanity into question.[20] Once their humanity is suspended, the legitimacy of governance and control can be rationalized with ease. The modern theological invention of the human as opposed to the non-human (or less than human) finds its historical root in sixteenth-century Renaissance theologians who played key roles in shaping the Valladolid debate, a historical milestone that sought theological legitimacy for the colonial enterprise of Europe in the Americas.

DEFINING THE HUMAN: PROPERTY AND OWNERSHIP

The juridico-theological debates in sixteenth-century Spain reveal important ideas that demonstrate how the Renaissance humanist conception of the human morphs into modern humanism through colonial encounter. These debates laid the foundation not only for modern humanism but also for the juridical-political ideas of sovereignty, just war, international law, and cosmopolitanism.

The sixteenth-century humanist debate on the natives of the new world was crucial in establishing basic political concepts essential to modern-liberalism such as reason, freedom, right to property ownership, and equality. Here, my reading centers on the notion of ownership and property as they seem to constitute the key defining elements of the human in the eyes of juridical and theological scholars at the dawn of modernity. This means, on the one hand, Spanish scholars regarded the faculty to own property as a key defining attribute of the human. On the other hand, once rendered less than human, natives were reduced to property subject to possession by the Spanish Crown. Thus, colonial others were reduced to body–as property subject to private ownership.

The colonial encounter and Europeans' treatment of natives were constant subjects of ongoing debates at the dawn of modernity. Most important of these was the Valladolid debate of the mid-sixteenth century. The central concern of these conversations was the humanity of Indians. Against Bartolomé de Las Casas who defended Indians' right to be treated equally, Spanish Renaissance humanist and theologian Ginés de Sepúlveda argued for slavery by resorting to Aristotelian natural law. Discussing just war theory, Sepúlveda evokes the Indians as an example of justifications for war. For Sepúlveda, justification for war can be sustained when it is against

> those barbarians vulgarly called Indians, whose defense you seem to have taken up, is as follows: That those whose natural condition is such that they must obey others, if they refuse that lordship and there is no other recourse, may be subdued by arms; and that this war is just according to the opinion of the most eminent philosophers.[21]

Sepúlveda invokes the Aristotelian natural law. In *Politics*, Aristotle lays out the notion of natural slavery based in the principles of natural law when the enslaved are considered to be a lower form of existence:

> It is both natural and expedient for the body to be ruled by the soul, and for the emotional part of our natures to be ruled by the mind, the part which possesses reason. The reverse, or even parity, would be

fatal all around. This is also true between man and the other animals; for tame animals are by nature better than wild, and it is better for them all to be ruled by man, because it secures their safety. Again, as between male and female the former is by nature superior and ruler, the latter inferior and subject. And this must be good for all mankind in general.[22]

Aristotle maintains that the slave is a man, but an incomplete, half man as he is inseparably dependent on his master. The slave is a "living but separate part of his master's frame."[23] It is also the master who thinks for the slave.[24] Reason constitutes the essential character lacking for those who are "slaves by nature." However, it is not just reason itself that separates free person from slaves. Rather it is the *possession* of it, for slaves can *participate* in it, yet not *possess* it.[25]

The association of humanity with ownership was predominant among Spanish humanists. A few decades before the debate, Spanish jurist Juan López de Palacios Rubios wrote an opinion on the legal legitimacy of Spanish presence in America per the request of King Ferdinand. While Palacios Rubios viewed the Indians as rational and peaceful beings, he observed that the lack of sense of ownership of land meant they did not understand the complexity of human custom and society: that they did not know how to rule themselves.[26] The same view regarding the association of the human with property is also found in Francisco de Vitoria, the founder of the school of Salamanca, whose thoughts were highly influential on Bartolomé de Las Casas. It was Las Casas and his colleagues in the Salamanca School who produced the most important documents countering Sepúlveda.

In the defense of Indians' humanity and their rationality, Vitoria uses Aristotle's notion of potentiality and actuality, and claims that Indians' rationality was in the stage of *potentia*.[27] The problem was not therefore in their nature. Like the poor peasants in Europe, the problem was the environment, the education.[28] Although fully human and with complete reason, Indians needed training. The immaturity of their reason, for Vitoria, is comparable to that of children. His view aligns very well with laws of Burgos which were comprehensive codes ordering colonists to relocate Indians away from colonists' homes and farms. The process of relocating Indians involved brutally violent measures such as burning down their old houses and entrusting sons of chieftains to Franciscan friars for four years. Most important, about one third of all of the Indian population was placed in gold mines: Labor was indivisible from education. In fact, the laws were sets of codes for protecting Indians from unregulated maltreatment: They included specific regulations preventing abuses.[29]

In the writings of Vitoria and other members of the Salamanca school, property ownership operates as the key constitutive characteristic of the human as the debate is centered on the notion of *dominium*, which is the right to ownership and control of property. At stake in these debates was the Spanish Crown's exercise of private and public *dominium* in the Americas.[30] In order to rationalize Spanish *dominium*, Vitoria develops the two meanings associated with *dominium*: jurisdiction and ownership. The Spanish activity in the Americas is a legitimate practice of human freedom in terms of exercising individual's right to private property over lawfully acquired goods—a right aided by *ius gentium* (law of nations).[31] Natural law teaches not only *dominium* but also exchange between humans (*vitae communicatione*). Along with possession and management of property, commerce was a vital sign of the ability for self-governance, another important constitutive element of the human. It is out of this juridico-theological concern regarding colonial governance, Indians' humanity, and Europe's interest in overseas commerce that the first system of modern international law and cosmopolitanism is born.

The notion of *dominium* provides the ground for installation of the modern liberal political subject characterized by self-possession. John Locke's political philosophy and the subsequent tradition of liberal political philosophy assume self-possession to be the defining feature that separates the rational Man from savages. The new world was the dialectical other of Europe in which the *terra nullius*, the empty land that was not possessed by Indians, was open to be occupied, appropriated, turned into commodity.[32] The commodification of the colonized other requires the reduction of the other's being to body, a theological sublation of the body. Aristotle's theory of natural law and natural slavery, which was used in Sepúlveda's argument, continues as following:

> Those whose condition is such that their function is the use of their bodies and nothing better can be expected of them, those, I say, are

slaves of nature. It is better for them to be ruled thus. For the slave by nature is he that can and therefore does belong to another, and he that participates in reason so far as to recognize it but not as to possess it (whereas the other animals obey not reason but emotions). The use made of slaves hardly differs at all from that of tame animals; they both help with their bodies to supply our essential needs. It is, then, nature's purpose to make the bodies of free men to differ from those of slaves, the latter strong enough to be used for necessary tasks, the former erect and useless for that kind of work, but well suited for the life of a citizen of a state, a life which is in turn divided between the requirements of war and peace.[33]

Being is reduced to sheer functionality of the body. The sole purpose of the slave's existence is to provide labor for the citizens of the state whose lives are marked with rational duties of ethical decisions. The slave provides the body for the bodiless master. He becomes a commodified body. The slaves' lack of capacity to possess property requires that their only possession (their bodies) be subject to management by the colonial master whose unmarked white Christian identity depends on the body of the slave, the depository of all negativity he believes he is free from. The slave *must be the body* for the master who does not need it. The white Christian subject does not need the body because it has delegated its body to the slave. The modern European subject must sublate its otherness, the colonial and racialized other who embodies the lack, the original sin.

Christianity and its theology disavow Christianity's own materiality by removing itself from its own fleshy body that signifies finitude. From its early origin, Christianity has, in J. Kameron Carter's words, separated itself from its Jewish origin that is the Jewish flesh and body of Jesus.[34] In reinventing its Christian self as the rational subject of the political state as opposed to the enchanted other, Christianity also removes itself from the sphere of religion. It instates itself as the secular embodiment of the divine, materialized in the sovereign power of the imperialist state. By lowering the status and significance of the body, the disenchanted (and disembodied) subject becomes the signifier of white Christian universality. The colonial other provides its body and labor so that the rational political subject reaffirms his possession of freedom to expand its property (Locke), navigate through the land of others (Vitoria), and eventually establish a cosmopolitan system of rational governance that promotes "perpetual peace" among sovereign nations (Kant).

"YOU BE MY BODY FOR ME . . .": BODY'S CAPACITY AS PRAXIS

Habeas corpus inscribes the illusion of *possessing* the body in which my subjectivity is securely contained, when in fact the body reveals itself to be a life stripped of *bios* subject to the necropolitical sovereign. Bodies are molded and conditioned by the vulnerability of exposure to continuous violence and surveillance. Following Hortense Spillers's distinction between body and flesh, Weheliye suggests *habeas viscus* in the place of *habeas corpus*: "You shall have the flesh," for flesh signifies the elemental materiality that preexists, exceeds, and eludes the abstraction of the body. The notion of body often abstracts the generative capacities of the flesh into an essentialized biological substance, a passive site for the inscription of social (and theological) signification. In contrast, the notion of the flesh turns our attention not only to body's generative capacity, but also its receptive nature. Calling our attention to the ambiguity of the flesh irreducible to body, Mayra Rivera writes, "Corporeal materiality is dynamically constituted in relation to social forces." Its creative and generative capacity does not indicate self-sufficiency or transcendence of sociality: "My body and its becoming are dependent on and bound to other bodies."[35]

The body is not an essentialized biological substance unaffected by the enactment of social norms. In Demetris Eudell's words, Frantz Fanon's notion of sociogeny demonstrates "as humans we cannot preexist our genres of Being Human or the representations of origins that give rise to them."[36] Fanon's *Black Skin, White Masks* demonstrates how sociality preconditions our modes of existence. Against the biocentric understanding of life, sociogeny indicates that symbolic and discursive registers are impressed into the fleshy surface of our bodily existence. Sociogeny, Walter Mignolo writes, "reveals the ontogenesis principle hides," that is how racism and its violence are not caused by genetic and biological differences, but are a sociocultural construct.[37] The body and its mode of existing in the world are culturally induced and instituted.[38] Man and his existence is an invention.

Seen this way, the body is the site of an active ongoing struggle and action. Africana critical theory invites us to think of the body as a social-material text in which we can read both the assemblage of racializing violence *and* new possibilities for resisting such biopolitics. The body understood in terms of possession points at mortality. When articulated as flesh, it signals the constant movement and unfolding of life, the creative force of action, solidarity, and praxis that make us human. Wynter calls it autopoiesis, after the Chilean biologists Humberto Maturana and Francisco Varela, who argue that biological organisms are self-generative and self-functioning.[39] The human articulated in terms of flesh reveals the condition of vulnerability to be a site of possibility. The human, Wynter suggests, is no longer understood as a noun, but a verb. Being a human becomes a matter of praxis.[40]

The Hegelian subject formation demonstrated in lordship and bondsman consists of (the struggle for) recognition. The subject is irrevocably bound to the other. Butler reads the master-slave dialectic in terms of the delegation of body. Even though Hegel does not use the word "body," Butler reads the process of subject formation as essentially the master's attempt to detach himself from the body and delegate it to the slave. The master's command thus is: "You be my body for me, but do not let me know that the body you are is my body."[41] This delegation, doubling of body, is impossible, a constant failure. The desire of detachment from the body shows, paradoxically, the master's attachment to it. It shows the master's attachment or boundedness to the other that is the slave. The desire for overcoming is equally bound by the necessity of preservation.[42] Butler's reading of the master-slave dialectic through the notion of body offers two important insights and questions on the complex relationships of body, possession, and otherness.

First, Butler's reading of the master-slave dialectic challenges the notion of a self-possessing subject, the foundational prerequisite of modern rational subjectivity, namely, the human. It interrogates the notion of body understood as property for the possession by the self. The desire to transcend signals its failure at the same time. Resignation of body reveals its attachment to it. The master is attached to the body, and he must preserve it. The master's disavowal reveals that he is bound to the other, the slave. The sovereignty of the self-contained subject is undone at the site of his encounter with the other. Bodies become. Bodies are shaped and produced by sociality, but they are also generative. They displace the sovereignty of self-possession. The autopoietic materiality of the flesh, its hetero-affective becoming indicates body's capacity for praxis, or rather, body's capacity *as* praxis—for resisting the colonial and necropolitical genre of the human.

Second, the self-possessed subject emerges only at the expense of the other. The bodiless master cannot emerge without the body of the slave.[43] The self-possessed individual cannot emerge without the unfree (propertyless) subject; without the savages who profess belief in animist cosmology, the monotheistic Christian truth cannot emerge; without the enchanted other, the secular subject of rationality cannot emerge; without the *death* of (killing of) the other, the desire to transcend the mortal body (and thus, the attachment to *life*) cannot emerge. The political theology of the necropolitical sovereign cannot emerge without sublating religion so that theology disappears from the public life and merges with the sovereign power of the state.

The possibility of undoing colonial political theology or necropolitical theology begins with the relearning of body, and Frantz Fanon has demonstrated this very well. Fanon questioned and rejected the body that was created by the white gaze and given back to him, the body that was enslaving the flesh and human that he was. Relearning and reconfiguring the body are crucial steps for the project of decolonization, which for Fanon is also the creation of a new humanity. The normative conception of humanity is a particular modality of being a human that is the Western bourgeois ideal of humanity masqueraded as a universal norm. Such a notion of humanity, for Fanon, operates only at the expense of dehumanization and murder, "negations of man."[44] Decolonization is inevitably a work of reconsidering the terms of humanity:

> Today we are present at the stasis of Europe. Comrades, let us flee from this motionless movement where gradually the dialectic is changing into the logic of equilibrium. Let us reconsider the question of mankind. Let us reconsider the question of cerebral reality and of the cerebral mass of all humanity, whose connections must be increased, whose channels must be diversified and whose messages must be re-humanized.[45]

As demonstrated in "Lordship and Bondage," the Hegelian dialectic is characterized by the trope of recognition. The dialectic illustrates the tension structuring the master and the slave who seek self-affirmation by way of negating each other. What holds the tension together is the desire for recognition. One becomes oneself only through the recognition from the other. But for both Butler and Fanon, the Hegelian dialectic overlooks the problem of unrecognition: Hegel takes recognition for granted. Recognition often takes place at the expense of unrecognition just as the normative conception of humanity depends on dehumanization (unrecognition) of other lives. If the abstracted body of the Hegelian subject is an object (as well as the subject) of recognition, the Black-skinned flesh of the slave confronting the master's self-consciousness in the colony is an object of subjection. The master expects nothing but labor and servitude from the slave. Similarly, for Butler too prevailing social norms render certain bodies and lives (such as the LGBT community), unrecognizable. Dialectics become motionless. The only way out of the impasse is to make oneself known, not by negotiating the terms of Western bourgeois humanity, but by creating a new humanity.[46] Fanon redefines the static notion of humanity as praxis, a self-making action that leads toward liberation.

The abstraction of body enables abstraction of labor. According to the Argentine Mexican philosopher Enrique Dussel's reading, Marx views labor as an irreducible site of alterity, a "living labor" that indicates the exteriority of capital, and thus, inappropriable.[47] In a similar way, Fanon articulates the indomitable possibility of life that refuses to be contained in the narrow modality of being. Flesh troubles categories that regulate life. But its possibility cannot be presumed to be inherently transformative. It takes the labor of unlearning the body, the terms of humanity, as well as prevailing modes of organizing life in the "free" economy of exchange that sustains necropolitical theology. Rearticulating the grammar of life and humanity demands the labor of relearning ways of reassembling the body and redistributing the affective-sociogenic registers that mold modalities of existence in ways that disarticulate humanity from the normative framework of property and ownership.

Rethinking the human in terms of flesh may open ways for reframing the liberal economy of freedom articulated in terms of property ownership, movement, and exchange as a problem of theology. The theology looming at the dawn of modernity in the works of Renaissance humanists is one that mediates its colonial political theology and the modern political subject it has invented under the banner of secular rationality. It consecrates freedom while covering its theological agenda with the discourse of liberal humanism. Such an idea of humanity along with the abstracted notion of body hides the operating mechanism of its necropolitical theology, which erects the self-contained, bodiless, rational subject at the expense of others' labor and deaths. The work of decolonizing this political theology demands rethinking the notion of the human by probing ways in which life is abstracted to body and constantly exposed to omnipresent threats of death, ways in which the appropriation and the extortion of labor take place behind the rhetoric of freedom.

Refusing the biological and essentialist conception of humanity and body, Fanon teaches us how the body and its humanly existence are achievements,[48] a work of praxis and movement toward liberation: "The thing colonized becomes a man through the very process of liberation." Lying in between the double demands, between transfer (of body) and suspension (of humanity), the body in its fleshy materiality signals its possibilities for becoming and praxis—the possibilities of be(com)ing fully human.

NOTES

1. Alexander Weheliye, *Habeas Viscus: Racializing Assemblages, Biopolitics, and Black Feminist Theories of the Human* (Durham, NC: Duke University Press, 2014), 2.
2. Giorgio Agamben, *Homo Sacer: Sovereign Power and Bare Life* (Palo Alto, CA: Stanford University Press, 1998), 125.
3. Sylvia Wynter, "Unsettling the Coloniality of Being/Power/Truth/Freedom: Towards the Human, After Man, Its Overrepresentation—An Argument," *CR: The New Centennial Review* 3, no. 3 (2003): 257–337.
4. Judith Butler, *The Psychic Life of Power: Theories in Subjection* (Palo Alto, CA: Stanford University Press, 1997).
5. Lewis Gordon, "African-American Philosophy: Theory, Politics, and Pedagogy," *Philosophy of Education* (1998): 39.
6. David Scott, "The Re-Enchantment of Humanism: An Interview with Sylvia Wynter," *Small Axe* 8 (September 2000): 199–200.
7. Pramod Nayar, *Posthumanism* (London: Polity, 2013), 4.
8. Cary Wolfe, *Animal Rites: American Culture, the Discourse of Species, and Posthumanist Theory* (Chicago: University of Chicago Press, 2003), 8.
9. Michel Foucault, *The Order of Things: An Archaeology of Human Sciences* (New York: Vintage, 1994), 386.
10. Wynter, "Unsettling," 275, 277.

11. It remains questionable whether we can label the Renaissance-modern ideal of the human as "Judeo-Christian" since Jews too have been for the most part racialized others of the Christian-Western subject through history.
12. Wynter, "Unsettling," 275–82.
13. Sylvia Wynter, "Beyond the Word of Man: Glissant and the New Discourse of the Antilles," *World Literature Today* 63, no. 4 (1989): 641–42.
14. Achille Mbembe, "Necropolitics," *Public Culture* 15, no. 1 (2003): 11.
15. Ibid., 12–14.
16. Ibid., 24.
17. The laws of Burgos endorsed the founding of encomiendas and natives' conversion into Christianity.
18. Sylvia Wynter and Katherine McKittrick, "Unparalleled Catastrophe for our Species? Or, to Give Humanness a Different Future: Conversations," in *Sylvia Wynter: On Being Human as Praxis*, ed. Katherine McKittrick (Durham, NC: Duke University Press, 2015), 21–23.
19. Sylvia Wynter, "Beyond the Word of Man," 639.
20. See David Chidester, *Savage Systems: Colonialism and Comparative Religion in South Africa* (Charlottesville: University of Virginia Press, 1996); David Chidester, *Empire of Religion: Imperialism and Comparative Religion* (Chicago: University of Chicago Press, 2014).
21. Juan Ginés de Sepúlveda, *Epistolario*, ed. and trans. Angel Losada, 2nd ed. (Madrid: Ediciones Cultura Hispanica del Centro Iberoamericano de Cooperacion, 1979), 94.
22. Aristotle, *Politics*, 1981 ed.: I, v, 1254, b2, b16.
23. Aristotle, *Politics* 1254 a 8.
24. Ibid.
25. Aristotle, *Politics*, 1981 ed.: I, v, 1254 b2, b6.
26. Anthony Pagden, *The Burdens of Empire: 1539 to the Present* (Cambridge: Cambridge University Press, 2015), 107.
27. Anthony Pagden, *The Fall of Natural Man: The American Indian and the Origins of Comparative Ethnology* (Cambridge: Cambridge University Press, 1987), 94.
28. Ibid., 96–104.
29. Lewis Hanke, *The Spanish Struggle for Justice in the Conquest of America* (Dallas: Southern Methodist University Press, 2002), 24.
30. Pagden, *Burdens of Empire*, 56.
31. Such an idea of private property becomes the basis of Vitoria's international law and sovereignty whose main concern is private property and freedom of exchange. See Marti Koskenniemi, *Empire and International Law: Historical Explorations* (Oxford: Oxford University Press, 2017), 16.

32. Catherine Kellogg, "'You be my body for me': Dispossession in Two Valences," *Philosophy and Social Criticism* 43, no. 1 (2017): 89–90; C. B. MacPherson, *The Political Theory of Possessive Individualism: Hobbes to Locke* (Oxford: Oxford University Press, 1972), 129.
33. Aristotle, *Politics*, 1981 ed.: I, v, 1254 b2, b6.
34. J. Kameron Carter, *Race: A Theological Account* (Oxford: Oxford University Press, 2008), 7.
35. Mayra Rivera, *Poetics of the Flesh* (Durham, NC: Duke University Press, 2015), 144.
36. Demetrius Eudell, "'Come on Kid, Let's Go Get the *Thing*': The Sociogenic Principle and the *Being* of Being Black/Human," in *Sylvia Wynter: On Being Human as a Praxis*.
37. Walter Mignolo, "Sylvia Wynter: What Does It Mean to Be Human?" in *Sylvia Wynter: On Being Human as Praxis*, 116.
38. Wynter, "Beyond the Word of Man," 640.
39. Wynter and McKittrick, "Unparalleled Catastrophe," 27–28.
40. Ibid., 23.
41. Judith Butler and Catherine Malabou, "You Be My Body for Me: Body, Shape, and Plasticity in Hegel's Phenomenology of Spirit," in *A Companion to Hegel*, ed. Stephen Houlgate and Michael Bauer (Malden, MA: Blackwell, 2011), 612.
42. Ibid., 632.
43. Kellogg, "'You be my body for me,'" 93.
44. Frantz Fanon, *The Wretched of the Earth* (New York: Grove, 1963), 311.
45. Fanon, *Wretched*, 314.
46. Fanon, *Wretched*, 163.
47. Enrique Dussel, *Towards an Unknown Marx: A Commentary on the Manuscripts of 1861–63*, trans. Yolanda Angulo (London: Routledge, 2001), xvii.
48. I borrow this term from Carol Wayne White, who contends that the humanity is not a given but an achievement. See *Black Lives and Sacred Humanity: Toward an African American Religious Naturalism* (New York: Fordham University Press, 2016), 32.

3. What It's Like to Be a Blackened Body, And *Why* It's Like That: A Preliminary Exploration

DESMOND COLEMAN

The issue of framework is perhaps one of the most important contemporary issues in religious studies. The traditional framework has been, as Manuel Vásquez has called it, "somatophobic."[1] That is, the philosophical anthropology underlying religious studies has tended toward an aversion to the role and position of the body in the formation of religious practices, experiences, ideas, and theologies. On Vásquez's reading of the history of Western study of religion, this aversion emerges through the coupling of a disembodied theory of mind with a Protestant exceptionalism that opposes Protestant "spirituality" to pagan fetishism and Catholic ritualism, two forms of religious practice easily associated with the body within the somatophobic framework in which the interpretation of texts and doctrines as products of disembodied minds, or more contemporarily, as simple products of language or discourse takes precedent.[2] Vásquez also points out that this somatophobia, even among scholars who desire to place the body at the center of their endeavors, has resulted in a blindness to the productivity of engaging the sciences in studies of religion, precisely because the body has been figured under the rubric of a certain kind of idealism and anti-scientific social constructionism.[3]

What I would like to do in this essay, then, is articulate a specific site where science, religion, and somatophobia intersect. Inspired by Sylvia Wynter's Nagelian and Fanonian inspired essay "Towards the Sociogenic Principle: Fanon, Identity, the Puzzle of Conscious Experience, and What It Is Like to Be 'Black,'" I will attempt to present an admittedly preliminary account—a prolegomena—of, as the title of the essay indicates, what it is like to be a blackened body, and why it is like that. In a manner similar to that of Wynter, I engage some recent work in cognitive neuroscience and neurobiology. Like Wynter, I also engage the role played by religion and science in the sociogeny of the blackened body, and the experience (the what-it-is-like) to be a blackened body. Where my investigation differs from Wynter's, however, is in my identification of the central role played by an important but overlooked religio-scientific tradition in the production of the blackened body, and the what-it-is-like (quality) to be it, namely, alchemy. What is more, the change from "what it is like to be black" to "what it is like to be a *blackened body*" is also consequential. The significance of this difference, however, will make sense only after I have said a little bit about alchemy.

I begin with a presentation of the work of two contemporary scholars from the disciplines of biological anthropology—Terrence Deacon (*Incomplete Nature: How Mind Emerged from Matter*), and interdisciplinary philosophy of mind—Andy Clark (*Supersizing the Mind: Embodiment, Action, and Cognitive Extension*). I begin with Deacon.

DEACON ON THE NEUROBIOLOGY OF THE SELF

My particular interest in Deacon's account of self is threefold. First, it provides a way to grapple with the abstract nature of self without losing sight of its relationship to the biological body. Second, it shows us that the insufficiency of "external" sensation to the self's relation to itself is an effect of the parasensorial aspects of the biological self. Third, it serves as a good background to a discussion of Clark's account of the extension of *cognition* beyond the biological body proper. Both, in turn, will aid me in my attempt to give a preliminary answer to the question: What is it like to be a blackened body, and *why* it is like that?

In the section on individuation in the "Self" chapter of *Incomplete Nature: How Mind Emerged from Matter*, Deacon discusses how individuation is not always or necessarily constituted by a membrane or skin separating the inside from the outside of the organism.[4] Although some organismal selves lend themselves to being individuated by a physical boundary, such as a single celled organism, this becomes much more difficult when we consider more complex kinds of biological selfhood/individuation. Deacon uses the example of multicellularity in embryonic development as a case in point of the ambiguity of the location and spatiality of the self/individual for complex organisms. During embryogenesis single-cell zygotes self-reproduce offspring cells, or self-copies. In the initial stages of embryogenesis these offspring cells still retain some semblance of autonomy. Eventually, however, these single-cell zygotes form a kind of "society" in which cellular-level individual autonomy decreases. "One level of individuation is sacrificed," writes Deacon, "so that a higher level of *compositional individuation* can form. What determines this transition in level of self (from the single zygote to the 'society' that is the embryo) is not the generation of an exterior skin, but rather a change in dynamical reciprocity."[5]

So, we see, even at the early stages of embryogenesis, the emergence of a complex biological self as the formation of "compositional individuation" forecloses the possibility of isolating a static material substrate to which we could point and say, "*That* is the self of the embryo," or "*This* is the individual." While we can point to the membrane, we cannot point to or see the *individuality* of the embryo. It can only be ascertained through the kind of research that Deacon as a biologist engages in, in which relational dynamics are discerned, relational dynamics to which our sensory capacities, for reasons just mentioned, are not alone adequate to discover. What Deacon calls dynamical reciprocity—that is, the give and take of potential realized and/or diminished—between selves creates new selves, selves that are individuated to the extent that there is a reciprocity between the parts that are currently functioning to preserve and sustain the organization. "Grasping" the individuality of the embryonic self requires a level of abstraction because the embryo itself is a dynamical and relational abstraction.

This, of course, also applies to a "mature" human body with a developed brain. In the same "Self" chapter of *Incomplete Nature*, Deacon emphasizes the difference between neurologically generated subjective experience and non-neurological selfhood/individuation, while highlighting the necessary interaction of the two.

The crucial difference between the mental selfhood possible because of brains and the biological selfhood shared by all multicellular organisms is that being an individual becomes even less correlated to physical boundedness or boundary. This discorrelation is in turn reflected in the *experience* of being an individual, an experience that gives us a sense of the difference of our self or "soul" from our bodies as reduced to sensation. As Deacon writes:

> Mental self is not a composite self in the same sense as is a multicellular organism body. Brains are composites of vast numbers of highly interdependent cells. And each neuron is extensively interconnected with other neurons. Brains evolved to enable multicellular animal bodies to move from place to place and intervene in the causality of extrinsic conditions, thereby altering the body's relationship to its local environment. Brains are in this respect part of the boundary that mediates between the teleodynamics intrinsic to the organism and the dynamics of the external world.[6]

The paradox here is that something inside the body, the brain, "opens" the body, and therefore the self or the individual, through complex mediation, to the dynamics of the external (i.e., bio-external, more on this later) world. Calling an internal organ a boundary that opens the self to the outside in unprecedented ways helps us see that the self/individual is *ecstatic*; that it is always already outside of the body proper, out of bounds so to speak. Put in still other words, the *interiority* that is the self/individual/subject is not equivalent to the *inside* of the body. (No ghost in the machine.) This openness allows, or indeed necessitates, biological and mental subjectivity or individuality, and their interrelation, to become entangled in the dynamics of the environment beyond the biological body.

CLARK ON THE EXTENSION OF COGNITION

Clark's central thesis in *Supersizing the Mind* is that bio-external objects, objects which are outside of the biological body, on the "other side of the skin" in the environment, can and do become systematically coupled with the body "proper." The biological body and bio-external objects sometimes form, in his words, "a coupled system that can be seen as a cognitive system in its own right."[7] According to Clark's thesis, while we typically think we are merely using an external object as a tool, it is better to say that the object is both an integral part of the physical activity as embodied and an integral part of the cognitive processes as extended beyond the body. Clark calls this reality "cognitive extension." In this section I focus on only one of the primary principles of Clark's account of embodied, embedded, and extended cognition, namely, what he calls the Principle of Ecological Assembly (PEA).

The PEA states that "the canny cognizer tends to recruit, on the spot, whatever mix of problem-solving resources will yield an acceptable result with minimum effort."[8] Importantly, the process of recruitment or integration of various "highly heterogenous" resources to solve a problem does not necessarily discriminate among neural, bodily, and environmental resources "except insofar as these somehow affect the total effort involved." The assumption here is that human beings exist in a world where they have to accomplish certain things, and by virtue of this, we confront problems which need solving in an ecologically efficient manner. In many instances, the most ecologically efficient manner involves an assemblage of neural, bodily, and environmental resources.

Clark uses a significant number of studies from artificial intelligence, neuroscience, and biology to expound this idea of cognitive extension and the Principle of Ecological Assembly. I will here focus only on a couple of these studies. The first study is "Tools for the Body (Schema)" by Angelo Maravita and Atsushi Iriki, which Clark introduces in a chapter titled "The Negotiable Body."[9] The second is a study titled "On Distinguishing Epistemic from Pragmatic Action" by David Kirsh and Paul Maglio, which Clark introduces in the chapter titled "Word, Incorporated."[10]

In "Tools for the Body (Schema)," Maravita and Iriki discuss how specific neural networks that hold updated maps of body shape and posture are affected by tool use. There are what they call "bimodal neurons," neurons that respond to, and form a map of, both *somatosensory stimuli* at a given region of the body (called the somatosensory Receptive Field or sRF) and *visual stimuli* near where the somatosensory stimuli is happening (called the visual Receptive Field or vRF). In other words, there are neurons that code two different sensory experiences. Functionally, this neuron links the somatosensory experience of the body, particularly the hands as they engage the world, and visual experience, so as to identify that which is close to the hand. This linkage yields "an action-relevant coding of visual space."[11]

Maravita and Iriki's discovery of these bimodal neurons took place during a study on tool use on a group of Japanese macaques. Put simply, during their research Maravita and Iriki discovered that while in their normal habitat the monkeys did not attempt to use tools to get food that was out of their reach; after two weeks in the contrived environment provided by the experimenters, the macaques learned to use a rake to reach food pellets. Crucially, and interestingly, Maravita and Iriki found that after only five minutes of the macaques using the rake to reach for the food, the visual Receptive Field, which originally represented stimuli at or near the hand, expanded to include the extent of the rake, *as if the rake were part of the monkey's body*. In effect, what happened was that the monkey's brain incorporated a bio-external object into (an "into" which includes still the *bio*-externality of the object) the body, or the "body schema." The same holds true for humans, as is demonstrated by Anna Berti and Francesca Frassinetti's study "When Far Becomes Near: Remapping of Space by Tool Use."[12] The significance of this is that for the brain, in important respects, the body is not just the organic matter of biology, but can also be the inorganic matter in and of the surrounding environment. The body, in the words of Clark's chapter title, is negotiable.

Now I move to the second study by David Kirsh and Paul Maglio on epistemic actions. Epistemic actions are bodily actions that are performed to extract or uncover information, information that would be relevant, or necessary, for solving some problem. In Kirsh and Maglio's own words: "We distinguish pragmatic actions—actions performed to bring one physically closer to a goal—from epistemic actions—actions performed to uncover information that is hidden or hard to compute mentally."[13] Kirsh and Maglio articulate this distinction in the context of an examination of expert Tetris players. While it may seem at first, upon simple reflection, that the zoid rotations made by Tetris players are first and foremost pragmatic actions, that is, performed to bring the player physically closer to a goal, in this case to fill a row, what Kirsh and Maglio discovered is that the rotation of the block is first and foremost an *epistemic* action, an action that the players performed to ascertain the shape (information) of the zoid. Kirsh and Maglio argue that the physical action of rotating the zoid takes the place of mentally rotating the zoid, as physical rotation is a much easier and efficient way to determine the shape of the zoid. In other words, the actual bio-external movement/rotation of the zoid, according to Clark, and Kirsh and Maglio, is incorporated into the cognitive routine of the Tetris players.

Clark suggests that the PEA is a good way to understand the idea of epistemic action.[14] The main point of the PEA is that the processes of recruitment to perform a task do not necessarily discriminate between neural (i.e., brain and internal), bodily, and environmental resources; PEA attempts to help us overcome the unhelpful assumptions within much cognitivist neuroscientific research that all cognition takes place in the brain.

An important idea here is the notion of "perception-action loop."[15] A perception-action loop emerges when an action is performed so as to perceive something, and when the perception in return contributes to the sedimentation in that action the assumption that the action guarantees such and such a perception or information discovery. One example of a perception-action loop, or more precisely, a sense-action routine, is when there is a flash of light and our eyes automatically saccade in the direction of the flash. Clark calls this an implicit "metacognitive commitment" embodied in the motor routine. In the case of an expert Tetris player, who has had extensive problem-solving practice, an implicit metacognitive commitment, which is not necessarily either *represented* consciously or unconsciously, is embodied in the player's rotation of the zoid. The call to the epistemic action, Clark writes, "does not depend on (consciously or unconsciously) representing the fact that such and such information is available by such and such a motor act. Rather, that fact is simply implicit, for example, in the learned associations between certain types of game positions in Tetris and the initiation of such and such an epistemic action."[16] It is in this sense that the game of Tetris, particularly the zoid, is incorporated into the cognitive routine. Expert cognition of Tetris, in other words, is extended beyond both the brain and the body, into the game itself.

Kirsh and Maglio's study of epistemic action in Tetris is but one example of a more general activity of human beings in their engagement of the environment. The studies require us to reject a neat inside-outside model of the relationship between mind and world. Mind is not simply in the head or in the body but also in the physical surround, and, what is more, the physical surround is itself incorporated into, or mediated by, sociohistorical relations and activities.

The extension of subjectivity/self and cognition beyond the biological body into the environment, and the consequent incorporation of the environment into the subjective and cognitive routines of the biological body, also necessitate the incorporation of the sedimented history of such incorporations and extensions into the subjective and cognitive routines of minded biological bodies. It is here, on this issue, that I must turn to Fanon and Wynter.

FANON AND WYNTER: SOCIOGENY, THE HISTORICO-RACIAL EPIDERMAL SCHEMA, AND WHAT IT IS LIKE TO BE BLACK

In "The Fact of Blackness," Franz Fanon writes: "In the white world the man of color encounters difficulties in the development of his body schema."[17] The body schema to which Fanon refers is, of course, the schema of the minded biological body I presented above through Deacon and Clark. To be "of" the color black means to have incorporated and been incorporated into a color, namely, blackness. But what is paramount is to recognize also that the blackness into which the Black person has been incorporated, and which they have also incorporated into themselves, has itself (qua color differentiated from race) been incorporated by and into histories of meaning. It is this that results in the "difficulties" experienced in the "development" of the Black person's body schema. Fanon names these difficulties "the historico-racial schema."[18] It is within this schema that particular minded biological bodies and their selves are "woven" as Negro and black.[19]

Sylvia Wynter, in her "Towards the Sociogenic Principle: Fanon, the Puzzle of Consciousness, and What It Is Like to Be 'Black,'" rightly links the historico-racial schema with Fanon's addition of the idea of sociogeny to Freud's ontogenetic addition to phylogeny. In other words, or rather in Fanon's, "black man's [sic] alienation" is neither a simple question of phylogeny, the evolutionary history of humanity, nor of ontogeny, the development of the individual human organism. Instead, the Black person's experience of alienation, and more specifically of alienation from himself as a minded biological body, can be understood only within the effective and productive history of the society within which minded biological bodies are Black.

In order to think through Fanon's suggestion of the sociogenesis of minded biological bodies' experience of themselves as Black, Wynter makes use of the work of philosopher of mind Thomas Nagel (*What Is It Like to Be a Bat*) and cognitive scientist David Chalmers (*The Puzzle of Conscious Experience*). What is key for Wynter in the work of both Nagel and Chalmers is their insistence on the irreducibility of consciousness and the sense of phenomenal, experiential self to the physical dynamics of the brain or biological body. While there are some important and technical differences between Chalmers and Deacon, and probably also between Chalmers and Clark, they all concur that mind and consciousness cannot be reduced to "the stuff behind the skin."

Wynter develops further Fanon's notion of the historico-racial schema in conversation with Nagel and Chalmers to understand the what-it-is-like, or experiential quality, of minds and consciousnesses of those biological bodies recognized as Black. Importantly, she does this with reference to the social history of Christianity. Making use of the work of Michel Foucault and Jacob Pandian, she posits that the modern notion of the human being as "Man" is a secularization of the "medieval religious identity of the *True Christian Self.*"[20] Moreover, in the place of the medieval "*Untrue Christian Self* (. . . *Idolaters and/or Infidels*)," was placed "the indigenous peoples of the Caribbean and the Americas." At the same time, it was those classified as Negro, she writes, who would be seen as embodying the Irrational Other in its most extreme form.[21] It is this specific religious dimension of the historico-racial schema which, on Wynter's account, generates the "difficulties" in the development of the Black person's body schema, which generates the experience of a "corporeal malediction."[22]

Again, inspired by Wynter's account, what I would like to do is consider the epidermal dimension of the historico-racial schema, what Fanon describes as the "racial *epidermal* schema."[23] More specifically, I would like to think about a specific relationship between a *blackened* racial epidermal schema and a particular religio-scientific tradition with an effective history in modernity and the present, namely, alchemy. In order to do this, it is necessary to first say a little bit about how a recent film, Jordan Peele's horror film *Get Out*, imagines what it is like to be Black.

JORDAN PEELE: THE SUNKEN PLACE

In Peele's film *Get Out*, a white family, the Armitage family, has developed a variety of techniques by which to sink Black people into what Peele describes in the script as "the dark abyss" of their own minds and bodies. The matriarch of the family, Missy, calls this dark abyss the Sunken Place. Importantly, these techniques of sunken-placing—preeminent among them romance, sexuality, hypnosis, surgery—are a service for their "order," which consists, interestingly, of white *and (East) Asians*. The service allows members of the order to inhabit the bodies of those who have been sunk and grants them complete control over their bodies from the "inside."

Although the film implicitly assumes a physicalist conception of consciousness insofar as the final step in the sunken-placing process, the "Coagula," involves a partial brain transplant, the film nevertheless offers a brilliant metaphor and imagination of what it is like, the phenomenological feeling, of being Black. According to the film, it feels like being Sunk. It feels like being sunk not only into the "dark abyss" of one's own mind, but also inside of one's own body. Indeed, the metaphor and filmic imagination of what it is "like" to be Black conjures a way into a genealogy of what it is like, to quote Fanon, to have no "ontological resistance" in the eyes of the white man, or woman, of what it is like to be "fixed in the sense in which a chemical solution is fixed by a dye."[24]

It is here, with Fanon's reference to chemistry, that I want to pinpoint a specific set of relations that concern the body (particularly the epidermis), a religio-scientific tradition, and conscious mindedness. That is, it is here that I would like to think about a genealogy of a religio-scientifically determined "racial epidermal schema." In order to do this, I must turn to a sixth-century (al)chemical text by Pseudo-Olympiodorus titled *On the Divine and Sacred Art*.

PSEUDO-OLYMPIODORUS:
KATAPAO AND THE SOMA HYPOSTATIKON

I want to focus on only a few of the linguistic and conceptual aspects that Marcellin Berthelot and Charles-Émile Ruelle develop in *Collection des anciens alchimistes grecs*. I quote an important and technical portion at length:

> What we call bodies that are sank . . . are sank to (their) constitution and are turned into ashes. And the hypostatic body, which they call "black lead," and which the Egyptian prophets desired to know and which the oracles of the demons delivered, are the ashes and the residues of Maria. For they have known that these have existed from the beginning. Blackening happens because of this. During the practice, un-blackening, that is to say, whitening (happens because of this). For nothing else signifies whitening if not the discolouration by privation of the black.

And see the concision, wise one. For you possess the entire work of the captive. You possess what has been sought for ages. I know that you have long endured the pain of wisdom. This is the key of the discourse, and it is the synopsis of the entire art. Do not overlook what is inside for it opens for you the doors of the contemplative and of the practical, knowing that the residues are the entire hidden doctrine. For all look for these and are hanging onto them. Countless allegories refer back to them and just as many books allegorise them.

For there are two colours that are diametrically opposed, white and black. White distinguishes but black comprehends. Zosimus allegorised this when he said: "it surrounds the pupil of the eye and the heavenly iris." Those who are ignorant do not realise what distinguishes and what comprehends. What comprehends and what is much compacted is extracted from the appropriate body. The nature of lead that is sunk is extracted from the liquid essence, as the divine Zosimus says—he holds fast to the whole truth of the knowledge of god. No longer revealing the invisible cosmos in itself [blackness], the soul reveals (itself) differently in another body of silver [whiteness], and in silver, the fiery blood, that is to say, gold.[25]

What I want to focus on, among the many aspects that demand attention, is the language of sinking (*kataspao*), blackening (*melanosis*), "hypostatic body" (*soma hypostatikon*), and extraction (*ekstrophe*). Within (al)chemical transmutation theory and practice *melanosis*, blackening, is a process of sinking and producing a blackened body out of which silver and gold can be extracted.

It is perhaps easy to discern a resemblance between the logic of transmutation as expressed in this text, and the logic of the Sunken Place as what it is like to be Black. The treatise indicates that "noble" metals (silver, then gold) are to be extracted after a process of sinking and blackening "base" metals (such as lead). The treatise calls the sunken and blackened "remains" a *soma hypostatikon*, which could be translated as "hypostatic body." Such translation is conceptually useful because it brings to mind the Christian notion of the "hypostatic union," the phrase used to define the unity of humanity and divinity in Jesus. The idea is that that which is "hypostatic" functions as the sediment or foundation for differences that are supposedly ontologically distinct and incompatible. The blackened and sunken hypostatic body is therefore, according to transmutation theory and practice at this moment in its history, that upon and out of which (paradoxically) ontologically superior metals are founded and extracted. This is so just as, in *Get Out*, the sunken-placing of Black people into the interior "dark abyss" of their minds and bodies functions to produce minds and bodies upon and out of which (paradoxically) the superior races (whites and Asians) realize their destiny of being and becoming gods.

The religious and theological dimensions of the Sunken Place and the Armitage family's practice of sunken-placing share important resemblances with theological dimensions of (some of) the alchemical literature. In order to elucidate this resemblance, it is necessary to indicate one theological significance and resemblance that Pseudo-Olympiodorus articulates between the sunken and blackened hypostatic body out of which gold is extracted above and the Egyptian God Osiris.

A little while later in the text, Pseudo-Olympiodorus writes that Osiris "tightens and binds the All of lead." By the "All" of lead Pseudo-Olympiodorus is presenting the alchemical notion that blackened lead, the sunken and hypostatic body mentioned above, is the containment and "comprehension" of the multiplicity of the "invisible cosmos." In saying Osiris binds and tightens the All of lead, he is saying that Osiris is the principle (*arche*) and end (*telos*) of *katapao* and *melanosis*, of sinking and blackening in their identity and unity. Of equal importance is that Osiris is the principle and goal of sinking and blackening because Osiris is, as he writes, "the principle of all *liquidity*."[26] It will be remembered from the passage quoted earlier that Pseudo-Olympiodorus speaks of "extracting" silver and gold from lead's "liquid essence." The notion of lead, upon becoming the sunken and blackened hypostatic body, having a liquid essence is repeated in the passage currently under consideration. Pseudo-Olympiodorus writes that the liquid essence "by its gravity tends toward ash and powers everything down toward itself."[27]

But why this link between Osiris and the sunken and blackened hypostatic body (blackened lead) upon and out of which nobler and superior metals (silver and gold) are built and extracted? The clue is given in the same passage in which Osiris is identified as the principle of liquidity and the binder and tightener of the All to lead. Pseudo-Olympiodorus writes of the "tomb of Osiris," calling him a "dead man bound and surrounded by strips."[28] This notion is of course a reference to the Egyptian theology of Osiris, specifically his death, resurrection, and subsequent becoming Lord of the Underworld (Duat). Not only does this reference establish for us the link between (al)chemy, the cult of Osiris, and the Egyptian artisans working in Egyptian temples, it allows us to understand the meaning of the (al)chemical imagination of the sunken and blackened hypostatic body's resemblance to Osiris: sinking and blackening, the production of the hypostatic body, is a violent *killing and death*, a kind of sacrifice. It is here that I would like to return more directly to the primary concern of this essay, "what it's like to be a blackened body, and why it's like that," and then attempt something of a conclusion.

MELANOGENESIS AND ALCHEMICAL *MELANOSIS*

In the opening two sections of this essay I presented the work of neuroanthropologist Terrence Deacon and analytic philosopher of mind Andy Clark. Both of these scholars' research into the relationship between consciousness, mindedness, and biological embodiment suggests (perhaps demonstrates) that consciousness and mindedness are irreducible to the biological/organic body. Its irreducibility is what allows, and even requires, conscious and minded biological bodies to become entangled in the dynamics of the "external" environment and world.

In the subsequent sections of the essay, I presented Sylvia Wynter's Fanonian inspired question "What is it like to be black?" I briefly articulated Wynter's development of Fanon's concept of sociogeny and the historico-racial epidermal schema within which conscious and minded biological bodies recognized by themselves and others as Black find themselves. The particular aspect of this historico-racial epidermal schema that Wynter presents, I noted, was the role of Christian theology in the formation of the historico-racial epidermal schema. On Wynter's account, the Negro came to occupy the category of the secularized *"Untrue Christian Self"* and embody the Irrational other in its most extreme form.

I then presented Jordan Peele's metaphor of the Sunken Place as another way into the question of what it is "like" to be Black. I suggested that the Sunken Place is a brilliant imagining of what it is like, as Fanon puts it, to experience no ontological resistance in the eyes of the white man or woman—of what it is like to experience oneself being "fixed in the sense in which a chemical solution is fixed by a dye."

I took Fanon's reference to chemistry as an opportunity to think about a tradition that is related but not reducible to Christianity, and which Peele's metaphor of the Sunken Place "conjures." This religio-scientific tradition is (al)chemy, and, more specifically, (al)chemical transmutation theory and practice. I then presented a very brief analysis of an early (al)chemical treatise by Pseudo-Olympiodorus. I emphasized a few ideas in that analysis, all of which came together in the notion of the sunken and blackened hypostatic body produced through alchemical *melanosis*, or blackening. Importantly, within Pseudo-Olympiodorus's understanding of the process of transmutation, the nobler metals of silver (signifying whiteness) and gold were extracted (Greek: *ekstrophe*) out of this sunken and blackened hypostatic body. I also indicated that the Egyptian God Osiris, and specifically his violent death, was identified as "symbolizing" the essence of this body.

The question now, then, is this: How does it all come together to help us come to an understanding of not only what it's like to be Black, but also *why* it is like that? The answer is suggested in the title. Part of the answer is suggested in formulating the question as: What is it like to be a *blackened body*? The notion of a blackened body suggested here is, of course, a reference to alchemical *melanosis*, the alchemical production of the sunken and blackened hypostatic body upon which and out of which the nobler metals of silver and gold are erected and extracted. Or, as one could also say, the transmutation of the sunken and blackened hypostatic body is the process by which this body is "turned out."

Thus, the formulation "what it is like to be a blackened body," should not only be understood as a reference to the blackened body/substance existing at the bottom of the (al)chemical retort, but also to those minded and conscious biological bodies that exist and are mediated by a historico-racial epidermal schema which *blackens* them. What is more, this formulation suggests that the historico-racial epidermal schema within which these minded and conscious biological bodies find themselves is shaped by, though not *only* shaped by, the effective history of alchemy and specifically this alchemical transmutation theory and practice in modernity and the present.

In short, the formulation "what it is like to be a blackened body" suggests a way to consider how the processes of *melanogenesis*, the chemical process by which eumelanin is produced in the epidermis, within certain minded and conscious biological bodies gets mediated by the effective history of alchemical *melanosis* within modernity and the present. There is, of course, a difference between melanogenesis and *melanosis*. Where melanogenesis is a biochemical process that makes black *skin*, the effective history of *melanosis* is a historico-social process that makes the fact of melanogenetic black skin signify melanotically blackened people. That is, sociogenic *melanosis*/blackening positions those whose skin is blackened through chemical melanogenesis as uniquely vulnerable in a variety of ways. Not only does sociogenic *melanosis*/blackening position black-skinned people as "sunken" into the bottom of the global social and political-economic reality, it also makes them/us uniquely vulnerable to premature death and to a predatory process of extraction. All of this is what sociologist Karen Fields and historian Barbara Fields call "the social alchemy of racecraft."[29]

CONCLUSION

Unfortunately, this essay does not allow me the space to elaborate further on this social, or rather, socialization of alchemy that is black racecraft; about the process of sociogenic *melanosis*/blackening, its specific connections to the role alchemy played in the scientific and financial revolutions and the chemical process of melanogenesis. I can say, though, that perhaps the what-it-is-like to be a blackened body is the experience of one's subjectivity and mind becoming sunk, in a certain sense, into the melanogenetic production of black skin. Becoming entangled in, and incorporating, melanosis (itself a complex of social relations and activities) makes the "natural" fact of epidermal melanogenesis a "difficulty" experienced by blackened people.

It is for this reason that this essay is only a prolegomena to a *future* study of a principle of sociogenic *melanosis*/blackening and the formation of a historico-racial epidermal schema. That study would articulate in more detail the relations between mindedness/consciousness, biological embodiment, melanogenesis, and the role that alchemy played in the enslavement of "Black" Africans, the colonization of Africa, and the racialization of the Africana more generally.

NOTES

1. Manuel A. Vásquez, *More Than Belief: A Materialist Theory of Religion* (Oxford: Oxford University Press, 2011), 22, 24.
2. Ibid., 28–30.

3. I say a "certain kind" of idealism because idealism as such is not anti-scientific or anti-naturalist. Idealism, as I understand it, has primarily to do with the privileging of *relations* as mediating and acting upon bodies, and with the understanding that relations *qua* relations are irreducible to either substance or subjectivity. Thus, the effectiveness of relations on bodies, and their irreducibility to either substance or subjectivity, constitutes the "ideality" of bodies. One kind or set of relational ideality that mediates the experience of being a minded biological body is that which can be called sociohistorical. This would include, of course, the socio-histories of "religions."
4. Terrence William Deacon, *Incomplete Nature: How Mind Emerged from Matter* (New York: W. W. Norton, 2013), 470–71.
5. Ibid., 470.
6. Ibid., 200.
7. Andy Clark, *Supersizing the Mind: Embodiment, Action, and Cognitive Extension*, Philosophy of Mind (Oxford: Oxford University Press, 2011), 222, 23.
8. Ibid., 13.
9. Ibid., 30–42.
10. Ibid., 61–68.
11. Angelo Maravita and Atsushi Iriki, "Tools for the Body (Schema)," *Trends in Cognitive Sciences* 8, no. 2 (2004): 81.
12. Anna Berti and Francesca Frassinetti, "When Far Becomes Near: Remapping of Space by Tool Use," *Journal of Cognitive Neuroscience* 12, no. 3 (2003): 415–20.
13. Ibid., 417.
14. Clark, 71, 72.
15. Ibid., 71.
16. Ibid., 73.
17. Frantz Fanon, "The Fact of Blackness," in *Theories of Race and Racism: A Reader*, ed. Les Back and John Solomos (London: Routledge, 2000), 258.
18. Ibid., 258.
19. Ibid.
20. Sylvia Wynter, "Towards the Sociogenic Principle: Fanon, Identity, the Puzzle of Conscious Experience, What It Is Like to Be 'Black,'" in *National Identity and Sociopolitical Changes in Latin America*, ed. Mercedes F. Durán-Cogan and Antonio Gómez-Moriana (New York: Routledge, 2001), 1.43.
21. Ibid., 43.
22. Fanon, 258.
23. Ibid., 258, 259.
24. Ibid., 257.

25. Marcellin Berthelot and Charles-Émile Ruelle, *Collection des anciens alchimistes grecs*, 3 vols. (Paris: Georges Steinheil, 1887–88), 91, hereafter CAAG.
26. CAAG, 92, 93. Emphasis mine.
27. Ibid.
28. Ibid.
29. Karen E. Fields and Barbara Jeanne Fields, *Racecraft: The Soul of Inequality in American Life* (London: Verso, 2014), 261.

4. The Rhizome and/as the Tree of Life: The Relational Poetics of Wisdom and Decolonizing Biblical Studies

A. PAIGE RAWSON

Wisdom is like a baobab tree; no one individual can grasp it.
—AKAN AND EWE PROVERB

[Wisdom] is a tree of life to those who grasp her and to whoever takes hold of her.
—PROVERBS 3:18

The root is not important. Movement is.
—ÉDOUARD GLISSANT

In the introduction to her monograph *Proverbs and the African Tree of Life*, Dorothy Akoto-Abutiate identifies the Baobab tree as an African manifestation of the biblical Tree of Life.[1] Like Akoto-Abutiate, I understand such a correlation to hold great significance for Africana and specifically Afro-Caribbean diasporic interpretations of the Bible, for Africana and biblical studies. I also consider such intertextual, intercultural, multilingual (symbolic) relationships to have profound implications for critical theory and to provide the alluvial soil from which we might imagine new hermeneutical horizons and intertextual exegetical entanglements. Both the Baobab and the Tree of Life are metaphors for Wisdom as well as its diffusion. Wisdom is comprehensive and beyond comprehension, accessible and intelligible, yet elusive in its opacity. Wisdom as the (Baobab) Tree of Life puts Wisdom in the hands of the people; within our collective grasp yet beyond sole proprietorship. For though Wisdom is a Tree, it is not Rooted in region but Relation and, therefore, beyond the constraints of demarcation. In this chapter, I proffer an archipelagic biblical hermeneutics of bibliorality[2] through and as a poetics of Relation.[3] Reading the Bible and its interpretation as an archipelagic assemblage and evoking the relational poetics of Édouard Glissant to disrupt traditional Western European episteme and its derivative exegetical analysis, I interpret Wisdom in Genesis and Proverbs[4] bibliorally as the rhizomatic Tree of Life according to a poetics of Relation rather than Eurocentric Root identity. For, as Glissant ruminates,

> The root is unique, a stock taking all upon itself and killing all around it. . . . [T]he rhizome [is] an enmeshed root system, a network spreading either in the ground or in the air, with no predatory rootstock taking over permanently. The notion of the rhizome maintains, therefore, the idea of rootedness but challenges that of a totalitarian root. Rhizomatic thought is the principle behind . . . the Poetics of Relation, in which each and every identity is extended through a relationship with the Other.[5]

Relation identity is to the archipelago and rhizome as Root identity is to territory and the Western European root-tree system.[6] As rhizome, then, I reason that Wisdom as (Baobab) Tree of Life cannot be colonized but may be grasped in and as the totality of the world in Relation (*tout-monde*).[7]

In the first section of this essay, I consider Wisdom's representation as the Tree of Life in Genesis, in distinction from the Tree of the Knowledge of Good and Bad/Evil (*etz ha'da'at tov v'rah*), and then look to Akoto-Abutiate, who, in her reading of the African and biblical Proverbs as Tree of Life, utilizes this shared sacred symbol to proffer an important African and Afro-Caribbean diasporic interpretive intervention and a corrective to Western European hermeneutical hegemony. I briefly attend to the relationship of the Baobab Tree and the Tree of Life (represented in Akoto-Abutiate's monograph), because I am primarily interested in the way the tree serves as a trope for Wisdom within African proverbs. Then, in the second section, I engage Glissant's oeuvre (*Caribbean Discourse* and *Poetics of Relation*) as exegetical intertext, en route to a radical re-interpretation of Proverbs *on* the Tree of Life, challenging and expanding (contemporary) understandings and interpretations of Wisdom as Tree of Life. In the conclusion, then, I read Wisdom as the Tree of Life according to a rhizomatic poetics of Relation not only in *distinction from* but in *resistance to* a Root Identity (represented by the Tree of the Knowledge of Good and Bad [as Evil]). Ultimately, I contend that while Wisdom, as Tree of Life, cannot be possessed or mastered (by an individual), Wisdom may be grasped in totality as the *tout-monde* of Relation, a proverbial proposition made manifest in the archipelagic interpretive assemblage I enact in this essay through bibliorality and one which is always already embodied in those bodies intentionally entangled in Wisdom's Relation. Wisdom as represented in Genesis and Proverbs functions as a rhizomatic route toward and vehicle of archipelagic epistemologies, of archipelogics.[8]

THE BAOBAB TREE OF LIFE

While Akoto-Abutiate does not engage Glissantian poetics (or Genesis) in her interpretation of the Tree of Life and Proverbs, the Ghanaian biblical scholar's exegetical interventions are unequivocally a subversion of the West's hermeneutic hegemony.[9] Akoto-Abutiate is an important interlocutor in this way, and her appeal to the African Baobab Tree as a materialization of the biblical Tree of Life is fecund. She is not interpreting biblical or African Proverbs *on* the Tree of Life, but engages the Tree as a common cultural motif and central metaphor for her *hermeneutic of grafting*, an interpretive lens whereby she reads the Proverbs and the Ewe peoples intertextually in a way that exemplifies an Africana oralituary epistemology. Intertext within biblical studies has traditionally referred to print-saved literature. Akoto-Abutiate, as an archipelagic thinker, thinks across mediums, where intertextuality encompasses (oralituary) print and lived cultural experience. Although the texts illuminate one another, Akoto-Abutiate explicitly privileges the African context, epistemologies, traditions, and folk proverbs as Root, approaching the biblical Proverbs as midrash on the Ghanaian wisdom sayings in what she describes as a "blending" which results in "a new hybridized fruit."[10] The biblical axioms, collectively conceptualized as Tree of Life, are thereby *grafted* onto the African Ewe proverbs, "translat[ing] meaning from the world of the Bible to the world of the African Ghanaian Ewe peoples."[11] More than translation, however, Akoto-Abutiate's hermeneutic appeals to Africa as Root to facilitate greater understanding of and engagement with the Bible in Africa and diasporic African communities, serving to empower African peoples as they interpret the Proverbs in an act of resistance, reparation, and re-membering.[12]

Though the Ewe ascribe to the widely held African belief in a mythical Tree of Life from which all beings originated, Akoto-Abutiate is primarily interested in the trope's ethical function.[13] More than a metaphor, the scholar understands the Tree as a "unique moral system" expressed in Ewe proverbs.[14] Proverbs are a hallmark of oral argumentation and epistemology. Although the Tree of Life represents a particular (Ewe) ethical code, like Wisdom, it is available to all.[15] In this way, the Baobab tree is, like the coconut tree in the islands, designated "the tree of life" for its material sustenance and physical appearance, and functions as a numinous symbol and real life representation of Wisdom, whose material existence strengthens its metaphorical force.[16] Citing a meditation on the Baobab tree, Akoto-Abutiate writes that its branches "stretch upward into the sky and when they lose their leaves and become bare, they look like roots," which is why the Baobab is designated "the upside down tree."[17] The diameter of the trunk, 7–11 meters (23–36 feet), makes it physically impossible to embrace it in its entirety; inspiring the Ewe proverb, "Wisdom is like the Baobab tree; no individual can grasp it."[18]

Proverbs are, in the words of A. T. Dalfavo, "expressions of culture," traditionally understood to support conventional values and order, and Akoto-Abutiate's explication of the Ewe Proverbs attests to this inclination. The biblical proverbs related to the Tree of Life, however, do not necessarily follow this understanding.[19] Because of Akoto-Abutiate's interest in the translation and application of the Proverbs *as* Tree of Life, she bypasses all biblical and Ewe references to the Tree of Life, including in Genesis.[20] Oddly, there are only two references to Wisdom and no deeper excavation of either source on Wisdom *as* Tree of Life, an unfortunate oversight when both the Ewe and Hebrew Proverbs demonstrate the exigency of seeking after Wisdom as Baobab and Tree of Life, respectively. Akoto-Abutiate's reflections are remarkable, however, for their enactment of a hermeneutic that in many ways reflects the *donner-avec* of Glissantian poetics, where meaning is made in the event of each novel encounter,[21] and her hermeneutic unambiguously challenges Western European, or Eurocentric, episteme, yet, in a way, its reliance on Root identity replicates continental thought.[22] Africana interventions such as Akoto-Abutiate's are vital and necessary for rethinking the relationship of the Bible, Africa, and Africana, for their explicit resistance to the empiracism of Eurocentric biblical interpretations, to the de-centering of "Western modes of thought and expression,"[23] and, therefore, the decolonizing of biblical studies. Working from Akoto-Abutiate's integral association of Wisdom and the Baobab Tree, I believe deeper engagement with Glissant's rhizomatic poetics of Relation *in relation* to Wisdom, the Baobab Tree and/as the Tree of Life will only strengthen the force of this decolonizing effort.

Relation, as rhizome, *maintains the idea of rootedness* even as it *challenges that of a totalitarian root*.[24] In an effort to read rhizomatically, I honor Akoto-Abutiate's arborescent hermeneutic of grafting[25] and seek to build upon this project by proposing a creolized, Afro-Caribbean, or archipelagic, intertextual biblical interpretation.[26] Like the islands of the Caribbean archipelago, texts as bodies touch and coalesce, their respective rhythms and flavors blend and blur, mottle and obscure, contaminating purity and creating something entirely otherwise: an assemblage ever in process, ever anew. Gilles Deleuze and Félix Guattari, two of Glissant's most generative interlocutors, describe a book in this way.[27] *A book is a multiplicity*, an assemblage, a rhizome, it is an archipelago of infinite intertextual islands, and the Bible is exemplary in this way, which is the value of interpretations that evince its diverse multiplicity.[28] Glissant's appropriation, that is creolization, of the rhizome is so relevant not only as we read Wisdom, but as we interpret the Bible, and particularly the Tree of Life in Genesis.

WISDOM, RHIZOME, AND THE TREE OF LIFE

As a transcultural symbol of prosperity, creation, creativity, and Wisdom, ancient oral traditions about the Tree of Life extend from Africa to Asia, but its earliest textual representations are ostensibly found in Genesis and Proverbs.[29] In Genesis, the Tree of Life emerges in the second creation account, in the middle of Eden.[30] There is debate over whether the Tree of Life is the Tree of the Knowledge of Good and Bad (as Evil),[31] and while I previously considered them one,[32] in reading Genesis 2–3 alongside Glissant, I now distinguish them. The former represents the rhizomatic Relation identity of Wisdom, which facilitates the diverse archipelagic entanglements of Life. The latter restricts us to the (unique, totalitarian) Root that divides and determines according to the hierarchical dualisms of continental thought (insular, auto-referential, static).[33] I maintain that such an understanding is evinced in the events that unfold after Eve and Adam ingest the fruit of the Tree of the Knowledge of Good/Bad.[34] The repercussions are dire; the characters become self-conscious;[35] and Yahweh Elohim exacts punishment via the binary gender system.[36]

As Ken Stone has convincingly argued in his Butlerian reading of Eden, rather than a blissful benediction and consecration of a union worth celebrating, the consequences of "The Fall" read more like a divine indictment and sanctioning of "forced submission to the constraints of the heterosexual contract . . . [and] opposite sex desire."[37] Stone reminds us that the presence of such legislation reveals not its primacy (as cause) but its necessity (as effect) and, therefore, the existence of deviations from the very norm it seeks to authorize.[38] There is much more than sexual dimorphism at stake in this passage, however. For Stone, the consumption of the fruit is only the means to an end, creating the conditions for Yahweh to institute the gender binary; it is not the Tree but Yahweh's contract that ordains the bifurcation and bespeaks underlying cultural anxieties about Diversity.[39] The symbolic significance of the Trees is of little consequence to Stone.[40] Yet if they are merely means to an end, what are we to make of Yahweh Elohim's perplexing prohibition and evocation of expiry, spoken to the *adam* before the one was made two?[41] "You may eat freely of every tree in the garden; but the tree of the Knowledge of Good and Evil, you shall not eat, for the day you eat of it, you will die."[42] And what of the ensuing dialogue between two characters heretofore entirely absent?

Just after his pronouncement, the Creator deems solitude unsatisfactory for the *adam* and fashions the *ishah*,[43] who moments later is conversing with a strange serpent, that inquires, "Did God say you couldn't eat from any of these trees?" "No," she replies, "only the one in the middle. If we *touch* it, we will *die*." The snake assures her they will not die, but will instead become like Elohim.[44] (Might this be the Nkrumahan God-complex from which idealism suffers?)[45] Intrigued, the woman and man eat from the Tree of the Knowledge of Good/Evil.[46] Their eyes are "opened," they see their bodies, create garments to cover their now "private parts," and hide from the non-omniscient deity. Once the god ascertains their whereabouts, the two confess, and in Genesis 3:16–20, Yahweh Elohim becomes, like his omnipotent counterpart in Genesis 1–2:4a, the great Dualizer, divine divider of the cosmos.

Beyond Stone's interpretation of Eden as divine inauguration of the binary gender system, there is a deeper dualism (Root structure) that has been read into in this pericope. I would argue, in distinction from Stone, that the couple's bifurcated judgment of their gender identity occurs the moment they *touch* the fruit, making the ante-Eve's summary of God's embargo prescient, for when they touch the fruit they do *di*. They do not *die*, as the serpent stated, but instead come to understand themselves as two diametrically opposed entities, having altogether lost sight of their original union (in one body).[47] While this dichotomy is gendered in Genesis 3, the name of the Tree from which they eat speaks to a more universal schema, reflective of Elohim in Genesis 1.[48] By eating from the Tree of the Knowledge of Good/Bad, they absorbed judgment (that discriminates in deferential dyads) rather than Life (consciousness),[49] and this is a sentence unto death.[50] *The Root takes all upon itself and kills everything around it.* Their contumacious consumption of that *dichotomous* fruit results in the ordination of a deep Root-structure of meaning, organizing bodily difference (as originary and) according to antagonistic hierarchical dualisms,[51] a deference that includes human and non-human bodies alike (good/evil, male/female, white/black, the West/the Rest, etc.). Though Glissant did not explicate the correlation, *this* is the Root myth of origins, which he claims animates and authorizes the West's ideal of Sameness.[52] It feeds off the Tree of the Knowledge of Good/Bad and seeks by whatever means necessary to starve the world of Wisdom's diverse multiplicity that is the Tree of Life.[53]

The institution(alization) of this oppositional ordering system restricts and regulates interpretations, iterations, identities, and their expression. Incapable of apprehending any other outside of the dehumanizing duality of its Root structure of meaning. As Glissant contends,

> The idea of civilization, bit by bit, helps hold together opposites, whose only former identity existed in their opposition to the Other.... The duality of self-perception (one is citizen or foreigner) has repercussions on one's idea of the Other (one is visitor or visited ... conquers or is conquered). Thought of the Other cannot escape its own dualism until the time when differences become acknowledged. From that point on thought of the Other "comprehends" multiplicity, but

mechanically and still taking the subtle hierarchies of a generalizing universal as its basis.⁵⁴

Thought of the Other can only escape dualism through the archipelagic awareness of and devotion to difference in terms of diverse multiplicity. The now unconscious, ubiquitous, and terminally bifurcated generalizing universal (worldview) to which Glissant is referring is unmistakably the product of Western European (ancient Greek, Roman appropriation of the Mediterranean) epistemological hegemony, which colonized Genesis and absorbed Eden as its primary Root myth. As such, it is unequivocally grounded in what Glissant identifies as *Root*, in distinction from Relation, *identity*. The former is rooted in a static sense of self and/as territory, whereby the Other is (unintelligible as human and therefore) assimilated, abjected, and/or annihilated; the latter is "produced in the chaotic network of Relation," circulating, extending, emerging in opacity, *giving on-and-with* rather than groping.⁵⁵ When the Tree of Life and the Tree of the Knowledge of Good/Evil are interpreted through a Glissantian Relational poetics, as representing rhizomatic Relation and totalitarian Root, respectively, the Wisdom sayings on the Tree of Life in Proverbs may then be grasped (in totality though never absolutely) according to Wisdom's rhizomatic reasoning *and* antipathetic refusal of the monolingual intolerance of the Root.⁵⁶ In this way, Wisdom represents the oralitury otherwise of an archipelogics, *the subterranean convergence*, the rhizome that unremittingly refuses the absolute (epistemological) colonization of (the activity of) creation, the Bible, and (their) interpretation.

WISDOM AS TREE OF LIFE AND THE RHIZOMATIC POETICS OF RELATION

It is in multiplicity and diversity, the correspondence and connection, distancing and divergence of the rhizome, that Glissant proffers his own sort of hermeneutics as a poetics of Relation. Although Glissant never identified his work as such (it was unequivocally a *poetics*), one might argue that his oeuvre represents both: elocution that frames interpretation and expression flavored by the landscape and experience of the Caribbean. In brilliant contrast to the Sameness of Western European intellectualism,⁵⁷ Glissant understands the archipelagos to embody an entirely other way.

These authorized "inherited categories must not . . . be an obstacle to a daring new methodology," which he advances, an approach that is able to adequately respond to the demands of our global climate.[58] For Glissant the "quarrel with history," evinces "the urgency of a reevaluation of the conventions of analytical thought."[59] And so it is within the fractured and freighted liminal space of our world becoming archipelago,[60] amid the fragments and shards of time represented as events, memories, and (hi)stories in the face of an unforeseen future, that the Martinican poet conceptualizes *creolization*, as the threshold and materialization of such *a daring new methodology*, instantiating the archipelagic (fluid and connective) thinking of a rhizomatic relational poetics.[61] Herein lies Glissant's "quarrel with history," this sacred and supreme symbolic signifying process can be subverted only through the resistance of the Root and the "reevaluation of the conventions of analytical thought," followed by strategic reimagination and revisioning (or re-membering) through archipelagic epistemologies.[62]

Creolization is the impossibility of racial or cultural "purity," exposed and superseded by the mixing of the blood and cultures of Indigenous Americans, Africans, and Europeans.[63] More than "the meeting and synthesis of two differences" (Retamar's *méstizaje*), creolization is, for Glissant, "a limitless *méstissage*" of inexhaustible diffraction and incalculable effects.[64] Creolization implicitly but also intentionally resists and revises Eurocentric episteme and, as such, becomes a vehicle for reinterpretation.[65] Perpetually pleasuring in paradox, Glissant asserts that creolization is "a form of expression through which we [may] consciously face our ambiguities and fix ourselves firmly in the uncertain possibilities of the word made ours."[66] (And, I would add, the *world*.) Glissant attributes the unique conditions within which creolization has emerged to the presence-absence of several factors that distinguish the Caribbean archipelago, but the true force of creolization might just be that while it is archipelagic, it is not exclusively Caribbean.[67] Caribbeanness, he explains, is "a form of disalienated relationship with the other, who in this way becomes our fellow [hu]man."[68] Identity in the Caribbean archipelago, unlike the European continent, is not found in the monolithic myths of ancestral origins, the ideal of Sameness, the dignity of individualism and nationalism, or the ownership of private property, but in diaspora, interbeing, Diversity, opacity, alliance, and shock.[69]

Comparing the Caribbean Sea to the Mediterranean, Glissant describes the latter as "an inner sea surrounded by lands, a sea that concentrates . . . ([and, therefore,] imposes the thought of the One)," while "the Caribbean is, in contrast, a sea that explodes the scattered lands into an arc. A sea that diffracts."[70] In this way, Glissant considers archipelagos an illustration of Relation.[71] In the perpetual motion of this rhizomatic reality creolization emerges, a dynamic of diversifying diffraction, "adventure of multilingualism and . . . the incredible explosion of cultures," the errantry, the chaos, the diasporic interdependence of the *tout-monde*.[72] The irruption of creolized bodies within space, time, and language, then, is in no way limited to Martinique or the Antilles. For Glissant, creolization is a global phenomenon and a cultural practice and not for the purposes of becoming one with the Other, but to establish "a cross-cultural relationship, in an egalitarian and unprecedented way."[73] It is process *and* practice; thought of the Other and the other of Thought; acceptance of alterity without alteration, yet entailing action, participation, and transformation; creating world beyond truth as singular and possessive.[74] Glissant offers an alternative approach to the expression and interpretation of bodies: human, textual, epistemological, civic, and geographical. More than a methodology and beyond *négritude* or *créolité*, Glissant engenders a distinctively Caribbean movement with the capacity to wrap itself around the world, not to dominate nor asphyxiate but in order to relate and re-create global politics through and as poetics, a poetics of Relation.[75] At its most rudimentary, a poetics of Relation is the creolized errantry of the poetic-political frustration of and revolt against Eurocentric episteme.[76]

Within a poetics of Relation, Glissant writes, "one who is errant (no longer traveler, discoverer, or conqueror) strives to know the totality of the world yet already knows that [s]he will never accomplish this—and knows that is precisely where the threatened beauty of the world resides."[77] Just as we find in the Wisdom of Hebrew and African Proverbs, a poetics of Relation perpetually *strives to know or grasp* that which is beyond possession, but *never* in order to possess.[78] "Wisdom is the Tree of Life to those who *grasp* her and anyone who takes hold of her" (Prov. 3:18).[79] The stratospheric striving to know *the totality of the world*, the all-world of Relation, is the search for Wisdom as the (Baobab) Tree of Life.[80] The process (and practice) is, however, not a purpose, for there is no telos, no end, no goal, which would imply arrival, finality, and, therefore, death. To have and to hold here is not synonymous with to claim or to own. To grasp and even to gain is not to grope and then retain. And the collateral beauty of our world as *chaos-monde* is threatened by the ignorance of this misinterpretation.

Wisdom, that is the *tout-monde* of Relation, is available in the capacity to acknowledge and honor the necessity of affectability, the impossibility of omniscience, and the absurdity of absolute origin or authority.[81] In Glissant's imagination, a poetics of Relation, like Wisdom as the (Baobab) Tree of Life, "is latent, open, multilingual in intention, [and] directly in contact with everything possible."[82] It not only emerges in the interaction of everything imaginable—the implicit potential for the entanglement of all bodies—it is the very possibility, the potentiality, of such contact.[83]

> Poetry's circulation and its action no longer conjecture a given people but the evolution of the planet Earth. . . . Every expression of the humanities opens onto the fluctuating complexity of the world. Here poetic thought safeguards the particular, since only the totality of truly secure particulars guarantees the energy of Diversity. But in every instance this particular sets about Relation in a completely intransitive manner, relating, that is, with the finally realized totality of all possible particulars.[84]

The circularity of a poetics of Relation is no circuit at all, not "a line of energy curved back onto itself" nor a trajectory.[85] It is rhizomatic and in this sort of dynamic, "we imagine the disclosable aesthetics of a Chaos, with every last detail as complex as the whole that cannot be reduced, simplified, or normalized," each part "implicated in the activity of every other."[86]

Of course, Glissant reminds us, "Chaos is not 'chaotic,'" but cha(o)smic; a lacuna, a womb, the χώρα of creation, yet not singular mythic Root.[87] Within the *chaos-monde* of Relation, we come to experience and appreciate "the aesthetics of the universe . . . cleared of a priori values."[88] Our *chaos-monde*, epistemological assemblage relating to and in relationship with itself, opening, closing, gathering, scattering, returning, rebelling, enduring, exploding, mending, morphing. A poetics of Relation "diversifies them infinitely yet brings them back, nonetheless, to a full burst of unity;" always irreducible either to the One or the Other.[89] Such is Glissant's illustration of identity, as he juxtaposes *Root* and *Relation*. According to Glissant, the immediacy and intensification of globalization has affected identity; no longer bound to "the sacred mystery of the root," it may now be conceptualized beyond permanence, "a capacity for variation."[90] As a result, *Root identity* is no longer adequate; rooted, as it is, in Eden-like myths of origin, establishing the self and territory, it "set[s] in motion the thought of the other and of voyage," and claims bodies *as* territory, where the birth of the colony is the death of the colonized Other.[91] *The single root kills all around it.* The Root originated in the West, Glissant observes, as the movement of the nomad became fixed as "nations declar[ed] themselves in preparation for their repercussions in the world."[92] The requisite of this fixing was expansion through colonization.[93] Gradually, as nations acquired autonomy from the West, they assimilated and replicated the West's (di)vision of power, which prevents *true* liberation[94] because animated by "the totalitarian drive of a single, unique root" and dualistic self-definition ("pitting citizen against barbarian").[95] The truly insidious and ironic implications of the Root are that rather than operating as source of sustenance for the life-force it grounds, it becomes the very condition for its termination.

Relation identity, in contrast, requires no cosmology because it emerges in "the conscious and contradictory experience of contacts among cultures . . . the chaotic network of Relation," the *echo-monde*.[96] Relation does not derive legitimacy from entitlement but "circulates, newly extended" and conceives of land as place "where one gives-on-and-with"[97] rather than territory to be claimed; it "exults the thought of errantry and of totality" (not absolutism or totalitarianism), reveling in opacity rather than transparency.[98] Glissant understands the rooted Rootlessness of Relation's creolized errantry to be exemplified in the rhizome, which is *the root that extends to meet other roots*, an enmeshed and ever-expanding network, root system sans colonizing rootstock.[99] Challenging the idea of totalitarian Root while retaining the notion of rootedness, *each and every identity is extended through a relationship with the Other* in dynamic poetic Relation, *rooted in the rhizomatic Wisdom of the Tree of Life*.[100]

"The tree is filiation," write Deleuze and Guattari, "but the rhizome is alliance, uniquely alliance." They continue,

> The tree imposes the verb "to be," but the fabric of the rhizome is the conjunction, "and . . . and . . . and . . ." This conjunction carries enough force to shake and uproot the verb "to be." Where are you going? Where are you coming from? What are you heading for?

> These are totally useless questions. . . . [Instead,] establish a logic of the AND, overthrow ontology, do away with foundations, nullify endings and beginnings.[101]

Entirely "unlike trees or their roots," the rhizome is assemblage, ever-expanding and connecting to any point without necessary or obvious correlation, composed, "not of units but . . . directions in motion."[102] Without beginning or end, the rhizome grows and overspills from *the middle*, in between.[103] A poetics of Relation is rhizomatic, *chaos-monde in relation*, a choreography of diverse bodies in motion, vibrating, migrating, diffracting, without absolute origin, telos, or terminus.[104] Is this not diaspora? Creolization of the *tout-monde* in our creative expression as a poetics of Relation.[105]

Errantry, opacity, interbeing, alliance, the resonances between rhizome and Relation are palpable, and the same is true of rhizome's relation to Wisdom as (Baobab) Tree of Life.[106] When we accept Glissant's formulation of Root identity as rooted in the binary logic of a single Root that must destroy Diversity, is this not the Tree from which Eve and Adam eat?[107] This Tree, like all Root-trees, is genealogical and defined by the ontological and axiological dualisms "between here and there . . . good and bad."[108] The Tree of Life, however, is Wisdom, Relation, and it is rhizome, *root extending to meet other roots*; Wisdom is a Tree entirely *unlike trees or their roots*.[109] So while this Wisdom-Tree is nominally arborescent, its value is not in its literal Tree-ness, but in its symbolic intensities and resonances (*echo-monde*).[110] Wisdom as the (Baobab) Tree of Life, according to a poetics of Relation, is never stagnant or idle, a rhizomatic assemblage perpetually in (creative) process, always connectable (and detachable), inexhaustible in its capacity for modification, variation, and offshoots (adjuncts if you will) because Wisdom is (the Tree of) Life lived in/as the *chaos-monde* of Relation.[111]

In Proverbs 3:19, we find that it is by Wisdom that God created and creates.[112] In 4:7a, we read, *Wisdom is superlative, therefore, gain Wisdom*; the word translated "gain," may also be translated "create," implying human participation in Wisdom's genesis.[113] This is an allusion to creation and a reference to Wisdom's self-assertion through creative expression, an expression in which humanity must actively participate in order for Wisdom to create and be created in all the earth—an expression which is, according to Glissant, poetics.[114] Addressing the necessary response to the disappearance, suffering, and economic exploitation of human lives,[115] Glissant appeals to poetics, arguing for poetics of Relation as political resistance to dehumanization. Poetics is, he explicates,

> the implicit or explicit manipulation of self-expression. . . . [it is] the only weapon that memory has against this human waste and the only place to shed light on it, both in terms of an awareness of our place in the world and our reflection on the necessary and disalienated relationship with the Other. To declare one's own identity is to write the world into existence.[116]

Wisdom is (a poetics of) Relation, and Wisdom is *in* Relation, leading us to declare our own identities and, thereby, to create, writing the world into existence otherwise. Although references to and representations of Wisdom abound in the Proverbs and elsewhere, Wisdom speaks *for herself, about herself,* and does so with exuberant and audacious self-expression.[117] In these chapters, *Chokmah* declares her own identity, writing the world into existence, as/in a poetics of Relation. And Wisdom is a Nasty Woman, who refuses to wait her turn.

Proverbs opens, and we find Wisdom brazenly shouting in the streets, in the heart of the city, at the borderlands, and the threshold. "Reject me and I won't beg for your attention, listen to me and I will lead you to Life."[118] She's not begging, but she's hard to ignore. Again, in Chapter 8, she's crying out in the center, on the fringes, at the gate.[119] From the heights to the wayside,[120] she's at the crossroads,[121] and once again at the threshold, taking a stand (in resistance),[122] inviting us all to listen, to love her, and to let her lead us as she led God at creation; Wisdom leads to Life.[123] "Find me, find Life. . . . (Dis)miss me and die.[124] . . . Come, taste, and eat of my fruit and drink the wine I have mixed. Let go of foolishness and Live!"[125] Wisdom takes us back to Eden to re-member, she is the Tree of Life and the creative expression of identity; and *we* have a choice: Root or Wisdom (as rhizomatic route other-wise)? The Root-Tree of the Knowledge of Good/Bad stands firm in malignant opposition to Life as and in Relation, denying Diversity through its delimitation of difference as definitively dual; a death-dealing dichotomy determined from a singular point of origin, peering down on its Other.[126] The Wisdom Tree of Life is our poetics of

Relation, manifest in the opacity and multiplicity of the *tout-monde*, our active participation, as affective archipelagic assemblage, in divinity expressing, creating, *writing the world into existence*.[127]

Reading the Bible rhizomatically and, therefore, relationally, intentionally averts universal, absolute, univocal, or even (more) "authoritative" interpretations, attributable to a particular (original) author or scholarly source, and instead strategically multiplies meaning. It eschews the West's representation of the book and literature, language and identity, as Root, grounding, authorizing, and colonizing history,[128] and invokes instead the Wisdom of African and Afro-Caribbean thinkers, poets, and iconoclasts, who, like Glissant, seek to disrupt continental thought.[129] Being that creation has been colonized by the Western European episteme, which read Relational rhizome as Root-Tree, it is far more fruitful to read Wisdom rhizomatically as Tree of Life, our creative expression of Relation.[130] Through poetics of Relation rather than Root, Wisdom as Tree of Life invites us to a radically Relational, (intertextually) diverse, (biblical) hermeneutics. Espousing *archipelagic thinking* instead of the sort of *continental thought* that has heretofore dominated the field, we can read Wisdom in/as the perpetual becoming of (self) creation-expression in opacity, rather than a means toward the possession/division of Knowledge/Territory (i.e., transparency).[131] In other words, when we displace Eurocentric episteme, in favor of African and African diasporic ways of knowing-being-interpreting, we may grasp the Tree of Life as the Wisdom of Relation in/as resistance to Root(ed)/Territorialism.[132] Wisdom as the Baobab Tree of Life is a (theo)poetics of Relation and the rhizomatic, archipelogical assemblage of our all-world entanglement, always already frustrating (hierarchal binarisms of) continental thought through the multiplicity-Diversity of our embodied hermeneutics, our verbal carnage, our bibliorality.[133]

Stretching upward into sky, beyond the eye . . . I . . . I . . . We are the rootless roots of the upside-down tree . . . We . . . We . . . Stretch (with) me. Grasp what My-nd cannot. What will not rot. Round and round, around we reach. We are the Wisdom of the Baobab Tree. Of Life. Not I, not you, not me. We are the Wisdom of the Baobab Tree.

NOTES

1. While I was working with Akoto-Abutiate, Willem Saayman edited an important volume titled *Embracing the Baobab Tree: The African Proverb in the 21st*

Century, which, like Akoto-Abutiate's monograph, appeals to the Baobab tree as cypher for African proverbs. See Saayman, ed., *Embracing the Baobab Tree: The African Proverb in the 21st Century* (Pretoria: University of South Africa Press, 1997).

2. *Bibliorality* is a neologism I created, which is inspired by Glissantian oraliture and Créolité and is a fusion of the Greek term for book, *biblion*, and orality. *Biblion* is a primary Western European (Greek and English) referent for the literary and in the so-called "proper" this noun inevitably became the signifier the principle sacred text of Judeo-Christianity (i.e., the Western world). It is also holy writ for the Rastafari. The term *orality* did not surface until the seventeenth century. A derivation of the Latin cognate for mouth, *orality* bears a wide semantic range that stems from what is spoken by mouth. Through the fusion of these concepts, I seek to represent a hermeneutic and a heuristic way of (conceiving) reading the Bible so as to foreground the already live action (*oraliturhythmic*) enterprise that is reading and interpreting, or re-membering, the Bible. I employ bibliorality to represent the coalescing of these two concepts in poetic Relation, expression, and interpretation, but at times I slide into using this term in the substantive as a synonym for oraliture, or that which is *oraliturhythmic* (i.e., oraliture as always already rhythmic). For an expansion on this notion and/as a hermeneutic as well as my neologism *oraliturhythmic*, see my as yet unpublished dissertation, "Re-Membering the Wor(l)d Other-Wise: An Archipelogical Hermeneutic of Bibliorality, Wisdom as Rhizome of Relation, & Other Poetic, Archipelagic Assemblages," defended at Drew University July 7, 2017.

3. What I alternatively consider a theopoetics of Relation.

4. Specifically, Genesis 2–3 and Proverbs 1, 3, 4, 8, and 9.

5. Édouard Glissant, *Poetics of Relation* (Ann Arbor: University of Michigan Press, 2014), 11.

6. It is for this reason that I employ the terms "archipelago" and "rhizome," *archipelogics* and rhizomatic epistemologies interchangeably. *Archipelogics* is a neologism I constructed in order to convey the logic of the archipelagos, and what Glissant deems *archipelagic thinking*. See below for further expansion on both concepts.

7. Not by an individual or as territory because Wisdom is assemblage and a collective process and practice, Wisdom implicitly and explicitly requires the participation of the *tout-monde*, all-world.

8. *Archipelogic(s)* is a neologism I conceived, which signifies [and is, therefore, synonymous with] the oraliturary archipelagic thinking (and epistemologies) Glissant identifies as emerging within the Caribbean islands through Créolité.

It thinks, writes, and imaginatively expresses the creolized creativity of a poetics of Relation (i.e., the *archipelagos*). The signifier represents what I consider to be an epistemology other-wise (i.e., Other than Western European, continental, Root episteme), which I use interchangeably with rhizomatic thinking. For more on archipelogics, please see Rawson, "Re-Membering the Wor(l)d Other-Wise."

9. Dorothy Akoto-Abutiate, *Proverbs and the African Tree of Life: Grafting Biblical Proverbs on to the Ghanaian Ewe Folk Proverbs* (Leiden: Brill, 2014). Akoto-Abutiate is but one African biblical scholar who draws on the power of symbol in the necessary work of intercultural and intertextual biblical exegesis, specifically tropes that are common in the Bible and the diverse cultures of the African peoples. Thomas G. Christensen, for his part, has also written extensively on the appeal to these shared symbols and specifically the Tree of Life. See Christensen, *An African Tree of Life* (Maryknoll, NY: Orbis Books, 1990).

10. Akoto-Abutiate, 13, 132.

11. Akoto-Abutiate, 18–20. Unlike Delanyo Adadevoh on the one hand and Noah K. Dzobo on the other, Akoto-Abutiate considers her work to be "strik[ing] a balance between both human development and spirituality by deploying pre-existing images in the life of the African peoples and blending them with the spiritual message of the Bible (Proverbs) to promote a better understanding and acceptance of the latter." See Adadevoh, *Approaches to Christianization in Africa: Hermeneutics in Ewe Christianity* (Orlando, FL: ILF Publishers, 2009); and Dzobo, "The Beginning of Life on God's Farm," paper presented at Pittsburgh Theological Seminary, Pittsburgh, Pennsylvania, May 1995.

12. Akoto-Abutiate, 13.

13. Akoto-Abutiate, 176. Since her aim is more pedagogical and even evangelical, Akoto-Abutiate does not address the African Tree of Life as oral antecedent to the biblical Tree of Life, which I believe could be an interesting and productive project. The scholar writes, "Teaching, learning, and understanding are more effective when they start from the known or the familiar system of knowledge to the unknown. Thus, it is important to make use of what is already a normal part of the 'receiving' culture in any attempt to present the Bible to that second culture." Akoto-Abutiate's goal is pedagogical and, even, evangelical, wanting to make "teaching and learning the message of the Bible" more accessible to African peoples (5).

14. Akoto-Abutiate, 176. Akoto-Abutiate considers the Ewe and biblical Proverbs to resonate implicitly with one another.

15. See Proverbs 8:4.

16. The Akan and Ewe Proverbs are both examples of an orality culture that recognizes a literal "Tree of Life" that signifies in these ways.
17. Akoto-Abutiate 3. See John Kirszenberg, "Meditation and Spiritual Growth: The Tree of Knowledge," http://meditationandspiritualgrowth.com.
18. Noah K. Dzobo, *African Proverbs: Guide to Conduct: The Moral Value of Ewe Proverbs* (Cape Coast, Ghana: University of Cape Coast, 1973), 45. Alternatively translated, "embrace it with both arms."
19. The former is a widely held assumption, not only in the Hebrew and the Ewe proverbs; Akoto-Abutiate's reflections on the "Order of Relationships" (59ff.) are exemplary in this way. As A. T. Dalfovo observes, "[Proverbs] are expressions of culture and thus they reflect reality because they stem from it and lead back to it. They are the very features that help to identify a specific culture . . . a genuine first-order philosophy . . . safeguarding African philosophy from undue exogenous influence" (43). See A. T. Dalfovo "African Proverbs and African Philosophy," in Saayman, *Embracing the Baobab Tree*, 197.
20. The scholar almost entirely focuses her exegetical attention on Proverbs 25:1–29.
21. Glissant, *Poetics of Relation*, 142. That is, *gives-on-and-with*.
22. Akoto-Abutiate, 23. The blending of the proverbs through grafting must always be "rooted in its African cultural contextual soil."
23. Akoto-Abutiate, 22. Akoto-Abutiate displaces Western methodologies in favor of what she considers a "dialogical approach." As a metaphor, however, grafting goes deeper than the dialogical. It involves the interpenetration of creolization in a way that a dialogical approach simply cannot. I believe, therefore, that "rhizome" is a better fit to represent this entanglement and the interdependence it entails.
24. Glissant, *Poetics of Relation*, 11.
25. Akoto-Abutiate might consider my intertextual intervention and interpretive approach to be an offshoot, grafted into her own. What Akoto-Abutiate began, I am expanding, probing the depths of imbrication that she may not have seen. Creolization, then, is archipelagic and as such enables us to think the rhizome in a way that grafting does not (and cannot because limited to the Root-tree).
26. Being that Glissant advocates for a rootedness without totalitarian Root, to appoint one "text" as "trunk" of an intertextual tree and graft another in is highly problematic (*hello, Romans 11:17!*).
27. Gilles Deleuze and Félix Guattari, *A Thousand Plateaus* (Minneapolis: University of Minnesota Press, 1987), 4. Deleuze and Guattari reflect, "In a book, as in

all things, there are lines of articulation or segmentarity, strata, and territories; but also lines of flight, movements of deterritorialization and destratification. Comparative rates of flow on these lines produce phenomena of relative slowness and viscosity, or, on the contrary, of acceleration and rupture. All this, lines and measurable speeds, constitutes an assemblage. A book is an assemblage of this kind and as such, is unattributable."

28. As scholars of the text, therefore, it is incumbent upon us not to seek one, universal, absolute, univocal, authorized interpretation, attributed or attributable to a particular (original) author, but to instead strategically multiply meaning. (Interpreters of the biblical text already often unwittingly demonstrate this truism.)

29. It is also referenced in the apocryphal books of 2 Esdras and 4 Maccabees, as well as the book of Revelation. In this essay, however, I will limit my biblical analysis to its representations in the TANAKH, specifically in Genesis and Proverbs. Of course, Jewish mysticism and Kabbalah have their roots in these texts as well. I will not, however, be including these discourses in the current analysis. I will briefly consider the *etz chayim* of Genesis before delving more deeply into the Proverbs.

30. Genesis 2:9–3:24.

31. See Tryggve N. D. Mettinger, *The Eden Narrative: A Literary and Religio-Historical Study of Genesis 2–3* (Winona Lake, IN: Eisenbrauns, 2007).

32. See Paige Rawson, "A Socioeconomic Hermeneutic of Chayim: The Theo-Ethical Implications of Reading (with) Wisdom," in *Common Goods: Economy, Ecology, and Political Theology*, ed. Melanie Johnson DeBaufre, Catherine Keller, and Elias Ortega Aponte (New York: Fordham University Press, 2015), 407–26.

33. There is, in fact, philological evidence of this very discrepancy in verse 6, which refers to the woman's apprehension of the tree, just before they eat. The statement conveys the woman's desire to eat of the tree for, among other things, its capacity to "make one wise." The Hebrew verb used here (*shkl*) is not the same root as the word for "wisdom" (used in Proverbs 3 in reference to the Tree of Life), which is *chokmah*. Therefore, the text indicates that the Tree of the Knowledge of Good and Bad/Evil is not explicitly associated with Wisdom, but instead signifies knowledge as that which discriminates between good and bad (as evil). Therefore, these two distinct concepts are represented by two distinct trees in Eden.

34. See Genesis 3:6. The importance and relevance of differentiating these Trees cannot be overstated, not only for the (re)interpretation of the (Hebrew) Bible but in order to expose Western cultural and epistemological imperialism and its claim upon biblical hermeneutics. Exegetically attending to the symbolic

difference of these Trees opens up an alternative anti-colonial analytical lens through which we might re-interpret/re-member this so-called *Root* (origin) myth and Wisdom within the Hebrew Bible. Eve and Adam chose the continental Tree of Knowledge as Good versus Bad, rather than eating freely from the Tree of Life, that is, the rhizomatic Relation of Wisdom.

35. Though it is unclear whether they see their difference as dual at this point in the narrative, their cognizance of bodily difference is substantiated by their assemblage of and adornment with "loincloths" (3:7). Accordingly, I interpret them to be self-conscious in distinction from becoming self-aware.

36. See Genesis system 3:16–20. Also see Ken Stone, "The Garden of Eden and the Heterosexual Contract," in *Bodily Citations: Religion and Judith Butler*, ed. Ellen T. Armour and Susan M. St. Ville (New York: Columbia University Press, 2006), 48–70. Previously published in *Take Back the Word: A Queer Reading of the Bible*, ed. Robert E. Goss and Mona West (Cleveland: Pilgrim Press, 2000), 57–70. Also see Stone, *Practicing Safer Texts: Food, Sex and Bible in Queer Perspective* (New York: T&T Clark, 2005), 23–45. As Stone submits, the bifurcated structure of these strictures reflects not only communal instability regarding gender scripts, but also the deity's own insecurity. One might argue that such a dimorphic view was apparent as early as verses 22 and 23 of chapter 2, when the *ishah* is created from the side of the *adam*. However, the fact that the nominal *adam*, rather than the male signifier *ish*, is employed up until 3:6, when the *ishah* hands the fruit to her *ish* (husband) suggests otherwise.

37. Stone, *Bodily Citations*, 65. For Stone, while binary sexual difference may be read prior to 2:23 (since "the text's instabilities allow it to be interpreted") and the textual inconsistencies here lend themselves to a queer reading of *ha-adam* as androgynous prior to explicit identification as *ish* beside (i.e., over and against) the *isha*. According to Stone, the first human creature is "what Butler might call an 'inconceivable' creature" because the original human created by Yahweh "may incorporate both 'man' and 'woman'" and, therefore, be entirely unintelligible as *either* "male" *or* "female" (63).

38. Stone is, of course, channeling Foucault and Butler. Stone, *Bodily Citations*, 65ff. See Michel Foucault, *The History of Sexuality, Volume I: An Introduction*, trans. Robert Hurley (New York: Random House, 1978); and Judith Butler, *Gender Trouble* (New York: Routledge, 1990).

39. Not to mention any sort of deviance and difference.

40. In fact, in his 2006 essay, he does not even mention the Tree or its infamous "apple."

41. I unequivocally associate the Trees and their fruits by appealing to Nkrumahan consciencism, where he identifies the "cardinal ethical principle of

philosophical consciencism" as the treatment of all humans "as an end in [themselves] and not merely as a means" (95).

42. Genesis 2:16b–17, my translation.
43. She is only "woman" at this point, since she is named Eve by Adam after the divine sentence.
44. Genesis 3:1–5. My translation. It also bears noting that the serpent does not say they will be like Yahweh Elohim, but Elohim "knowing good and bad." In this way, the serpent conjures the deity from the first creation story in Genesis 1–2:4, whose main activity was separating by dividing entities in two.
45. Kwame Nkrumah, *Consciencism* (New York: Monthly Review Press, 1964), 19.
46. Ironically, the first time the man speaks in the entire narrative, it is in response to Yahweh Elohim, when he identifies his location and states that he is afraid, naked, and hiding (Genesis 3:9–10). The second time he speaks, he blames the woman for the predicament they are in (Genesis 3:11–12). See Phyllis Trible, "Depatriarchalizing in Biblical Interpretation," *Journal of the American Academy of Religion* 41, no. 1 (1973): 42–47; Phyllis A. Bird, "Images of Women in the Old Testament," in *Religion and Sexism*, ed. Rosemary Radford Ruether (New York: Simon and Schuster, 1974); Phyllis Trible, "Women in the OT," in *The Interpreter's Dictionary of the Bible: Supplementary Volume*, ed. Keith Crim, Lloyd Richard Bailey, Sr., Victor Paul Furnish, Emory Stevens Buck (Nashville, TN: Abingdon Press, 1976), 963–66; Carol Meyers, "The Roots of Restriction: Women in Early Israel," *Biblical Archaeologist* (September 1978): 91–103; Phyllis A. Bird, "'Male and Female He Created Them': Genesis 1:27b in the Context of the Priestly Account of Creation," in *I Studied Inscriptions from Before the Flood: Ancient Near Eastern Literary and Linguistic Approaches to Genesis 1–11*, ed. Richard S. Hess and David Toshio Tsumura (Winona Lake, IN: Eisenbrauns, 1994): 329–61; and Judith Ochshorn, *The Female Experience and the Nature of the Divine* (Bloomington: Indiana University Press, 1981).
47. As indicated by their body awareness and covering in 3:7. As Stone, and others have conceded, while one might argue that gender dimorphism was apparent as early as verses 22 and 23 of chapter 2—when the *ishah* is created from/at the side of *ha-dam*—like much of the Hebrew Bible, this is not incontrovertible. The fact that the nominal *adam*, rather than the male signifier *ish*, is employed up until the *ishah* hands the fruit to her *ish* (husband) in 3:6, suggests otherwise. (Though Stone makes no mention of this point.)
48. See Genesis 1–2:4a.
49. I understand life, through Wisdom, to be as awakened awareness, conscienticization, and like Nkrumah's consciencism. The dualistic discrimination of the Tree of Knowledge of Good/Bad is *either/or* where *good and bad* might be bet-

ter represented as *good/bad, good vs. bad*, by which I mean, *good always triumphs over bad* (because good is God and bad is evil).
50. In *Consciencism*, Kwame Nkrumah identifies consciencism over and against Western European rationalism and idealism, whereby the entire universe is "neatly tucked away in our minds" (19). Consciencism on the other hand honors the value and humanity of all persons, recognizing the importance and "the objectivity of different kinds of being" (90).
51. A structure of intelligibility according to dichotomy rather than diversity, which instantiates dualisms that are only secondarily or retrospectively demarcated by divine decree.
52. See Édouard Glissant, *Caribbean Discourse* (Charlottesville: University of Virginia Press, 1999), 72–73, 97–98.
53. Cf. Genesis 3:24. Also see Rawson, "Reading (with) Wisdom."
54. Glissant, *Poetics of Relation*, 14, 17.
55. Ibid., 140–44, 190–92.
56. A Root whose neurotic obsession with narcissistic bifurcation impedes life and inevitably induces death.
57. As well as the Christianizing mission.
58. Glissant, *Caribbean Discourse*, 65.
59. Ibid. Akoto-Abutiate's hermeneutic is but one example of the sort of African diasporic interventions that represent this effort and seek to disrupt Western epistemological hegemony.
60. Édouard Glissant, *Traité du Tout-Monde* (Paris: Gallimard, 1997), 194.
61. I consider *Poetics of Relation*, like all of Glissant's work post-1980, to be an expansion on and extension of his theorizing of creolization as/in *Caribbean Discourse*.
62. Glissant, *Caribbean Discourse*, 65. Akoto-Abutiate's hermeneutic is but one example of the African diasporic interventions that represent this effort and seek to disrupt Western epistemological hegemony.
63. Creolization is a process manifest in the Creole language and its deployment by Martinicans. "The 'function' of Creole languages, which must resist the temptation of exclusivity, manifests itself in this process, far removed from the fascines (linked facet, fascination) of the fire of the melting-pot. We are also aware of the mysterious realm of the unexpressed, deep in all we say, in the furthest reaches of what we wish to say, and in the pressure to give weight to our actions" (Glissant, *Caribbean Discourse*, 250–51). Glissant (re)appropriates the term Creole *as* creolization, repurposing it as process rather than persona, language, or identity (a *how* more than a *what*), and he does so in order to represent a uniquely Martinican counterpoetics with global resonance.

64. Glissant, *Poetics of Relation*, 34. I am here appealing to Glissant's elaboration on creolization in *Poetics of Relation*. Although his ruminations on the concept in *Caribbean Discourse* are ample, they are amplified and all the more lucid (in their brilliant opacity) when brought into conversation with his later musings. Further illuminating his distinction between the two, Glissant proceeds, "Creolization diffracts, whereas certain forms of *méstissage* can concentrate one more time. Here it is devoted to what has burst forth from lands that are no longer islands." According to Glissant, the Creole language functions as the most conspicuous symbol of creolization, for its "genius consists in always being open, that is, perhaps, never becoming fixed except according to systems of variables that we have to imagine as much as define."

65. See Glissant, *Caribbean Discourse*, 162–70. In his essay "An Exploded Discourse," Glissant illustrates the specific ways in which French is manipulated through the creolizing of French phrases. In Martinique, for example, the instruction, "Do not drive too closely" takes a variety of forms, which play on French terms for driving, rolling, and being nearby or close and, thereby, poke fun at the original restriction. This playful refusal to acquiesce and perfectly mimic French is akin to Bhabha's postcolonial ruminations on mimicry ("not quite, not White"), but is itself not quite mimicry because, according to Glissant, it both intentionally and unintentionally sabotages the mastery of the French Caribbean elite over the Martinican. Glissant also points to carnivalesque as exemplary of this sort of playful subversion.

66. Ibid., 168. Glissant is here motioning to the ways in which Creole is strategically deployed in popular protest movements. In this way, Creole is released from its "irresponsibility" and fashioned into "a weapon in its own struggle." He continues, "All the people together or an elitist group, liberated poetics or defiant anti-poetics, we must force self-expression into existence because it does not have the time to mature through some slow evolution. Perhaps we do not have the time to wait for the precious linguists. When they catch up with us, it could well be to explore the traces of what has already happened."

67. Ibid., 249–50. He expounds upon each in the following ways, Creole is the presence/absence of "compromised languages, accompanying the survival of vernaculars and the development of major languages," the presence-absence of "a cultural 'ancestral' hinterland" he understands to have allowed for "the systemic success of techniques of survival," the presence-absence of "an extensive physical hinterland" is due to the "success of cultural accretion based on *marronage*," and, finally, there is the presence/absence of the potential "to create or maintain an autonomous system of production." "[R]einforced by the colonial need for isolation," Glissant understands each of these distinct

dynamics to have shaped the various strategies of struggle deployed by Caribbean peoples, resulting not so much in the obliteration of nationalism but in an entirely new conceptualizing of a nation, one not contingent upon exclusion.

68. Ibid., 250.

69. Glissant writes that the "shock of relating . . . has repercussions on several levels." Since Martinique is a composite culture, it is always vulnerable to the intolerances of other countries *entering into its composition*. Therefore, he contends, "This composition culture is fragile in the extreme, wearing down through contact with a masked colonization." Martinique is but one country in the West Indies that is postcolonial, yet still very much negotiating its own decolonization. The primary dilemma is whether or not to "just go along with it," which results in "privileged disquiet"; "the one that comes from having to consume the world without participating in it, without even the least idea of it, without being able to offer it anything other than a vague homily to a generalizing universal" (145). Resistance in Martinique, Glissant continues, is not only in traumatic reaction, but in their relationship to and protection of the Caribbean, Creole, and the ecology.

70. Glissant, *Poetics of Relation*, 33. The idea of the One is common to Greek, Hebrew, and Latin antiquity and later in the emergence of Islam.

71. Ibid., 34. Careful not to confer advantage onto the Caribbean, Glissant highlights the universal quality of archipelagic connectivity. He observes, "The reality of archipelagos in the Caribbean or the Pacific provides a natural illustration of the thought of Relation."

72. Ibid. Glissant considers the main themes of such a poetics, to which he intentionally and repeatedly returns in *Poetics*, to be "the dialectics between the oral and the written, the thought of multilingualism, the balance between the present moment and duration, the questioning of literary genres, the power of the baroque, the nonprojectile imaginary construct." He then concedes that his own repetition of these thematics evinces that "such a poetics never culminates in some qualitative absolute." For, in reality, he continues, "Relation is not an absolute toward which every work would strive but a totality—even if for us this means disentangling it, something it never required—that through its poetic and practical and unceasing force attempts to be perfected, to be spoken, simply, that is, to be complete" (35).

73. Glissant, *Caribbean Discourse*, 249. Glissant weaves into this discussion... the interrelated histories within the Caribbean. He sees "the civilization of cassava, sweet potato, pepper, and tobacco" as pointing to the future of "a cross-cultural process," which is, he contends, why the Caribbean "struggles to repossess the memory of its fragmented past." He continues, "This practice of

cultural creolization is not part of some vague humanism, which makes it permissible for us to become one with the next person. It establishes a cross-cultural relationship, in an egalitarian and unprecedented way." Which is also why his might be considered a utopian vision.

74. Glissant, *Poetics of Relation*, 155. Glissant proffers, "The other of Thought is always set in motion by its confluences as a whole, in which each is changed by and changes the other."

75. Glissant, *Caribbean Discourse*, 169. Glissant defines poetics as "the implicit or explicit manipulation of self-expression." Akin to *négritude* and *créolité* and even *testimonios*, Glissant understood this self-expression to be cultural, collective, and Caribbean, distinctive, however, in its expansive inclusivity.

76. Glissant, *Poetics of Relation*, 34. The poetic, in Glissant's imaginary, is always already political. In *Poetics*, Glissant confirms, "What took place in the Caribbean, which could be summed up in the word *creolization*, approximates the idea of Relation for us as nearly as possible." Glissant affirms that creolization instantiates a poetics of Relation as the frustration of myths of origin and purity as well as the subversion of hierarchical binaries of empirical-colonial epistemologies (that seek to know so as to name, to understand in order to own), which in its latter form is articulated in/as an errantry accessible to and embodied in the (totality of the) world, the *tout-monde*. Relation revolts against the West's machinic assemblages which claim Root identity as "legal"/lethal sovereign over bodies through the governance of language, literature, history, global socioeconomic and political relations. Also see Deleuze and Guattari, *A Thousand Plateaus*, 7.

77. Glissant, *Poetics of Relation*, 20.

78. In distinction from Glissant, implicit in my application of "grasp" is the impossibility of ownership or propriety. "Grasp," in this way, contains the wisdom of the Akan proverb above, signifying a concept akin to Glissant's *com-prendre*, or "giving-on-and-with" rather than implying "the movement of hands that grab their surroundings and bring them back to themselves" (Glissant, 191–92).

79. Proverbs 3:18, My translation; HALOT 303; 1751. *Chzq*, hif, 3p, plural. The root signifies to be strong or to grow strong, to have courage in the *qal*, and to make firm or strong, gird, repair, or sustain in the *piel*. Here, in the *hiphil* (*chaziqim*), the verb signifies to seize, to grasp, to take and keep hold of. In the preceding verse, Wisdom claims herself as the path to peace and the way to true wealth. See Rawson, "Reading (with) Wisdom."

80. In Glissant's poetics, there may be echoes of the Pythagorean Monad, the Platonic Khora, as well as the Plotinian One (which he indirectly grants), yet his

argument for totality immanently and explicitly frustrates these Eurocentric (Ancient) Mediterranean paradigms, appealing not only to the history (manifest in the very present absences) of the Caribbean but according to its geography and ecology.

81. See Glissant, *Poetics of Relation*, 141. In his introductory remarks on the disruption of "the old idea of identity as root," in light of our global situation, he writes, "the violence of poverty and mud but also an unconscious and desperate rage at not 'grasping' [*com-prendre*] the chaos of the world. Those who dominate benefit from the chaos; those who are oppressed are exasperated by it."

82. Ibid., 32.

83. And here, I understand Wisdom, the Baobab Tree of Life, and (Derrida's rendering of) Plato's χώρα to converge.

84. Glissant, *Poetics of Relation* 32.

85. Ibid.

86. Ibid., 32–33. Glissant asserts that "each of its parts patterns activity implicated in the activity of every other," and then expounds, "The history of peoples has led to this dynamic. They need to stop running on their own momentum to join in this movement, since they are inscribed in it already. They cannot, however, 'give-on-and-with,' until they reach the point at which they go beyond assenting to their linear drive alone and consent to global dynamics—practicing a self-break and a reconnection."

87. Ibid., 94, 5. In Glissant's excogitation, "Chaos is not devoid of norms, but these neither constitute a goal nor govern a method there. *Chaos-monde* is neither fusion nor confusion: it acknowledges neither the uniform blend—a ravenous integration—nor muddled nothingness. Chaos is not 'chaotic.' But its hidden order does not presuppose hierarchies or pre-cellencies—neither of chosen languages nor of prince-nations. The *chaos-monde* is not a mechanism; it has no keys. The aesthetics of the *chaos-monde* . . . embraces all the elements and forms of expression of this totality within us; it is totality's act and its fluidity, totality's reflection and agent in motion." And Relation, according to Glissant, is "the *chaos-monde* relating (to itself)" for Relation is that "which simultaneously realizes and expresses this motion." Also see Glissant, ibid., 136–40. "[T]he danger of being bogged down, diluted, or 'arrested' in undifferentiated conglomerations" must always be resisted (142). For expansion on the notion of the "chaosmic," see James Joyce, *Finnegans Wake* (London: Faber & Faber, 1939); Gilles Deleuze, *Difference and Repetition*, trans. Paul Patton (New York: Columbia University Press, 1995); and Umberto Eco, *The Aesthetics of*

Chaosmos: The Middle Ages of James Joyce (Cambridge, MA: Harvard University Press, 1989). Also see Félix Guattari, *Chaosmosis: An Ethico-Aesthetic Paradigm* (Sydney: Power, 1995).

88. Glissant, *Poetics of Relation*, 94. It is found in the presence-absence, the institution and abolition of order, in "the impassioned illustration and refutation" of pre-established norms. Χώρα, like *chaos-monde* of Glissantian poetics of Relation, is fluid and perpetually in motion. A mirror of the be(com)ings s/he hurls into the cosmos as cosmos. Characterized, then, by her "suchlike"-ness (τοιουτον), χώρα is "manifest but never as itself" (Plato 49d–e). She is "the same" yet never the same (50b). The space of (the becomings) of all beings, χώρα is never (a) "being" but perpetually becoming because always changing—transformed by the matter transforming within her. "Being moved and marked by the entering" and exiting figures, χώρα is matrix (εκμαγειον), imprinted or "stamped" by her process as perpetual place birthing life. Indirectly equated by Plato to the excessive desire of the woman's womb, χώρα is constantly on the move within the universe, blocking up its normal processes, thereby disrupting the well-ordered cosmos through her incessant and excessive desire to birth new life (88d–e). Χώρα's is a chaos which, like Relation, in its motion is, in fact, the exact opposite of what is typically understood as "chaotic." Chaos, according to Glissant, opens onto an entirely new phenomenon that is Relation or "totality in evolution, whose order is continually in flux and whose disorder one can imagine forever" (133).

89. Glissant, *Poetics of Relation*, 140. Also see Deleuze and Guattari, *A Thousand Plateaus*, 21. In this section, Glissant might as well be speaking about khora and is most certainly ruminating rhizomatically. And it is in this hyphenated space where creativity is differentiated from (the) origin and branches are mistaken for roots that the amorphous shape (or *shapelessness*) and manifold fecundity of the rhizome replaces the root as metaphor of be(com)ing.

90. Glissant, *Poetics of Relation*, 141. Glissant proposes that this shift has also resulted in the exacerbation of inter- and intra-communal violence, dominated and dictated as they are by "the flash agents of Communication." He contends that identity is understood more now as "a variable—either under control or wildly fluctuating."

91. Ibid., 143–44. Glissant asseverates that myths of origin, such as the Garden of Eden, are "sanctified by the hidden violence of a filiation" rather than Relation. This process, promoted and preserved through conquest and its authorization, is most readily apparent in colonization. Though Glissant privileges opacity, he is absolutely clear in his distinction of land from territory. He asseverates, "Territory is the basis for conquest. Territory requires that filiation be planted

and legitimated. Territory is defined by its limits, and they must be expanded. A land henceforth has no limits. That is the reason it is worth defending against every form of alienation" (ibid., 151).

92. Ibid., 14. This "fixing" is colonization, the expansion and declaration through domination and subjugation. The poet's next move is surprising, for in order to establish a correlation between the rhizome, skeptics (atheists), nomads, (orphans), and anarchy (in distinction from "a settled way of life, truth, and society") en route to his critique of Western imperialism, Glissant turns to none other than Immanuel Kant. However, Glissant points out, this "parallel" with Kant's reflections on anticonformism does not indicate that rhizomatic thought is necessarily subversive, nor that it "has the capacity to overturn the order of the world," since that would entail "ideological claims presumably challenged by this thought." From here, Glissant proceeds to delineate/narrate the development of Western civilization, and its obsession with power as control of land (as territory) and people through colonization, from the nomadic to the nation.

93. And the progressive subsumption to imperial intolerance and intransigence.

94. See Gilles Deleuze and Félix Guattari, *Anti-Oedipus: Capitalism and Schizophrenia* (New York: Penguin, 1977), 382. In *Anti-Oedipus*, Deleuze and Guattari speak to this exact process in terms of the economy of flow and the possibility or preclusion of collective expressions of desire. "For a revolutionary group at the preconscious level remains a *subjugated group*, even in seizing power, as long as this power itself refers to a form of force that continues to enslave and crush desiring-production. . . . A subject-group, on the contrary, is a group whose libidinal investments are themselves revolutionary, it causes desire to penetrate into the social field, and subordinates the socius or the forms of power to desiring-production; productive of desire and a desire that produces, the subject-group always invents mortal formations that exorcize the effusion in it of a death instinct; it opposes real coefficients of transversality to the symbolic determinations of subjugation, coefficients without a hierarchy or a group superego."

95. Glissant, *Poetics of Relation*, 14.

96. Ibid., 93, 144. Rather than *the hidden violence of filiation*, Relation identity materializes within the chaotic network that is the totality of the *chaos-monde*.

97. Glissant's *donner-avec*.

98. Ibid., 144. "The opaque is not the obscure, though it is possible for it be so and be accepted as such. It is that which cannot be reduced, which is the most perennial guarantee of participation and confluence. We are far from the opacities of Myth or Tragedy, whose obscurity was accompanied by exclusion and

whose transparency aimed at 'grasping.' In this version of understanding the very desire to grasp contains the movement of hands that grab their surroundings and bring them back to themselves. A gesture of enclosure if not appropriation. Let our understanding prefer the gesture of giving-on-and-with that opens finally on totality" (192).

99. Ibid., 11. A rhizome is "a network spreading either in the ground or in the air, with no predatory rootstock taking over permanently." First acknowledging Gilles Deleuze and Félix Guattari's aversion to notions of the root and of being rooted, Glissant proceeds to offer a gloss on the rhizome, which though a type of root is advanced in distinction for the single, unique Root (tree). In *A Thousand Plateaus*, Deleuze and Guattari identify the root-tree as representing a Western European epistemological framework. The philosophers understand "the East" and "Oceania in particular" to offer "something like a rhizomatic model opposed in every respect to the Western model of the tree" (18).

100. Glissant, *Poetics of Relation*, 11. Rhizomatic thinking is "the principle behind . . . the Poetics of Relation." This concession, however, is merely a lacuna for Glissant, a sort of threshold opening onto a vast landscape of possibility in the creolized errantry and opacity of Relationality.

101. Deleuze and Guattari, *A Thousand Plateaus*, 25.

102. Ibid., 21. In *A Thousand Plateaus*, Deleuze and Guattari engage and theorize the rhizome (as thought assemblage) in order to resist binary logic (as root-tree) and to think multiplicity. In the former, the rhizome is made manifest in and functions to sustain their articulation of the economy of flows. In their larger project, which includes *Anti-Oedipus*, the philosophers, like Glissant, are interested in power, its neuroses, apparatus, its effects and affects, particularly in the neurotic (egoic) compulsions of colonization, politically, economically, intellectually, and psychically. Remember, "[U]nlike trees or their roots," Deleuze and Guattari explicate, "the rhizome connects any point to any other point, and its traits are not necessarily linked to traits of the same nature. . . . It is composed not of units but of dimensions, or rather directions in motion."

103. Ibid. They write, "neither beginning nor end, but always a middle (*milieu*) from which it grows and which it overspills . . . between things, interbeing, *intermezzo*" (25). Recall that the Tree of Life grows in the middle of Eden (Gen. 3:9).

104. What Derrida and Caputo after him might call a khora-graphy. See John D. Caputo, *Deconstruction in a Nutshell* (New York: Fordham University Press, 1996).

105. Our variegated expressions of self, culture, and creativity.

106. Particularly when we read Wisdom as Relation and in relation to the Root-Tree of the Knowledge of Good and Bad/Evil.

107. Deleuze and Guattari, *A Thousand Plateaus*, 21. Interestingly, in Proverbs 8:36, Wisdom actually states that those who miss Wisdom destroy themselves.
108. Ibid., 20. The Tree of the Knowledge of Good and Bad/Evil is "defined by a set of points and positions, with binary relations between the points and biunivocal relationships between the positions."
109. Ibid., 21. An *acentered, nonhierarchical, nonsignifying*, anti-structure system and anti-genealogy map—I believe Wisdom displays these characteristics especially in Proverbs 8. Also see Glissant, *Poetics of Relation*, 93.
110. Ibid. Wisdom and the Tree of Life "is not the object of reproduction: neither external reproduction as image-tree nor internal reproduction as tree-structure."
111. Ibid. Wisdom is perpetually produced and constructed over and again; reinterpreted, re-membered, reimagined otherwise.
112. Proverbs 3:19. (And, I would add, continues creating through us.) The verse is translated, "The Lord founded the earth by wisdom" in the TANAKH. A closer exegetical exploration alerts us to two terms utilized here which have broader significance in the Hebrew Bible (and for the people of Yehud): *yasad* and *aretz*. The former is a verb which can be translated "to found, establish; destine, allocate; or allow," while the latter could be translated "ground, earth; piece of land; territory, country; regions; or the underworld" (HALOT 90–91). What I would like to highlight is that in addition to a more overt reference to creation, this text might (among other things) potentially imply God's allocation of land, which could be as territory (possession), but might also be as earth equally created by and distributed among all creatures.
113. HALOT 1169–70. *Resith*, typically translated "beginning," derives from the Hebrew word *rosh*, which signifies *head, the top, that which comes first* or *the very best thing*, which is why I chose to translate it as "superlative" here. In 4:7a, we find translators attempting to make sense of what appears to be syntactical ambiguity (*"reshith chokmah qanah chokmah"*). The translators of the TANAKH and most other versions of the text render this sentence: "The beginning of wisdom is—acquire wisdom." However, the opacity of Hebrew syntax, particularly in a situation such as this, offers more possibility than this translation allows. Therefore, I translate *qanah*, "create," which signifies not only generation or production but acquisition, ascription, and attribution.
114. Édouard Glissant, *Poetic Intention* (Lebanon, NH: Nightboat Books, 2010), 94. The poet, for Glissant, strives to "experience the world [in its] actuality" and in so doing enacts "the creation of that which does not exist" (70, 78). The poem, then, "reaches toward that indistinction [between creator and created] which is not confusion but synthesis" (79). In this affective-creative process,

knowledge "no longer impede[s] *immediate contact* with the world. On the contrary: knowledge of things is knowledge of the self as a function," it is "a condition of the Ensemble."

115. As always, Glissant's scope includes and extends beyond the Caribbean.
116. Glissant, *Caribbean Discourse*, 169.
117. Descriptions of Wisdom are interspersed throughout the book of Proverbs' beginning, and the majority of these statements are third person endorsements of Wisdom's great worth. In chapter 3, for instance, the orator of the Proverbs speaks hyperbolically of Wisdom's value, asserting that nothing can surpass or even compare to Wisdom's ways; Wisdom is greater, better, and more precious than anything (3:14–17). In Proverbs 1, 8, and 9, however, Wisdom speaks in the first person.
118. Proverbs 1:27–33, my translation.
119. HALOT 1246–47; HALOT 1212. The allusion to creation in 1:20–21 is often lost in (mis)translation. The referents of the most common translation, "squares," include the expanses of land and/or water. The verb typically translated "cries aloud," in Proverbs 8, *teronah* (from rnh), signifies both a "cry of jubilation, rejoicing" and a "cry of lament, wailing." Either way, it is clear that Wisdom is making a racket. Also see Rivera 2010; Rawson, "Reading (with) Wisdom."
120. HALOT 231–2. The use of *drk* here may be an allusion to Genesis 3:24, where God stations the cherubim and the sword to safeguard the *etz chayim*. If God is guarding the way (*derek*) to the Tree of Life with the fiery ever-turning phallus and Wisdom is standing in resistance "along the way" (*ale-derek*) asserting that s/he is available to all people, might it be that Wisdom is, in fact, resisting God's attempts to guard and, therefore, prevent, access to the Tree of Life? This might, then, also explain why Wisdom seems to be asserting herself so strongly (and) in relation to God in Proverbs 8.
121. HALOT 732. The phrase here is literally "between pathways."
122. HALOT 714–15. The Hebrew word here represents positioning oneself and/or to be in opposition.
123. The extent of Wisdom's self-assurance in self-assertion in 8, surpasses her previous self-revelations, as Wisdom speaks in greater detail and determination and particularly of her*self* in relation to God. Reiterating and, therefore claiming what was previously professed of her (particularly in chapter 3), *Chokmah* then makes some strange and significant moves in her self-affirming soliloquy, moves which might be interpreted as part of an earlier rhetorical tradition that established her co-equivalence with the divine, which in later transcription was quashed. Among these instances are Wisdom's repetition of the phrase "I am," Wisdom's allusion to Jeremiah 29:13 in verse 17, and Wisdom's representation

of creation in verses 22–31. I actually understand there to be more evidence of Wisdom's claim of co-divinity, but believe these examples to be sufficient within the scope of this project. The phrase "I am" is present in 8:12, 14, 17, and 27. Although the phrase is not identical to that of Elohim in Exodus 3:14, which is verbal (the first person form of the verb "to be") rather than substantive (first person nominative). It also bears noting that this phrase holds such profound symbolic valence that the writer of John places these words in the mouth of Jesus in 6:35, 48; 8:12, 8:58; 9:5; 10:9, 11; 11:25; 14:6; and 15:1. Which holds particular import when one considers that in John's midrash on creation in the first chapter of the gospel, the author is all but stating that Jesus is Wisdom (Sophia-Logos) and that Proverbs evinces Jesus' presence at creation (1:1–4). Proverbs 8:7 is most often translated, "Those who love me I love, and those who seek me will find me." Likewise, Jeremiah 29:13 is typically rendered, "You will search for me and find me, if only you seek me wholeheartedly." The only equivalence in Hebrew is the word translated "find" in both verses. The translations, however, suggest a deeper correlation between seeking God and seeking Wisdom (wholeheartedly). Proverbs 8:7a, I would add, might alternatively be translated, "I am love to/for those who love." (See HALOT 17–18.)

124. Proverbs 8:35, 36; HALOT 305; 329. Wisdom closes, saying, "All who hate me love death."

125. See Proverbs 9:5–6. HALOT 526; 806–7; 984. "Walk in the way of understanding." *Asher*, the verb often translated "walk" in 9:6b, also signifies leading and happiness. In chapter 9, Wisdom speaks in the first person one last time, as the Tree of Life offers a final, personal invitation to partake of Wisdom's resources and live. Wisdom speaks out (for and of herself), inviting us all as s/he does, and in so doing, we participate in/as the divine Wisdom (of) creation creating—we respond through our own creative self-expression and we participate in and embody Wisdom as Tree of Life. Wisdom, like Glissant, exhorts us to embrace and express ourselves in the fullness of our divine Diversity, refusing to deny the multiplicity making us wise/Wisdom. Glissant's creolized, errant, tout-monde poetics of Relation, in fact, offers the rhizomatic reasoning necessary to interpret the Bible as archipelagic assemblage and to grasp Wisdom as Tree of Life. A rhizomatic poetics of Relation offers us the space/vehicle in/by which to reflect upon how the Bible (as the oral tales of folk and official literature) can, is, and will always be (re)appropriated, re-presented (oraliterarily), and re-membered. Wisdom as Tree of Life in the Hebrew Bible is the/our expression of Relational identity/poetics, politically revolutionary *because* radically (inter)relational and, as a result, profoundly relevant in our twenty-first-century global context.

126. It is defined in binary (hierarchical) opposition where the One is Good over and against the Evil Other/s.
127. While Wisdom in Proverbs is represented as wo/man, rather than female subordinated to male or vice versa, Wisdom is the all-world Relation identity necessary to/for divine creation-expression. The complementarity that is Wisdom-God is not in the binary opposition of Sameness, but manifests in the Diversity of creation creating.
128. The book is only one node for Deleuze and Guattari, for assemblages themselves are ubiquitous. In fact, all of life can be understood as or in terms of assemblage (*agencement*). In this way, they are intentionally subverting the book in the History of the West, which has signified cultural, political, and epistemological power.
129. He does so, of course, through the rhizomatic, or archipelagic, thinking of a relational poetics. Glissant speaks to our infinite intertexts when he writes, "No matter how many studies and references we accumulate (though it is our profession to carry out such things), we will never reach the end of such a volume; knowing this in advance makes it possible for us to dwell there. Not knowing this totality is not a weakness. Not wanting to know it certainly is. Consequently, we imagine it through a poetics: this imaginary realm provides the full-sense of all these always decisive differentiations. A lack of this poetics, its absence or its negation, would constitute a failing" (*Poetics*, 154).
130. Acknowledging Eden's hijacking by the Root-Tree of the Knowledge of Good/Evil, reading Wisdom in this way resists the Western Root. In this way, Relation identity becomes a creative communal theopoetics. Wisdom as rhizomatic tree rather than Root-Tree through a poetics of Relation is the perpetual frustration of all claims to origin through originality; such a poetics is a claim to originality but not as origin.
131. Glissant, *Poetics of Relation*, 61–62. Elucidating the connections he identifies between opacity and Relation, on the one hand, and transparency and continental thought's rooted filiation, on the other (but also the West's devious deployment of opacity in its production of myth of/as origin, not to mention the frustration of any absolute distinction), Glissant notes, "If it is true that the intolerant violence of filiation was formerly buried in the sacred mystery of the root, and that entering into the opacity of this mystery was tragically grated, and if this opacity therefore both signified the mystery and simultaneously masked its violence—this always took place in function of a final underlying transparency in the tragic struggle. This same transparency, in Western History, predicts that a common truth of Mankind exists and maintains that what approaches it most closely is action that projects, whereby the world is

realized at the same time that it is caught in the act of its foundation. Against this reductive transparency, a force of opacity is at work. No longer the opacity that enveloped and reactivated the mystery of filiation but another, considerate of all the threatened and delicious things joining one another (without conjoining, that is, without merging) in the expanse of Relation. Thus, that which protects the Diverse we call opacity." Let us "return," then, Glissant advises, "not to a replenished outrageous excess of specificities but to a total (dreamed-of) freedom of the connections among them, cleared out of the very chaos of their confrontations." Of course, this returning is only to once again depart. Of Glissantian opacity, Michael Wierdorn posits that it "serves as a sort of protective mechanism insulating the radical difference of the other from the self's at times depredatory search for knowledge. Opacity thus dictates that in the other an unknowable remainder persists . . . Glissant uses opacity and the set of paradoxes that accompany it as part of a larger enterprise of creation: that is, not only the creation of an ethical mode of being between self and other but also the impetus for creation of new literary forms. Through accommodating contradiction and allowing paradox to perdure, opacity points us towards possibilities for new forms of literary creation." See Michael Wierdorn, "Go Slow Now: Saying the Unsayable in Édouard Glissant's Reading of Faulkner," in *American Creoles: The Franco-Caribbean and the American South*, ed. Martin Munroe and Celia Britton (Liverpool: Liverpool University Press, 2012), 184.

132. Rather than the imperial, nationalistic, neoliberal territorialism of the Root, we enter, extend, and emerge in the Wisdom of Relation as entanglement. We grasp the Wisdom and profoundly revolutionary implications of a poetics of Relation *in* Relation to and as the *chaos-monde*.

133. A conceptualizing of humanity that pushes Césaire's and Fanon's efforts to articulate a transcendent notion of the human even further than either imagined.

5. Senghorian Négritude and Postcolonial Biblical Criticism

ALIOU CISSÉ NIANG

How did Aimé Césaire and I launch the word "négritude" in the years 1933–35? Together with a few other black students, we were at the time in the depths of [panic-stricken] despair. The horizon was closed. There was no reform in the offing, and the colonizers were legitimizing our political and economic dependence by the tabula rasa theory. They deemed we had invented nothing, created nothing, written, sculpted, painted, and sung nothing. Dancers, perhaps! . . . To institute a worthwhile revolution, our revolution, we first had to get rid of our borrowed clothing—the clothing of assimilation—and to assert our essential being, namely our négritude. Nevertheless, négritude, even when defined as "the total of black Africa's cultural values" could only offer us the beginning of a solution to our problem and not the solution itself. We could not go back to our former condition, to a négritude of the sources. We were no longer living under the rule of the Askias of the Songhai, or under Chaka the Zulu. We were twentieth-century students in Paris, and one of the realities of this twentieth century was the awakening of national consciousness; another, even more real, however, is the interdependence of peoples and continents. To be really ourselves, we had to embody Negro African culture in twentieth-century realities. To enable our négritude to be, instead of a museum piece, the efficient instrument of liberation, it was necessary to cleanse it of its dross and include it in the united movement of the contemporary world. This was, after all, the conclusion of the First Congress of Black Artists and Writers, which gathered symbolically at the Sorbonne in September 1956.

—LÉOPOLD SÉDAR SENGHOR[1]

Strange dawn! The morning the Occident in Black Africa was spangled over with smiles, with cannon shots, with shining glass beads. Those who had no history were encountering those who carried the world on their shoulders. It was a morning of accouchements: the known world was enriching itself by a birth that took place in mire and blood.... We must ask them: we must go to learn from them the art of conquering without being in the right.
—CHEIKH HAMIDOU KANE[2]

Janet Vaillant prefaced her homage to Léopold Sédar Senghor with the following words:

> Léopold Sédar Senghor was a "great baobab." The image of Senghor as baobab tree ... recognizes Senghor's ability to survive as a distinct personality through seasons of flowering and drought, success and failure, while continuing to draw from his African roots.[3]

Similarly, our Transdisciplinary Theological Colloquium invites us to talk about our variegated diasporic self-definition and ruminate on what it means to be "a Baobab tree"[4] for our times.

I stand in a long tradition of Senegalese leaders who resiliently worked to face the colonial trauma that almost destroyed Senegalese precolonial culture and faith traditions and to free the country from colonial trapping. They did so by staking their own lives and the destiny of Senegal on a daring existential journey which the above epigraphs framed as a "strange dawn" and "a panic-stricken despair."[5] The "strange dawn" of which Cheikh Hamidou Kane spoke is the abrupt French colonial intrusive presence in Senegal and the resulting state of bewilderment it inflicted on the colonized which Kane recounts as a fictionalized lived experience of his Diallobé people as well as other Africans. Senghor's "panic-stricken despair" experience is the realization of the failure of assimilation to foster equity between Africans and French in Senegal and Metropolitan France.

Kane, in the voice of la Grande Royal, "The most Royal Lady," introduces a way in which leaders of his Diallobé community negotiated life and deliberated on how a liberation of his Diallobé people might be achieved. The only way out of colonial cultural annihilation, she insists, is to send their own children to France beginning with her cousin Samba

Diallo. *"We must ask them; we must go to learn from them the art of conquering without being in the right,"* she said. Samba Diallo, one of the finest Muslim students of the Qur'an, must take the lead to learn this art—a process also called the art of joining "wood to wood."[6] Her influence was breathtaking as she was able to convince her fellow Diallobé community to send their children to the "new school," the French colonial school that is the most effective French weapon for assimilating Senegalese people in order to subvert colonial ideology. Her proposal was radical and prophetic. She opines:

> The School in which I would place our children will kill in them what today we love and rightly conserve with care. Perhaps the very memory of us will die in them. When they return from the school, there may be those who will not recognize us. What I am proposing is that we should agree to die in our children's hearts and that the foreigners who have defeated us should fill the place, wholly, which we shall have left free . . . remember our fields when the rainy season is approaching. We love our fields very much, but what do we do then? We plough them up and burn them: we kill them. In the same way, recall this: what do we do with our reserves of seed when the rain has fallen? We would like to eat them but, we bury them in the earth. Folk of the Diallobé, with the arrival of the foreigners has come the tornado which announces the great hibernation of our people. My opinion—I, The Most Royal Lady—is that our best seeds and our dearest fields—those are our children. Does anyone wish to speak?[7]

The words of The Most Royal Lady echoed some striking features of Pauline eschatology in 1 Corinthians 15:37–44.[8] Samba Diallo would forever symbolize those first Senegalese immigrants who bore on their shoulders the future survival of Senegalese, if not West African, cultural heritage. The lived experiences of French colonization and the cultural displacement it engendered, I argue, shaped the life and thought of Senghor[9] and inspired his Négritude. This essay argues that the concept of Négritude as articulated by Léopold Sédar Senghor repositions and reclaims African cultural values. It is a *Poetics of Postcolonial Biblical Criticism*, as I argued in my recent book,[10] that seeks to liberate and rehabilitate victims of French occupation during and after the colonial era.[11] Often wrongly accused of being the most assimilated African to French culture, Senghor was determined to free Senegalese people from being assimilated to French culture. Despite his level of comfort with some aspects of French culture, this is a less known fact about him. He worked assiduously to inspire Africans to relearn, as Kane's character maintains, and reclaim some of their indispensable African cultural values that were being suppressed by French assimilation policy. I will now show how Senghor's repositioning process is echoed by postcolonial theorists such as Edward Said, Homi Bhabha, and Gayatri Chakravorty Spivak.

POSTCOLONIAL THEORISTS AND SENGHORIAN NÉGRITUDE

The Senghorian epigraph captures the process of and the making of the Négritude concept well before Said's *Orientalism*. Words like cultural exegesis, liberation exegesis, Négritude, or postcolonialism, to name a few, are concepts coined to name agency that in most cases predates the terms themselves. Robert J. C. Young traces the making of colonialism, imperialism, neocolonialism, and postcolonialism to offer invaluable insights into the variegated ways conquered people responded to the European invasions of their spaces and bodies.[12] Despite the fact that the nomenclature of the body of literature produced varies, it can be appropriately termed proto-postcolonialism. Postcolonialism as a lived experience predates the coining of the term, which scholars date between the 1970s and the 1980s.[13] That being said, I am using *proto-postcolonial literature* or postcolonial literature as a body of literature that denotes the variegated lived experiences from colonial to postcolonial times[14] being voiced against injustices of colonization inflicted on them—both at home and in the diaspora. My point is that the multifaceted responses to colonization that Musa Dube rightly describes begin with inceptive acts of some forms of colonial occupation. Writing for their respective locations, the colonized seek freedom from colonial control.

Orientalism is Said's way of denouncing Western supremacist epistemology constructed to bolster European transfer of their cultural values to the colonized that did much to disguise European exploitation of the colonized. This geopolitical discourse that Said calls Orientalism has devastating psychological and practical consequences for non-Europeans, for it functions as

> a collective notion identifying "us" Europeans as against all "those non-Europeans," and indeed it can be argued that the major component in

European culture is precisely what made that culture hegemonic both in and outside Europe: the idea of European identity as a superior one in comparison with all the non-European peoples and cultures. There is in addition the hegemony of European ideas about the Orient, themselves reiterating European superiority over Oriental Backwardness, usually overriding the possibility that a more independent, or more skeptical, thinker might have different views on the matter. In quite a constant way, Orientalism depends for its strategy on this flexible positional superiority, which puts the Westerner in a whole series of possible relationships with the Orient without ever losing him the relative upper hand.[15]

As main orientalists, the French and the British ensured that the overseas colonial academic institutions through their curriculum actualize and permanentize their supremacist ideology. This is exactly how Kane understood the function of the French colonial efforts in Senegal as being the quintessential colonial weapon that instills a lasting effect and affect in the psyche of the colonized. Like Senghor and Kane, Said's reflections on orientalism have important autobiographical elements. He writes:

> Much of the personal investment in this study derives from my awareness of being an "Oriental" as a child growing up in two British colonies. All my education, in those colonies (Palestine and Egypt) and in the United States, has been Western, and yet that deep early awareness has persisted. In many ways my study of Orientalism has been an attempt to inventory the traces upon me, the Oriental subject, of the culture whose domination has been so powerful a factor in the life of all Orientals. This is why for me the Islamic Orient has had to be the center of my attention. . . . My own experiences of these matters are in part what made me write this book. . . . I have been able to put to use my humanistic and political concerns for the analysis and description of a very worldly matter, the rise, development, and consolidation of Orientalism.[16]

Clearly, Said echoes some of the concerns Senghor had and is determined to subvert European geopolitical discourse with a view to freeing and repositioning his people from the liminal spaces created by empires.[17] Bhabha reinvents the liminal space and finds himself turning it into a "productive space of the construction of culture as difference, in the spirit of alterity or otherness."[18] Such a space will be permeated by new epistemological and ontological realities at work to create an alternative "space for a subject peoples"[19]—"a hybrid" or "third space" that "gives rise to something different, something new . . . a new area of recognition of meaning and representation."[20] Such an "affective experience of social marginality,"[21] as he conceived of it, is fruitful space where the colonized can reposition themselves. This is the space of which Spivak spoke, insisting that she finds "the demand on" her

> to be marginal always assuming . . . I am tired of dining out on being an exile because that has been a long tradition and it is not one I want to identify myself with. I think there is nothing that is central. The center is always constituted in terms of its own marginality. However, having said that, in terms of the hegemonic historical narrative, certain people have always been asked to cathect the margins so others can be defined as central. Negotiating between these two structures, sometimes I have to see myself as the marginal in the eyes of others. In that kind of situation the only strategic thing to do is to absolutely present myself at the centre. And this is theoretically incorrect. But one of the things I've said, about deconstruction is that none of its examples can match its discourse. If I can't keep my hands clean anyways, why not take the center when I am being asked to be marginal? I've never defined myself as a marginal in India, I can assure you.[22]

Constructed narratives embed an ideological interest that serves their producers at the expense of those omitted from these discourses and thus reduced to liminality. So to subvert such a liminal space and position herself within that sphere of existence calls for the deconstruction of those narratives. A quintessential endeavor for the inclusion of those whose lived experiences and needs are eclipsed by those ideologically constructed narratives Spivak calls a "radical acceptance of vulnerability."[23] This blatant and intentional omission of the humanity of others recalls the geopolitical aims on the so-called *tabula rasa* which Senghor, Léon-Gontran Damas, and Aimé Césaire assiduously strove to expose. To me what Said, Bhabha, and Spivak are theorizing are sustained and resilient acts of repositioning within imperially manufactured liminal spaces and for our purpose—colonized bodies and spaces. They all suggest that effective repositioning rests on endless possibilities that avail themselves in the assigned margins, as bell hooks has long reminded us. The daring move to carve space within liminality for self-repositioning within assigned margins is the beginning of emancipation[24]—that is liberation and rehabilitation. To me this is what Kane's Most Royal Lady persuaded her Diallobé compatriots to explore as we have already seen earlier.

The founders of Négritude, Damas, Césaire, and Senghor, as I argued elsewhere, saw Négritude as a problematic and yet heuristic concept to articulate and then practice.[25] Senghor tells us that the idea of Négritude came to him during his earliest school years in Dakar—his lived experiences of marginalization in his native home of Senegal during his school years and in France shaped his later formulation of it.[26] Authors in this period wrote from their lived experiences and most became powerful leaders who, after receiving their training in France, returned home to move their countries to independence and beyond. While acquiring the "art of conquering without being in the right" might have been a strong spur for repositioning, its positive outcomes in the case of Senghorian Négritude outweighed its negative ones. I was trained and fully immersed in the kind of interpretation of the Bible that has little to do with my Senegalese context, let alone my African or transnational status. I soon realized that I needed a new way of reading scripture that does not abrogate my Senegalese Diola cultural values. I followed in the footsteps of Léopold Sédar Senghor; his Négritude became my *fortress and refuge, a beginning and a cause* to read scripture with my Senegalese Diola values. My question is: In what way can Senghorian Négritude be conceived as a poetics of postcolonial criticism? To that question I now turn.

SENGHORIAN NÉGRITUDE AS A POETICS OF POSTCOLONIAL BIBLICAL CRITICISM

Writing from one's postcolonial lived experience is a central aspect of Senghor's prolific writings. Born in 1906 in a Sérère village, Joal, which was then in the French protectorate (about eighty miles from Dakar, Senegal, West Africa) to parents who firmly valued both their Sérère and Christian faith traditions,[27] he embraced his Sérère culture and faith traditions that shaped him since infancy.[28] While a youth, he converted to Christianity and was schooled by French Catholic missionaries, seminarians of Father Francis Libermann, in Joal, Ngazobil and Dakar.[29] The embedded Sérère culture and faith traditions of his "childhood kingdom," the villages of Joal and Djilor/Dyiloôr, were soon in dialogue with his newfound Christian faith in Ngazobil introduced by missionaries, especially under the tutelage of Father Lalouse and others at the Libermann College.[30] As we will see later on, Senghor was able to assimilate Christian faith with elements of his ancestral faith traditions.[31]

What is striking is that even as a young boy growing up in Senegal, Senghor was not completely sold on the missionary version of Christianity, especially that which tended to denigrate his African culture. Senghor was born and reared in an African family—a family unit that includes the living and those who transitioned into the world of ancestors. Senghor's father, Basile Diogoye Senghor, practiced his Sérère faith traditions and Catholicism—an inculturated Christianity practiced by most members of his beloved childhood kingdom and other Senegalese to this day. This context shaped his reception of Christianity, and it is remarkable that at an early age he not only interrogated the seeming normative construction of French missionary Christianity, he began to work out a dialogue between his inherited Sérère Faith Traditions with his newfound Christian faith. As a subject living in the protectorate, a marginal space created by French colonists, instead of a citizen of the center, the Four Towns of colonial exercise, Senghor had to prove himself—to learn the French imperial *"art of conquering without being in the right."* Gradually equipping himself with the making of this art of domination, Senghor was able to migrate to metropolitan France, where he steadily mastered its main vehicle of dissemination, transmission, and construction of reality—the French language as means for the transfer of French cultural values. As a result of hard work, he became a teacher, poet, president of Senegal from 1960 to 1980, and later a member of the prestigious l'Académie Française from 1983 to 2001.[32]

In France, he was the first African to earn his agrégation in 1935, a rigorous diploma in Grammar akin to a PhD—a degree that enabled him to philologically study Senegalese languages.[33] Senghor earned the respect of his peers—admirers and critics alike.[34] I am bewildered that despite much interest in Senghorian Négritude in humanities in North American universities and colleges,[35] little if nothing is done to delve into the multivalence of his life and thought—worse a deafening silence about Senghorian

Négritude permeates much of contemporary postcolonial biblical critical lenses. His work is often mentioned for its shortcomings just to be ignored. Some of the criticisms leveled against his work are well meaning but, I must say, overdrawn in many ways for failing to take into account the strategic counter-geopolitical breadth of his arguments framed as *"Africanité or Négritude"* and *"Arabité."*[36] Critics who would rather focus on the contributions of Aimé Césaire, and mostly Frantz Fanon, fail to recognize that Senghor significantly influenced their thoughts.[37] That being said, in what way is Senghorian Négritude a poetics of postcolonial biblical criticism? The answer to my question is found in Senghor's own words in the above epigraph. Négritude, as he, Césaire, and I must add, Damas, conceived of it—"the total of black Africa's cultural values," engaged the colonial geopolitics of *tabula rasa* theorized to eclipse their lived experiences or reduce their civilization to nothingness. They saw in the founding of this concept, a process to resolve their "problem and not the solution itself." They were not calling for a return to a precolonial "condition, to a négritude of the sources." Rather, in a retort to his critics about the aims of Négritude in the years 1933 to 1935, Senghor said, "To be really ourselves, we had to embody Negro African culture in twentieth-century realities. To enable our négritude to be, instead of a museum piece, the efficient instrument of liberation, it was necessary to cleanse it of its dross and include it in the united movement of the contemporary world."[38] Fanon chillingly echoes this profound disjunction, speaking about colonization as something that forces the colonized person into a profound identity crisis that gives rise to the bewildering introspective cry: "In reality, who am I?"[39] What Senghor meant by "we had to divest ourselves of our borrowed attire—that of assimilation—and assert our being" was the gradual process of ridding themselves "of complexes inculcated by the former colonizers." I am referring to this process as *repositioning*.

The act of repositioning, for Senghor and his fellow diaspora students of African descent, comes in the form of writings that gave rise to the bulletin titled *L'Étudiant de la France d'Outre-mer: Chronique des Foyers*, issued in 1943. The bulletin was a healing fortress, the first medium through which immigrant students such as Senghor openly voiced their distasteful lived experiences of alienation. It was a space that allowed them to begin the process of actualizing the "art of conquering without being in the right" and denounce it in order to reposition themselves. An anonymous author (probably Senghor himself) wrote an apt introductory piece to the bulletin's first edition chillingly describing the African student in France as being a person "in transition, mentally a hybrid. Neither native, since his French education has made him so different from his ancestors, nor European, since he has been brought up elsewhere."⁴⁰ The lived experience that Senghor characterizes as being in a state of "panic-stricken despair" prompted the following comments on the condition of African students in France by Vaillant. She writes:

> He is a person without a stable self. . . . When he goes to France, he is at first overwhelmed, but also happy and hopeful. He works hard. But then he comes to feel uprooted from his world until he learns that he is not well adapted to European civilization. He then has a crisis. He has three choices: to resist, to capitulate or to adapt. At worst, the result can be suicide. Even at best, he experiences confusion and pain.⁴¹

She went on to conceive of this marginal space as having the fruitful sphere of existence that yielded new possibilities for emancipation and repositioning on which Senghor assiduously worked to negotiate both worlds. He found it expedient to reevaluate, accept, and preserve elements of his beloved childhood kingdom, which appeared to have been fleeting away under the imperial assimilation policy. These elements shaped his identity and were quintessential for the making of his new self as a person with a new voice as Black African who happened to be French—against Vaillant who conceives of this Senghorian new voice as being "neither French nor African" but "a new personage, the French Negro."⁴²

Although Vaillant saw in Senghor a resilient ability to make a positive use of marginal space, I disagree with her characterization of Senghor as a person who was "neither French nor African." Her position overlooks his firm embrace of his African roots, which she actually admits. Senghor relentlessly warned African leaders not to jettison some of their traditional African values for the political freedoms independence proclaims because they are indispensable for a lasting national and cultural inspiration. As president of Senegal, Senghor questioned what post-independent African head of states were doing with their newfound freedom from their former colonizers and found their consciousness wanting.

> It is evident that freedom without consciousness is worse than slavery. The slave at least is conscious of his own slavery. We too often forget that cultural imperialism is the most dangerous form of colonialism; it deadens consciousness. The most striking thing about the Negro peoples who have been promoted to autonomy or independence is precisely the *lack of consciousness* of most of their chiefs and their disparagement of Negro-African cultural values.[43]

Ousmane Sembène, a disciple of Senghor, leveled a similar criticism against Senegalese elites through the voices of his fictional characters in his novel titled *The Last of Empire*. It goes like this:

> In the years 1945–50, Leon Mignane would say during his election campaigns: "I will free you from the serfdom of native status. . . . I will make you . . . French citizens." That was why the peasants supported him. Twenty years after our independence, our thinking still bears the marks of serfdom. . . . Similarly, I've known Africans who were highly critical of certain regimes or ideologies, without realizing that their opinion was based on the European system, their gold standard. . . . Exactly, exclaimed Djia Umrel. What model of society are we offered through the media? We are made to swallow outdated values, no longer accepted in their countries of origin.[44]

Sembène's blistering critique of Négritude for evolving into a strategic attempt by founders "living in Europe to be accepted by Western culture"[45] appears to have missed the crux of the arguments Senghor and his colleagues were making. Repositioning is conscientization through dialogue not a soliloquy. His fears however were echoed by Senghor's warning African heads of state whom he found to be "proud of the political freedom of their people, but they do not realize that true freedom is not of the body but of the mind. And we see them importing just as they stand the political and social institutions of Europe, and even their cultural institutions."[46]

Négritude is somewhat a model Senghor uses to think and explain how repositioning works—that is the determination to reclaim the once objectified "whole complex of civilized values—cultural, economic, social, and political which characterize the black peoples, or, more precisely, the negro-African World."[47] This is not a mere return to precolonial African culture. Négritude is participatory—a work of many hands, a corporate "WE" that his *Anthologie de la nouvelle poèsie nègre et malgache de langue Française* clearly reflects.[48] Jean-Paul Sartre saw the importance of the collaborative dimension of Négritude and described it to his metropolitan French audience. He rhetorically asked his compatriots, "What were you hoping for when you removed the gag that was keeping these black mouths shut?"[49] This question overlooks the nature of things. Founders of Négritude fought hard for the independence of their countries. At least his third question rhetorically pinpoints the culpability of his ancestors and the brave struggle Africans mounted in order to reclaim their freedom. He further interrogates them.

> Did you think that when they raised themselves up again, you would read adoration in the eyes of these heads that our fathers had forced to bend down to the very ground? Here are black men standing, looking at us, and I hope that you, like me, will feel the shock of being seen. For three thousand years, the white man has enjoyed the privilege of seeing without being seen. . . . The whiteness of his skin was a further aspect of vision, a light condensed. . . . Today, these black men are looking at us, and our gaze comes back to our own eyes; in their turn, black torches light up the world and our white heads are no more than Chinese lanterns swinging in the wind.[50] . . . If we want to crack open this finitude which imprisons us, we can no longer rely on the privileges of our race, of our color, of our technics: we will not be able to become a part of the totality from which those black eyes exile us, unless we tear off our white tights in order to try simply to be men.[51]

Despite my discomfort with his first question, Sartre got it right in the rest of his analysis with the foundation provided by his two subsequent questions. To me, his words aim at forcing his audience to cultivate introspective skills and see the evils perpetrated on Africans by their ancestors and reimagine their privileged status in the making, especially when he says, "Here are black men standing, looking at us, and I hope that you, like me, will feel the shock of being seen." I will return to this crucial point later. Having rightly addressed the need for European introspection with reference to the slave trade and colonization, Sartre fails to follow through in his conscientization, and his argument becomes somewhat misleading as he ends up reducing Négritude to an antiracist racism.[52] Sartre seems to be arguing that the manner by which Négritude confronts racism does little more than become another form of racism. Strings of negative criticisms follow suit reducing Négritude to nothing less than cultural essentialism,[53] an outdated trope,[54] or, in the words of Reiland Rabaka "a roguish regurgitation of white supremacist colonial antiblack racism by another name: "Négritude" or "Africanity."[55] In the same vein, Said reduces Senghorian Négritude to a nativism which he thinks is very much part of Rastafarianism. Such a nativism, he opines,

> reinforces the distinction even while revaluating the weaker or subservient partner. . . . has often led to compelling but demagogic assertions about a native past, narrative or actuality that stands free from worldly time itself. One sees this in such enterprises as Senghor's *négritude* . . . to accept nativism is to accept the consequence of imperialism, the racial, religious, and political divisions imposed by imperialism itself . . . to leave the historical world for the metaphysics of essences like *négritude* . . . is to abandon history for essentializations that have the power to turn human beings against each other; often this abandonment of the secular world has led to a sort of millenarianism if the movement has had a mass base, or it has degenerated into a small-scale private craziness, or into an unthinking acceptance of stereotypes, myths, animosities, and traditions encouraged by imperialism.[56]

Said, like some of the critics mentioned above, misread the complex and multivalent dimensions of Senghorian Négritude. Senghor insists they "could not go back to our former condition, to a négritude of the sources."[57] Ironically Senghor welcomes these criticisms, in the sense that they were formulated by those he considers to be "good writers" of a younger generation and finds their criticisms "legitimate" in their aims to deepen and innovate on Négritude.[58] In other words, some of these criticisms are well taken, but most of them are overdrawn.

Incipient Négritude was an organic repositioning trope for Senghor and his West Indies colleagues. Some Black American leaders of the Harlem Renaissance who influenced the making of Négritude participated in the

First International Conference of Negro Writers and Artists held in Sorbonne in 1956 and collaborated as much as possible to advance the Black cause at home and the diaspora.[59] The Americans of African descent in Paris were respected for intellectual and artistic accomplishments. Founders of Négritude earned a similar reputation, especially among the French educated.[60] Concerning Négritude and as one might expect, Americans of African descent who attended the First International Conference of Negro Writers and Artists in 1956, Richard Wright and James Baldwin in particular, had mixed feelings when they heard Senghor's speech on the vibrancy of African culture and its contributions to world civilization that colonial powers had objectified as nothing more than a *tabula rasa*. Wright's frustration was echoed offstage in the Senghorian construction of African culture.[61] Here are some of his remarks.

> I want to speak as carefully as I can. . . . I was stupefied with admiration with what Léopold Senghor said here today. . . . It was a brilliant speech and a revelation to me—a brilliance poured out in impeccable, limpid French, about the mentality and sensibility of the African—a poetic world, rich, dynamic, moving, tactile, rhythmic. Yet, as I admired it, a sense of uneasiness developed in me. . . . I wonder where do I, an American Negro, conditioned by the harsh industrial, abstract force of the Western world that has used stern, political prejudices against the society (which he has so brilliantly elucidated)—where do I stand in relation to that culture? . . . The modern world has cast us both in the same mould. *I* am black and *he* is black; I am an *American* and he is *French,* and so, there you are. . . . The ancestor cult religion with of all of its manifold, poetic richness that created a sense of self-sufficiency—did not that religion, when the European guns came in, act as a sort of aid to those guns? Did that religion help the people to resist fiercely and hardily and hurl the Europeans out? I question the value of that culture in relationship of our future. I do not condemn it. But how can we use it?[62]

His uneasiness in no way impeded his determination to cultivate a mutual relationship with Pan-Africanists and the founder of Négritude in order to fight for freedom of the people of African descent. Despite Wright's professed uncertainties about how African culture might unify people of

African descent, as Babacar M'Baye observes, he saw European exploitation and alienation of Black people a shared plight.[63] Similarly, James Baldwin saw stark differences on how Africans and people of African descent in America saw themselves in Paris vis-à-vis colonial Europe, especially France. He writes:

> In Paris, the African Negro's status, conspicuous and subtly inconvenient, is that of a colonial: and he leads here the intangibly precarious life of someone abruptly and recently uprooted. His bitterness is unlike that of his American kinsman in that it is not so treacherously likely to be turned against himself. He has, not so very many miles away, a homeland to which his relationship, no less than his responsibility, is overwhelmingly clear: his country must be given—or it must seize—its freedom.[64]

These existential remarks that Baldwin makes are based on his lived experience of the African intellectuals he saw, heard, and cultivated a rapport with while he was in Paris, who, he admits, "endured privation, injustice, medieval cruelty" but have yet to suffer "the utter alienation of [themselves] from [their] people and [their] past."[65] Despite this cultural difference, Baldwin admits in hearing Senghor's speech that

> it became clear as the debate wore on, that there was something which all black men held in common, something which cut across opposing points of view, and placed in the same context their widely dissimilar experience. What they held in common was their precarious, their unutterably painful relation to the white world. What they held in common was the necessity to remake the world in their own image to impose this image on the world, and themselves, held by other people. What, in sum, black men held in common was their ache to come into the world as men and this ache united people who might otherwise have been divided as to what a man should be.[66]

Many diaspora people of African descent do acknowledge the cultural distance that separates them from those who live on the continent. Ralph Ellison agrees with both Wright and Baldwin on the meaning and relevance of the African cultural unity of which Senghor spoke. The American Negro, Ellison writes:

is North American in origin and has evolved under specifically American conditions. . . . it takes its character from the experience of American slavery and struggle for, and the achievement of, emancipation . . . and from living in a highly industrialized and highly mobile society possessing a relatively high standard of living and an explicitly stated equalitarian concept of freedom. Its spiritual outlook is basically Protestant, its system of kinship is Western, its time and historical sense are American (United States), and its secular values are those professed, ideally at least, by all people of the United States.[67]

Senghor was fully aware of the concerns Wright, Baldwin, Ellison, and others raised about the African culture he was passionately describing for them as alienated people of African descent. The end of the arguments Senghor and Alioune Diop were making centered on paving the way to freedom to be themselves, fully participate in and contribute to world civilization, and live, in Diop's observation, with other human beings to cultivate "peace and understanding."[68]

Affirming Blackness and appealing to some African cultural values were indispensable dimensions for this repositioning journey of which Senghor spoke. The cultural essentialism or nativism of which some critics accused him ignores his resilient work to promote a civilization that welcomes the contributions of other cultures. Critics of Négritude should not ignore the fact that French colonizers were the first ones to essentialize European culture, which they imposed on other cultures to adopt as normative. The failure of the assimilation policy precipitated the need for the reclamation of some elements of their African culture once objectified by imperial France. In this case, Négritude had a deconstructive role (undoing the foundation of the assimilation policy) and a reconstructive role (reaffirming some African values) in paving the way to freedom—a space to reembrace Back culture as something good and worth celebrating, but also a contribution to world civilization. African culture matters.

Sartre's "antiracist racism" point may be well taken, but he failed to do justice to the Black cause, not just to Frantz Fanon, who thought that to dub Négritude as "antiracist racism" was destructive to the "black zeal,"[69] but also to Senghor who, in response to Sartre, wrote:

> What then is this NÉGRITUDE that scares the delicate, that was presented to you as a new racism? It is in French that it was first expressed, sung, and danced. This alone should reassure you. How would you like us to become racist, we who have been for centuries, innocent victims, black hosts of racism? Jean-Paul Sartre was not quite right when, in "Black Orpheus," he defines négritude as "antiracist racism"; he is surely right when he presents it as a certain emotional attitude to the world.[70]

Kane's *"art of conquering without being in the right"* is a sociocultural, spiritual, and economic quest that required voluntary immigration to Metropolitan France. This is a risky journey during which the immigrant might be culturally uprooted, as Kane shows in the spiritual and cultural death of his hero Samba Diallo. The chief of the Diallobé prophetically made this point when he spoke about sending their children as being fraught with dangers. His point is that, in France, children "would learn all the ways of joining wood to wood . . . they would also forget. What they forget is themselves, their bodies, and the futile dream which hardens with age and stifles the spirit. So what they learn is worth infinitely more than what they forget."[71] To the chief, Western education might lead to forgetting one's cultural and spiritual roots, but it does not preclude or inhibit relearning those very suppressed values.[72] This was the dangerous quest Senghor, Kane, and a handful of Senegalese intellectuals embarked on. I will now turn to the key dimensions of Senghorian Négritude that I believe constitute repositioning, namely a poetics of postcolonial biblical criticism.

REPOSITIONING

As I noted earlier, Said, Bhabha, and Spivak all spoke in one way or another about the need to reposition themselves and create space for emancipation from colonial marginalization—a task Senghor and his colleagues started much earlier. R. S. Sugirtharajah is onto something in positing that liberationist readings of biblical texts critique reform programs that serve the rich and not the poor.[73] The lifeblood of these programs is the internal oppression they create and sustain, that generates wealth for the rich. Liberation theologians use Gospel and prophetic texts to critique any form of dehumanization with a view to effecting freedom from this new form of oppression. Seen from this perspective, it would not be overdrawn to consider liberation hermeneutics and postcolonial criticism companions in the struggle for liberation, as does Sugirtharajah. Both ways of reading share the daunting task of subverting the dominant paradigm of imperialism and neocolonialism, but their commitment is not limited to liberation as it intersects at a crucial juncture in the lived experience of the oppressed—the indispensable need to empower or precisely to rehabilitate the freed-oppressed. The complementarity of liberation and rehabilitation is central to emancipation. It is also important to recognize the religious pluralism and the variety of religions and confessional traditions that postcolonial biblical criticism welcomes.[74] Senghor championed both liberation and rehabilitation as quintessential to the emancipatory journey. Two main dimensions of Négritude relevant to my contribution to postcolonial biblical criticism are, as I noted earlier, liberative and rehabilitative.

The Liberative Dimension of Négritude
In his book titled *Liberté 1*, Senghor asserted that the first task of Négritude is to "liberate"[75] colonized people. Senghor, Damas, Césaire, and even young Fanon were confronted by the failures of the French colonial policy of assimilation to promote equity between the French and people of African descent and the resulting ugly and blatant racist attitudes directed against them in Metropolitan France. Senghorian contradictions and tendencies toward nativists' reactions that critics such as Said detected in Négritude were very much entrenched in the naïve and demeaning colonial experimentation of the assimilation policy. To present French culture as normative for colonized people is not just problematic; it is cultural genocide.

Despite the criticism leveled against his embrace of some aspects of French culture, Senghor believed French education was instrumental to debunking as well as subverting the French colonial ideology that inculcated a sense of cultural inferiority in the mind of the colonized. Senghor thought that French colonial ideology attempted to teach Africans to be educated by forgetting their African culture and heritage. In reality, no one owns language. Being well read (classical literature, Western philosophers, Africanists, and his Sérère orature), with a view to reposition himself and

Africans, Senghor argued that the Western emphasis on the primacy of reason is wanting. In reality "intuitive reason" is solely "capable of an understanding that goes beyond appearances, of taking in total reality."[76] The Cartesian emphasis on the primacy of reason missed an indispensable dimension of life. Reason, Senghor argues, is analytical; intuitive reason is very much participatory. As Senghor's epigraph reminds us, the theory of tabula rasa denies Africans any ingenuity, and unfortunately, many Africans believed it. Senghor is determined to liberate Africans from such a denigrating construction of their identity. Hence, the nuanced reader of Senghor might begin to perceive efforts he made to relearn much about his African values suppressed by the French colonial policy of assimilation.

In Joal-Djilor, Senghor was socialized to live and construct reality in relation to the Sérère villagers of his childhood kingdom. The identity of each villager, in this rural context, hinges on corporate participatory experience through which she or he learns and loves with others—a shared life echoed in the famous Senghorian riddle: "'I feel, I dance the Other; I am.'"[77] To dance, as Senghor sees it, is an *other-centered* performative act expressing the *vital force* that animates the person and empowers her or him to know the "Other" through "the *reason of touch* . . . the *reasoning-embrace.*" The act of dancing has ontological and epistemological dimensions as a performed act of discovery and re-creation; especially, "when it is a dance of love . . . re-creation and recreation, after the model of God."[78] It is for this reason that Senghor conceives of human relationships and self-knowledge as an expression of "vital force" (*l'élan vital*),[79] which, he also thinks, is integral to rhythm. Rhythm shapes ontology as it sends a "system of waves" to other beings as

> the pure expression of *vital force*. . . . The force that, across the senses, seizes us at the root of life. . . . For the African, it is in the same measure that rhythm is embodied in the sense that it illuminates the spirit. . . . From the preeminence of the Word, it is the rhythm that gave it efficacious fullness that transformed it into *Verbe*. It is the verb of God, which is the rhythmed word that created the world.[80]

Elements inherent in the making of the universe manifest the *vital force* that emanates from God. It is personified in human existence as a *life-force* that gives rise to a mystical relationship—the divine and nature, visible and invisible world. As an African Christian who values his Sérère faith traditions, Senghor finds Marxism wanting for its critique of religion. Nevertheless, he embraces its dialectics as useful for freeing colonized and oppressed people. The conflict theory championed by Marxism failed to see religion as a matrix for fomenting revolution. If myth and intuitive reason permeate scripture, how might a Senegalese Christian contextualize scripture?

The Rehabilitative Dimension of Négritude
If liberation is the first task of Négritude, the second, Senghor insists, is to rehabilitate. The long-suppressed contributions of precolonial Africa to world civilization, in particular the contributions of the kingdom of Wagadou under King Kaya Magan later absorbed by the kingdom of Mali under Sundiata Keita, must be reconstructed, reassumed, and reaffirmed by Africans.[81] The unfortunate colonial ploy to denigrate Africans that facilitated the inculcation of the theory of *tabula rasa* in the mind of many Europeans and Africans to ensure it sticks indelibly must be deconstructed and subverted. Senghorian Négritude seeks to liberate Africans and rehabilitate the image of Africa and her leaders—a double-edged tool to *affirm* and *assume*, as he conceived of it.[82] However, to decolonize effectively, one had to debunk the failed promises of assimilation in order to rehabilitate. Senghor's realization was revelatory in the sense that it shaped his Négritude, incubated, and sustained its multivalence,[83] all in the effort to deconstruct France's claim to superiority based on her presupposed normative culture for the world.[84]

First, with his poem titled "Shaka," he rehabilitates Shaka Zulu, once characterized as a bloodthirsty tyrant by Western geopolitical discourse, into an exemplary African leader and hero.[85] Put differently, Senghor staged a conversation between Western geopolitical colonial discourse he calls *la Voix Blanche* (White Voice) that takes the Hegelian view of an infantile and savage Africa at face value and casts Shaka positively as a freedom fighter. Instead of a bloodthirsty leader who terrorized and killed his own people, as "the White Voice" would have us believe, Shaka becomes an African hero whose resistance against colonial occupation provides didactic political lessons for Africans to emulate. In fact, he died, not as vanquished but as a freedom fighter who gave his life for his people—a portrayal that echoes the soteriological and Christological significance of Jesus Christ.

Shaka as liberator might not sit well with some South African readers. These themes of liberation echo the words of Jesus, who spoke of being sent "to proclaim release to the captives and recovery of sight to the blind, to let the oppressed go free, to proclaim the year of the Lord's favor" (Luke 4:18–19) and "to serve, and to give his life as a ransom for many" (Mark 10:45). To Senghor, Africa is not the Dark Continent as European colonists and some missionaries would like to have us believe. Africa is the cradle of humanity, civilization,[86] and a beautiful Black woman embodies African civilization.[87]

Second, colonial attempts to erase African culture and faith traditions were traumatizing to Senghor, lived experiences he characterized as "panic-stricken" despair that only liberation and rehabilitation can address. Rehabilitation involves rereading scripture from an African cultural lens. As I lamented earlier, the exclusion of these dimensions of Senghorian Négritude in postcolonial biblical criticism is surprising. Francis August Schaeffer, an evangelical philosopher, theologian, and Presbyterian minister found Senghorian speeches on African socialism moving and then made the following observations:

> If a man stood up in any of the Western countries and delivered these as political speeches, very few Christians would understand their real significance. The fact that Senghor is an African underlines the need to train our overseas missionaries in a new way, for the problem of communication in our day extends beyond the Sorbonne, Oxford, Cambridge, Harvard, or Massachusetts Institute of Technology to those places which we have traditionally thought of as the mission-field. The problem of communication does not end at our own shores.[88]

Schaeffer critiques Western missionary claims to be sound, intellectually persuasive, and normative ways of conveying ideas. He insists that the utterance of the word God "by itself is meaningless until given content."[89] He concurs with Senghor's interpretation of Marx, Engels, and Teilhard de Chardin that prioritizes the dialectic optic for apprehending "religious forms."[90] Schaeffer is correct. Senghor reads biblical texts dialectically, a lens that shaped his inculturation of scripture.

In response to what he thought was the Europeanization of the African Church, Senghor insisted that the church in African and non-European countries should mirror liturgical elements of their own cultures in their theological language and ritual performance instead of European ones. To impose European Christianity on Africans is to ignore the multivalence and adaptability of scripture itself as echoed in Pauline traditions and the Acts of the Apostles. Rereading scripture in conversation with African cosmology introduces the kind of symbiosis institutionalized Christianity of Senghor's time denounced as being syncretistic and by definition inferior. Senghor rejects syncretism for inculturation and prefers symbiosis, which, to him, allows both his Christian faith and Sérère faith traditions to inform each other.[91] To Senghor, this dialogical reading of scripture has an inspiring rehabilitative aspect the once colonized and denigrated Africans need for their self-actualization.

Critics who think Senghorian Négritude is anti-racist racism or cultural essentialism missed his *robust Christian humanism*. It underpins and permeates his work and infuses it with biblical and African religious themes and images, and shapes his vision for a cultural and religious symbiosis he persistently calls *la civilization de l'universel*—a "cultural mixing" he thinks will grow in the twenty-first century.[92] There is not a consensus on whether Senghor coined the expression *la civilization de l'universel*. What is clear is, as Baidy Dioum observes, the idea pervades his poems, speeches,[93] and I would add his appropriation and interpretation of African traditional sources.

NÉGRITUDE AS POETICS OF POSTCOLONIAL BIBLICAL CRITICISM

Many postcolonial themes and issues biblical scholars unearth from scripture have liberative dimensions. Studies emphasize the transfer of cultural values that legitimates a plethora of colonial oppressions and exploitations. Empire critics raise similar concerns, and intersectionality is of the essence here. I am not rejecting a nuanced contrast between postcolonial and empire critical reading optics. As I noted above in this essay, it suffices to recognize that empire critical studies raise concerns similar to those voiced by postcolonial critics especially on the role of empires.[94] The overlap and divergence between liberation hermeneutics and postcolonial biblical criticism is clearly noted by Sugirtharajah[95] and need not to be addressed here. It is pertinent, however, to mention one key aspect of the divergence, namely the fact that liberation hermeneutics does not draw on nonbiblical religions. I am interested in this critical point by virtue of the fact that Senghor engages both scripture and his Sérère faith traditions in his poems as well as his other writings, as I will show.

How does Senghor read scripture? As Senghor fights to free colonized people in Africa and the diaspora, he also focuses on rehabilitating them from the psychological trauma inflicted on them for centuries—a condition that left many Africans in cultural, religious, and spiritual disarray. His faith traditions (Sérère-Christian) in conversation with his education were foundational. Having refuted his first missionary teacher's assumed environmental determinism, Father Lalouse, one of the Holy Ghost missionaries, Senghor insists that nurturing Africans into European civilization or intellectual acumen is denigrating, unsustainable, and must be rejected. Like many French colonial officials then, Father Lalouse must have forgotten Father Libermann's charge to Catholic missionaries: *Faites-vous Nègre avec les Nègre*, "Become Negro with the Negros."[96] Black Africans are as human as Europeans are. Africa has a great and beautiful civilization, Senghor maintains. These formative counter-thoughts shaped his proto-Négritude sentiments.[97] So what makes Senghorian Négritude a Poetics of Postcolonial Biblical Criticism? To respond to this question, I must turn to his use of biblical and African traditional imagery.

Senghorian Négritude is *A Poetics of Postcolonial Biblical Criticism*, as I argued in my recent book. First, many of the poems Senghor wrote, especially the ones grouped under the heading *Black Hosts (Liminary Poem, Prayer for the Senegalese Soldiers, Assassinations, To the Black American Troops,* and *At the Call of the Race Sheba)*, express his deepest take on the suffering of people of African descent—variegated forms of oppression that often led to the death of many Africans at the hands of colonial Europe, especially France. Echoing biblical and African ancestral faith traditions in the excerpts of poems below, Senghor prays fervently for people of African descent—Africans and Americans who fought for the freedoms of the very empires that oppressed them: France and America. In my second essay in this book, I translated the title *Black Hosts* to mean *Black Wafers to capture Senghor's intention to present Black bodies (African soldiers drafted from French colonies) sacrificed to liberate France for Nazi Germany*. He prays as follows:

You Senegalese Soldiers, my black brothers with warm
hands under ice and death
Who can praise you if not your brother-in-arms, your
brother in blood?

. . .

You, Senegalese soldiers, my brothers with warm hands,
Lying under ice and death?[98]
Lord, if I speak to You, You who are the Unknown Presence,
It is not because the Republic has appointed me
The good king of my people or deputy of the Four
Communes.
I grew up in the heartland of Africa, at the crossroads
Of castes and races and roads, and now I am a second-class
Soldier

. . .

Landed on this European soil, disarmed of weapons,
Left for sale to the dead.

. . .

Lord listen to the offering of our militant faith
Receive the sacrifice of our bodies, the selection
Of all these gloomy perfect bodies, black victim decoys.
We offer You our bodies along with those of French
Peasants . . .[99]
There they lie stretched out by the captive roads along the routes of
Disaster

. . .

Senegalese prisoners lying gloomy on French soil.

. . .

O black Martyrs, immortal race, let me say the words
That forgive![100]
I did not recognize you in your prison of sad-colored uniforms
I did not recognize you under the calabash helmet without plumes

. . .

I just touched your warm brown hand and said my name,
"Africa!"

. . .

Black brothers, fighters whose mouths are singing flowers,

O, the delight of life after winter—I salute you
As messengers of peace.[101]
Bless you Mother!
I hear your voice as I surrender to the cunning silence of this European
night
A prisoner of cold, tightly drawn, white sheets,
Of fits of anguish intertwining me inextricably,
when sudden falls upon me the bitter panic of yellow
leaves
Or the panic of black fighters in the fury of thundering tanks
When their leaders fall with the great scream, his whole body
writhing . . .
I remember the days of my fathers, Dyilôr evenings . . .
Haven't these colonial days bled our dawns
For more than two generations and colored your eyes . . .
For nine years, Mother, you have mourned the deserter
At the weak moment just before sleep,
Worried if the doors were locked and the dogs
Were barking only at spirits.
And I, your son, I meditate, I forge my mouth wide
To resound in the shade with the echo and trumpet of
Liberation . . .[102]

Reaching out to his African ancestors in the set of poems titled *Shadow Songs*, Senghor solemnly prays in *Black Mask* and *Totem* appealing to the power of memory of lived experience to inform his poetic/prophetic protest. As in the lines above, Senghor continues to protest against oppressive Europe and bemoans the suffering of the children of Africa.

Masks! O Masks!
Black mask, red mask, you white-and-black masks
Masks of the four cardinal points where the Spirit blows
I greet you in silence!
. . .
On an altar of blank paper
And in your image, listen to me!

The Africa of empires is dying—it is the agony
Of sorrowful princess
And Europe, too, tied us at the navel.
Fix your steady eyes on your oppressed children . . .
Who else will teach rhythm to the world
Deadened by machines and cannons?
Who will sound the shout of joy at daybreak to wake
orphans and the dead?[103]
I must hide him down in my deepest veins
The ancestor whose stormy skin streaks with lightning and thunder
He is the guardian animal I must hide
Lest I burst in the dam of scandal
He is my loyal blood demanding loyalty,
Protecting my naked pride against myself
And the arrogance of fortunate races . . .[104]

Second, Senghor was grateful to the Jesuit Father Pierre Teilhard de Chardin whom he credited for restoring his faith—a lived experience that shaped his critical reading and contextualization of scripture. Built on Teilhard de Chardin's, Senghor's socialism is more than a political and economic theory; it includes a crucial spiritual dimension that emphasizes "the nature and role of love in socialization" and union in differentiation. It is *"the technical and spiritual organization of human society by the intelligence and the heart*. After satisfying their animal needs and acquiring well-being by democracy and planning, men will then be able, in union, which is love, to realize their maximum-being."[105] The love and unity of which he speaks are both foundational biblical themes. Their theological significance for developing the counter-imperial movements of Jesus and Paul cannot be underestimated. The earliest followers of Jesus such as Paul, John, and James[106] used love and unity as themes to anchor their constructions of alternative communities under empire. They permeate Jesus' and Pauline community constructions that centered on communalism. A Pauline example best illustrates this reality in an imperative

> "For the whole law is summed up in a single commandment, 'You shall love your neighbor as yourself.'" (Gal 5:14)

"... the fruit of the Spirit is love, joy, peace, patience, kindness, generosity, faithfulness, gentleness, and self-control. There is no law against such things." (Gal 5:22–23)

"Be united in the same mind and the same purpose." (1 Cor 1:10)

Johannine Jesus exhorts his disciples this way: "I give you a new commandment, that you love one another. Just as I have loved you, you also should love one another. By this everyone will know that you are my disciples, if you have love for one another" (John 13:34–35). In their Greco-Roman contexts, Jesus and Paul gave these exhortations to inspire the construction of alternative communities under imperial Rome.

Senghor agrees with Teilhard de Chardin that Christ is the goal and crown of the natural and supernatural worlds—the inextricable connection of Jesus Christ to the cosmos as the "Alpha" but also "Omega."[107] The expression the "Alpha and the Omega" symbolizing Jesus Christ is the theological anchor of Revelation (Rev 1:8, 21:6, 22:13). Teilhard de Chardin speaks of the resurrection of Jesus Christ in this way:

> In a system of Creative Union, it is not only the Universe but God himself who is necessarily "Christified" in Omega, at the upper limits of Cosmogenesis . . . "evolved" Monotheism, around which all that is best in the Earth's religious energies undoubtedly seems to be concentrating, is moving to its logical and biological fulfilment in the direction of some Pan-Christism. With no limit to this capacity for being extended and adapted to the world's new dimension and, in addition, with an inexhaustible charge of evaluative energy for our hearts—so there is growing in our firmament, to the scale of and at the demand of the *Ultra-human*, a true *Super-Christ*, in all the radiance of *Super-Charity* . . . assumed the dominating position of all-inclusive Center in which everything is gathered together. . . . as mankind emerges into consciousness of the movement that carries it along, it has a continually more urgent need of a Direction and a Solution ahead and above, to which it will at last be able to consecrate itself. Who then is this God, no longer the God of the old Cosmos but the God of the new cosmogenesis . . . you, Jesus, who represent him and bring him to us?[108]

The divine revelation Teilhard de Chardin describes does not contradict Senghorian African cosmology and ontology, as I discussed earlier. God has always been, in the Negro-African ontology as the uncreated Creator, the Force from which creation proceeds and is sustained—a symbiosis that resists any dichotomy between the natural and supernatural order.[109]

Third, myth and intuitive reason that permeate biblical cosmology in the First Testament/Hebrew Bible are concretely realized in the Second Testament/New Testament, especially the Johannine prologue (John 1: 1–14) and Paul (Gal 2:20)—a realized phenomenon inherent in African cosmology.[110] Senghor read and theologically appropriated the P (Priestly) and J (Yahwist) myths of creation. For instance, P (Priestly) emphasizes the divine creative act through speech that creates and orders space for creatures. "Then God said, 'Let there be light'; and there was light" (Gen 1:3 NRSV). The creative speech of God is an integral aspect of the incubating and life-giving power of the wind (rûah) of the deity (Gen 1:2 NRSV). Divine speech orders existing matter and enlivens by *wind-life force-spirit* that rhythms all forms of life.

. . . "Let there be a dome in the midst of the waters, and let it separate the waters from the waters" (Gen 1:6).

. . . "Let the waters under the sky be gathered together into one place, and let the dry land appear" (Gen 1:9).

. . . "Let the earth put forth vegetation: plants yielding seed, and fruit trees of every kind on earth that bear fruit with the seed in it" (Gen 1:11).

. . . "Let there be lights in the dome of the sky to separate the day from the night; and let them be for signs and for seasons and for days and years, and let them be lights in the dome of the sky to give light upon the earth" (Gen 1:14–15).

. . . "Let the waters bring forth swarms of living creatures, and let birds fly above the earth across the dome of the sky" (Gen 1:20).

. . . "Let the earth bring forth living creatures of every kind: cattle and creeping things and wild animals of the earth of every kind" (Gen 1:24).

. . . "Let us make humankind in our image, according to our likeness; and let them have dominion over the fish of the sea, and over the birds of the air, and over the cattle, and over all the wild animals of the earth, and over every creeping thing that creeps upon the earth" (Gen 1:26).

... "Be fruitful and multiply, and fill the earth and subdue it; and have dominion over the fish of the sea and over the birds of the air and over every living thing that moves upon the earth" (Gen 1:28).

Humans, the Yahwist tells us, were made by direct inspiriting[111] with "the breath of life"—a divinely embodied *enlivening wind-life force-spirit*.

... "LORD God formed man of the dust of the ground, and breathed into his nostrils the breath of life; and man became a living being ..." (Gen 2:7).

God's "vital force" (*l'élan vital*) or the Word (*logos*)[112] that was the agent of divine creative power became human in John 1:1, 14[113]—making the biblical creator God accessible to humans in the person of Jesus. The Word, in Johannine theology, animates all human life and creation—an expression of divine creative love.

"In the beginning was the Word, and the Word was with God, and the Word was God ...

And the Word became flesh and lived among us. ... God so loved the world (*kosmon*) that he gave his only Son, so that everyone who believes in him may not perish but may have eternal life. (John 1:1, 14; 3:16)

God, in African philosophical and religious thought, is "Force," namely "force of forces." To Senghor, Christians should understand this African view of God to mean, "And the Word was made flesh and dwelt among us." Therefore, "it is by animating the visible and invisible universe with art, by singing and rhythmating it, that humanity strengthens the force of God and becomes, at the same time, similar to God. This is why, as Africans say, 'God needs humanity.'"[114]

Senghor boldly exploits parallels between biblical and African Faith Traditions (especially Bambara, Dogon, and Sérère, but not limited to them)[115] to show how divine revelation encounters humans to shape the divine-human relationship, which in his estimation is similar to how the African people, including the Sérère, experience the divine daily. He was convinced that the "intuitive reason" and the "mythological thought" he finds in biblical cosmology are close to African cosmology. As a follower of Jesus Christ, he builds on these parallels to reread scripture through an African lens with colonial antecedents that shaped his Négritude in France. Admittedly, imperial Christianity that was poised to change Senghor into a Black-skinned French was repulsive to him—a realization that almost obliterated his faith on the brink of spiritual death. He was unable to reconcile the bourgeois Catholic expression of Christianity in France with his African beliefs until his discovery of the works of Teilhard de Chardin. Reading his writings resuscitated and empowered his faith and spirituality. Invigorated with a new sense of purpose, Senghor developed a lively prophetic and poetic voice that contains a conciliatory and yet resilient and radical critical stance that defiantly prays for colonized and their colonizers alike.

> Lord Jesus, at the end of this book, which I offer You
> As a ciborium of sufferings . . .
> —Yet I know that my brothers' blood will once more redden
> The yellow Orient on the shores of the Pacific
> Ravaged by storms and hatred
> I know that this blood is the spring libation
> The Great Tax Collectors have used for seventy years
> To fatten the Empire's lands
> Lord, at the foot of this cross—and it is no longer You
> Tree of sorrow but, above the Old and New Worlds,
> Crucified Africa,
> And her right arm stretches over my land
> And her left side shades America
> And her heart is precious Haiti, Haiti who dared
> Proclaim Man before the Tyrant
> At the feet of my Africa, crucified for four hundred years
> And still breathing
> Let me recite to You, Lord, her prayer of peace and pardon. . .
> O bless this people who break their bonds,
> Bless this people at bay who defy the hungry mob of
> Bullies and torturers. And with them bless
> All the peoples of Europe, all the peoples of Asia,
> All the peoples of Africa, and the peoples of America
> Who sweat blood and suffering. And in the midst
> Of these millions of waves, see the surging heads
> Of my people. And give their warm hands
> A band of brotherly hands so they can embrace the land
> Under the rainbow of your peace . . .[116]

To me this closing poem anchors the depths of Senghor's postcolonial theological thought uttering the unutterable that can only be captured through poems. He denounces enslaving Imperial Europe for its role in the dehumanizing transatlantic slave trade, colonization, and rampant exploitation in the post-independent era. As if he were taking his cues from the Psalmist, Senghor foregrounds his prayer with a strong hope for the liberative power of forgiveness and conciliation thus epideictically stabbing right at the heart of France's colonial geopolitics. These words encapsulate a Senghorian *Black Theology of Liberation* etched at the core of his Négritude. Senghor fought to liberate France from Nazi Germany. He knew that the racism of the Nazi was nothing less than "hate and violence. . . . Science at the service of Death, not Life."[117] His prayers include elements of lament that analogically echo those of peoples of African descent in America—"I am a Man"[118] and "Black Lives Matter"[119] are laments and resilient assertions of life. They vehemently reject human injustice and affirm life against the odds by asserting the humanity and dignity of the oppressed, summoning and forcing oppressors to examine their own humanity. This is what Frantz Fanon, a junior participant in the First International Conference of Negro Writers and Artists held in 1956, meant when he said:

> I am a man, and what I have to recapture is the whole past of the world. . . . Every time a man has contributed to the victory of the dignity of the spirit, every time a man has said no to an attempt to subjugate his fellows, I have felt solidarity with his act. In no way should I derive my basic purpose from the past of the peoples of color. In no way should I dedicate myself to the revival of an unjustly unrecognized Negro civilization.[120]

In the same vein, engaging racism in America, James Cone argues that Americans of African descent struggle "'to make a living' in a society labeled 'for whites only'. . . By definition, whiteness is 'being,' and blackness is 'nonbeing.' And the killing and caging of black leaders make us think that black genocide has already begun. Blacks live under sentences of death . . . to breathe in white society is dependent on saying yes to whiteness, and blacks know it."[121] He went on to say that God deeply experiences Black suffering and identifies with Black experience of racism.[122] The God who suffered injustice on the Roman Imperial cross and on the lynching tree of white supremacists is the only God who can free whites from the idolatry of racism and at the same time be a safe haven for Black people. Whites must engage in this radical ontological journey to undo racism.[123] Building on the dictum of Father Libermann and the poetic reflections of Arthur Rimbaud,[124] Senghor insisted that it is imperative for Catholic missionaries and European colonists to ontologically "become Negro with the Negros."[125] As prophet, poet, and apostle of Négritude speaking from his *pathos* like that of eighth-century Hebrew prophets, Senghor chillingly laments: "At the feet of my Africa, crucified for four hundred years and still breathing."[126] As if to say to some breath-sucking imperial colonists or contemporary Western law enforcement officers, there is *intrinsic breath* they will never be able to take away, just as Cone argues that lynching is not the final word.[127] That mysterious divine inbreathing that enlivens earthlings into human beings (Gen 2:7) cannot be murdered, and therefore it never dies. This is the intrinsic breath neither the lynching tree nor life-negating imperial powers can annihilate.

Biblical themes permeate Senghor's *Prayer of Peace*. His are not the words of a coward, sellout, or assimilated Black African, but a subversive activist who builds on the power of the cross of Jesus Christ to change, heal the human heart, and resurrect human distorted perceptions of others, even colonists. As I have written elsewhere, to fight violence with violence (Fanon and Amilcar Cabral)[128] leaves no room for reconciliation and forgiveness. As the Matthean Jesus warned millennia ago, "all who take the sword will perish by the sword" (Matt. 26:52).

Inspired by his faith, Senghor seized on the revolutionary power of prayer—a prayer of peace that denounces France for abusing and crucifying Africans for centuries, beginning with the atrocities of the transatlantic slave trade and colonization. Such a blistering critique through the biblical lens is an expression of liberation theology foregrounded in the mystery of human vulnerability and invites colonists to kneel at the foot of the cross of Jesus Christ. It summons colonial France to examine itself in order to find strength to denounce its participation in the slave trade and colonization and be inspired to seek forgiveness and reconciliation. Jesus became a model for emulation. Despite suffering the trauma of being nailed to a cross, and as he was dying, Jesus absorbed pain and suffering as many Africans did and still do. Jesus said, "Father, forgive them; for they do not know what they are doing" (Luke 23:34). This is nothing short of a *daring activism with a redemptive edge*—a way of being in the world with others that firmly denounces injustice and oppression of any kind tempered with a conciliatory vision. Wrong done to any group of human beings affects all and thus must be righted.

CONCLUSION

Despite negative criticisms leveled against Senghor, his Négritude shaped the country of Senegal and the political and religious sphere of most Francophone West African countries. Négritude influenced decisions reached at Vatican II, especially on the importance for African followers of Jesus to contextualize the gospel, namely to affirm their African identity(ies), cultural, and Christian liturgical expression. In other words, Négritude invigorated many Senegalese-born priests such as Farther Nazaire N. Diatta to inculturate the Bible[129]—a gradual hammering out of an African biblical hermeneutics and liturgy informed by African lived experience.[130] Most francophone politicians and clergy are now embracing a central dimension of Senghorian Négritude, namely Senghor's humanism and vision for the world. The denigrating speech President Sarkozy of France delivered on January 15–16, 2008, at the University of Cheikh Anta Diop in which he called Africans primitive was not incidental.[131] French colonists' denigrating characterizations of Africans before him used similar epithets. Arrogance must have undermined his memory or it was a cavalier display of white supremacy that ignored Senghor, the African academic and president of the Republic of Senegal as well as many of his interlocutors who earned PhDs and teach in the most prestigious institutions in the West and Senegal.

Reoccurring interreligious dialogues held in Dakar, as I have argued elsewhere, built on Senghorian Négritude to effect peacemaking—especially to address the interethnic conflicts and religiously inspired violence that have plagued many African countries. Participants appeal to the Senghorian conciliatory approach to life, intentional practice of dialogue, cultural, and religious symbiosis.[132] Senghor's prayer of peace embraces the practice of forgiveness as an effective weapon for humanity's well-being and rejects colonization and other forms of oppression.

This is why I am arguing that the relevance of Senghorian Négritude to current postcolonial discourses is not just as a theory but a Poetics of Postcolonial Biblical Criticism that may help people of African descent relearn and reposition themselves should they forget. In the steps of Senghor, I, as a diaspora Senegalese biblical scholar, now read biblical texts in America and I am convinced that twenty-first-century theorists and critics will do well to revisit Senghorian Négritude as a *Poetics of Postcolonial Colonial Biblical Criticism*. I believe it fosters a hopeful vision of life against the odds that overcomes despair and repositions objectified people to live and proclaim liberty. Senghor knew that the sustainability of a peaceable future of humanity hinges on an intentional exercise of cultural and religious symbiosis—*a cultural symbiosis in which Black lives and their contributions to world civilization matter*. Senghorian symbiosis is an expression of *ubuntu* that, in the words of Desmond Tutu,

> speaks of spiritual attributes such as generosity, hospitality, compassion, caring, sharing. . . . Those who had *ubuntu* were compassionate and gentle, they used their strength on behalf of the weak, and they did not take advantage of others—in short, they *cared*, treating others as what they were: human beings. . . . We matter because we are made in the image of God and belong in one Family—God's family, the human family.[133]

Analogically, *Ubuntu* calls for the practice of well-being that sustains life of persons in community—the kind of communalism Senghor emphasized in his *On African Socialism*.[134] This symbiosis was in many ways crucial to peoples of African descent who participated in the First and Second International Congresses of Negro Writers and Artists in Paris and Rome.[135] I believe Senghorian liberation and rehabilitation should be reimaged for our times to help twenty-first-century activists and advocates of justice confront the rise of the kind of racist nationalism that has no room in the robust humanism of Senghorian Négritude. This is nothing short of postcolonial biblical criticism—a proto Black Liberation theology—that invites people of faith to do the will of God on earth[136] by practicing a sustained critique of injustice tempered with the art of forgiveness and reconciliation.

NOTES

In my book titled *A Poetics of Postcolonial Criticism: God, Human-Nature Relationship, and Négritude* (Eugene, OR: Cascade Books, 2019), 19–32, I argued for

Senghorian Négritude as *A Poetics of Postcolonial Criticism* focusing on its relevance for how Diola people relate to God and nature. I also discussed some aspects of Senghorian Négritude as a postcolonial reading lens in a forthcoming essay in "Négritude and Minoritized Criticism: A Senegalese Perspective," to be published by the Society of Biblical Literature in a project titled *Reading in These Times* edited by Tat-Siong Benny Liew and Fernando F. Segovia.

1. Léopold Sédar Senghor, "Rapport sur la doctrine et la propagande du Parti," Congrès constitutif du Parti du rassemblement africain (P.R.A., 1959), 14, quoted in Lilyan Kesteloot, *Black Writers in French: A Literary History of Négritude*, trans. Ellen Conroy Kennedy (Philadelphia: Temple University Press, 1963/1974), 80, with some adaptation based on Silvia Ba's translation in her *The Concept of Négritude in the Poetry of Léopold Sédar Senghor* (Princeton, NJ: Princeton University Press, 1973), 12. "Panic-stricken despair" will be used henceforth.
2. Cheikh Hamidou Kane, *Ambiguous Adventure*, trans. Katherine Woods (Portsmouth, NH: Heinemann, 1962), 48.
3. Janet Vaillant, "Homage to Léopold Sédar Senghor: 1906–2001," *Research in African Literature* 33, no. 4 (2002): 17.
4. https://www.drew.edu/theological-school/theology-programs-traditional-interdisciplinary. Indeed, the baobab tree metaphor captures "an image of the growing, branching vitality of the many connected strands of diasporic discourse."
5. The former happened in Senegal to Samba Diallo (fictionalized Cheikh Hamidou Kane himself, his Diallobé and Senegalese people) and the latter in metropolitan France (with Senegalese colonial antecedents) to Léopold Sédar Senghor and his fellow Senegalese and West Indian student immigrants.
6. Kane, *Ambiguous Adventure*, 38.
7. Kane, *Ambiguous Adventure*, 46–47.
8. "But someone will ask, 'How are the dead raised? With what kind of body do they come?'. . . What you sow does not come to life unless it dies. And as for what you sow, you do not sow the body that is to be, but a bare seed, perhaps of wheat or of some other grain. But God gives it a body as he has chosen, and to each kind of seed its own body. . . . So it is with the resurrection of the dead. What is sown is perishable, what is raised is imperishable. It is sown in dishonor, it is raised in glory. It is sown in weakness, it is raised in power. It is sown a physical body, it is raised a spiritual body. If there is a physical body, there is also a spiritual body" (1 Cor 15:35–44).
9. Kane himself along with others pioneered this daring experiment and negotiated it as best as they could from the first generation to the second.
10. Niang, *A Poetics of Biblical Criticism*, 19–32.

11. Léopold Sédar Senghor, *Liberté 1. Négritude et Humanisme* (Paris: Éditions du Seuil, 1964), 417; Niang, *A Poetics of Biblical Criticism*, 23–32.
12. Robert J. C. Young, *Postcolonialism: An Historical Introduction* (Oxford: Blackwell, 2001).
13. Georg M. Gugelberger, "Postcolonial Cultural Studies: 1. Origins to the 1980s," in *The John Hopkins Guide to Literary Theory & Criticism*, 2nd ed., ed. Michael Groden, Martin Kreiswirth, and Imre Szeman (Baltimore: John Hopkins University Press, 1994, 2005), 756–60; Diana Brydon, "Postcolonial Cultural Studies: 1. 1990 and After," in *The John Hopkins Guide to Literary Theory & Criticism*, 2nd ed., ed. Michael Groden, Martin Kreiswirth, and Imre Szeman (Baltimore: John Hopkins University Press, 1994, 2005), 760–68.
14. Musa W. Dube, "Post-Colonial Biblical Interpretation," in *Dictionary of Biblical Interpretation*, vol. K–Z, ed. John H. Hays (Nashville, TN: Abingdon Press, 1999), 299–303; idem, *Postcolonial Feminist Interpretation of the Bible* (New York: Orbis Books, 2000), 3–43.
15. Edward Said, *Orientalism* (New York: Vintage, 1979), 7.
16. Said, *Orientalism*, 23.
17. Said, *Orientalism*, 4–8, 329–52.
18. Homi Bhabha, "The Third Space: Interview with Homi Bhabha," in *Identity, Community, Culture, Difference*, ed. Jonathan Rutherford (London: Lawrence & Wishart, 1990), 209.
19. Homi Bhabha, "The Other Question: Difference, Discrimination and the Discourse of Colonialism," in *Out There: Marginalization and Contemporary Cultures* (New York: New Museum of Contemporary Art, 1990), 75.
20. Bhabha, "The Third Space," 211.
21. Homi Bhabha, *The Location of Culture* (New York: Routledge, 1994), 246.
22. Gayatri Chakravorty Spivak, "Strategy, Identity, Writing," in *The Post-Colonial Critic: Interviews, Strategies, Dialogue*, ed. Sarah Harasym (New York: Routledge, 1990), 40–41.
23. Gayatri Chakravorty Spivak, "The Post Modern Conditions: The End of Politics?" in *The Post-Colonial Critic: Interviews, Strategies, Dialogue*, ed. Sarah Harasym (New York: Routledge, 1990), 18.
24. bell hooks, *Yearning: Race, Gender and Politics* (Boston, MA: South End Press, 1990), 145–53.
25. Niang, *A Poetics of Biblical Criticism*, 19–32; idem, "Négritude and Minoritized Criticism," in *Reading in These Times*, forthcoming.
26. Léopold Sédar Senghor, *La poésie de l'action* (Paris: Editions Stock, 1980), 51.
27. Janet Vaillant, *Black, French, and African: A Life of Léopold Sédar Senghor* (Cambridge, MA: Harvard University Press, 1990), 12. The subjects lived in the pro-

tectorate "indigénat" as uncultured as opposed to so-called évolués "civilized or evolved" who were the dwellers of the Four Colonial Towns "Quatres Communes" (Saint Louis, Dakar, Gorée, and Rufisque). These towns were the centers where French colonists lived, introduced, and experimented with the assimilation policy from 1887 to 1960.

28. Lilyan Kesteloot, *Comprendre les poèmes de L. S. Senghor* (Paris: L'Harmattan, 1986), 14–22; idem, *Black Writers in French*, 195–200. Djilor is also spelled as Dyiloôr.

29. Jean-Pierre Biondi, *Senghor ou la tentation de l'universel* (L'aventure Colonial de la France) (Paris: Éditions Denoël, 1993), 13–21, 113–15, 117.

30. Léopold Sédar Senghor, *La poésie de l'action: conversation avec Mohamed Aziza* (Paris: Éditions Stock, 1980), 90. See the second picture on page 11 in Joseph Roger de Benoist, *Histories de L'église catholique au Sénégal: Du milieu du XVe siècle à l'aube du troisième millénaire* (Dakar: Editions Clairafrique, 2008). Father Lalouse sitting. Senghor is standing second from the left.

31. Léopold Sédar Senghor, *Œuvre Poétique* (Paris: Edition du Seuil, 1990), 393. First published in 1964.

32. Kesteloot, *Comprendre les poèmes*, 3–7.

33. Vaillant, *Black, French, and African*, 88.

34. Vaillant, *Black, French, and African*, 70–71.

35. Souleymane Bachir Diagne, *African Art as Philosophy: Senghor, Bergson and the Idea of Négritude*, trans. Chike Jeffers (New York: Seagull Books, 2011); Gary Wilder, *The French Imperial Nation-State: Négritude and Colonial Humanism between the Two World Wars* (Chicago: University of Chicago Press, 2005); idem, *Freedom Time: Négritude, Decolonization, and the Future of the World* (Durham, NC: Duke University Press, 2015).

36. Léopold Sédar Senghor, *Foundations of "Africanité or Négritude" and "Arabité,"* trans. Mercer Cook (Paris: Presence Africaine, 1971), originally published in French as *Les Fondements de l'africanité ou Négritude and Arabité* in 1967.

37. Aimé Césaire, *Discourse on Colonialism*, trans. Joan Pinkham (New York: Monthly Review Press, 1972), 86, 94. Fanon had an aversion to Senghor for reasons I will not discuss here. Suffice it to say that he thought of Senghor as a sellout but still wanted to work with Senghor in Senegal probably because of the kind of political stability Senghor was able to create for Senegalese people, as Hussein Abdilahi Bulhan, *Frantz Fanon and the Psychology of Oppression* (New York: Plenum Press, 1985), 210, said against Peter Geismar, *Fanon: A Biography* (New York: Grove Press, 1969), 58–59, who noted Fanon's need for medical equipment to practice psychiatry that would have been accessible to him in Martinique.

38. Senghor, "Rapport sur la doctrine," 14, quoted by Kesteloot, *Black Writers in French*, 80.
39. Frantz Fanon, *The Wretched of the Earth*, trans. Constance Farrington (New York: Grove Press, 1961/1963), 250.
40. Quoted by Vaillant, *Black, French, and African*, 181. Prior to Bhabha's use of this term, the idea of hybridity was already used by this anonymous author who could have well been Senghor, Césaire, or Damas.
41. Vaillant, *Black, French, and African*, 181.
42. Vaillant, *Black, French, and African*, 128, 128–46. The language of "new person" echoes Harlem Renaissance voices of the "new Negro." In fact, many American leaders of the Harlem Renaissance were very much conversant with the pioneers of Négritude and some participated in the first 1956 conference in Paris that featured Richard Wright, Fanon, and Césaire. They spoke about life through poems by evoking their distasteful lived experiences. On the Harlem Renaissance, see Alain Locke, *The New Negro: Voices of the Harlem Renaissance* (New York: Simon & Schuster, 1997).
43. Léopold Sédar Senghor, "Constructive Elements of a Civilization of African Negro Aspiration," *Présence Africaine* 2 (March 26–April 1 1959): 290.
44. Ousmane Sembène, *The Last of Empire: A Senegalese Novel*, trans. Adrian Adams (London: Heinemann, 1981), 135.
45. Samba Gadjigo, *Ousmane Sembène: The Making of a Militant Artist* (Bloomington: Indiana University Press, 2007, 2010), 142–43.
46. Léopold Sédar Senghor, "Constructive Elements," 290.
47. Léopold Sédar Senghor, "What Is Négritude?" *Atlas* (1962): 54–55. Italicized words are his.
48. Léopold Sédar Senghor, *Anthologie de la nouvelle poésie nègre et malgache de langue française* (Paris: Quadrige Presses Universitaires de France, 1948).
49. Jean-Paul Sartre, "Orphée noir," in *Anthologie de la nouvelle poésie nègre et malgache de langue française* (Paris: Presses Universitaires Française, 1948), IX.
50. Sartre, "Orphée noir," IX.
51. Sartre, "Orphée noir," XI.
52. Sartre, "Orphée noir," XIV.
53. Ezekiel Mphahlele, *The African Image* (London: Faber and Faber, 1974), 67; Wole Soyinka, *Myth, Literature and the African World* (Cambridge: Cambridge University Press, 1976), 134.
54. René Depestre, *Bonjour et Adieu à la Négritude* (Paris: Éditions Laffont, 1980).
55. Reiland Rabaka, *Forms of Fanonism: Frantz Fanon's Critical Theory and the Dialectics of Decolonization* (New York: Lexington Books, 2010), 178.

56. Edward Said, *Culture and Imperialism* (New York: Alfred A. Knopf, 1993), 228–29, 275–279, surprisingly mischaracterized Négritude as nativism, failing to take seriously Senghorian humanism (discussed in detail in *Liberté 1: Négritude et Humanism*) and persistent advocacy for *la civilization de l'universel*, "universal civilization" (dealt with extensively in *Liberté 3: Négritude et civilisation de l'universel*) (Paris: Éditions du Seuil, 1977).
57. Senghor, "Rapport sur la doctrine," 14.
58. Senghor, *La poésie de l'action*, 90.
59. Michael Fabre, *Black American Writers in France, 1840–1980: From Harlem to Paris* (Urbana: University of Illinois Press, 1991), 146–59, highlights the crucial contribution of women that often gets lost in the profuse debates over whose perspective best reflects the Black cause and did much to provide a crucial dimension of Négritude that is sadly reduced to a handful of publications. For more on women's contribution to Négritude, see Paulette Nardal, *Beyond Négritude: Essays from Women in the City*, trans. T. Denean Sharpley-Whiting (New York: State University of New York Press, 2009); T. Denean Sharpley-Whiting, *Négritude Women* (Minneapolis: University of Minnesota Press, 2002).
60. Ousmane Oumar Kane, *The Homeland Is the Arena: Religion, Transnationalism, and the Integration of Senegalese Immigrants in America* (New York: Oxford University Press, 2011), 242–43. See also how Dominic Thomas, *Black France: Colonialism, Immigration, and Transnationalism* (Bloomington: Indiana University Press, 2007), 4–12, 73–81, 185–205, recounts the experiences of the pioneers of Négritude in France and subsequent changes after that generation. Kane and Thomas agree that the French attitude toward Black African immigrants went from admiration to scorn, especially against those with limited education who were illiterate.
61. See Richard Wright, "Discussion," *The 1st International Conference of Negro Writers and Artists* (Paris: Présence Africaine 1956): 65–68.
62. Wright, "Discussion," 66–67.
63. Babacar M'Baye, "Richard Wright and African Francophone Intellectuals: A Reassessment of the 1956 Congress of Black Writers in Paris," *African and Black Diaspora: An International Journal* 2, no. 1 (2009): 29–42.
64. James Baldwin, *Notes of a Native Son* (Boston, MA: Beacon Press, 1955), 123.
65. Baldwin, *Notes of a Native Son*, 124.
66. James Baldwin, *Nobody Knows My Name: More Notes of a Native Son* (New York: Dial Press, 1961), 28–29.
67. Ralph Ellison, *Shadow & Act* (London: Secker & Warburg, 1967), 262–63.
68. Alioune Diop quoted in Lilyan Kesteloot, *Intellectual Origins of the African Revolution* (Washington, DC: Black Orpheus Press, 1972), 113.

69. Frantz Fanon, *Black Skin, White Masks*, trans. Charles Lam Markmann (New York: Grove Press, 1967), 135.
70. Senghor, *Liberté 1*, 316–17.
71. Kane, *Ambiguous Adventure*, 34.
72. Cheikh Hamidou Kane, *Les Gardiens du Temple* (Abidjan, Côte d'Ivoire: Nouvelle Éditions Ivoiriennes, 1997), 48–49, 51–54. Compare with idem, *Ambiguous Adventure*, 34, 45–47.
73. R. S. Sugirtharajah, *Postcolonial Criticism and Biblical Interpretation* (New York: Oxford University Press, 2002), 102–22. Like any methodology or theological construct, liberation hermeneutics places too much emphasis on texts, disparages many religions, and tends to misconstrue the poor by an approach that teeters on homogeneity. It tends to prioritize the eradication of poverty first and then reinterprets texts in this direction. From this vantage point, reality is seen as one, and liberation is all encompassing: it privileges the poor and their interpretations, directs biblical scholarship to deal with problems of people and leave the refuge of theoretical debates, and rejects a neutral reading of the text, taking the side of the poor and using their context as the one necessary for a reading. The credibility of the Bible depends on reading it from the liberation perspective. Liberation as the central focus is important, and biblical narratives of exodus and Jesus Christ show the divine revelation in history. Jesus is rightly seen through acts of God mediated in solidarity with humanity. Yet it often becomes a liberation theology of the poor instead of a theology of liberation of the poor.
74. Ibid. Sugirtharajah rightly points to the limitations of liberation hermeneutics for its parochial and exclusivist tendencies. Postcolonial biblical criticism views the Bible as both problem and solution because it promotes freedom and slavery simultaneously. A trained postcolonial eye will see the biblical voices promoting freedom and slavery as a necessity and thus maintaining an unresolved binary tension—freedom versus slavery.
75. Senghor, *Liberté 1*, 417.
76. Senghor, *Liberté 1*, 246.
77. Léopold Sédar Senghor, *On African Socialism*, trans. Mercer Cook (New York: Frederick A. Praeger, 1964), 73, 93–94. Similarly, John S. Mbiti, *African Religions and Philosophy*, 2nd ed. (Oxford: Heinemann Educational, 1969), 106, who, four years later, agrees that the African's self-understanding hinges on the corporate personality of the group: "I am, because we are; and since we are, therefore I am."
78. Senghor, *On African Socialism*, 73.
79. Diagne, *African Art as Philosophy*. See Henri Bergson, *Creative Evolution*, trans. Arthur Mitchell (New York: Dover, 1998).

80. Senghor, *Liberté 1*, 211–12. Emphasis is his.
81. Léopold Sédar Senghor, "Éthiopiques," in *Œuvre Poétique* (Paris: Edition du Seuil, 1990), 107–9. See also Papa Gueye N'Diaye, *Éthiopiques: Poèmes de Léopold Sédar Senghor* (Dakar: Les Nouvelles Éditions Africaines, 1974), 25–27; Kesteloot, *Comprendre les Poèmes*, 23–24.
82. Senghor, *Liberté 1*, 417. Contra Fanon, whose refutation of the Senghorian approach to decolonization called for meeting the violence of colonization with violence (see Fanon, *Wretched of the Earth*, 35–37).
83. Souleymane Bashir Diagne, "Négritude," *Stanford Encyclopedia of Philosophy*, http://plato.stanford.edu/archives/spr2014/entries/négritude. Négritude has ontological, aesthetic, epistemological, and political dimensions. According to Diagne, Négritude is still relevant today as a tool to fight against racism, and it would be a serious mistake to dismiss it as irrelevant, especially when our twenty-first-century experiences at home and in the diaspora still tell us that "Black lives matter" today more than ever.
84. Vaillant, *Black, French, and African*, 12.
85. Senghor, "Éthiopiques," in *Œuvre Poétique*, 122–36. See also Baïdy Dioum, *La trajectoire de Léopold Sédar Senghor: Du Terroir à l'universel* (Paris: L'Harmattan, 2014), 66.
86. Léopold Sédar Senghor, *Ce que je Crois* (Paris: Grasset, 1988), 30–113. Senghor echoes Césaire, *Discourse on Colonialism*, 33, who spoke against European lampooning of Africa and Africans as pagans and savages.
87. Léopold Sédar Senghor, "Chants d'Ombre," in *Œuvre Poétique* (Paris: Edition du Seuil, 1964/1990), 18–19.
88. Francis August Schaeffer, *The Francis Schaeffer Trilogy: The Three Essential Books in One* (Wheaton, IL: Crossway, 1990), 44.
89. Schaeffer, *The Francis Schaeffer Trilogy*, 45.
90. Schaeffer, *The Francis Schaeffer Trilogy*, 89.
91. Henri Biram N'Dong, "Inculturation et non syncrétisme," *Éthiopiques*, no. 59 (1997). See Mamadou Diop, *La multivalence du sacré dans l'œuvre de Léopold Sédar Senghor: Négritude, Universalité, Géopoétique* (Allemagne: Editions Universitaires Européennes, 2010), 53–85. His Jesus must not be confused with the Jesus of institutionalized Christianity he encountered in Ngazobil, West Africa, and metropolitan France.
92. Senghor, *Liberté 1*, 22–23, and *Liberté 3*, 8–9. They display his main thoughts on what he meant by universal civilization. To understand his robust humanism, it is imperative to read the entire set of five volumes (*Liberté 1–5*).
93. Dioum, *La trajectoire de Léopold Sédar Senghor*, 229.

94. Musa W. Dube and Jeffery L. Staley, *John and Postcolonialism: Travel, Space, and Power* (Sheffield: Sheffield Academic Press, 2002); Stephen D. Moore and Fernando F. Segovia, eds., *Postcolonial Biblical Criticism: Interdisciplinary Intersections* (T & T Clark International, 2005); Sugirtharajah, *The Postcolonial Biblical Reader* (Malden, MA: Blackwell, 2006); Fernando F. Segovia and R. S. Sugirtharajah, eds., *A Postcolonial Commentary on the New Testament Writings* (New York: T & T Clark, 2007); See *Union Seminary Quarterly Review* 59, no. 3–4 (2005); Adam Win, ed., *An Introduction to Empire in the New Testament* (Atlanta, GA: SBL Press, 2016).
95. Sugirtharajah, *Postcolonial Criticism*, 103–23.
96. Senghor, *La poésie de l'action*, 50. Italics are his.
97. Senghor, *La poésie de l'action*, 50–51.
98. Senghor, "Liminary Poem," in *Léopold Sédar Senghor Collected Poems*, trans. Melvin Dixon (Charlottesville: University of Virginia Press, 1991), 39–40.
99. Senghor, "Prayer for the Senegalese Soldiers," in *Léopold Sédar Senghor Collected Poems*, 50–52. His inclusion of French peasants suggests that they might have been victimized and exploited by their compatriots, perhaps the French bourgeoisie whose Christianity he deplored.
100. Senghor, "Assassinations," in *Léopold Sédar Senghor Collected Poems*, 57–58.
101. Senghor, "To the Black American Troops," in *Léopold Sédar Senghor Collected Poems*, 66–67.
102. Senghor, "At the Call of the Race Sheba," in *Léopold Sédar Senghor Collected Poems*, 39–43.
103. Senghor, "Prayer to the Mask," in *Léopold Sédar Senghor Collected Poems*, 13–14.
104. Senghor, "Totem," in *Léopold Sédar Senghor Collected Poems*, 14.
105. Senghor, *On African Socialism*, 146.
106. "You do well if you really fulfill the royal law according to the scripture, 'You shall love your neighbor as yourself'" (James 2:8).
107. Pierre Teilhard de Chardin, *The Heart of Matter*, trans. René Hague (New York: Harcourt Brace Jovanovich, 1976).
108. Teilhard de Chardin, *The Heart of Matter*, 55–57.
109. Senghor, *Liberté 1*, 252–68.
110. Senghor, *Liberté 1*, 419.
111. Sana Nahum, *Genesis*, JPS Torah Commentary (New York: Jewish Publication Society, 1989), 17. The expression "living being" appears in Genesis 1:30.
112. Traduction, *Océanique de la Bible*, 1988, et la *Bible de Jérusalem* (logos "Verbe") contrasté par *Louis Segond*, 1910 (logos "Parole") et la Nouvelle Édition de Genève, 1979.

113. Senghor, *Liberté 3*, 61.
114. Senghor, *Ce que je crois*, 113. For more on his framing of African culture and religious thought, see pages 77–113.
115. Philippe Laburthe-Tolra, "Le Mysticisme dans l'œuvre de Léopold Sédar Senghor," in *Rencontre des traditions religieuse de l'Afrique avec le Christianisme, l'Islam et la laïcité à partir d'écrits de Léopold Sédar Senghor* (Paris: UNESCO, 2008), 35–43.
116. Léopold Sédar Senghor, "Prayer for Peace," in *Léopold Sédar Senghor Collected Poems*, 69–72. The prayer foretells of the story of peoples of African descent in the hands of European slave traders and colonists.

    . . . "Dragging out Ancestors and spirits by their peaceful beards.
    And they have turned their mystery into a Sunday
    entertainment
    For the sleepwalking bourgeois. . .
    For You must forgive those who hunted down my children
    Like wild elephants. And they disciplined them
    With whips and turned into black hands those whose hands
    were white. . .
    Yes, Lord, forgive France, who hates occupying forces
    And yet imposes such strict occupation on me
    Who offers a hero's welcome to some, and treats
    The Senegalese like mercenaries, the Empire's black
    Watchdogs. . ."

117. Léopold Sédar Senghor, *Pierre Teilhard de Chardin et la Politique Africaine* (Paris: Éditions du Seuil, 1962), 21.
118. Steve Estes, *I Am a Man: Race, Manhood, and the Civil Rights Movement* (Chapel Hill: University of North Carolina Press, 2005).
119. Christopher J. Lebron, *The Making of Black Lives Matter: A Brief History of an Idea* (New York: Oxford University Press, 2018).
120. Fanon, *Black Skin, White Masks*, 226.
121. James H. Cone, *A Black Theology of Liberation* (Maryknoll, NY: Orbis Books, 1986/1990), 11.
122. Cone, *A Black Theology of Liberation*, 62–66.
123. Cone, *A Black Theology of Liberation*, 65–66; idem, *The Cross and the Lynching Tree* (Maryknoll, NY: Orbis Books, 2011), xix.
124. Arthur Rimbaud, *Collected Poems*, trans. Martin Sorrell (New York: Oxford University Press, 2001), 219, who writes in his poem titled *A Season in Hell*; "I am . . . a negro."
125. Senghor, *La poésie de l'action*, 50. Italics are his.
126. Senghor, "Prayer for Peace," in *Léopold Sédar Senghor Collected Poems*, 69–72.

127. Cone, *The Cross and the Lynching Tree*, 23, 28.
128. Fanon, *Wretched of the Earth*, 35, 63. See Tsenay Serequeberhan, *The Hermeneutics of African Philosophy: Horizon and Discourse* (New York: Routledge, 1994), 79, 55–85.
129. Nazaire N. Diatta, "Participation du Joola chretien aux rites traditionnels," *Téléma* 46 (April–June 1986): 67–81; idem, "Et si Jésus-Christ est, le premier ne d'entre les morts, était l'initie?: La personnalité de l'initie Joola face au Christ," *Téléma* 57 (January–March 1989): 49–73; idem, "Rites funéraires traditionnels et liturgie chrétienne: Lieux du dialogue interreligieux," *Téléma* 67–68 (July–December 1991): 61–72.
130. A. Abble et al., *Des Prêtres Noirs s'interrogent: cinquante ans après* . . . (Paris: Présence Africaine, 1956).
131. Philippe Rey, *L'Afrique répond à Sarkozy: Contre le discours de Dakar* (Paris: Éditions Philippe Rey, 2008).
132. Philippe Rey, *Rencontre des traditions, religieuses de l'Afrique avec le Christianisme, l'Islam, et la laïcité à partir des écrits de Léopold Sédar Senghor: La voix de l'Afrique dans le dialogue interreligieux* (Paris: UNESCO, 2008); Bassirou Dieng et Geneviève N'Diaye-Corréard, *Senghor: Colloque de Dakar Université Cheikh Anta Diop 10–11 Octobre 1996* (Dakar: Presses Universitaire de Dakar, 1996).
133. Desmond Tutu, *God Is Not a Christian* (London: Rider, 2011), 21–24.
134. Senghor, *On African Socialism*, 73; See Aliou Cissé Niang, "Political Ethics of Léopold Sédar Senghor," in *The Palgrave Handbook of African Social Ethics*, ed. Nimi Wariboko and Toyin Falola (Cham, Switzerland: Palgrave Macmillan, 2020), 257–81, and Mogobe B. Ramose, "The Philosophy of *Ubuntu* and *Ubuntu* as a Philosophy," in *The African Philosophy Reader*, ed. P. H. Coetzee and A. P. J. Roux (New York: Routledge, 1998), 270–80.
135. Léopold Sédar Senghor, "The Spirit of Civilization or the Laws of African Negro Culture," *Présence Africaine* 1 (1956): 51–64; idem, "Constructive Elements," 262–95.
136. Senghor, *Liberté 1*, 305. It is clear that Senghor was implicitly referring to Matthew 6:10, a central line of the Lord's Prayer—a prayer significant for both Christians and Muslims.

PART II

⌘ Africana Activism

LITANY ON THE LINE

PAMELA MORDECAI

Bad news again on the long distance line: a growth flourishing in my sister's throat. I think if one can spill hot coffee on oneself and sue the restaurant and win, perhaps a legal eagle with a well-tuned bill could whistle up a case against AT&T and Mama Bell. Two years ago on this same phone, Lizzie told me and Mary Joan that they'd shot Richard dead. Across the trans-Atlantic line I hear the ocean sizzle where infected earth burning with fever oozes pus along a rupture in its crust. I see the flickering photospores inside the eyes of deep-sea fish. I hear the cries of jettisoned black men, women and children, not yet slaves, just worth less than insurers paid for cargo spoiled en route. Slitting this Carib basin's diamond skin they flung its glints aside and burrowed in. A person dies. It changes everything. They died. No alteration? Nothing changed? Except forever afterwards ships, boats and planes with trained, skilled crews and honed and hardened pilots fell into that grave triangle for the Human Trade. And flying now above the blue Bermudas, look and you will see, along a coral ridge of white, dark looping t's, like long canoes, like open crypts. o, lay the ancestors to rest inside these cursive curls with litanies. Anoint their necks, their ankles, wrists, with sacred oil. Put wampum shells upon their eyes and set bouquets of trembling anemones between their fingers and their toes.

Sing sankeys, beat the drums to dredge up greed, harpoon it like Leviathan and beach it where the carrion birds will pick its pink meat from its bones. Blessed are you buried in this blue dirt. Blessed are you who never reached this side. Blessed are you who listen as the tribe burbles its grievous news across these fibre-optic threads. Blessed are you.

6. God Killed! God Interrupted, Long Live the People!: Political Theory in Religious Act

NIMI WARIBOKO

Long before Nietzsche's madman in the market shouted, "God is dead.... And we have killed him," the Kalabari people (Izon, Niger Delta, Nigeria) on September 27, 1857, announced to Africans and Europeans in the Niger Delta that they had just killed one of their gods (Owu Akpana, the Shark-god) and proceeded to celebrate the deicide and its ensuing freedom.[1] This act, which was not metaphysical but historical, involved eating the divine flesh and drinking the blood of the god, incorporating the divine into the human and thus recognizing sovereignty in the people. Like a mole, they burst asunder the carapace of spiritual-political hegemony that divided them from their sovereignty, so that the hegemony crumbled away. All gods in Kalabari—except one, the supreme being Tamuno/Tamarau—became vulnerable to death at the hands of their worshippers as a community.[2] Put differently in Lacan's felicitous phrase, the gods were always already dead, they just did not know it. The Shark-god found out the hard way. Indeed, the September disruptive act mobilizes three ethico-political elements: Human beings are the immanent obstacle that prevents the sacred from achieving full self-identity; the political is the immanent Spirit of the community; and materialization of some higher or untouchable power or reality could be cast down to *nothing*.

Before Nietzsche's madman threw his lantern on the ground on seeing the astonishment on the faces of his listeners and declared, "I have come too early, my time has not come yet," the death of God was already functioning as a *concept* in Kalabari, and not as a mythopoetic thought to awaken people from their slumber of transcendence. With the execution of Owu Akpana, the pre-conceptual thought of deicide instantly transformed from thought to material act to an *ideal entity*. This is precisely the moment two revelations traversed Tamarau herself: (a) The people as *demos* as well as Spirit (a community of organized believers as divine, sacred energy, *amatemeso*) is a disruptive, interruptive power, and (b) *natality* as a political notion haunts all claims of exception and givenness.[3] The divine-human relationship became scarred by traces of this "hubris," social antagonisms/agonisms, or trauma. And its scarred character is, arguably, the interpretative frame through which the Kalabari people perceive and relate to the dense network of relationships that define or mark human existence. More specifically, interactions that appear to Kalabari people as hierarchic relationship, "big other," "objective order," or "hyperobject" are "already transcendentally constituted through a horizon of meaning sustained by" the metonymic 1857 event, the volcanic core of divine-human interaction.[4]

The people (an emancipatory political collective), at least for a moment in 1857, hovered "above the entire life of the state" and all forms of realization of the divine.[5] How can this tradition be retrieved to illuminate democratic politics or counter the politics of near-divine impunity by leaders on the continent? What social-ontological power did the revolutionary act of deicide recognize, reveal, or portray? (Perhaps, it is the capacity to initiate something new amid ongoing social-political processes, the possibility of radical new beginning.) What is the implication of all this for democratic sovereignty in Africa?

This essay endeavors to provide a fuller narrative, explanation, and analysis of the 1857 *event* and deploy it to offer a diagnostic of Africa's present political situation under late capitalism. To accomplish this, I bring in themes from the *Ozidi Saga*, a highly acclaimed Izon national epic,[6] to critically accentuate the disruptive effects of an awakened demos marked by *the capacity to begin*.[7] According to Isidore Okpewho, who is arguably the most distinguished expert on African oral literature, "The Ozidi story is easily the best known of tales told among the Ijo of Nigeria's delta country, who have drawn worldwide attention to themselves for resisting what they consider the collusion between the country's federal government and some multinational corporations in the exploitation of the area's petroleum resources."[8]

The Ozidi story paints a portrait of people with a restless subjectivity, republican polis, and emancipatory politics of interruption. In a sense, void resides always at the core of power in Izon society, and the *Ozidi Saga* can be interpreted to point to the passion of natality/rebellion, rage for justice/withdrawal of consent that swirls around established (enchanted, entrusted, or heteronomous) power as a form of concealment or occultation of the void. The killing of god and the subsequent emphasis on Izon republicanism (in the sense that political power belongs to no one person) suggest that there is a disincarnation of power: Political leadership depends on the consent of the citizens, and no leader can function as an incarnation of the divine. A leader can refer neither to an *outside* (to a god or sacred mandate) nor to an *inside* singular appropriation of the democratic power of the community to privilege his or her authority. Power is groundless and unfounded, and thus open to endless interrogation and alteration.[9]

In the *Ozidi Saga*, we encounter an Izon community in quest for its own democratic foundation while also raising questions about divine-human relationship. Ozidi, the hero of the saga, killed all men in politico-military power and some supernatural beings (gods) to rid himself of the burden of justice placed upon him after the assassination of his father at the hands of his father's political rivals. In his victory, we see the rapture that makes two bodies of power (political and divine) vanish and "replaces them with no body at all."[10] He becomes neither a ruler (monarch) nor a materialization or moderator of the divine. The political throne of the community becomes void, an empty space of power; which it was already always in a democratic, republican *polis*, except that it became visible. His action and his very identity are now marked by the void, revealing power as an empty place (to be occupied by the *polis* in its entirety, in its differential multiplicity)[11] and as "the capacity of human beings to alter radically the forms and structures they inherit."[12]

What do all the preliminary analyses and discussions I have so far set forth mean for comprehending Africa's current political situation? Preparing the reader to adequately respond to this question through the lens of a historically derived political theory is the main task of this essay. Now let us put aside for a moment theoretical ruminations and delve into the historical event, the politico-religious earthquake of 1857, which anchors our deliberations today and animates the political philosophy I am constructing in this essay.

THE EXECUTED GOD

> Monday, 28th [September 1857]
> [I] went up to [New] Calabar town this morning and while there heard that the chiefs had a meeting in their palaver house yesterday, in consequence of several of the natives having been killed lately by their big Jew Jew [juju, god], the Sharks, they came to the conclusion that it no be use for have wowo jew jew [useless god] all same shark no more and it is therefore no longer held as such, but the natives are catching them as fast as possible and now allow "white men" to do the same if they like which of course we shall do whenever we have a chance as the shark is the sailor's greatest enemy.[13]

A Liverpool trader, Mr. William Oates, who was in New Calabar (Elem Kalabari, the headquarters of the Kalabari people at the time), recorded this event in his diary. When growing up as child in the 1970s, I heard the elders in my town, Abonnema, talk about this event and later I read about the same story recorded as oral history by British anthropologists such as P. Amaury Talbot, G. I. Jones, and Robin Horton. On one hand, there was always some suspicion that the event did not happen; my people could not have killed their god. There was no written record to support the tale told.[14] But there were enough insights in the native worldview or philosophy that were repeated often as proverbs to suggest that my Izon ancestors were capable and even fond of killing their gods.[15] There is a popular Kalabari aphorism that says: If a god becomes too furious or demanding, we will tell it from which wood it was carved (*agu nsi*[16]*owi baka kuma en ke o kara sin en dugo o piriba*). This means that a community can unanimously annul the power of a god by refusing it worship.[17] Robin Horton interprets the aphorism this way.

> Literally, if a spirit's demands become too burdensome, the whole congregation can join together to destroy its cult objects, and by this unanimous act of rejection render it powerless to trouble them further. . . . Broadly, then, the more people lavish offerings, invocations, and festivals upon any spirit, the more powerful it becomes both to

reward and punish them. And conversely, the less they attend to it, the less powerful it becomes—up to the point at which unanimous rejection results in the complete loss of power. Generally, of course, a single man cannot reject a spirit at will; for while he is only one among a congregation of many, it will have the power to punish him.[18]

This idea that when a people stop praying or worshipping a god the god ceases to exist can be interpreted through the lens of two principles in Izon political philosophy. First, there is the Indigenous conception of freedom. In the light of the traditional African spirit of communality, freedom is not something enjoyed in private, but in public: concerted participation in public action for the common good with one's peers. Freedom is the power to act together, to initiate new possibilities in the community, to think and act in new ways. It is about appearing to others as a distinct, irreplaceable individual in the public space, the shared world, and performing immortal deeds.[19]

This notion of freedom embeds the idea of *capacity to do*, to do what a person needs to do irrespective of the obstacles, burdens, or circumstances, a striving to achieve the improbable—one who can bring something new into an already existing situation. One way this capacity to do is rendered in Kalabari is *"I ye gbaye ye."* This is the pure capacity to do—the "I can." The focus is neither on the will—"I will," which can be defeated by interior (mind versus body struggle) and exterior circumstances—nor is it dependent on the intellect, which can be paralyzed by analysis of future desirability of aims. *I ye gbaye ye* is pure doability—it is sufficient to act, to manifest one's being in the presence of others, to manifest the human character as an acting with the initiative to begin again, to establish a new reality. *I ye gbaye ye* demands doing or acting to bring in the new, even the unexpected. Usually a series of events is ongoing and action is needed to interrupt it. Within it there is always this freedom to act, to begin afresh, which is the key quality of the intercourse among fellow citizens. The man or woman is free if he or she can disrupt automatic political, historical, and religious processes by persuading other citizens to act collectively with him or her rather than be a slave to them.

Quintessential freedom of the individual in Kalabari involved three dimensions. First, the person was not a slave to another human being. Second, he or she was not a servant of necessities of life. Finally, she or he could act (*ori ine o ye gbaye ye ba*), exhibiting the capacity to begin, to do and act, to start something new in the midst of others (world). To be free is to thrive on the basis of the unprecedented. Kalabari say, "*ala-okolo poku pila-maa,*" which literally means "a chief's (great person's) feces do not pollute the holy." The phrase is generally understood to mean that a great man or woman is above the law. But the inherent meaning of the saying goes beyond seeing chiefs as above the law. Law in general imposes limitations of action, and such containment is founded on precedent, but every action (which law is attempting to police or contain) is inherently boundless and unpredictable, and thus thrives in the realm of the unprecedented.[20]

The divine-human relationship is not above these sentiments of freedom or the belief in the human capacity to begin something new. As the event of 1857 in Elem Kalabari and other similar stories in Izon communities in the nineteenth century demonstrate, Izon people are willing to start afresh with their gods. Thus, if a god starts a process that is not conducive to human flourishing, they can disrupt the process to start something new. If a god becomes too violent, they will cause it to cease to exist.

This brings us to the second political principle used to interpret the event of 1857: The withdrawal of worship from or worshipful dependence on the god deprives the god of its power and authority to act on humans or control human activities. From the standpoint of Kalabari worldview and political philosophy, the deicide of 1857 is not at all surprising once we grasp the importance of relations as constitutive of both society and personhood in Kalabari communities. Worship is not just reverence, obeisance, praise, and exaltation, or appropriate response to deity, but the dynamic maintenance of deep, thick relations, a social bond with a deity. All forms of power, be it political or spiritual, are always predicated on the strength of social bonds among persons, and the fracture or rupture of the bond or the displacement of harmony in the bond means erosion of power and authority.

The idea that the holy emerges from social practice has long been something that many in traditional Izon culture take for granted. Among the Kalabari of the Niger Delta in Nigeria, the holy, godliness, is an emergent phenomenon of human worship; like social systems, it realizes itself through practices. The holy emerges and is ensconced in the social practice of worship. The gods arise from such practice insofar as their power of being is in it. The gods are conceived as a source of tremendous power. But the power that the gods possess is believed to depend on the social practice of human worship, and thus humans can reduce or completely efface the power of any god by withdrawing worship.[21] The Kalabari believe that spirits and gods do not have intrinsic powers of their own, maintaining that a god that is not worshipped loses its power.

POLITICS OF INTERRUPTION:
THE VOLCANIC CORE OF SOCIAL RELATIONS

I have so far deployed Kalabari understanding of freedom and relationship to frame the 1857 deicide. This enframing can be expanded by a third factor: action as an interruptive force. Kalabari people interpret action as the capacity to interrupt, disrupt the power dynamics, or lob in a voice, or do something that halts or diverts an ongoing system or process. Persons or institutions that have this kind of power to maximally interrupt others' lives become gods. For instance, the British colonial imposition as consulate authority in the life of the Kalabari people caused so many disruptions in their everyday life and the workings of local institutions in the early twentieth century that the consulate became a "god." In the 1970s, years after Nigeria's independence, you could still hear old folks invoke this terrible god against an adversary: *"Konsin bere ibu paka,"* may you be persecuted by the consulate. Consulate as a god that interrupted local power dynamics was now called upon to visit its form of interruption on an adversary, to deploy its wickedness and impunity to interrupt a person's ongoing life.

Gods are interruptive forces even as human beings can interrupt them also. The British colonial government knew well that under the influence of a local deity, the people could summon collective energy to disrupt its oppressive imperial rule. Under the guise of Christian civilization that frowned on the worship of local gods, it proceeded to discredit them. In some cases, colonial authorities destroyed the shrines of deities and even passed laws against people invoking the name of their gods against their opponents in a dispute. In the early 1940s, Mrs. Kalawanyi Wariboko Young-Jack, a Christian widow in her thirties, invoked the name of a local deity against a powerful chief of her Jack compound in Abonnema. The chief's son had severely flogged her ten-year-old daughter while playing a masquerade during a festival in the public square.[22] She wanted the young man to be punished for the infraction. But his father refused. Having no regular political power to bring the chief and his son to justice, she summoned (*oru gbo*) one of the local deities to punish the chief, to interrupt his smugness of unassailable power. He dragged the aggrieved woman to the colonial native authority court (in which he was one of the judges), charging her with breaking the law by invoking the name of a local god against him, though it was still common in the town to call down the judgment of gods in disputes. Another man, Chief Graham Douglas, a cousin of hers from a different compound and a member of the native authority court, saved the woman from the wrath of the colonial authority. He interrupted the plan of the power-drunk chief to bring negative judgment against her. After she was cleared she changed her name back to its maiden form, Ms. Kalawanyi Daketima Douglas, interrupting her shared belonging (as in common last name) with the overbearing chief.

The key principle I want to highlight here is that *oru gbo*, calling on a god, is a way Kalabari culture gives voice or speech to persons who are not supposed to be heard, affords them a way to be heard among the powerful. The rupture of Mrs. Young-Jack, her calling up a deity to secure justice for her regardless of the colonial ban, is publicly interruptive of the hegemonic order symbolized by her rich and powerful adversary. The part-of-no-part speaks when they are expected to be silent, and it is one way the gods become involved in politics, the politics of interruption, dissensus of the uncounted and excluded, as Jacques Rancière informs us.

The power of community to interrupt powerful people or agents is asserted or enacted in the ceremony of becoming chiefs. One of the questions a would-be chief must answer is this: "If you are with a beautiful woman, a new woman and you are about to have sex or already engaged in it, will you interrupt the coitus and come when the community calls?"[23] If the aspirant is not capable of resisting libidinal impulses to promptly leave for community services when he hears a clarion call for action in the face of a new naked lover who is alone with him in the room, then he does not qualify for leadership and he has exhibited a failure to understand a basic requirement of citizenship. The man is questioned so the community can learn something about his willingness to consciously move from the private realm to the public, to interrupt his private interests for the sake of the public.

This perchance to interrupt or gauge the preparedness of citizens for interruption is also evident in one of the primordial relations Kalabari Izon believe exists between God (the supreme being, Tamarau/Teme-órú/Tamuno) and them. Here we are talking about the tension between *fiyeteboye* and *bibibari*. In the Kalabari theory of personhood, the individual is believed to have a two-part personality. The component parts of this personality act as separate "persons." One is conscious, the other unconscious. Before the person is born, the unconscious part (the soul) decides on the person's destiny (*so* or *fiyeteboye*), the life-course of the whole person on earth. When a soul (spirit) is about to come to earth the would-be soul of the person goes before *Teme-órú* and decides on a set of possibilities for the life of the individual it is going to inhabit. The other part (the conscious), which is the physical embodiment of the soul, works to actualize the chosen set of possibilities in history. If a person does not like the course of her life on earth she goes to a diviner to change her *so* or *fiyeteboye*. The process of changing destiny is called *bibibari* (altering or nullifying the spoken word, recanting). The person visits a diviner to let Teme-órú know that she would like to change how she wants to live her life-course on earth. Once the change of destiny is effected, the new *so* conditions the person's whole course for the remainder of her life on earth.[24]

What does this example add to the portrait of the Izon political philosophy we are developing in this essay? If *fiyeteboye* is the "timeless," ontological structuring of the range of possibilities within a person's life, *bibibari* is the radical temporality of subjectivity as an openness to the future in Kalabari thought. The individual has the opportunity or right to interrupt the primal voice, the pre-existence speech in her life. Here the person is actually interrupting the voice speaking from the throne room of the supreme being. Yes, in the beginning was the word, but there is always a re-beginning of the beginnings.

The Kalabari-Izon person is not only culturally formed to interrupt his speech-agreement with God, but also to interrupt his very being or own desire. This is enacted in a set of practices I have named elsewhere as *counterfoil choice*.[25] The characteristic feature of counterfoil choice is that whenever A is offered, the Kalabari put its negative (non-A), to show the person where a decision should not go or to gauge his willingness to interrupt his desire. In moments of rites of passage or situations where it is necessary to make citizens rethink their actions or behavior, they are given a forced choice between A or non-A. One other question is asked of a would-be chief: "Are you willing to pick yam or cannon ball?" Yam represents the ability to feed his household and cannon ball represents risk-taking on behalf of the community, being willing to put his capability and financial resources toward defending it in times of war and upholding its freedom. He has to pick cannon ball to make it through the ceremony, going against his self-centered well-being. His upbringing has prepared him on how to respond to tests like this.

Fathers tell their sons and nephews that if given the forced choice of freedom or death, you choose death to keep your freedom of choice. Choosing freedom under the threat of death is unmanly, cowardice, offering no proof of freedom. Young men are told that a proper Kalabari man in such a condition laid before him (a kind of declaration of war) should be able to quietly cut off his breath instead of "eating phlegm." In such a condition, he should be willing to sacrifice the very thing that he cares most about, betray his paramount interest in life, the very natural desire to preserve and promote life that makes the forced choice so palpable, personal, and painful in order to demonstrate that he has the freedom of choice. He chooses freedom by choosing its negation (non-A). He interrupts the flow of his life so as not to give up on who he is.[26] He interrupts his very being, his ownmost desire that in the first place brings him to the point of sacrifice.

This idea of interruption runs so deep in the culture that, as we have already seen, the very gods that could be used to interrupt the speech of powerful men who govern can in turn be interrupted or put out of existence, can experience the ultimate interruption. As a matter of fact, Kalabari say that they create sculptures for their gods for the precise reason of interrupting the flow of their movement in order to exercise control over them. As an informant told anthropologist Robin Horton: "If you invoke a spirit without sculpture to act against someone who had wronged you, where will you call it off? Maybe, the place where you invoke, the spirit will not be there: and the place where you do not invoke, the spirit will be there."[27] And Kalabari say gods stay and come in their names, and a wooden sculpture (*oru fubara*, literally, "forehead of the god"[28]) is a form of a name of the god that confines it for interactions in a shrine. In this way, a sculpture of a god "enjoys the same intimate link with the spirit it represents as would any other kind of name: whatever is done to the one *ipso facto* affects the other."[29]

The politics of interruption, as we have laid it out, is akin to the notions of freedom and relationship that also define the interaction between gods and humans. They all point to the limitations of power, whether supernatural or natural, and that the citizens, worshippers, or subjects under authority must always have something to disrupt ongoing social processes, to overturn overbearing power. So when Kalabari say, "If a spirit becomes too violent, they will tell him from which stick it was carved," in everyday speech it is a reminder, as Horton informs us, about the limitations not only of supernatural power, "but also the pitfalls that lie in wait for the overbearing human being. Its use is based on the fact that 'the stick they carved him' is a figure of speech for the instrument of their power over him."[30] The people as a collective always have something through which they control or use successfully to revolt against a god or person in authority. This something is their action or their capacity to begin. The generative impulse of the political is that the actions of human beings work to eliminate the impossible by creating new possibilities. Simply put, coexistence (among humans and between human beings and gods) carries a high voltage charge of disruptive possibility and is delicately balanced on a fragile consensus of each actor not overstepping her bounds.

The shark deity transgressed its limits, and it was killed; portions of its blood and flesh were put into the town's drinking well for all citizens to consume.[31] The mixing of shark's blood in the town well says to the people as a collective: "This is the blood of Owu Akpana shed by us for us. Drink this in remembrance of our triumph, liberation and in fidelity to our collective destiny and our collective guilt." There is here an intersection of the political theological, political economic, and the democratic. The political theological and the democratic do not need to delay us here as we have been shedding light on it, and we will say more about them below. The Akpana lineage (surviving remnants of the ancient Amabiame house of Elem Kalabari) which produced the priests for the shark cult (Owu Akpana) refused to partake in the communion and eucharistic feast on the flesh of the shark deity. For this the lineage was tried and heavily fined, and they were unable to pay. "King Karibo redeemed its members by paying the fine and they thus became absorbed into his house and the independence of the [Amabiame] house finally came to an end."[32] The divine flesh secured by the citizens acting in concert was commodified.

The transformation from the political theological and democratic to the political economic took place against the background of international trade with European merchant capitalists. The wrong that the shark deity did for which it was executed and consumed cannot be adequately understood apart from the slave trade and so-called legitimate commerce between the people of the Niger Delta and Europeans from the fifteenth century to the nineteenth. The unanswered question here is what caused the increased contact between human beings and sharks that led to the increased shark attacks on children that fueled the decision to commit deicide? Historians inform us that sharks followed European ships (during the slave and legitimate trades) into the coasts to feed on scraps and dead bodies thrown into the waters. Thus, it is arguable that European ships coming into the Niger Delta brought the sharks closer to areas of human residence and play.

Indeed, the shark's flesh teems with signification, standing at the jointure between the normative, the somatic, and the democratic.[33] The flesh provokes the quest for meaning and justice, generates the feeling of satisfaction at wrong, consumption of divine meat, and acceptance of redemption money, and enacts the praxis of coming together with others and acting in concert.

The deicide also gestures in other directions, apropos to the political theological and the democratic. First, it points to a devouring relation, feasting on carrion of the god, and to the deed as a sponge that wiped away an entire horizon of religious meaning, so to speak.[34] The people were called to accept with enjoyment the very deicide, the letting go of protective powers of a god, a spiritual umbrella, which is generally horrifying. Second, the eating and drinking of the substance of the god symbolizes a communal decision, a collective action; no one individual can defeat a god, but the community can with a triumphant yes-saying to itself. The power of the defeated god is now incorporated into the human body. The sacred in this case is no longer an external force that rules over them, but a mark of their capacity to create new possibilities by altering the form and structure of the sacred they inherit. Finally, the story of the 1857 deicide offers a productive way of thinking about religion and political theory creatively through a critical lens of the politics of interruption.

Indeed, the story of the Izon people that we have narrated here offers the reader a way to imagine Rancière's characterization of the political being-together as "a community of interruptions, fractures, irregulars and local, through which egalitarian logic comes and divides the police community from itself."[35] We will further explore this characterization of Izon political community through a critical discussion of the famous epic *Ozidi Saga*. This text explores the issues of interrupting establishments, challenging natural and supernatural powers, and initiating something new amid ongoing social processes. Our engagement with this text will enable us to further explore the practice and concept of interruption for both religion and political theory. We seek to explore not because we want to excavate deep truths others do not know about the Izon spirit, but rather to revivify the epic for the present African political moment, learn more about initiating something new amid increasing vulnerability, fragility, and mortality on the continent, and seek ways of reorienting political imagination toward the politics of interruption. As Hannah Arendt puts it, "The lifespan of man running toward death would inevitably carry everything human to ruin and destruction if it were not for the faculty of interrupting it and beginning something new, a faculty which is inherent in action like an ever-present reminder that men, though they must die, are not born in order to die but in order to begin."[36] The *Ozidi Saga* points us to where to look for the source of the new, the impulse for the capacity to begin, to initiate something new in the space of responsibilities. In this epic, the community is made "right" (mainly) from inside. We will see in just a moment how the hero, Ozidi, and his grandmother, Oreame, relied less on Tamarau, the transcendental power, for their success than would be expected in a typical gods-drenched traditional African society. It was from within (immanent) rather than from outside that the source of the new lies: In the performance of their herculean tasks, they relied more on people, flora, fauna, and forces of nature within the natural Izon world than on God (Tamarau).[37]

THE WEIGHT OF OZIDI: LONG LIVE THE PEOPLE!

The *Ozidi Saga* is the story of a boy hero named Ozidi who set out to avenge the assassination of his father (Ozidi Senior). Ozidi Sr., a brave warrior, was killed by some of the most powerful generals of the city-state of Orua of the Tarakiri-Orua Izon (Ijo, Ijaw) clan in the Niger Delta area of Nigeria. His body was also desecrated. His colleagues colluded to murder him when they all went to secure a human head to honor the installation of a new king, Temugedege, a mentally challenged man and the elder brother of Ozidi Sr. The right to rule has come to the lineage of Ozidi by rotation based on the Izon notion of republicanism—govern and be governed—but the other leaders in the town resented the coronation of Temugedege because he was an "idiot."

In resisting the right of Temugedege, the aristocratic generals were contesting the very foundation of the notion of democracy, the complete absence of distinguishing quality or entitlement to govern. "Democracy," Rancière teaches us, "is the specific situation in which it is the absence of entitlement that entitles one to exercise *arkhè*."[38]

John P. Clark in his play *Ozidi*, which is based on the saga itself, interprets the military generals' reluctance to go through with the coronation rites by giving gifts to Temugedege as also based on the fear that a fool made a leader might turn out to be too demanding, like a god. One of the citizens of Orua in conversation with others on the issue makes this connection clear, as well as points to the fecundity of the tension in any divine-human or hierarchic relation.

> I have no water in my mouth as I stand
> Here speaking. You all know a god is
> A god once you make him so. After
> The ceremony, he ceases to be mere wood. Give him
> Palm oil then, and he'll insist on blood.[39]

We should also interpret this conversation in the light of a political philosophy that founds the immanence of sovereign power on resistance to any political paradigm which facilitates a creator becoming enslaved to her creation, an effect "transfiguring" into its own cause.

Nine months after the assassination of Ozidi Sr., his widow, Orea, bore a son and the son's maternal grandmother, Oreame, a famed and powerful sorceress, carefully trained him. She raised him to eliminate all those who conspired to kill his father and any supernatural being or force of the community that would oppose his lineage claim to kingship and prominence in the land. Altogether, Ozidi the hero fought fourteen epic battles, vanquishing all foes, including human and non-human beings alike, "who constitute a menace to life and leadership in his society."[40] The fights were marked by revolutionary terrors and horrors. In all his fights, he was ably supported by Oreame, who encouraged him with words to shore up his energies in moments of weakness and equipped him with supernatural powers. In their first eight fights they battled human figures who had a hand in the assassination of Ozidi Sr. In the last six, we see the interruptive impulse of the Izon warrior spirit going against non-human figures. "Having disposed of the assassins, Ozidi and Oreame emerge as the supreme powers in the society. They therefore incur the resentment of other forces, of far less human order, who long claimed such a position and will not brook any competition."[41] The reputation of the Ozidi-Oreame team reached the supernatural beings from the citizens of Orua who were running into the bush because of excessive bloodshed in their city.

The Ozidi story is suffused with magic and the supernatural. One easily gets the impression that the boy-grandmother team won their fights because of the unrivaled magic prowess of Oreame, even as we know that they were propelled by a sense of justice. Magic or the supernatural in this context should not be conflated with powers from beyond-history space, a transcendental realm. The noumenal is often an *intensification* of the phenomenal perception. As Okpewho puts it, "The supernatural power quite often consists in exploiting the virtues [the pharmaceutical virtues] inherent in the surrounding nature."[42] Tamarau herself plays a minor role in the story. For instance, in the midst of a very strong battle, Oreame flies to heaven to meet God (Tamarau) to gain reassurance about the justice of the mission of her grandson and to get the Creator to confirm that justice is on her side, but Oreame did not get any assistance from Tamarau.[43] "It is clear that the Oreame-Ozidi team owes its triumph far less to whatever aid the higher beings might offer than to the occult power of magic derived from exploiting the latent qualities of the flora and fauna of the natural Ijo world."[44]

No doubt Ozidi and Oreame accomplished great feats in the name of justice, yet there is some reluctance on our part to declare them as champions of the Izon republican spirit. Were the victories of the Ozidi-Oreame team really a triumph since it became the supreme power in town in which the citizens of Orua have run into the bush in fear of the team's revolutionary terrors and horrors? Was it not because of the fleeing of Orua citizens into the bush that provoked the non-human forces to challenge Oreame and Ozidi? We want to now explore the meaning of all this for theory of democratic sovereignty, Izon republicanism, and the politics of interruption that we are attempting to craft in this essay.

In the Ozidi story, the details of the reality of republicanism, the wrestling of power from hegemonic forces, are spectralized and the moment or the realism of liberation is experienced as a nightmarish dream. Herein lies a crucial difference between the 1857 historical revolutionary act and the fictional (historical mythic) account of revolution. While Ozidi, the main protagonist in the epic, fights to sustain Izon republicanism by the heroic assuming of his historical destiny as an authentic son of Orua, his calling politically fails, in a sense, by his inability to expand his work—the conjunction of his authentic existence and historical destiny—onto collective modes of being. Yet the failure of Ozidi (individual) and the success of the Kalabari (community) are not two different things. They are two sides of the same process. They interpret one another. His failures are part of the identity of Izon emancipatory political praxis. Ozidi accepted the basic premise of Izon emancipatory politics; his alleged failures are only its unexpected or disavowed consequences. Excess revolutionary terror and the emergence of an individual who directly embodies the political collective are just two of the consequences. (Is the elimination of all gods, higher powers and not only Shark-god, not an immanent utopian vision of the 1857 multitude? Is revolutionary terror to correct all wrongs at once not an inherent fantasy of every successful emancipatory struggle?) We can add a third consequence: The singular leader can be "sublated" in the "living spirit of the community": His very failure does not signal a renunciation of the community or its ethos, but "functions as a founding gesture of universal mobilization."[45] Ozidi (or rather what this fictional character represents) has come to function as a master signifier of the collective national praxis of freedom in the social imaginary of the Izon people.

In summary, the failure and success we are speaking about here are of one thing because Ozidi's revolutionary horrors are the result of the immanent antagonisms of the Izon praxis of freedom. Ozidi, an innocent boy, "directly embodies/assumes the excess," the surplus violence that makes an act a revolutionary one.[46] A revolutionary act mobilizes two elements of the praxis or decisionism of freedom; and this is the source of its inherent imbalance.[47] The exercise of freedom in a novel, revolutionary context is marked by a tension between these. First, the ensuing decisions are unpredictable, marked by non-knowledge insofar as it is unprecedented, and the actors are guided by their audacity. (But once the decision or action is taken, it retroactively changes the reality within which the actors acted. As described by Jean-Pierre Dupuy, "If an outstanding event takes place, a catastrophe, for example, it could not have taken; nonetheless, insofar as it did not take place, it is not inevitable. It is thus the event's actualization—the fact that it takes place—which retroactively creates its necessity."[48]) Second, there is a recognition of the domain of objective knowledge or experience of reality. There is always tension between these two elements, and the opposition between them can break down, and the first element dominates and appears as the capriciousness (abyss) of human will and the power of a leader.

There is another dimension to the immanent antagonisms of freedom in the Izon praxis of freedom: Ozidi's story reveals the passage from republic to empire, emancipatory politics to totalitarian temptation. Ozidi and his grandmother not only performed his historical destiny, they succeeded in driving away almost all members of the community, taking total control of the mythical city of Orua, and yet Ozidi after killing the mentally challenged old king (who is his uncle Temugedege) could not crown himself the new king. The epic ends in a deadlock.

Simultaneously, it is impossible for Ozidi to become king and impossible for him to rid himself of the desire to be king. By the republican rule of Izon community—"partake in ruling and being ruled," and rotating leadership—the new king after the death of Temugedege cannot come from Ozidi's lineage. But since he has eliminated all rivals and emptied the town of its citizens, he is *de facto* king. When there are no citizens or equals to recognize him, reigning as master is worthless. This is the fundamental deadlock of desire and structural reason in the relationship between Ozidi and Orua.

This logical impasse is hinted at another depth of the story: The empty town after Ozidi's career of blood symbolizes the impossibility of a person representing, assuming, or embodying the People. Ozidi cannot be a "Leader who *is* the People," cannot be a singular leader who is not sublated in the spirit of the people.[49] Okabou Ojobolo in his narration succinctly captured the deep Izon impulse for republicanism and equality by not depicting the people of Orua dancing and celebrating their freedom under the Great Leader. The genius of Ojobolo is to keep the city empty, resisting filling the city square with an adulating, ululating crowd, and with ideological projections of harmonious organic unity of the city under a great Hero. Ojobolo's deep appreciation of Izon homebred political philosophy is further revealed in the dialectical shift he makes in the character of Ozidi or the flow of the story itself. He moves us from the chaotic abyss of Ozidi's killing, the void of destructive fury, "which swallows everything to [a] Frame within which the New can emerge."[50] Ozidi's seven-pronged killing sword moves from being magically stored in his *inside*, his inner being, to being given physically to his grandmother, Oreame. At the same time, for the first time, he learned to have sex, pointing to the future birth of children, natality, a new beginning. Perhaps, then, Ozidi's failure or impossibility to represent the people opens a new space, "zero-point of a new beginning," the space for sublation.[51]

CONCLUSION

Let us sum up some of the key dimensions of the theological revolution of Izon religion that have implications for political theory. First, Izon society, like most traditional cultures, believes that norms of their society preexist them, are substantially given to them. But there is tension in that, given its politics of interruption, its citizens also see them as expressions of their spirit, their capacity to begin. They make their norms or institutions real by taking them as real, by weaving the spirit of the new out of the old. Clark, armed with the metaphor of dance, illustrates the appearance or finding of the new through a process of making the old.

Traditional Ijo dance, as seen in the story of Ozidi, apparently has no beginning, no middle, no end within a time structure. The dancer, submerged in the stream of everyday chores, rises spontaneously to the beat of the drum, to the sound of the song, and the dance flows on for as long as there is a tidal wave of drum and song sweeping through the town. It is the special quality of such experience that in its seeming monotony and fixity a dancer may in fact attain a new fluidity of movement, achieving freedom of spirit from this material world. This surely is transfiguration, whether pejoratively termed "a state of possession" or "auto-intoxication" by those outside such an area of experience.[52]

Second, in most religions when the relation between god and human beings has been severely fractured because of sin, the adherents strive to purify themselves so as to elevate themselves to overcome the alienation from god. In Izon religion, on the contrary, the god is likely to be abandoned, rejected, or killed. The alienation of human beings from god is projected into god as disparity within god: between immortal divine and finite mortal supernatural being, gap between the glory of power and its foundationless void, alienation between godliness and worshipful fidelity within the god itself.

Third, the place of power is empty. Izon recognize that in this perspective of seeing the gods and power against the background of nothingness is the supreme gift of freedom. This should not be construed to mean that freedom or democratic sovereignty emerge from the void which is in the very heart of power, but from constraints on void. "Constraints means here an inner obstacle or limit which prevents some possibilities of being realized, some roads not to be taken, not accidentally but necessarily (even if it appears that it happens only by accident)."[53]

In this essay, I have made explicit some of the norms of emancipatory politics that are implicit in Izon divine-human relationship and democratic tradition, which are always incomplete. The question for us is: How do Africans grapple with this ethos and attempt to creatively follow it to craft a democratic governance that is accountable to the people? We should think along the lines of politics of interruption, disrupting the usual flow of things as a form of resistance. This requires enacting social practices of freedom and radical emancipatory politics at the grassroots, and building popular institutions for massive political organization and mobilization to adequately respond to Africa's current political moment. There are two Africas now: a subjugated Africa that is an instrument of global capital that changes things all the time only to remain the same and an incipient Africa of emancipatory politics. Stasis versus natality. For those of us who hinge the wagon of Africa's development only to emancipatory radical politics there is another choice: The option is between natality as demand for what is possible within the current system and natality as a demand for the impossible. Izon religious acts and political theory gesture to the impossible as the soul of politics, which is a subjective openness to swerve from equilibrium, an inclination to being otherwise.

NOTES

1. See Liverpool merchant William Oates's diary notes of September 28, 1857, D/o/18, National Museums of Liverpool, Maritime Archives and Library. See also G. I. Jones, *The Trading States of the Oil Rivers: Study of Political Development in Eastern Nigeria* (Oxford: Oxford University Press, 1963), 217.
2. This exception does not signify a sovereign's power to overdetermine reality; rather, it is a symbol of a cultural creativity that puts absence of divine

vulnerability at the same level as presences of divine vulnerability. Simply put, the exception points to a logic of differentiality.

3. Nimi Wariboko, *Ethics and Time: Ethos of Temporal Orientation in Politics and Religion in the Niger Delta* (Lanham, MD: Lexington Books, 2010), 60–61n13.

4. Slavoj Žižek, *Disparities* (London: Bloomsbury Academic, 2016), 70.

5. Carl Schmitt, *Political Theology: Four Chapters on the Concept of Sovereignty*, trans. George Schwab (Cambridge, MA: MIT Press, 1985), 49.

6. J. P. Clark-Bekederemo, *The Ozidi Saga: Collected and Translated from the Oral Ijo Version of Okabou Ojobolo* (Washington, DC: Howard University Press, 1991).

7. See Nimi Wariboko, *The Pentecostal Principle: Ethical Methodology in New Spirit* (Grand Rapids, MI: Eerdmans, 2012).

8. Isidore Okpewho, *Blood on the Tides: The Ozidi Saga and Oral Epic Narratology* (Rochester, NY: University of Rochester Press, 2014), 1.

9. Stathis Gourgouris, *Lessons in Secular Criticism* (New York: Fordham University Press, 2013), 130–37, inspired these lines. His comments are on Claude Lefort's contribution to political theory.

10. Gourgouris, *Lessons in Secular Criticism*, 141.

11. Gourgouris, *Lessons in Secular Criticism*, 143.

12. Gourgouris, *Lessons in Secular Criticism*, xvii.

13. Oates, Diary notes, D/O/18.

14. Until I discovered Oates's diary in July 2009 at the International Slave Museum, Liverpool, UK.

15. The people of Bonny, another Izon group, also killed two gods that they considered wicked. "Kunbuyana and Tolofari . . . were wicked and capsized many Bonny canoes, going and coming from market, unless a small offering of palm-oil was thrown into the river. They so molested Bonny that my [Mr. B. M. Pepple] ancestor, King Dappa Pepple, went off and cut off their heads, which he brought back to Bonny. This happened long years ago." P. Amaury Talbot, *Tribes of the Niger Delta: Their Religions and Customs* (London: Frank Cass, 1967), 52. I have heard of another case in Okrika, another Izon community, where the god Kun-ma (which is called *Ogboloma* in Kalabari) was also "disrobed."

16. "Agu-nsi" is an Igbo word that has been adopted in Kalabari. The Kalabari word for carved or sculptured idol is *ẹkẹkẹ-tamụnọ*; and *ẹkẹkẹ* means stone, piece of stone, or rock.

17. Robin Horton, *Kalabari Sculpture* (Lagos: Department of Antiquities, Federal Republic of Nigeria, 1965), 8–9. See also Robin Horton, "The Kalabari Worldview: An Outline and Interpretation," *Africa* 32, no. 3 (1962): 204. Horton relates the story of how a spirit who misbehaved was summoned before an assembly of its worshippers, found guilty, and fined. (Robin Horton, "A Hundred Years

of Change in Kalabari Religion," in *Black Africa: Its People and Their Cultures Today*, ed. John Middleton [New York: Macmillan, 1971], 194–98).
18. Horton, "The Kalabari Worldview," 204.
19. See Nimi Wariboko, *The Depth and Destiny of Work: An African Theological Interpretation* (Trenton, NJ: Africa World Press, 2008) for the role legacy and social immortality play in the ethical formation of subjects in an Izon community.
20. Wariboko, *Ethics and Time*, 46–49.
21. Wariboko, *Depth and Destiny of Work*, 37–39.
22. My mother was the daughter who was flogged. My grandmother told me this story.
23. See a reinstatement of this question in the form of a public announcement in J. P. Clark, *Ozidi* (Ibadan: Oxford University Press, 1966), 18.
24. Wariboko, *Ethics and Time*, 66–70.
25. Nimi Wariboko, *Pattern of Institutions in the Niger Delta: Economic and Ethological Interpretations of History and Culture* (Port Harcourt, Nigeria: Onyoma Research Publications, 2007), 301–37.
26. I am indebted to Bonnie Honig for the language to interpret Izon counterfoil choice. See Bonnie Honig, *Antigone, Interrupted* (New York: Cambridge University Press, 2013), 177–79.
27. Horton, *Kalabari Sculpture*, 8.
28. "Now the forehead is that part of the person associated with the *so* [destiny] that rules the fortunes of his life; hence *oru fubara* implies not just something which is intimately linked to a spirit, but something which exercises a kind of control over it." Horton, *Kalabari Sculpture*, 8.
29. Horton, *Kalabari Sculpture*, 10.
30. Horton, *Kalabari Sculpture*, 8.
31. Jones, *Trading States*, 217.
32. Jones, *Trading States*, 217.
33. Eric L. Santner, *The Weight of All Flesh: On the Subject Matter of Political Economy* (New York: Oxford University Press, 2016).
34. We only need to read Captain Crow's account of the Kalabari relationship with the shark deity decades before they murdered it to appreciate the enormity or radicality of their deed. This was a very powerful god in their world and riverine environment. Captain Hugh Crow, *Memoirs of the late Capt. Hugh Crow* (London: Longman, Rees, Orme, Brown, and Green, 1830).
35. Jacques Rancière, *Disagreement: Politics and Philosophy*, trans. J. Rose (Minneapolis: University of Minnesota Press, 1999), 137.
36. Hannah Arendt, *The Human Condition* (Chicago: University of Chicago Press, 1958), 246.

37. Okpewho, *Blood on the Tides*, 19, 33. See Isidore Okpewho, "The Ozidi Saga: A Critical Introduction," in Clark-Bekederemo, *The Ozidi Saga*, xiii.
38. Jacques Rancière, *Dissensus: On Politics and* Aesthetics, trans. Steven Corcoran (London: Continuum, 2010), 31.
39. Clark-Bekederemo, *Ozidi Saga*, 15.
40. Isidore Okpewho, "Performance and Plot in the Ozidi Saga," *Oral Traditions* 19, no. 1 (2004): 64.
41. Okpewho, *Blood on the Tides*, 124.
42. Okpewho, "The Ozidi Saga: A Critical Introduction," xiii.
43. Clark-Bekederemo, *The Ozidi Saga*, 82–83.
44. Okpewho, *Blood on the Tides*, 33.
45. Žižek, *Disparities*, 271.
46. Žižek, *Disparities*, 268.
47. Žižek, *Disparities*, 249–54.
48. Jean-Pierre Dupuy, *Petite metaphysique des tsunamis* (Paris: Seuil, 2005), 19, quoted in Žižek, *Disparities*, 249–54.
49. Žižek, *Disparities*, 368–69, inspired this insight.
50. Žižek, *Disparities*, 371.
51. Žižek, *Disparities*, 372.
52. Clark-Bekederemo, *The Ozidi Saga*, li.
53. Žižek, *Disparities*, 39.

7. "Doing the Will of God" as Loving God Whose Way Is Peace

ALIOU CISSÉ NIANG

Not everyone who says to me, "Lord, Lord," will enter the kingdom of heaven, but only the one who does the will of my Father in heaven.
—MATTHEW 7:21[1]

No good comes from much of their private discussions, except [from] those who enjoin charity, kindness, or peace-making among people. And We shall bestow a tremendous reward upon whoever does this, seeking the good pleasure of God.
—AN-NISĀA, 4.114

The goal of Islamism and Christianity . . . is to realize the will of God. For in order to realize this will, for the purpose of gaining heaven, we must realize, here on earth, human kinship through justice for all people.
—LÉOPOLD SÉDAR SENGHOR[2]

In my chapter in this book titled "Senghorian Négritude and Postcolonial Biblical Criticism," I noted that Léopold Sédar Senghor was eulogized as being "a great baobab" for his "ability to survive as a distinct personality through seasons of flowering and drought, success and failure, while continuing to draw from his African roots."[3] I also pointed out how our Transdisciplinary Theological Colloquium encouraged us to embody and reimage ourselves as baobab trees[4] for our troubling times. Historians remind us that ours is a century that witnessed tremendous human suffering. Human causes of suffering range from colonial occupations, religious (near genocidal) wars, to economic collapses and near collapses. Although natural disasters (floods, droughts, and famines) have threatened human life, some can be traced to human causes, such as global warming due to carbon emissions. Many concerned peoples of faith, including Jews, Christians, Muslims, and other faith traditions, are holding interreligious dialogue conferences with a view to conscientize and actualize sustainable peace guided by love and purpose.[5]

I was born in Senegal, the oldest French colony in West Africa—a poor country but known as one of the most stable of all the West African countries. My mother was a Diola Christian and my father a Sufi Muslim. As history would have it, I was raised by grandparents who practiced Diola religion which I consider to be one of the many expressions of African Traditional Religion.[6] It was when I moved to Dakar, the political and economic capital of Senegal, that I practiced Islam, like a Senegalese Sufi Muslim would. Later on I came in contact with American missionaries who built a compound in the village of Fanda, in the arrondissement of Niaguis of the Casamance region, about fourteen miles from the largest city of southwestern Senegal, Ziguinchor. I met a missionary from Alabama named Bernice Clara Martin, who befriended my mother. She was an English teacher of missionary children preparing them for college education in the United States. She refrained from quoting scripture to me, but rather, she invited me to read the Bible.

As I was reading it for the first time, I noticed surprising parallels between the Hebrew Bible/Old Testament and the Qur'an. Days of reading led to many discussions that shaped my formal decision to follow Jesus and his teachings in conversation with other religious traditions that guided my faith in God. What I am saying is simply this: My spiritual journey was and is being shaped by my Diola religion, Islam, and Christianity. In many conversations where I have revealed this conviction, my listeners wonder whether I am truly a Christian—for them, it is inconceivable for a person to be a Christian and still embrace healthy ethical values exercised by Muslims and African Traditionalists.

Needless to say, my life, teaching, and reading of sacred texts is shaped by my Senegalese worldview. Prior to the arrival of Islam and Christianity in Senegal there was, I would argue, *Téranga* ("hospitality") informed by a sense of mutuality. Senegalese people take great pride in their exemplary exercise of *Téranga* and a good socioreligious symbiosis of 94 percent Muslim, 5 percent Christian, and 1 percent Indigenous faiths (each group has an expression of *Téranga*). The fact that Senegal was peacefully governed for two decades by a Catholic president, Léopold Sédar Senghor, with no religious conflict between Christians, Muslims, or other religious groups, says much about the country's socioreligious symbiosis.[7] To reiterate the epigraph, "The goal of Islamism and Christianity . . . is to realize the will of God. For in order to realize this will, for the purpose of gaining heaven, we must realize, here on earth, human kinship through justice for all people."[8] Senghor addressed these words to a people of faith the same year they were delicately transitioning from the French colonial trappings to independence in 1960.

My question in this essay is if the "goal of Islam and Christianity . . . is to realize the will of God," might that purpose help people of both faith traditions to actualize the peace of God for our time? Building on the above Senghorian words, I am arguing that Christians and Muslims might do well to refocus on the common purpose of their respective faith traditions to provide a constructive and lasting answer to the persistence of religiously inspired conflicts, objectification, and exclusion. Jewish, Christian, and Muslim scriptures provide helpful clues on how we might engage and learn from our Christian and Muslim ancestors in the faith for our time. As a person shaped by three religious traditions and trained in biblical interpretation, I am reading Deuteronomy 6:5; Leviticus 19:18; Genesis 2:7; 9:13–17; and Luke 10:33–37 in conversation with *Al-Ḥijr* 15:28–29 and *Hūd* 11:25–49 to argue that practicing the will of God is very much an act of *Loving God Whose Way Is Peace*. Doing so affirms our common humanity, which belongs to God—a quintessential dimension of life indispensable for practicing and lasting peace.

EXERCISING THE WILL OF GOD AS LOVING GOD

Years ago, I came across a significant publication in response to a letter from concerned Muslim leaders addressed to Christians titled "A Common Word between Us and You."[9] Other equally important works along the same lines were published in a compilation of moving speeches given during the First and Second Baptist-Muslim Dialogues.[10] The intention behind these events was to facilitate and inspire a constructive dialogue between Christians and Muslims in a post-9/11 (2001) world. These publications should be commended as they were designed to help faithful children of Abraham recover their common divine vocation—the practice of the will of God as a concrete expression of loving God. They provided good insights into what has been done, expected outcomes, and a future prospect I call a resilient hope for a healthier action-oriented future. In my keynote speech at the Second Baptist-Muslim Dialogue in 2012, I reminded conference participants that we were not the first to engage in an interreligious dialogue, rather we are building on what our ancestors in the faith started.

Millennia ago, an author or authors under divine guidance, faced with sociopolitical, economic and religious crises of the day,[11] wrote a daring command into Jewish and Christian scripture that reads, "You shall love the LORD your God with all your heart, and with all your soul, and with all your might" (Deut. 6:5). These words are integral to the *shēma'* (Deut. 6:4–9). They are also echoed in the Decalogue where they emphasized loyalty to God and a healthy interrelationship between community members (Deut. 5:7–21). Leviticus 19:17–18 restates key elements of the Decalogue (Exod. 20:3–17) by stressing obedience to God as a relational loving act practiced between neighbors and aliens (Exod. 20:10; 22:21; 23:9–12; Lev. 16:29; 19:10, 33–34; Num. 15:14; Deut. 5:14; 24:17–21; 27:19). The resulting intertext, according to Jacob Milgrom, yields a "New Decalogue."[12]

Love, *'ahab / 'āhēb* also rendered as *agapáō* by the translators of the Septuagint (LXX),[13] is the practice of love toward the neighbor and resident aliens. It is an expression of one's love of/for God (Lev. 19:18, 34) or obeying divine commandments (Deut. 6:5; 10:12; 11:13, 22; 19:9; 30:6, 16, 19–20). Words such as heart *lēbab* (Masoretic Text) or *kardia* (Septuagint), soul *nepesh* or *psyche* (LXX), and might *me'ōd* (MT) or *dunamis* (LXX)[14] express the whole person's unwavering loyalty to God (Deut. 6:4–5). Loving God is a lived experience in the household and the community at large. Community members must faithfully instruct their children to keep this commandment forever etched in their individual and collective memories. The three terms, heart (*lēbab/kardia*), soul (*nepesh/psyche*) and might (*me'ōd/dunamis*), resist any compartmentalization of the human body. Each of these terms symbolizes the whole person in Hebrew anthropology.[15] The meaning of the term *nepesh*, however, reaches back to the myths[16] of creation in Genesis 1–2. God created humans in God's image (Gen. 1:27) by a direct inspiriting[17] of "the breath of life," empowering them to breathe—that is enlivening them as physical and spiritual beings.[18] God is the source of life.

Patrick Miller posits that the *Shema* affirms "the breath of life" (Gen. 2:7) with love `ahab as its active strong verb, thus moving it from a mere commandment to "what makes human life possible."[19] My point is this, as Miller states, "All claims on human life are relativized and subsumed within the one total claim of God so that the demand is ultimately the gift of grace."[20] So, whether taken metaphorically or literally, exercising the *shēma`* in daily life would have been understood to have something to do with one's neighbor (Deut. 6:4–19; Lev. 19:18; Prov. 6:20–22). It is an other-centered praxis that turns it into the theological anchor of the Jewish, Christian,[21] and Muslim faith traditions (Al-`Aḥzāb 33:4; Al-Baqarah 2:165; Az-Zumar 39:23).[22]

Rabbinic traditions provide good insights into how some teachers understood and exercised the command to love God. For instance, Rabbi Bekhor Shor, cited by Milgrom, considered loving God to be a remedy to overcoming one's hatred toward one's perceived enemy. Viewed from this vantage point, hating a human being is more than "an emotion or attitude but also deeds."[23] Milgrom also cites Rabbi Hillel who exhorted his pupils not to do what they hate to others (b. Sabb. 31.a). This is nothing short of a summary of Torah vision one hears from Jesus in Matthew 7:12 and Luke 6:31—a saying known as the Golden Rule. The reception of this divine exhortation throughout scripture and rabbinic literature can be seen as an invitation for the people of faith to imitate God by doing something good for those in need and to practice good deeds toward other people as "a giant step toward achieving holiness."[24]

Jesus commands his followers to love their enemies and pray for them (Matt. 5:45–48), and to love God and neighbor (Mark 12:30–31; Matt. 22:37–39; Luke 10:27). Gospel authors redacted Leviticus 19:18 and Deuteronomy 6:5 to encourage their readers and hearers to imitate God amid Roman imperial occupation with a view to subverting empire.[25] Differences in wording reflect contextual needs rather than disagreements.[26] Loving the neighbor sums up the Torah (Gal. 5:14; James 2:8). It is a divine gift that should be practiced by everyone who receives it (James 4:7–10) with deference to the neighbor (James 4:20–21).

Luke presents his story of Jesus with a promissory angelic proclamation of joy and peace for all people (Luke 2:10), and he presents Jesus as harbinger of good news to the poor and freedom from socioeconomic oppression

(Luke 4:18–19). As the story unfolds, one soon realizes that joy, peace, and freedom are not abstract concepts but concrete expressions of an other-oriented practical life, that is loving the neighbor as oneself; namely, doing to others as we would have them do to us (Luke 6:31). Of the synoptic authors, Luke is the one who crafted an illustration of how the practice of loving God and neighbor might look. Often missed or altogether ignored is the context that gave rise to this example riddle, the Parable of the Good Samaritan (Luke 10:23–37), that underscores a perennial ethical conundrum. Jesus told this story under the Roman imperial occupation of Palestine through puppet kings to emphasize human agency (Luke 10:30–37). At its core is an invitation to read, hear, and practice Deuteronomy 6:5 and Leviticus 19:18 as one commandment with two interconnected dimensions.[27] Loving God should translate into a nonnegotiable and unconditional act of loving neighbor. It transcends the social constructions of identity that thrive on ethnic, religious, and cultural exclusivism. The Jewish and Samaritan binary echoed in some scriptural passages (Mark 10:5–6; Luke 10:33; 17:16; John 4:7, 9, 22; 8:48), I would argue, was highlighted just to subvert it (Luke 10:33–37; 17:16; Acts 8:25; John 4:39–40) with radical acts of compassion. Luke echoed the socioreligious struggles of a community trying to understand its function as bearer of the good news of God's reign under Imperial Rome. A successful mission (Luke 10:17–24) and practices of neighborliness (Luke 10:25–33) are public manifestations of God's peaceable and just reign. Successful mission creates communities of good neighbors as they exercise the will of God.

What lessons does Jesus want us to learn from this parable? There are many illustrations that can be drawn from this story but I will highlight just two I find pertinent to my argument. First, the Samaritan is the *othered one* whose theology about the ways of God is suspect and subject to scrutiny. He is not only a heretic but also a dangerous neighbor and enemy we hardly know but consider an existential threat to the secure world we fight hard to construct and preserve under God's name. Second, the Samaritan is our indispensable guide to help tear down our parochial configurations of society and correct distorted perceptions of others.[28] He symbolized divine agency, arguably Jesus himself, God *incognito* extending mercy to the needy who cannot ask for help as well as a path to find ourselves, say the pathway to the practice of sustainable communal life and peace. His daring compassion invites us to regrind our parochial lenses and uncover what it means to "do likewise" and enter God's peaceable reign. In the words of William C. Spohn, "... likewise, it is up to each person to figure out in different situations. Anyone who can use her analogical imagination to stand in the place of the lawyer in Luke 10:25 has a new model for looking at others. It instructs the imagination, goads our sympathy beyond its usual parochial limits, and calls us to acknowledge that we too have received undeserved mercy from others and from God."[29]

The Qur'an states, "No good comes from much of their private discussions, except [from] those who enjoin charity, kindness, or peace-making among people. And We shall bestow a tremendous reward upon whoever does this, seeking the good pleasure of God" (*An-Nisāa'*, 4.114). Self-serving secrecy and indifference to the needs of others are poisonous to the ongoing construction of mutuality[30] which is foundational to the cultivation of communal peace and individual empowerment. Like the lawyer in the story, we, too, are reminded that the aim of the dialogue is not only to help us think but also to exercise the inextricable dimensions of the love command by constantly probing ourselves to unearth the meaning of self in relation to the other—neighbor.[31] Garret Keizer is probably right in saying that "God has been trying to tell us something since at least the Axial Age, and the message is both clear and generic, namely that we are in this world to help each other or, in the words of the Torah, to love our neighbors as ourselves."[32]

In his exploration of the global rise of religious violence, Mark Juergensmeyer writes that those engaged in terrorizing acts are convinced that their communities are besieged—a worldview that turned them into "cultures of violence."[33] A divine mandate is often invoked to legitimize the objectification of their would-be enemies and labeling them "cosmic foes" who turned the world into a dangerous place filled with evil that must be obliterated.[34] In this *imaginaire*, killing a neighbor who dares to disagree with their worldview is the divinely legitimated course of action. Juergensmeyer offers five ways to address violence—destroying, terrifying, winning with violence, "separating religion from politics," and healing politics and religion.[35] Juergensmeyer's work is an alarming reminder about the enormous task at hand. How would loving God help us see the neighbor as a divine creation in our modern context? Is the Samaritan a parable to help us transform an enemy from within?[36] Probably!

DIVINE PEACE AS A WAY TO SUSTAINABLE LIFE

I believe peace as God's way with humanity and creation is a motif embedded in Deuteronomy 6:5 and Genesis 2:7, 9:13–17. As I noted earlier, Genesis 2:7 describes God's creation of humanity (an account considered by many scholars to be older than the one recorded in Gen. 1:26–28) while also insisting that the act of loving God is an act of affirming and exercising one's humanity which is "the breath of life" God infused in humanity. God made life possible—a reality conveyed through a myth. Here are the striking biblical and Qur'anic renditions of this reality. Whereas Jewish and Christian scripture says the "LORD God formed man from the dust of the ground, and breathed into his nostrils the breath of life; and the man became a living being" (Gen. 2:7), Muslim scripture states, "Behold I am about to create mortal man out of sounding clay, out of dark slime transmuted; and when I have formed him fully and breathed into him My spirit, fall down before him in prostration!" (*Al-Ḥijr* 15:28–29; *As-Sajadah* 32:9). Parallels between "breathed into his nostrils the breath of life" and "breathed into him My spirit" are striking. Commenting on the latter, Muhammad Asad posits that "God's 'breathing of His spirit' into man is obviously a metaphor for His endowing him with life and consciousness: that is, with a soul."[37] In other words, the idea that God created humans and nonhuman creatures is clear in Jewish, Christian, and Muslim traditions. The significance of the *nefeš ḥayyâ* ("living being/soul") is crucial for our dialogue especially as we consider God's decision after the flood.

After surveying the disaster on creation wrought by the effects of the flood, God initiated a covenant with Noah, humans, and nonhuman creatures never to obliterate "life" by another flood (Gen. 9:11–17). Scholars agree that God, in effect, starts a *new creation* with Noah's family by suspending God's bow of war. As it would have been true of Ancient Near Eastern mythology, the bow was viewed as a divine weapon of war, and the decision to suspend it meant "divine bellicosity and hostility has been transformed into a token of reconciliation between God and man."[38] Our modern insights into the making of the rainbow informed by our technological advances do not preclude its promissory meaning—an extension of divine mercy (Gen. 9:13–14). God cares for creation and is and always will be merciful to creation—a determined unconditional divine agency embedded in God's covenant with Noah and humanity.

The Qur'an offers an insightful picture of God's relationship with Noah and his family. Noah is delivered from the flood but violates God's command not to plead for those who will perish in the flood. Upon realizing that his son perished, Noah probed God for an answer (*Hūd* 11:37; 45–46). God rebuked him, leading to Noah's repentance and plea for divine "mercy and forgiveness,"[39] and thereafter sent Noah out of the Ark saying, "O Noah! Disembark in peace from us and with [Our] blessings upon thee" (*Hūd* 11:25–49).[40] Noah leaves the Ark guided by divine mercy and peace. This is an excellent picture of God being the source of intrinsic mercy and sustaining peace modeled by the deity for humans to emulate in the new creation. By emulate, I mean practice with concrete acts that create organic communities of peace.[41] After experiences of global/local disaster, God's pathway with humanity in God's new creation was anchored by divine mercy and peace in both the biblical and Qur'anic accounts.

Although the word "peace" is not mentioned in Genesis 9:13–17, the idea, I would argue, is implicitly embedded in God's promissory mercy that undergirded God's new creation. The Qur'an however makes an explicit mention of the word "peace" (*Hūd* 11:48). Peace, *shalôm*, lexicographers tell us, belongs to a broad semantic field with meanings ranging from *being whole, intact, prosperity, peace, ease, unaffectedness, success, well-being, state of health, kindness to salvation*[42] and has the same meaning in Arabic,[43] as Asad rightly confirms.[44] *Shalôm* is "an iridescent word" with "iridescent dimensions"[45] throughout the Hebrew Bible/Old Testament. It is:

> more than the somewhat bland definition of "wholeness" or "totality." It is more than absence of warfare and hostility. It is a state of positive friendship and security between two parties, often the result of restitution and reconciliation. . . . The Mosaic laws show that a necessary corollary of peace with God is peace between his people.[46]

The pairing of *shalôm* with *mishpat* ("justice"; Isa. 59:8) and *tsedaqah* (Ps 72:7; Isa. 48:18; 54:13–14; 60:17) appears to be a way of emphasizing the imperfection of peace and presenting it as a "work in progress" that can function as a theology of hope, a large-scale promissory vision of what will one day surely be. Seen this way, the practice of *shalôm* is a strong spur against despair and a hasty settlement for an unfinished system.[47]

If *shalôm* is indeed a divine delicate "gift" and "work in progress," as Walter Brueggemann argued, then it must be handled with care due to its fragile nature and character—"present gifts are always fractured and incomplete when confused with expectations."[48] Therein lies the invitation for Jews, Christians, and Muslims to work together not to reduce peace or peacemaking to a trivial category, as Willard M. Swartley rightly laments.[49] It is unfortunate how a profound theological term such as *peace* can easily be distorted, silenced, or tamed for political, religious, or economic reasons. Luke writes about *erenē* ("peace")[50] initiated by God's reign to a community that already heard news of the peace of Rome—the empire ordained by Jupiter to rule the known world according to poets such as Virgil (*Aen.* 1.278–282; 1.231–6.278–83; 6.791–807, 851–53) and Ovid (*Fasti*. 1.315–17, 587–616), and historians such as Pliny (*NH*. 2.189–90; 3.5.39–42) and Livy (*Hist*. 1.310–4.3). Augustus Caesar, the so-called son of god in Rome's imperial theology, claimed to have liberated and brought peace to the state (*Res Gestae*, 1.1), ended civil wars on land (*Res Gestae*, 34.1), and liberated the sea from piracy (*Res Gestae*, 25.1), and his birth was the inception of good news to the Romans.[51]

In contrast, the Bible talks about the "mercy of God" who guides the faithful in the way of peace" (Luke 1:78–79). An angel delivers "good news" of "peace on earth" (Luke 2:14). Jesus says peacemakers are not only blessed but they "will be called children of God" (Matt. 5:9). He dismisses those whose needs he met "in peace" (Mark 5:34; Luke 5:34; 8:48), and the disciples are encouraged to exercise peace (Mark 9:50; Matt. 10:13; Luke 10:5–6; John 14:27). Greetings often pairing grace and peace (*charis kai erenē*) permeate the New Testament epistles (Rom. 1:7; 1 Cor. 1:3; 2 Cor. 1:2; Gal. 1:3; Eph. 1:2; Phil. 1:2; Col. 1:2; 1 Thess. 1:1; 2 Thess. 1:2; 1 Tim. 1:2; 2 Tim. 1:2; Titus 1:4; Phlm. 3; 1 Peter 1:2; 2 Peter 1:2; Rev. 1:4) or placing mercy between grace and peace (1 Tim. 1:2; 2 Tim. 1:2; 2 John 3 and Jude 2). As for the Apostle Paul, the "God of peace" initiates restorative acts that pave the way for humans to have a new and peaceable relationship with the deity (Rom. 5–8; 1 Thess. 5:23) moved by the indwelling presence of the "peace of God" (Phil. 4:7–9). Jesus' exercise of peace was ironically met with the terrorizing, lethal, and unjust peace of Rome crucifying him, but God intervened with a divine pathway to peace practiced by his followers.[52] What do these ideas discussed above have to do with "doing the will of God" as stated by Léopold Sédar Senghor? To answer this question, I first address how Senghor came to the idea of doing the will of God as a common word for the people of faith.

INTERRELIGIOUS DIALOGUE IN GOD'S MIND

As I noted in my chapter in this volume titled "Senghorian Négritude and Postcolonial Biblical Criticism," Senghor, as a teenager, challenged the normative view of Christianity presented by some of the missionaries associated with the Holy Ghost Fathers. His response was to contextualize Christianity in such a way that his inherited Sérère Faith Traditions would help strengthen his Christian faith. He was shaped by a culture that embraces the multivalency of the sacred and thus made of him a person of conciliation. As Abou Bakr Moreau writes,

> Léopold Sédar Senghor est lui-même le produit d'un brassage; c'est peut-être ce qui fait de lui un homme de conciliation. Issu de l'intérieur du Sénégal, rural, catholique, aise, enracine et chauvin, et ouvert aux Lettres, a la politique et aux sciences humaines, Senghor a puisé à toutes les théories de son temps. Il est le produit d'une histoire et d'une singularité. Dès l'âge de sept ans déjà, lorsqu'il est confié aux Peres missionnaires, le jeune Senghor peut observer et affirmer: ' Les esprits de l'animisme et le Dieu catholique, avec ses Anges et ses Saints, vivaient en bonne intelligence chez moi.' Les réflexions du poète qui jaillissent quelques fois de la Bible attestent de l'éducation et de la pratique religieuses catholiques reçues. Le Catholicisme qu'il adopte, l'animisme qu'il reçoit en héritage et qui est inné en l'homme africain traditionaliste bien enracine, et l'évolution du poète dans une société largement musulmane forment divers courants qui élèvent son sens de l'Homme et de la tolérance en lui inculquant des vertus théologales: l'espérance à la suite de l'échec, la foi en Dieu et aussi en l'Homme, la charité qui est une forme de solidarité sociale et de miséricorde humaine.[53]

[Coming from the interior of Senegal, rural, Catholic, comfortable, rooted and chauvinistic, and open to literature, politics and the human sciences, Senghor drew on all the theories of his time. It is the product of a story and a singularity. Already at the age of seven, when entrusted to the missionary Fathers, the young Senghor can observe and affirm: "The spirits of animism and the Catholic God, with his angels and his saints, lived in good intelligence at home in me." The poet's reflections, which spring up a few times from the Bible, attest to the Catholic religious education and practice received. The Catholicism he adopts, the animism he inherits, and which is innate in the deeply rooted African traditionalist man, and the evolution of the poet in a largely Muslim society, form various currents that elevate his sense of humanity and tolerance by instilling in him theological virtues: hope as a result of failure, faith in God and also in humanity, charity which is a form of social solidarity and human mercy.]

Senghor found a way to fulfill his earlier wish to enter the Catholic priesthood, according to Birahim Thioune, by making himself *Prêtre hors du Temple* "priest outside the Temple"[54]—namely the church.

Many critics of Senghorian Négritude failed to see this heavily theological dimension of the poet, as I argued in my "Senghorian Négritude and Postcolonial Biblical Criticism." In his collection of poems titled *Hosties Noirs* ("Black Wafers"), Senghor takes on the function of a priest presiding over a communion in a world affected by the atrocities of the transatlantic slave trade, French colonization, and World War II. The poems echo profound postcolonial theological and ethical themes exposing the ills of French domination, cultural imposition, and exploitation, countered by sacrifices made by the colonized to liberate and humanize imperial France. Senghor ingeniously communicated this lived experience through the Christian theme of the Eucharist (1 Cor. 11:23–26) which he took up in *Hosties Noirs* as *black bodies* not just offered but publicly portrayed as sacrificed to liberate France from the German occupation.[55] Pauline echoes of Jesus Christ publicly crucified (Gal. 3:1) are very much part of Senghorian poetic characterization of the agency of black bodies, including his to liberate France from the Germans.[56]

Clearly Senghor's construction of a sacred cosmogony informed his hermeneutics of the crucifixion of Jesus and the Eucharist.[57] The world was created and sacralized by one supreme deity worthy of reverence and worship. Since it was the Spirit of God who animated all creation (Gen. 1:1–2; John 1:1–5), empowered biblical figures, and mysteriously birthed Jesus (Matt. 1:20–21; John 1:14)[58] and the Church (Acts 2:1–20), it is not surprising therefore that Senghor conceived of the crucifixion and resurrection of Jesus as having a cosmic implication (Gal. 3:1a, 3:1, 6:14–16; 2 Cor. 5:17). The Eucharist, resurrection, and post-resurrection appearances of Jesus established his eternal presence in the world among nonhuman and human creatures (Rom. 8:19–23).[59] In effect, Senghor constructed the sacred cosmogony in which the birth, crucifixion, resurrection, and appearance of Jesus have universal contours that affect all spaces where people of all faiths meet for their respective religious services—Jews, Christians, Muslims, and African Traditionalists. Clearly, Senghor understands the function of religion as a mediator that is a vehicle to a healthy end—interreligious dialogue. Its nature is extrinsic since it begins in the mind of God.

INTERRELIGIOUS DIALOGUE IN THE MIND OF HUMANS

I once had a conversation with a missionary who thought actions that demonstrate a person's love of God are a virtue found only in Christianity. I was baffled by his assertion and found it unfounded, reductionist, and sadly ignorant of the teachings of my then Sufi and African Traditional religious communities. What my friend was really after, I thought, was the formal or exact biblical language of love in other religions—a quest that does not take into consideration the need to grasp language, culture, religious, and textual translatability.[60] The practice of the will of God, as Senghor conceived of it, has at least two interconnected dimensions rooted in the double commandment—love God and neighbor. The African Traditional Religion that shaped most of the African constructions of reality has practical expressions of love found in Abrahamic religions. I have already offered my take on ill-informed dimensions of Senghorian Négritude that fueled overdrawn criticism of his overall argument in my "Senghorian Négritude and Postcolonial Biblical Criticism."

The importance of the contributions Senghor made outweighs some of the controversies he might have caused, as one of his staunchest critics Wole Soyinka eulogized.

> I can think of two areas in which Senghor can be considered an exemplar, a medium, and mediator for the future of the continent. One is his philosophy of conciliation, which, considered profoundly, may be regarded as the precursor of South Africa's seemingly miraculous resolution of a potentially destructive conflict.[61]

The second area Soyinka rightly finds worthy of consideration and emulation by African leaders is Senghor's

> lesson in power, one that brings with it the transcendence of the humanist over the trappings of office, a lesson that one wished so desperately that other African Heads of State would heed. That bequest is perhaps best demonstrated by an incident that took place after he ceased to be the President of Senegal. It took place in a Scandinavian country. Senghor had retired from office and embarked on his new career as poet, sage, and traveling statesman. When he arrived at the borders of this country, however, he discovered that, having probably become used to such minor matters being taken care of by a well-trained staff, he had overlooked the expiry date on his passport. So there he was, the ex-president of a well-respected nation at the frontier of a foreign state, technically without an identity. He was afforded every courtesy, remained at the VIP lounge with the Senegalese Ambassador and his staff who had come to receive him—but he could not cross the border into that nation where he had so often been an honored guest, had indeed been received on state visits. Senghor took it stoically. . . . Senghor, I was informed, took the greatest pains to assure the embarrassed immigration officers that he was not in the least offended, indeed, congratulated them on the performance of their duty. Both outside and within Senegal, our colleagues testify to similar episodes that affirm that Senghor's relinquishing of power was not simply symbolic. After years of pomp and circumstance of power, he accepted and fully lived his transformation into a private citizen. As recent events in Zimbabwe have demonstrated, the sermon that Léopold Sédar Senghor, priest *manqué*, has preached with his life remains as urgent and pertinent as ever: there is life after power.[62]

Another dimension of Senghor's life and thought, I argue, anchors his practice of conciliation, humility, respect, and compassion, of which Soyinka spoke highly. Senghor was probably the only African head of state who cared to financially assist the war-torn East Timorese people[63]—a concrete demonstration of the moral vision of his *Africanité*. The robust nature of the legacy Senghor left must be unearthed and practiced. This is clearly stated in Elhadj Abdoul Hamidou Sall's homage to Nelson Mandela. Sall relates how Senghor, during Mandela's visit to Senegal in 1962, firmly agreed to support the South African struggle against the apartheid regime through diplomacy which he believed to be a more effective weapon for dismantling the apartheid regime than through armed conflict.[64] Mandela was perplexed at Senghor's lone and stern position on a diplomacy path as the only viable option since the other African heads of state he visited backed him financially. Senghor made good on his promise to create an office in Dakar to jump-start, equip, and strengthen the diplomatic front to subvert apartheid.

First, Senghor begins with love in African Traditional Religion, which he thinks is enshrined in the French word *connaissance* ("knowledge")—philologically, "*con-naître* is to die to self in order to be reborn in the OTHER."[65] This idea of God has as its essence love in the sense of the giving of oneself to the neighbor—a divinely inspired virtue Jews, Christians, and Muslims share[66] despite some of their theological differences. These words were shaped by a Senegalese practical as well as spiritual experimentation of *laïcité* that, according to Souleymane Bachir Diagne, "exemplifies the project of constructing a version of secularism, characterized as a 'well understood and properly practiced *laïcité*'" by Senghor's successor, Abdou Diouf.[67] Senghorian approach to interreligious dialogue is honest and courageous as it does not shy away from emphasizing the theological differences between the Bible, the Qur'an, and African Faith Traditions. Whether it is important to address these differences textually, scholars differ. Some thinkers see little or no benefit in focusing on the texts of the Bible and Qur'an as a basis for an interreligious dialogue whereas others find both textual agreements and disagreements invaluable, helpful, and unavoidable. I agree with the latter position. Senghor does not shy away from acknowledging theological differences but did so to build on common agreements.

Second, as a humanitarian Christian influenced by the ideas of Pierre Teilhard de Chardin and Henri Bergson,[68] Senghor believed in "doing the will of God" as the common obligation between Christians and Muslims—an expression that became the anchor for future interreligious dialogues in Senegal, especially Rencontre des traditions religieuses de l'Afrique avec le Christianisme, L'Islam et la laïcité held in January 2008.[69]

As a Christian who embraced the positive aspects of his Sérère African faith traditions such as love, Senghor initiated what few Christian clerics and Muslim clerics would have entertained in the 1960s. He saw the need to move beyond Christian and Muslim doctrinal differences to focus instead on the devotion to one supreme God as common ground for exercising the will of God. He was after the kind of mutuality that binds humans culturally in a common cause regardless of their faith traditions and made this clear in a lecture he delivered at the University of Cairo on February 16, 1967, titled "The Foundation of Africanité, of Négritude and 'Arabité.'"

> If we hope to build a united Africa, we must do it solidly, and for that we must found it on points of cultural convergence, not on our political differences. I have said that there are two cleavages, two obstacles to the realization of African unity: The gap between Francophones and Anglophones, and the gap between Arabo-Berbers and Negro-Africans. The Second seems to me the more important, because it is older and stems from the ambivalent nature of Africa.[70]

To be clear, the cultural convergence he called for is by no means cultural homogeneity. Rather, he was advocating a way of being in the world with others which he conceived as being the ontological underpinning of his *civilization de l'universel*.[71] His vision and determination to create such a universal civilization guided his construction of Négritude and informed his role as one of the founding fathers of Francophonie—the now blossoming international organization.[72]

I hear in Senghorian "Négritude" or "Africanité" a Senegalese *Téranga* or Diola *Kassoumay*, which for the Diola of Senegal, is integral to human mutuality and liberation as exemplified in the prophetic ministry of Aline Sitoé Diatta (1920–1944). When accused of leading an insurrection against French colonial authorities, she retorted that she was "a messenger of God who appeared to her many times" whose oracles she was transmitting.[73] Amid French colonial pressures on Diola people, Sitoé Diatta preached the "merciful God" of creation who is shaping "a universal communion marked by divine grace" and creating an inclusive communion of a people.

Her ministry was inclusive—welcoming all people regardless of their religious background, ethnicity, gender, and social status—a healthy *Kassoumay*. Pertinent to my argument, Sitoé Diatta, who was neither Christian nor Muslim, received into her community Christians, Muslims, and people of other faiths. Her *Kasila* "ministry," like Senghor's "doing the will of God," exemplified the hope enshrined in the common vision people of faith share but must act on. The Christian practice of loving God and neighbor, as far as Senghor was concerned, is integral to Muhammad's saying that "no one of you will be a believer if he does not love his brother as he loves himself."[74] Loving the *other* or neighbor as oneself in both faith traditions is more expedient than ever. A healthy discipleship that seeks the reign of God and its justice (Matt. 6:33; *An-Nisāa'*, 4.114) is the lasting antidote to the inhumane resurgence of unexamined nationalism and religious intolerance. To Senghor, history has never ceased to remind us that a "common desire to live together without religious tolerance—and racial—, without fraternity," [75] and I would add, well-being without peace, is unthinkable. Healthy interreligious dialogue is, to me, interfaith or better a socioreligious conscientization. This is extrinsic interreligious dialogue that is dependent on God's initial intention for human kinship. It requires people of faith to love God with one's whole being,[76] echoed in the *shēma'* and innovations on the Golden Rule.

Reading the *Fort Worth Star-Telegram* in 2006, I came across a striking message from the newspaper's editorial cartoonist, Etta Hulme. At first I thought it was nothing more than a satirical take on the then president of the United States, George W. Bush, for his administration's interpretation of the Geneva Conventions to bolster the treatment of Taliban prisoners. As I continued to make sense of the cartoon, I began to notice the genius of Hulme's profound theological take on the Golden Rule. The chilling questions it proffers are: What would become of human interrelationship if it were to be regulated by a version of the Golden Rule reduced to *doing to others as one would*? What would acts of *doing the will of God* be like with such a revised riddle? How might a common goal between people of different faith traditions be attainable, much less practiced?

This cartoon raises delicate existential, theological, and ethical questions for the people of faith serious about their vocation as practitioners of love, peace, and justice. Senghor as a *Baobab* left a towering legacy for Senegalese politicians, clergies, and clerics to build on and transmit to future generations. This is happening even in some conflict-ridden and war-torn West African countries. Senegal has its share of internal conflicts engendered by concerns other than those based on religion that cannot be treated in this essay. It suffices to say that most of those conflicts, which claimed some of my family members, had much to do with the country's postcolonial condition.⁷⁷ I am neither touting the Senegalese interreligious success nor setting it as model to emulate. Rather, I am simply saying that the Senegalese model is worth studying because Senegal remains the most stable of all West African countries since its independence in 1960. Here are some actionable ideas.

A SENEGALESE EXAMPLE OF INTERRELIGIOUS DIALOGUE

Mutuality among Muslims, Christians, and other faith traditions in Senegal predated the arrival of Islam and Christianity. I would argue that Senghor's life and thought were shaped by this Senegalese temperament. Moustapha Tamba's recent work sheds much light on how Senegal-born virtues such as *jom* (dignity), *jambar* (courage), *jambur* (peace), *téranga* (hospitality), *sutura* (discretion), and *muñ* (patience) are shared by Muslims and Christians.⁷⁸ Semantically, each one of these words evokes this deep Senegalese temperament anchored in mutuality. Speaking of the Diocese of Saint Louis, Senegal, Léon Diouf writes:

> Au temps où la ville brillait encore d'un passé où elle avait présenté les Cahiers de doléances des Quatre Communes aux Etats Généraux de la Révolution Française de 1789, et d'un passe plus récent ou elle était la capitale du Sénégal Indépendant, la coexistence et la convivialité entre chrétiens et musulmans était telle que les prénoms et même les conjoints franchissaient la frontière particulièrement perméable entre communauté musulmane et communauté chrétienne. Les mariages avec disparité de culte n'étaient pas rares, de même que les amitiés entre parents chrétiens et musulmans faisaient porter des prénoms chrétiens à des enfants musulmans et des prénoms musulmans à des enfants chrétiens. Ainsi le risque que courait la paix était-il facilement évité. Ce que l'on qualifie aujourd'hui d' 'exception sénégalaise', faite de relative stabilité politique repose sans doute sur cette 'culture saintlouisiènne' mais aussi sur un phénomène culturel n'appartenant pas qu'au Sénégal: 'parenté à plaisanterie.' Tolérance mutuelle entre ethnies et entre patronymes, par individus interposes, la 'parenté à plaisanterie' a désamorcé plus d'une fois les conflits latents, et pourrait désamorcer les conflits entre Etat et institutions religieuses, à condition que les protagonistes soient encore assez imprégnés de leur culture locale.⁷⁹

[At the time when the city was still shining a past when she presented lists of grievances of the Four Communes to the States General of the French Revolution of 1789, and a more recent past where it was the capital of independent Senegal, coexistence and conviviality between Christians and Muslims were such that the first and second spouses crossed the particularly permeable boundary between the Muslim community and Christian community. Mixed religious marriages were not rare, as well as friendships between Christian and Muslim parents in which Christian names were given to Muslim children and Muslim names to Christian children. Thus the risk peace might run would be easily avoided. What is described today as a "Senegalese exception," made of relative political stability, is undoubtedly based on this "Saint-Louisian culture" but also on a cultural phenomenon not only in Senegal: "joking kinship." Mutual tolerance between ethnicities and between surnames, by individuals interposed, the "joking kinship" has defused latent conflicts more than once, and could defuse conflicts between state and religious institutions, provided that the protagonists are still sufficiently imbued with their local culture.]

The stability of Senegal compared with other West African nations does not mean that the country is free from internal tensions or conflicts. To maintain a lasting stability is a daunting task for any country, especially postcolonial Africa, much less amid the shifting sands of African politics that never ceased to be heavily shaped by foreign geopolitical interests.

To return to my initial point, the arrival of Islam[80] and Christianity[81] in Senegal as well as other African countries gave rise to the need for inculturation or Africanization[82] of each religion, as many authors have already documented. Whether one acknowledges this fact or not, the Traditional African Religious lens never ceased to shape how both religions are lived in Senegal. African Traditional Religion is a silent and yet robust conversational partner, a reality Senghor and many Senegalese-born clerics and clergies affirm, that, I would argue, constitutes the bedrock for the Senegalese stable and mutual interreligious lived experience of which many have written.

Finally, my point is healthy peacemaking is a work of many eyes, ears, feet, hands, and voices. Just as the work of committed farmers, who know that their life depends on caring for sprouts engendered by a delicate mutuality with nature, so is the work for a lasting peace. The delicate nature of peace demands a labor of love for God and God's nonhuman and human creatures. It requires, as Diouf maintains, a devotion to one's religious vocation, practice of mutual respect, rejection of "political confiscation of religion," corporate and ongoing participation in "social, intercultural, and interreligious dialogue," refusal to give in to the pressures of petty secularism be it religious or secular fundamentalism, and alertness and timely handling of inherent social conflicts.[83] The delicate nature and ubiquity of the wish for peace in Jewish, Christian, Muslim, and Senegalese greetings suggests that it is always in a state of permanent construction. For example, in Wolof, the desire for peace pervades daily greetings as in *Jamma nga am?* which expresses a "sympathetic questioning" wish meaning "'Do you have peace?' But also 'May you have peace!'. . . . If peace is so often desired, it is not so much because a conflict threatens it directly as because it must never be stopped."[84] In the same vein, the Diola *Yo, Emitay ekati Kasumay* means "May God bless you" or "Yes/Good, May God preserve your well-being, happiness, peace."[85]

CONCLUSION

Juergensmeyer and contributors to the Baptist-Muslim dialogues and *A Common Word* all grapple with the daunting task and pressing need for viable alternatives to religiously inspired conflicts and wars.[86] They echo the resilient human will to live like baobab trees in the arid socioreligious and cultural spaces where *doing the will of God* is heresy. As shown by many participants of our interdisciplinary conversation, our twenty-first century is haunted by our human tilt to destroy life, fueled by unexamined nationalism, religious intolerance, violence, or indifference to the dignity of human and nonhuman creatures. The lack of rigorous historiography and scriptural exegesis has been the culprit that continues to inspire and underpin bad hermeneutics and ethics. Hulme has rightly captured the danger we face when memory is fossilized into a specimen rather than an organically embodied and practiced reality. As a follower of Jesus in the Baptist faith tradition shaped by Diola Traditional Religion and Islam, I see *Loving God Whose Way Is Peace* not as a human invention but a divine vision for not just humans but all creation that, when experienced, forces us to pause and expose the potential enemy within—both in the self and corporately. It is also that fragile, gracious divine gift and path for us to tread on cautiously because it is divine PEACE. Christians such as those engaged in peace initiatives and interfaith dialogues and faithful humanitarians understand the mystery of God that inspired them to assiduously advocate for peace and justice, help the needy, and last but not least, promote religious liberty.[87] They know the "breath of life" which made us "living beings" according to Genesis 2:7 belongs to God.

Loving God and neighbor is the theological anchor of our faith, rooted not only in the Jewish, Christian, and Islamic traditions, but also, as noted in the first National Baptist-Muslim conference, "our common word." Exercising it would help us foster cultures of peace rather than violence. It is not until we learn to love God and become empowered to exercise this love in concrete ways that emulate divine peace that we can say with Emmanuel Assante, "I am related . . . therefore I exist."[88] Relatedness grows out of the exercise of mutuality and the central goal of life inspired by the love of God and neighbor. Lamin Sanneh's insights are worth noting.

What religions offer in terms of salvation and ultimate truth cannot in the nature of the case be separated from the practices laid down to attain truth, and dialogue must not drive a wedge between the means and end of religion, between path and goal. The view we have of God is not unconnected to the path by which we ascend to that view, so that dialogue and witness, therefore, belong together. . . . Interfaith engagement proceeds by what is common to being religious as well as by the exigencies of complex human deeds and situations, but most indisputably by what is unique and determinative of faith tradition.[89]

Inherent in the greetings children of Abraham extend daily is the promise of peace.[90] Life infused with such a constant mutual wish is performative—a spontaneous practical theology of hope of something achievable based on the kind of relatedness that acknowledges and transcends our common and uncommon words, political affiliations, and socioreligious traditions to the concrete exercise of God's will. Doing to others as we would have them do to us (Matt. 7:12; Luke 6:21) is our only viable path to a just and peaceable future life with God and one another—a life of loving *God Whose Way Is Peace* only those faithful persons as resilient as a baobab tree can faithfully lead.

NOTES

1. "Not everyone who says to me, 'Lord, Lord' will enter the kingdom of heaven, but only the one who does the will of my Father in heaven." Although Luke's

wording omits key Matthean elements, Luke emphasizes failure to practice Jesus' words. "Why do you call me 'Lord, Lord,' and do not do what I tell you?" (Luke 6:46).

2. Léopold Sédar Senghor, *Liberté 1: Négritude and Humanisme* (Paris: Les Éditions du Seuil, 1984), 305. Le but de l'Islamisme et du Christianisme . . . est de *réaliser la* volonté *de Dieu.* Car pour la réaliser, cette volonté, en gagnant le ciel, il faut réaliser, ici-bas, la fraternité entre les hommes par la justice pour tous les hommes.

   It is clear that Senghor was referring to the Matthean version of the Lord's Prayer (Matt. 6:10) and Hadiths such as *Sahih Al-Bukkari, Kitab al-Iman, Hadith* 13; *Sahih Muslim Kitab al-Iman,* 67-1 and *Hadith* 15.

3. Janet Vaillant, "Homage to Léopold Sédar Senghor: 1906–2001," *Research in African Literature* 33, no. 4 (2002): 17.

4. Transdisciplinary Theological Colloquium, https://www.drew.edu/theological-school/theology-programs-traditional-interdisciplinary. Indeed, the baobab tree metaphor captures "an image of the growing, branching vitality of the many connected strands of diasporic discourse."

5. *Rencontre des traditions religieuses de l'Afrique avec le Christianisme, L'Islam et la laïcité: À Partir des écrits de Léopold Sédar Senghor* (VADI; Paris: UNESCO, 2008).

6. African Traditional Religion will henceforth be abbreviated as ATR.

7. Aliou Cissé Niang, "A Model for Our Time: Fulfilling the Will of God in Dakar, Senegal, West Africa," *West African Research Association* (2016–17): 14.

8. Senghor, *Liberté 1,* 305–6.

9. Miroslav Volf, Ghazi bin Muhammad, and Melissa Yarrington, eds., *A Common Word: Muslims and Christians on Loving God and Neighbor* (Grand Rapids, MI: Wm. B. Eerdmans, 2010).

10. "Baptist-Muslim Dialogue," *American Baptist Quarterly* 28, no. 1 (2009): 3–138 and "Second Baptist-Muslim Dialogue," *American Baptist Quarterly* 31, no. 3 (2012): 291–350.

11. Richard D. Nelson, *Deuteronomy. A Commentary* (OTL; Louisville, KY: Westminster John Knox Press, 2002), 2–12; Ronald Clements, "Deuteronomy," in *The New Interpreter's Bible,* ed. Leander E. Keck (Nashville, TN: Abingdon Press, 1998), 280.

12. Jacob Milgrom, *Leviticus: A Book of Ritual and Ethics* (Minneapolis: Fortress Press, 2004), 241.

13. HALOT, "`ahab,*"* 179; LEH, *"agapáō,"* means "like, love, love doing something" or "lovable." For more details, see William Klassen, "Love," ABD 4.381–96.

14. See DBD, *"lebab,"*4760; *"nepesh,"* 6250; *"me'ōd,"* 4975; LEH, *"kardia," "psyche,"* and *"dunamis."*

15. Hans Walter Wolf, *Anthropology of the Old Testament*, trans. Margaret Kohl (Minneapolis: Fortress Press, 1974), 7–58. See also Patrick D. Miller, *Deuteronomy* (Louisville: Westminster John Knox Press, 1990), 102–3.
16. Myth here means a story with profound meaning about life that cannot be told in any other way, namely the why of creation.
17. Sana Nahum, *Genesis*, JPS Torah Commentary (New York: Jewish Publication Society, 1989), 17. The expression *nišmat ḥayyîm* "living beings" appears in Genesis 1:30.
18. Claus Westermann, *Genesis: A Commentary*, trans. John J. Scullion (Minneapolis: Augsburg, 1984), 207.
19. Miller, *Deuteronomy*, 104.
20. Miller, *Deuteronomy*, 104.
21. "An Open Letter and Call from Muslim Leaders," *American Baptist Quarterly* 28, no. 1 (2009): 9–28, shows how the Qur'an implies similar meaning.
22. Cited in Volf, et al., *A Common Word*, 30–46.
23. Milgrom, *Leviticus*, 234.
24. Milgrom, *Leviticus*, 236.
25. Richard A. Horsley, *Jesus and Empire: The Kingdom of God and the New World Disorder* (Minneapolis: Fortress Press, 2003); John Dominic Crossan, *God and Empire: Jesus against Rome, Then and Now* (New York: HarperCollins, 2007).
26. For instance, whereas Mark combines Deuteronomy 6:5 and Leviticus 19:18, and adds "mind" between soul and strength, Luke has "mind" at the end of the injunction (Luke 10:27). Matthew replaces strength with "mind." Synoptic authors are not compartmentalizing the human body with these words; rather, they are expressing a totality, namely the whole person—a "living being."
27. Paul Furnish, *The Love Command in the New Testament* (Nashville, TN: Abingdon, 1972), 34–37. I would also add that Matthew and Mark had this reading in mind using "greater than these" (Mark 12:28) or "like it." Even when read from the gospels of Matthew and Mark, the command to love God is implicitly interpreted throughout these accounts as one.
28. William C. Spohn, *Go and Do Likewise: Jesus and Ethics* (New York: Continuum, 1999), 91.
29. Spohn, *Go and Do Likewise*.
30. Muhammad Asad, *The Message of the Qur'an: The Full Account of the Revealed Arabic Text Accompanied by Parallel Transliteration* (London: Book Foundation, 2003), 114. See *An-Nisāa'* 4.114n138. See `Abdullah Yūsuf `Ali, *The Holy Qur'ān*, 11th ed. (Beltsville, MD: Amana, 2009), 222 on *Al-Nisā'* 4.114n625. Clearly, concerns raised in this Qur'anic passage echo Jesus' concerns when it comes to benevolent deeds in Matthew 6:2–3 saying "whenever you give alms, do not

sound a trumpet before you, as the hypocrites do in the synagogues and in the streets, so that they may be praised by others. Truly I tell you, they have received their reward. But when you give alms, do not let your left hand know what your right hand is doing."

31. Garret Keizer, *Help: The Original Human Dilemma* (New York: HarperCollins, 2004), 22–33.

32. Keizer, *Help*, 24.

33. Mark Juergensmeyer, *Terror in the Mind of God: The Global Rise of Religious Violence*, 3rd ed. (Berkeley: University of California Press, 2000), 12.

34. Juergensmeyer, *Terror in the Mind of God*, 14, 58, 180.

35. Juergensmeyer, *Terror in the Mind of God*, 229–43; Nathalie Wlodarczyk, "African Traditional Religion and Violence," in *OHRV*, ed. Mark Juergensmeyer, Margo Kitts, and Michael Jerryson (New York: Oxford University Press, 2013), 153–66.

36. Martin Luther King Jr., "Loving Your Enemies," in *A Knock at Midnight: Inspiration from the Great Sermons of Reverend Martin Luther King, Jr.*, ed. Clayborne Carson and Peter Holloran (New York: Warner Books, 1998), 41–60. In his sermon titled "Loving Your Enemies," Martin Luther King Jr. encouraged his audience to always seek to transform enemies or would-be enemies into friends—a process that can only begin with self-transformation.

37. Asad, *The Message of the Qur'an*, 431n26.

38. Nahum, *Genesis*, 63.

39. John Kaltner, *Ishmael Instructs Isaac: An Introduction to the Qur'an for Bible Readers* (Collegeville, MN: Liturgical Press, 1999), 69. See *Hūd* 11:47–48.

40. See *Hūd* 11:48 for the entire account.

41. I understand fully that the persistence of violence in the Bible poses serious challenges to my argument—a troubling theme I will address in a forthcoming project. In the meantime, it suffices to say there are texts as such Ezekiel 34:25; 37:26 that have God initiating a covenant of peace.

42. See HALOT, "Shalôm," 9627, and BDB, "Shalôm," 10001.

43. HALOT, "Shalôm," 9627, in Arabic "*salm* and *silm* peace; *salāam* soundness, intactness, well-being, peace, security."

44. Asad, *The Message of the Qur'an*, 168–69n29 (cf. 36n71), notes differences with the Christian understanding of salvation and the doctrine of original sin.

45. See also Willard M. Swartley, *Covenant of Peace: The Missing Peace in New Testament Theology and Ethics* (Grand Rapids, MI: Wm. B. Eerdmans, 2006), 27, 414.

46. P. A. Barker, "Rest, Peace," in the *Dictionary of the Old Testament: Pentateuch*, ed. T. Desmond Alexander and David W. Baker (Downers Grove, IL: Intervarsity Press, 2003), 690.

47. Walter Brueggemann, *Peace* (St. Louis, MO: Chalice Press, 2001), 5.
48. Brueggemann, *Peace*, 5.
49. Swartley, *Covenant of Peace*, 1–10.
50. William Klassen, "Peace," *ABD*, 5.207–8, discusses other terms such as *galēnē* ("calmness") and *homonoia* ("concord") that should not be confused with *erēnē* "peace." Whereas the former is found in Mark 4:39, Matthew 8:26, and Luke 8:24, the latter is missing from New Testament texts but is present in the Apostolic Fathers' writings.
51. *OGIS* 458; ca. 9 BCE. See a discussion of this inscription in relation to the gospel of Mark in Craig Evans, "Mark's Incipit and the Priene Calendar Inscription: From Jewish Gospel to Greco-Roman Gospel," *Journal of Greco-Roman Christianity and Judaism* (2002): 67–81.
52. Marcus Borg, "Executed by Rome and Vindicated by God," in *Stricken by God?: Nonviolent Identification and the Victory of Christ*, ed. Brad Jersak and Michael Hardin (Grand Rapids, MI: Wm. B. Eerdmans, 2007), 150–63; N. T. Wright, "Reasons for Jesus' Crucifixion," in *Stricken by God?: Nonviolent Identification and the Victory of Christ*, ed. Brad Jersak and Michael Hardin (Grand Rapids, MI: Wm. B. Eerdmans, 2007), 78–149.
53. Abou Bakr Moreau, *Léopold Sédar Senghor et Walt Whitman: Pour l'idéal Humaniste universel* (Paris: L'Harmattan, 2010), 87.
54. Birahim Thioune, *Léopold Sédar Senghor: Un Combattant parmi les hommes, un poète devant Dieu* (Paris: L'Harmattan, 2014), 37; Moreau, *Léopold Sédar Senghor et Walt Whitman*, 86–91.
55. The characterization of African soldiers drafted to fight alongside the French against Germans as *Tirailleurs* ("Riflemen") literally conveys the idea of soldiers who shoot their rifles away or aimlessly perhaps because of their inability to master their rifles or simply that they do make good soldiers. Despite their dire need for liberation, the French still held onto their sense of supremacy over the Africans by derogatorily calling them clumsy and unsophisticated snipers, the same African soldiers who lay down their lives to liberate France.
56. Janet Vaillant, *Black, French, and African: A Life of Léopold Sédar Senghor* (Cambridge, MA: Harvard University Press, 1990), 200.
57. Thioune, *Léopold Sédar Senghor*, 64.
58. Senghor, "Hosties Noirs," in *Œuvres poétiques, Poésie* (Paris: Les Éditions du Seuil, 1990), 57–100.
59. Senghorian exegesis builds on many biblical texts such as Gen. 1:1–2; John 1:1–5, 14; Matt. 1:21–23; 18:20, 26–28; 28:18–20; Luke 1:26–35; 22:19–20; 24:13–37; John 20:10–27; Acts 1:1–9; 2:1–23; 1 Cor. 11:23–26.

60. Lamin Sanneh, *Translating the Message: The Missionary Impact on Culture* (Maryknoll, NY: Orbis Books, 1989); idem, *Piety and Power: Muslims and Christians in West Africa* (Maryknoll, NY: Orbis Books, 1996).
61. Wole Soyinka, "Senghor: Lessons in Power," *Research in African Literatures* 33, no. 4 (2002): 1–2.
62. Soyinka, "Senghor: Lessons in Power," 2.
63. Soyinka, "Senghor: Lessons in Power," 1.
64. Elhadj Abdoul Hamidou Sall, "Mandela et le Senegal, Mon Hommage a Madiba," http://www.leral.net/Mandela-et-le-Senegal-Mon-Hommage-a-Madiba-Par-Hamidou-Sall_a100899.html.
65. Senghor, *Liberté 1*, 414, "La notion de Dieu, en Afrique, aura toujours eu pour essence l'AMOUR dans le sens du don de soi à l'AUTRE."
66. Senghor, *Liberté 1*, 414.
67. Souleymane Bachir Diagne, "A Secular Age and the World of Islam," in *Tolerance, Democracy, and Sufis in Senegal*, ed. Mamadou Diouf (New York: Columbia University Press, 2013), 36.
68. Souleymane Bachir Diagne, *African Art as Philosophy: Senghor, Bergson, and the Idea of Negritude*, trans. Chike Jeffers (New York: Seagull Books, 2011), 42–136.
69. Meeting of African Religious Traditions with Christianity, Islam, and Secularism.
70. Léopold Sédar Senghor, *The Foundations of "Africanité" or "Négritude" or "Arabité,"* trans. Mercer Cook (Paris: Présence Africaine, 1971), 86.
71. Senghor, *The Foundations of "Africanité,"* 7–88.
72. Papa Alioune Ndao, *La francophonie des pères fondateurs* (Paris: Karthala, 2008). It is inspiring when once colonized peoples, who have every reason to reject anything that belonged to imperial France instead joined forces to create an institution that not only outlives them but is receiving many nations to date despite much skepticism from Metropolitan French leaders such as Charles de Gaulle. The other African co-founders of Francophonie are the Tunisian Habib Bourgguiba and Diori Hamani of Niger.
73. Aliou C. Niang, *Faith and Freedom* in *Galatia and Senegal: The Apostle Paul, Colonists and Sending Gods*, Biblical Interpretation Series 97 (Leiden: Brill, 2009), 118; see also pages 90–135; Marilyn Robinson Waldman and Robert Baum, "Innovation as Renovation: 'The Prophet' as an Agent of Change," in *Religious Traditions: Essays in the Interpretation of Religious Change*, Religion and Society 31 (Berlin: Mouton de Gruyter, 1992), 250.
74. Senghor, *Liberté 1*, 305, "personne d'entre vous ne sera croyant s'il n'aime pas son frère comme il s'aime lui-même."

75. Senghor, *Liberté 1*, 306, "il n'y a pas commun vouloir de vie commune sans tolérance religieuse—et raciale –, sans fraternité."
76. Wolf, *Anthropology of the Old Testament*, 7–58.
77. Jean-Claude Marut, *Le conflict de la Casamance: Ce que disent les armes* (Paris: Karthala, 2010); Paul Diédhiou, *L'identité jóola en question: La bataille idéologique du MFDC pour l'indépendance*, Hommes et sociétés (Paris: Karthala, 2011); Mohamed Lamine Manga, *La Casamance dans l'histoire contemporaine du Sénégal* (Paris: L'Harmattan, 2012). The war broke out in 1982 and the cease-fire introduced in 2004 was often interrupted by nagging flare-ups culminating in independence advocates suing the Senegalese government in 2014. Diola people engaged in this war often cited economic disparities inflicted in the region by Senegalese politicians.
78. Moustapha Tamba, *Histoire et sociologie des religions au Sénégal* (Paris: L'Harmattan, 2016), 302–3.
79. Léon Diouf, "Postface," in *L'Église et L'état au Sénégal: Acteurs de développement?* (Paris: L'Harmattan, 2015), 360.
80. On the Muslim side of internal stability and tension, see Mamadou Diouf, "New Perspectives on Islam in Senegal: Conversion, Migration, Wealth, Power, and Family," in *New Perspectives on Islam in Senegal: Conversion, Migration, Wealth, Power, and Family*, ed. Mamadou Diouf and Mara Leichtman (New York: Palgrave Macmillan, 2009), 1–18; Rudolph T. Ware III, "The Longue Durée of Quran Schooling, Society, and State in Senegambia," in *New Perspectives on Islam in Senegal: Conversion, Migration, Wealth, Power, and Femininity*, ed. Mamadou Diouf and Mara Leichtman (New York: Palgrave Macmillan, 2009), 21–50; Mara Leichtman, "The Authenticity of a Discursive Islam: Dhi'a Alternatives to Sufi," in *New Perspectives on Islam in Senegal: Conversion, Migration, Wealth, Power, and Femininity*, ed. Mamadou Diouf and Mara Leichtman (New York: Palgrave Macmillan, 2009), 111–38; Eric Ross, "Christmas in Cambérène, or How Muhammad Begets Jesus in Senegal," in *Muslims and Others in Sacred Space*, ed. Margaret Cormack (New York: Oxford University Press, 2013), 74–107; Douglas H. Thomas, *Sufism, Mahdism and Nationalism: Limamou Laye and the Layennes of Senegal* (New York: Continuum, 2012).
81. On the Christian side of internal stability and tension, see Jean Lecourt, *Histoire Religieuse du Sénégal* (Dakar, SN: Éditions Clairafrique, 1976); Geneviève Lecuir Némo, *Anne-Marie Javouhey: Fondatrice de la congrégation des Sœur de Saint-Joseph de Cluny (1779–1851)* (Paris: Éditions Karthala, 2007); Joseph Roger de Benoist, *Historie de l'Église catholique au Sénégal: Du milieu du XVe Siècle à l'aube du troisième millénaire. Mémoire d'Églises* (Dakar, SN: Édition Clairafrique, 2008);

Bengt Sundkler and Christopher Steed, eds., *A History of the Church in Africa* (Cambridge: Cambridge University Press, 2000); Jean-Claude Angoula, *L'Église et L'état au Sénégal: Acteurs de développement?* (Paris: L'Harmattan, 2015).

82. Sanneh, *Piety and Power*; idem, *Whose Religion Is Christianity?: The Gospel beyond the West* (Grand Rapids, MI: Wm. B. Eerdmans, 2003); idem, *Summoned from the Margins: Homecoming of an African* (Grand Rapids, MI: Wm. B. Eerdmans, 2012).

83. Diouf, "Postface," 357–64.

84. Diouf, "Postface," 358.

85. Christian Sina Diatta, *Parlons Jola: Langue et Culture des Diolas* (Paris: L'Harmattan, 1998), 103. *Kasymay* is polygenous and means well-being/peace, and when stated as a question, it means how are you doing? Are you well? Do you have peace?

86. Juergensmeyer, *Terror in the Mind of God*, 3–138; "Baptist-Muslim Dialogue," 3–138; "Second Baptist-Muslim Dialogue," 291–350; Volf, Muhammad, and Yarrington, eds., *A Common Word*.

87. Robert Sellers, "What Baptist Traditions Teach Us about Loving Our Neighbors," *American Baptist Quarterly* 28, no. 1 (2009): 111–22. See also Paul Dekar, "Baptist Peacemakers in the Nineteenth-Century Peace Societies," *Baptist Quarterly* 34, no. 1 (1991): 3–12.

88. Emmanuel Asante, "The Gospel in Context." *Interpretation* 55 (October 2001): 355.

89. Sanneh, *Piety and Power*, 6.

90. I have already discussed the polygenous nature of *shalom* in both the Bible and the Qur'an. For a detailed discussion, see Klaus Wengst, *Pax Romana and the Peace of Jesus Christ*, trans. John Bowden (London: SCM Press, 1986); Perry B. Yoder and Willard M. Swartley, eds., *The Meaning of Peace: Biblical Studies* (Louisville, KY: Westminster John Knox Press, 1992).

8. Mysticism and Mothering in Black Women's Social Justice Activism: Brazil/USA

RACHEL ELIZABETH HARDING

THE OVERVIEW: ANCESTORS, REVENANTS, AND OTHER
UNORTHODOX TOOLS OF SCHOLARSHIP

In the introduction to *Wizards and Scientists*, Stephan Palmié's magnificent reflection on meanings of modernity and tradition in Afro-Cuban religion, the anthropologist writes about a ghost.[1] The spectral presence is a former slave named Tomás, who remains close to Palmié, watching him from behind and perhaps aiding and influencing Palmié's attempts to engage a more nuanced meaning of Caribbean history as represented in Afro-Cuban experience.

For Palmié and his collaborators in Cuba (he consciously resists the terminology "informants"), Tomás is representative of the *muertos*, the spirits, the *pretas velhas*, the *eguns*, the ancestors—the millions of our dead whose continued presence in the ritual life of African diasporan religions embodies a means toward an-other discourse on history, another meaning of history.

A fugitive slave notice in the March 20, 1841, issue of the *Correio Mercantil* newspaper in Salvador, Bahia, Brazil, refers to a woman named Maria who ran away from enslavement with her ten-month-old son. Maria is described as having "some scars of wounds she received between her breasts, others on her forehead and another in the middle of her back."[2] Scholar of Afro-Brazilian women's history, Isabel Reis, ponders Maria's disfigurements, likely the results of punishments, horrifying forms of cruelty not infrequently suffered by many enslaved women and men.

Maria carried her burdens annealed to her body as she carried her son in her arms. And like Tomás, she represents a meaning and an experience of modernity that is all but unnoted, indeed structurally concealed, by conventional Western understandings of historiography. The ancestral presences in diasporic communities are the ghosts on the edges ("notionally remote areas") of the meaning of the modern world and, Palmié insists, our inability to see and acknowledge them is more a result of our particular beliefs about what constitutes "history" than proof of their inexistence.[3]

The historical construction of modernity has allowed little room for the stories of its excesses—the great sufferings of Indigenous people in Africa and the Americas, whose genocides, enslavements, and colonizations are the bases of the creation of the world we live in. Palmié and Reis join other scholars of religion, literature, and history—including Charles Long, Edouard Glissant, Sylvia Wynter, Veve Clark, Patrick Chamoiseau, Milton Santos, Toni Morrison, and Muniz Sodré, whose work urges us to find ways to disocclude what lies hidden, muted in the interstices of conventional understandings of how the world we live in came to be and at what sacrifice it continues.

"Unorthodox" sources of meaning—such as visions and dreams, literature, music, dance, and the collective remembrances of the marginalized—are necessary tools in the more complete excavation of our hemispheric history. Other important implements are the religious and spiritual traditions created by those on what Long calls "the underside of modernity" as a way to navigate and survive within it. Included in these Afro-Atlantic and Indigenous ritual traditions are the spectral presences of the past, the ghosts, the revenants, the spirits of those who lived and died in slavery and who, in ritual and metaphysical ways, are recognized as having a great deal to say about what it all means.

Of course, none of these interpretive tools is generally recognized as "rational." Still, such alternative modes of making sense of the world are more widely recognized, explicitly and implicitly, than some academics may be comfortable admitting. In this essay, I hope to offer a small contribution toward the collective effort at disocclusion, that is to say, the effort to open space, to build an alternative framework of rhetoric and experience that specifically acknowledges the spiritual histories, insights, traumas, and resiliences of Black women in a way that creates more complicated, more nuanced meanings of what is happening in their lives and the societies where they find themselves.

THE APPROACH: A WOMANIST INTERDISCIPLINARY RECLAMATION

The analytical framework from which I write incorporates history of religions of the Afro-Atlantic diaspora, ethnographies and historiographies of contemporary social justice movements, oral histories, and womanist theology and ethics. My research explores the moral and mystic universe of Afro-Brazilian and African American women activists in the mid-twentieth-century South of the United States and in the Brazilian northeast in the late twentieth and early twenty-first centuries. The resources of mysticism and mothering discussed here are among the interpretive tools that African American and Afro-Brazilian women can offer toward a collective effort at disocclusion and recovery of some other kinds of intelligence about the New World—an intelligence replete in the communities, histories and strategies of Black women but which has been hidden, muted, in conventional scholarly conversations about their history, and even in conversations about the tools of social transformation and community building.

I am both a scholar and an initiate of the Afro-Brazilian religion, Candomblé, one of the major African-based ritual traditions in the Americas. Candomblé is a re-elaboration of West and Central African understandings of the world with some aspects of Catholicism and Amerindian influences from the late colonial and imperial periods in Brazil, during which the religion developed the formal structure it now carries. Like most Indigenous spiritual traditions, Candomblé is centered on cycles of human connection to the life force and natural elements—wind, earth, water, fire, etc.—and rites of balance and healing. I am also the daughter of historians and activists grounded in traditions of African American religion. This text is informed by years of reflection and participation in Candomblé communities in Salvador, Bahia, Brazil, as well as by oral histories I've collected of African American women who were participants in the southern freedom movement (civil rights movement)—including my own mother's story.

Brazil is home to the largest population of people of African descent outside of the continent of Africa. It shares with the United States and other countries in the Western hemisphere a centuries-long history of enslavement and structural marginalization of Black people. Following in the wake of the civil rights and Black Power movements in the US, cultural and political mobilizing efforts for Afro-Brazilian human rights grew significantly in the 1970s, '80s, and '90s. Though these movements successfully challenged some of the country's entrenched racial inequalities (most notably perhaps in federal commitments to affirmative action in education), Blacks in Brazil, like their diasporic cousins in North America, continue to suffer disproportionately from poverty, unemployment, health and education disparities, state-sponsored violence, incarceration, and inadequate political representation.

Scholars of political organizing in both Brazil and the United States indicate that while men are often the most visible representatives of racial justice struggles, women are commonly the principal organizers at the grassroots level. In the case of the U.S. southern freedom movement of the 1950s and '60s, for example, Black women's participation in civic and religious associations, their work as full-time activists in movement organizations such as SNCC and CORE, and their radically inclusive hospitality was essential to campaign successes as well as to the nurturance of a sense of family and "beloved community" among those who joined in the struggle to bring the American nation more in line with its stated ideals of democracy and justice. In more recent years, women in working-class Afro-Brazilian neighborhoods in the state of Bahia have taken important leadership roles in developing community responses to a range of problems including drug violence, land dispossession, police killings, and neo-evangelical Protestant attacks against religions of African origin. My work looks primarily at this comparison—Black women in Candomblé communities who are active in social movements in Brazil (with a focus on the state of Bahia), from the 1980s to the present, and Afro-North American women involved in racial justice organizing in the U.S. in the 1960s and '70s.

In many of the oldest and most traditional *terreiros* (or Candomblé temple communities), women are the supreme ritual leaders, *iyalorixás*, who direct the ceremonial cultivation of divinized forces of nature (known as *orixás*, *nkisis*, and *voduns*). In the working-class neighborhood of Engenho Velho da Federação, where there are over a dozen terreiros, and where I have concentrated my study and participation, female adherents in Candomblé are central to community-building efforts and activist campaigns around a variety of racial, gender, and economic justice issues. In exploring the moral and mystic universe of Afro-Brazilian and African American women activists, my intention is to suggest a way of bringing Black women's voices, wisdoms, and experiences of spirit into the academic sphere in a manner that approaches their meaning on their own terms and avoids exoticization of these mystic engagements with the world. My approach is essentially that of a womanist analysis.

A WORD ABOUT TERMS: WOMANISM, MYSTICISM, AND MOTHERING

Womanist and *womanism* are concepts that entered the national lexicon in the mid 1980s with the publication of Alice Walker's collection of essays, *In Search of Our Mother's Gardens*. And although the terms may have been new, womanist analysis focused attention on political, social, and historical phenomena in light of values that have long been important to the survival of Black communities in the Americas—inclusivity, a strong motivation to struggle collectively against structural inequalities, creative/unorthodox approaches to problem-solving (a willingness to "make a way out of no way"), and concern for the well-being of women, their families, and their communities. The approach is similar to feminist, subaltern, and postmodern theoretical frameworks in that it privileges the moral and ethical perspectives of people who have been marginalized by the structures and processes of modernity. Womanism, however, is marked by a profound intersectionality that addresses not only race, gender, class, and sexuality but also joins these in an integral way with spirituality/religion as a vital element in the lives of women of color. As Layli Phillips writes, "Black women and other women of color are generally not afraid of or skeptical about spirituality. . . . In this light, [they] are emblematic of the majority of humans, for whom a relationship with the spiritual world is actual, palpable, meaningful and valued. Black women and other women of color also recognize the political implications of this spiritual relationship in ways that few more academically or ideologically inclined perspectives do."[4]

In the plainest sense, *mysticism* can be understood as unmediated, intimate encounter with the sacred. In the context of religions and cultures of the Afro-Atlantic diaspora, I use the term to refer to a variety of practices that emphasize attention to the presence of spirit. Simplistically seen sometimes as "superstitious," or worse, as "demonic," the attention to dreams and visions, interpretation of signs, embodiment of spiritual presence/"possession," transformative prayer and singing, divination, sacred dance, healing and cleansing rites, communication with ancestors, communion with nature, ritual retreat or cloistering, and *obrigação* (ritual initiation) are all mystic elements that have historically been found to greater or lesser degree in the religious life of Black communities throughout the diaspora. These are also elements that Black women activists in Brazil and the United Sates have utilized in their efforts to build and sustain, defend and transform communities under great duress, and to organize collective resistance to a range of structural injustices.

"Mothering," as understood by womanist scholars such as Phillips, Delores Williams, and Cheryl Townsend Gilkes, is a concept that includes the biological birthing process but extends to encompass the generation of ideas and solutions to family and community problems as well. Mothers are also those who provide spiritual guidance and divination, eldering and mentoring of younger people, and who create *kitchen table* spaces for conversation and collective discernment, women-centered spaces of hospitality and inclusion. Women who embody these roles are often identified as mothers in Afro-Atlantic religious and community contexts whether or not they have birthed children from their own bodies.

For this essay, I've identified four examples—three from the U.S. and two from Brazil—that demonstrate some of the ways in which Black women in both societies make use of mystic means and mothering strategies in the context of social justice work. The women profiled here make explicit connections between their activism and the ways they connect with Spirit—whether understood as ancestors, Orixás/Nkisis/Voduns, Caboclos,[5] or God, for help and guidance. Again, although such connections are not unusual in the world, they have not begun to be explored by scholars with the fullness and sincerity they deserve.

EXAMPLE I: THE COURAGE SONGS

Scholar, musician, and former SNCC activist Bernice Johnson Reagon writes about the transformative power of African American religious music—in particular the sacred songs of the Black church that became anthems of protest and instruments of audacity in the midst of the southern freedom movement. In an interview in 1997, Reagon discusses how she and fellow SNCC workers and other community members in Albany, Georgia, in the early 1960s used African American congregational singing to alter the energy in mass meetings or on demonstration lines such that people who might realistically be fearful for their lives would instead gather the confidence to face violence (and sometimes to move would-be attackers to a less offensive position). The experience of Episcopalian public theologian Ruby Sales, who is also a former SNCC activist, highlights one of the ways in which African American sacred singing is understood to embody and enable connections to ancestral tenacities in the face of hardship and injustice.

In 1963, in Haynesville, Alabama, Ruby and three colleagues (two white men and another Black woman) approached a gas station to buy sodas after protesting at a segregated swimming pool with a group of young movement volunteers. Ruby was first to reach the door of the establishment and was met there by the armed white owner of the station who immediately cursed her and threatened to kill her. Within seconds, Ruby's friend, Jonathan Daniels, an Episcopalian seminarian, pushed Ruby out of the way of the loaded gun and in almost the same instant, the station owner opened fire and killed Jonathan instead of Ruby. In the months that followed, Ruby received threats that she too would be killed if she testified against the murderer. In her interview with the Veterans of Hope Project in 1998, Ruby explained that she was able to conquer her fear of testifying by singing the sacred music that had been created by her enslaved ancestors and taught to her by her grandmother—spirituals. Songs like *How Did You Feel When You Come Out the Wilderness?*, *Couldn't Hear Nobody Pray*, and *We've Come This Far by Faith*. Ruby said that even before this particular tragedy, when she was learning the songs at her grandmother's side, she experienced the eliding minor tones of the music as links to the suffering and the strength of people who had come before her. And in her own distress, the young activist instinctively called up the music that she associated with the moral and spiritual courage of her community. Ruby says that as she sang the songs, she felt her ancestors rising in her voice, accompanying and encouraging her. Ultimately, she was able to get up on the courtroom stand and tell her story.

Even today, as she continues her activism through the Spirit House Project and investigations of state-sponsored violence against Black men, women, and children, Ruby sings the old songs for strength. And when she sings, "I don't just sing it in my voice. There is a rattle in my throat as deep and old as my grandmother's voice. It connects me. It allows me to move from one historical period to the next and to really get to the souls of where Black people were. It is in that moment, through song, that I am able to feel something other than myself. I become part of a community. I become part of a struggle."[6] This use of African American sacred sound to induce courage, and the ancestral connection that Ruby Sales infers from the singing, are examples of the way a mystic sensibility functions among many of the southern Black women who were active in the freedom movement.

EXAMPLE 2: THE ANCESTRAL CALL

Ruby Sales's impulse to action, via the songs of her ancestors, is echoed in the experience of another activist for Black people's human rights, Valdina Pinto. Valdina Oliveira Pinto, who passed in 2019, was a Makota, a ritual elder in the Angola tradition of Candomblé who assists the terreiro leader and is responsible for training new initiates, caring for incorporated *nkisis*, and offering instruction to the religious community as a whole. She was one of the best known and most widely respected environmental justice advocates in Bahia, and her activist work was firmly grounded in her experience as a devotee of Candomblé. In her memoir, *Meu Caminhar, Meu Viver*, Makota Valdina wrote about an experience she had in the early 1970s at a *mukondo*—a Candomblé funeral ceremony. At the time, Valdina was a primary school teacher and a catechist in the Catholic church where, due to her growing awareness of racial justice issues, she was beginning to question the demonization of Afro-Brazilian religions by Catholicism. At the funeral rite, she watched from outside the circle of participants, as she was not at the time initiated in Candomblé, and she recalls that it was an odd and uncomfortable feeling for her, standing as a mere witness to this striking moment, a ceremony of remembrance of the African origins of the person who had recently passed. Valdina remembers hearing the voices of her grandmother and great-grandmother—not so much as distinct sounds in her ear, more like a sensation of knowing, still with great clarity and directness. She says her ancestors were asking her why she was standing on the outside, telling her that she needed to be part of the ceremonial circle. Valdina writes, "It was as if I was surrounded by all of my relatives who had passed on, even those I hadn't known, and even ones who were not Candomblé devotees. I think that's the best way to explain what happened to me in that ritual—the ritual which, I think, is the most profound in Candomblé." This event marked the activist in a very significant way, and it was at that moment, she explains, that she determined to leave the Catholic church *and* to work for the respect and human rights of Afro-Brazilian people from within the tradition of Candomblé.

EXAMPLE 3: DREAMING STRENGTH AND GUIDANCE

Dreams and signs are a very common, but again infrequently discussed, mystic resource in the lives of activist African American women. Although these aspects of Black spirituality are not usually disparaged by institutional religion, Yvonne Chireau notes that the historiographic emphasis of scholars on the Black church, as such, has often obscured the many examples of African American affinity for mystic and supernatural understandings of the world.[7]

When her fourteen-year-old son was brutally murdered in Money, Mississippi, in 1955 for saying "Bye baby" to a white woman as he walked out of a general store, Mamie Till-Mobley was undone. Compounding her grief was the horror of the way her child had been maimed as his life was taken, his body so horribly mangled that the only way she could positively identify him for the coroner was by a school ring. For a generation of African Americans who were children and teens in the fifties, the image of Emmett Till, lying in an open casket, his face barely human from the ravages of his mutilations, was a watershed moment in their lives (similar to the way the murders of Trayvon Martin, Sandra Bland, George Floyd, and Breonna Taylor, et al. have settled into the bones of more recent generations). Despite pressure from white Mississippians who urged her to bury Emmett in the state where he died and avoid additional public scrutiny, Mrs. Till-Mobley decided to bring her son's body back to Chicago and hold an open-casket funeral, "so that all the world could see what they did to my boy." Till-Mobley said that in determining what course to take, she first discussed her decision with her mother. Then, she said, she had a dream that convinced her of the rightness of her choice—it confirmed for her that she was capable of going through the trauma of a public funeral for her son, and that this activist gesture was a good and needed thing to do.

Till-Mobley is in a long line of Black women who have taken guidance and encouragement from dreams and visions in the service of justice and human rights. One of the most striking examples of this approach to wisdom comes from the experience of Harriet Tubman, perhaps the best known of the conductors of the Underground Railroad—that network of women and men who risked their lives to help enslaved people make their way to freedom in the nineteenth century. Harriet is recognized as having freed hundreds of people and served during the Civil War as a spy, a scout, and a leader of the raid on Combahee Ferry in South Carolina where Union forces liberated an additional 700 African Americans. In telling her story to writer Sarah Bradford, Harriet said very little if anything about her relationship to formal structures of church during her childhood, but was very conscious of what she described as a family legacy of spiritual gifts that included her father's ability to foretell the future and her own capacity to access unmediated divine guidance for the well-being of her passengers and for her own strength and perception as she navigated woods and rivers, towns and backcountry roads, leading people out of slavery.

Tubman had received a head injury as a child, and she was said to have suffered from frequent fits of somnolence or "sleeping spells" as a result, for the rest of her life. Often her uncanny foresight and discernment came to Harriet in the midst of the "spells," at other times they came via dreams in sleep, in waking visions, and in what she described as miraculous answers to prayer. Biographer Jean Humez writes that there are many stories of Harriet avoiding capture while she was rescuing enslaved people, which Tubman attributed to God answering her pleadings. Humez writes, *"God was Tubman's name for the source of visionary guidance for her antislavery action. Prayer enabled her to tap directly into the source of such guidance."*[8] For Harriet, the successes of her activism on behalf of her people, her bravery in the face of overarching odds, are to be understood in terms of her intimate communications with spirit and the aid that came as a result of prayer.

EXAMPLE 4: THE CORN BLESSINGS

Another example of the combined uses of mystic and mothering sensibilities as resources for community activism comes from the Terreiro do Cobre in Salvador. Late one night, in August 2006, loud gunfire sounded just outside the ritual community's walls, and soon people were heard running along the narrow, maze-like alley descending from the side of the terreiro into the heart of the urban neighborhood where the Candomblé temple is located. Two young men had been killed and two young women wounded. The community was in shock. Crack cocaine and other drugs were a growing problem, compounded by persistent structural unemployment and a tradition of vicious state-sponsored anti-Black violence in one of the largest cities in Brazil. Although the violence of the city had not reached the notorious proportions of Rio de Janeiro, there was tremendous fear and anxiety about what the murders, practically at the doorstep of the temple, meant for the tight-knit working-class Afro-Brazilian community.

The *iyalorixá*[9] of the Terreiro do Cobre, Mãe Val, had been organizing in the neighborhood for more than a decade—sponsoring literacy and citizenship education classes, and arranging training projects in traditional folk arts, hoping to steer the many young people who had dropped out of school to finish their educations and develop skills that would enable them to make a living. Her own teenage son had been killed a few years prior in similar violence in another city. From her position as an activist, a religious leader, and a community mother, Mãe Val consulted with the *orixás* and *caboclos* of the temple and determined that in addition to increased demands for employment and quality education for the neighborhood's youth, there were rituals of cleansing and healing that needed to be done for the community as a whole.

The following year, on a Friday (the day of the week consecrated to *Oxalá*, the orixá of peace) close to the anniversary of the murders, Mãe Val gathered her initiates, members of other Afro-Brazilian religious temples in the vicinity, as well as any community members who wanted to participate—and with donations of white corn and borrowed heavy-gauge extra-large steel pots, the *iyalorixá* and other women prepared large quantities of unsalted, boiled white corn kernels. When these were cooked and cooled, the *caboclos* were invited to come and bless the community with their healing energy. They manifested in the bodies of devotees and threw the corn, in a ritual of cleansing, from the roofs of nearby houses, tumbling the sacred food onto the streets below so that the asphalt roads and concrete walkways looked as if they were covered in snow. White corn is a sacred food of *Oxalá* and is often used in rites of purification in Candomblé. The *caboclos* offered the kernels as a head-to-toe ritual bath to anyone who wanted it. The ceremony, held annually now, is an intense moment of reflection, remembrance, and psychological healing for the Candomblé communities and for the larger neighborhood.

CONCLUSION

These examples, across a span of geographies and time, offer a glimpse of the ways in which Black women in the U.S. and Brazil have employed and sustained resources of community, history, ancestry, and spirit in their work for the rights and well-being of their communities. Whether in the case of Palmié's spectral collaborators, the ancestral voices that led Makota Valdina into her work as an activist and ritual leader, or the dreams and prayers that clarified Harriet Tubman's routes to freedom, these alternative modes of making sense of the world have had profound meaning for the peoples who have employed them in their daily lives and collective struggles. Absent a means to engage traditions and understandings of Africana mysticism, academic discourses about the experience of women and men of African descent in the Americas can occlude more than they reveal, obstructing the histories, insights, traumas, and resiliences of those whose ancestral sources of meaning and power represent uncomfortable yet incontrovertible revenants of the making of the New World.

NOTES

1. Stephan Palmié, *Wizards and Scientists: Explorations in Afro-Cuban Modernity and Tradition* (Durham, NC: Duke University Press, 2002).
2. Isabel Cristina Ferreira dos Reis, *Historia de vida familiar e afetiva de escravos na Bahia de século XIX* (Salvador: EDUFBA, 2001), 96.
3. Palmié, *Wizards and Scientists*, 7.
4. Layli Phillips, Introduction to *The Womanist Reader*, ed. Layli Phillips (New York: Routledge, 2006), xxvi, xxxix.
5. Caboclos, spiritual energies representing the original, Amerindian inhabitants of Brazil, are widely understood as capable of great healing work.
6. *Ruby Sales: Standing Against the Wind*. Veterans of Hope Pamphlet Series 1, No. 3 (Denver: Veterans of Hope Project, 2000), 6-7
7. Yvonne Chireau, "The Uses of the Supernatural: Towards a History of Black Women's Magical Practices," in *A Mighty Baptism: Race, Gender and the Creation of American Protestantism*, ed. Susan Juster and Lisa MacFarlane (Ithaca, NY: Cornell University Press, 1996), 177.
8. Jean Humez, "In Search of Harriet Tubman's Spiritual Autobiography," in *This Far by Faith: Readings in African American Women's Religious Biography*, ed. Judith Weisenfeld and Richard Newman (New York: Routledge, 1996).
9. The *iyalorixá* is literally *mother of the orixá*, ritual mother of the Candomblé temple.

9. A Theopoetics of Exodus and the Africana Spirit in Music

SHARON KIMBERLY WILLIAMS

RHYTHM OF BREATH: AN EXODUS POETICS OF BECOMING

All throughout the African Diaspora
the Spirit is manifest
as an exodus of human souls
dispersed the world around
with a common purpose
carrying a certain rhythm
in the souls of the people
A uniquely syncopated African breath that is
simultaneously
individual and collective
African, Caribbean, African-American, Latino and Latina
An exodus rhythm of
dislocation, displacement, dispersal, exile
sometimes erasure—not often return—
a syncopated cycle
of breath for the African Diaspora
What happens when the rhythm is disrupted?
Keeping in time with the rhythm
of exodus is essential breath
for an African Diaspora whose
survival depends on
keeping faith

with this rhythm
which dictates the
movement of a people
through a wilderness toward *becoming*
more divine after
being dehumanized
We keep with the rhythm lest the cycle stop!
Wisdom chooses to keep time
with the rhythm of this world order
which was predestined by the colonizers
when they decided
who will be "the first" and
who will be "the last"
For black bodies, for "the last,"
who refuse to be dislocated
the cycle stops at erasure
What does this movement reveal?
what revelation does it conceal?
Could we ever divine its divine purpose?
Perhaps it is the colossal dislocation
of the African Diaspora
that is in due time to create
a sustained, stabilizing
rhythm for all of humanity
But at what cost?
But at what cost?

BLACK SUFFERING AND THE CREATION OF SOUND IN THE MIDDLE PASSAGE

> The images of ships in motion across the spaces between Europe, America, Africa, and the Caribbean—a living micro-cultural, micro-political system in motion—focus attention on the Middle Passage, on the various projects for redemptive return to an African homeland.
>
> PAUL GILROY, *The Black Atlantic*

Imagine if Spirit in the African Diaspora could be interpreted as a manifestation of one exodus journey measured across generations through the continuum of time by African ancestors. Human spirits connected by the memory of the singular experience of crossing the Atlantic. Human spirits dislocated and dispersed around the world with a particular purpose. Human spirits interconnected by one syncopated world rhythm. This is the enchanted rhythm of the African Diaspora that is created by the movement of its people. Like the Spirit that animates, the rhythm of an exodus represents the many movements of diasporic life—dislocation, displacement, dispersal, exile, erasure (not often return)—which all become more rhythmic when these cycles are systematized. It is this exodus rhythm of movement that represents the Spirit of the Diaspora in foreign lands far beyond the shores of the African continent. Exodus movement allows the African Diaspora to animate itself as Spirit for the sake of its own survival and the survival of the world.

But the ends do not always justify the means. What did the slave owners conceal as they manipulated the King James Bible to justify the unjustifiable crimes against humanity and God? Their actions cannot simply be explained away as a "necessary evil." To fully understand the purpose of African migration that forced black bodies into chattel slavery one must be willing to imagine the meaning of exodus movement in divine terms.

It is this exodus narrative that moves the African Diaspora from an offbeat rhythm of despair to a soaring song of hope bound together by one transcendent, ancestral spirit. The Hebrew text begins with a genealogical introduction of names: *we'elleh shəmōṯ* or וְאֵלֶּה שְׁמוֹת ("these are the names"). The title "exodus" is an English translation of the ancient Greek word ἔξοδος, which means "departure" or "going out." The rhythmic kinship list of names signaled by the Hebrew text converges with the motif of departure that the story has come to represent. One could imagine the African Diaspora as an exodus movement of the *Spirit* of a people that needed to "depart" or "go out," away from its homeland. The slippage from the rhythms of names to the grand departure is not lost in Africana poetics; instead, the slippage and erasure are summoned into recognizing that forced African migration was primarily driven by the economic desire for mass commodification of black bodies for advancing the transatlantic slave trade.

The 1619 maiden voyage from West Africa through the Middle Passage to Virginia is a symbolic marker of the birth of American capitalism with the haunted image of slave ships that carried black bodies as human cargo.

This concept continues throughout the development of American culture and evolves into the rise of the commodification of black bodies in popular music. It is with the creation of *The Spirituals* that the legacy of exploiting black bodies as part of popular music culture first begins in America and is then shared around the world. On its own exodus journey, it is the spirit of black music that "departs" or "goes out" from the homeland to make its maiden voyage around the world.

The Africana spirit in music is an exodus movement of the sound of a people that "departs" or "goes out" and reflects black suffering as lament in the soul and spirit of a people. The people of the African Diaspora cannot be separated from the ancestral sounds created in the hulls of those haunted slave ships. The cries of the ancestors, as they were being ripped from their native lands, were not met with compassion but with the whip and the socioeconomic justification that the ends would ultimately justify the means. Slaves were not even the owners of their own sorrows. In the legacy of *The Spirituals*, even their laments were stolen and commodified as their heritage songs were sold as popular music for the benefit of whites. As we learn from W. E. B. Du Bois, one must remember that when it comes to black music, the commodification of black sound is the very commodification of the souls of black folks. Furthermore, as Paul Gilroy has argued,

> Successive generations of black intellectuals had their rhizomorphic systems of propagation anchored in a continued proximity to the unspeakable terrors of the slave experience.[1]

It is from the terror chamber of the Middle Passage where one can dare to imagine the African Diaspora as a manifestation of an exodus journey of human spirits. Human spirits dressed in black bodies and relegated to the status of *The Other*—dispersed around the world for the socioeconomic purpose of being consumed by the insatiable appetite of the empire. In *Get Out*, the 2017 Academy Award–winning feature film by Jordan Peele, the issues of race and horror are addressed through satire. This screenplay depicts psychological domination as a tool that subjugates the black psyche to a fictional, unconscious state of being known as "the Sunken Place." Once the human spirit is relegated to the Sunken Place, their disembodied black flesh is then sold to whites at an auction so the new owners can transfer themselves into experiencing the world through the eyes of blackness. What is most compelling about this film is that it demonstrates how the commodification of black bodies begins with the control of the mind and the dislocation of the spirit. It is time for the people of the Black Atlantic to, in the words of Bob Marley, "Emancipate yourself from mental slavery. None but ourselves can free our minds." What we learn from this film is that the exodus narrative of spirit in the African Diaspora, the "departure" or "going out" of human spirits in this horrific, hypnotic state of the Sunken Place is parallel to survival in the Middle Passage. In both instances it is rhythm, movement, and sound that hold the spirit captive inside the body or sets it free.

In the Middle Passage, black sacred sound in the form of lament echoes from the ocean's floor and cries out to the heavens seeking its source beyond the cosmos. It is a sound that began in the slave ships. A sound that is cut in half by hope and horror. The womb of the Black Atlantic beats like a drum whose sound echoes against the sunken places of the unknown. What drowns and what floats is the difference between fantasy and reality—afrofuturism and afropessimism—the balance between hope and skepticism. What one believes about the fate of the descendants of the African Diaspora is a delicate question that must be tempered and balanced. For most, the debate between afrofuturism and afropessimism serves to balance hope and skepticism, but the people on this exodus journey want to find their way back to humanity. After enduring the realities of the horrors of slavery, the people of the African Diaspora were left in varying states of trauma. Thus, pessimism in the Africana context can be understood as a term that grounds one in the reality of the depths of the problems facing the Africana world so that the work of liberation and systematic change can be strategically executed over time. The balancing act of maintaining both hope and pessimism simultaneously also has a rhythm that keeps time with the political strivings of societal wants and desires. The real hope is in the Africana world's ability to transcend the realities of pessimism with hope for a better future. This exodus journey will connect current generations to this past reality with three central concepts that are expressed through *The Spirituals* and Psalms: (1) "Go Down, Moses!," (2) "Lord, How Come Me Here?," and (3) "How Can We Sing in a Strange Land?"

GO DOWN, MOSES!

When Israel was in Egypt's land,
Let my people go!
Oppressed so hard they could not stand,
Let my people go!
Go down, Moses,
Way down in Egypt's land.
Tell old Pharaoh,
Let my people go!

Negro Spiritual

Then the LORD said unto Moses, "Go in unto Pharaoh, and tell him, Thus saith the LORD God of the Hebrews, Let my people go, that they may serve me."

Exodus 8:1

Music and its rituals can be used to create a model whereby identity can be understood neither as a fixed essence nor as a vague and utterly contingent construction to be reinvented by the will and whim of aesthetes, symbolists, and language gamers.

PAUL GILROY, *Black Atlantic*

In this spiritual, Egypt can be likened to the Sunken Place where the Pharaoh's empire systematically holds the Israelites in a psychological form of bondage that suppresses them to the margins of society. The spiritual commands Moses to go "Way Down" to a faraway location to reach God's people. This is just how far the psychological oppression of the people of the African Diaspora has gone in this horror narrative that began with the Middle Passage and ended in exile. Way down to the Sunken Place in the recesses of their mind. This is the place where Spirit survived the terror of the reality of chattel slavery. The balance between hope and pessimism in the struggle for liberation engages in the fantasy that songs of liberation facilitate the transcendence of the Spirit from the Sunken Place of the unconscious being that clings for survival. In the "Way Down" spaces of the margins of the Sunken Place, one finds altered realities that steal the souls to possess black bodies believed to be in fashion and so that they can be commodified in new ways. This spiritual commands and demands before God that the people need a liberator to deliver them from the hypnotic state of race inferiority for the sake of superiority.

The line "Let My People Go!" reminds us that the Africana Spirit has been trying to escape the Sunken Place for over 400 years. Like the film's title, the people have been trying to "get out" of the place where they have been trapped, which is why the exodus of the Africana Spirit is measured on a continuum through time and generations. The question becomes, "Where are we now?" And the witness of the ancestors becomes the best tool for understanding. Time kept against the infinite for the purpose of escaping the inescapable systematic oppressions of an empire that controls with psychological tools that break spirits and fracture black psyches for the purpose of safeguarding power from *The Other*. Oppressed so hard they could not take a stand for justice, so they needed Moses to deliver them from the hypnotic place that justifies the kind of evil, which predetermines who gets to be rich and who gets to be poor, who gets to be slave and who gets to be free. This is our story, this is our song!

A Moses emerges for the community to deliver the command of God for Pharaoh to "Let My People Go!" so that they might serve God, not empire. Does God understand the suffering of the people trapped in sunken places? "Go Down, Moses! Let My People Go" is a direct, prophetic call that challenges empire and commands release of the black human psyche that holds black bodies in bondage by controlling the mind and disembodying the spirit. This Spiritual is a prophetic wake-up call that names both the oppression and the oppressor, Pharaoh. Being held in physical and psychological bondage indefinitely is likened to the science fiction aspects of the Sunken Place as the image of the free-falling soul spiraling through time haunts us. The film emphasizes the fact that the first step before the body is taken and completely dominated is to conquer the mind; this serves as a sobering reminder that psychological tools are often used to oppress large groups of people. *The Spiritual*, "Go Down, Moses!" emphasizes the fact that Moses, the deliverer, will have to fight the powerful infrastructure of the empire and go to great depth to release the spirit of his people from bondage. Like transcendence in the paradoxical understanding of afropessimism, the hope for the African Diaspora lies in its ability to balance reality and skepticism with liberation of both the spirit and the mind.

> Spirit of Truth keep a song in our hearts,
> That lets justice prevail in our spirits as we remain,
> Until the revelation of hope is unveiled,
> Strengthen us in our middle state,
> From a perilous passage through a cramped middle space,
> That hosts humans layered in its haunted hull,
> Where future lynched spirits enter the gateway,
> And land in the home of the free to remain ever chained,
> To a backward system of justice,
> That hangs in the balance of the sacred middle space,
> Where only Spirit sings.

Who are the people of the African Diaspora within the larger continuum of human suffering? Are we not God's children even in our suffering? At these moments of injustice, are we not most like God? What does it mean to be a black child of God within the context of suffering? For the descendants of the African Diaspora who have suffered disproportionately, to be black is to be like the quality of dissonance in music—ever creating tension and clashing against the consonances of conventionalism and established societal and cultural norms. African Americans have created music within this same dichotomy—against all the established norms of the dominant culture within the sociopolitical sacred space of oppressed groups—"Way Down" on the margins of society.

So how does one locate the voice of God in the suffering of the people of the African Diaspora? Perhaps one could imagine the African ancestors crossing the Atlantic during the Middle Passage as a way of examining the voice and the sound quality of lament as a primal, soul response to black suffering. Voices commanding and demanding remain ingrained within the human stain of slavery—the soul laments, "Where is God?" Deafened by the silence of God, the voice of the soul rises out of the slave ship hull and sustains, crescendoing through time and space—identifying itself as the voice of God—as a co-companion of the people on the journey into the unknown—as the One giving voice to the voiceless. We are still one with that ancestral lament that was started in the Middle Passage—the original sacred space of the margins.

HOW CAN WE SING IN A STRANGE LAND?

By the rivers of Babylon, there we sat down, yea, we wept, when we remembered Zion.
> We hung our harps upon the willows in the midst thereof.
> For there they that carried us away captive required of us a song;
> and they that wasted us required of us mirth, saying, Sing us one of the songs of Zion.
> How shall we sing the LORD's song in a strange land?
Psalm 137:1-4 (NRSV).

The struggle against the commodity form has been taken over in the very configuration that black mass cultural creation assumes.
PAUL GILROY, Black Atlantic

How can we sing when we're in a strange land? A land where black bodies are commodified, disposed of, possessed, and overconsumed to feed the insatiable appetites of a dominant culture that wants to consume African American culture simply because it is fashionable to do so. How do we sing when we are paralyzed and in the Sunken Place? That is, psychologically paralyzed and left to die when black bodies often cannot breathe let alone sing! How does one sing in this condition? In crossing the Atlantic during the slave trade—rather than coming to a strange land, some captured Africans chose to drown. Like Pharaoh's army in the Red Sea—sinking instead of singing—those were the only options. To sink into the deep meant that the spirit would never know bondage or exile. The spirit never descending beyond the ocean's floor, it is this control of singing that demonstrates how the people of the African Diaspora consciously chose to live or not live in a sunken place carved out for them. For people in exile choosing to sing or not sing can be likened to negotiating the very terms of life or death: To live or die. To sing or not to sing? That is the existential question to be asked in the Sunken Place known as exile. I sing, therefore I am? Not exactly. But the ability or decision to sing in the face of suffering does denote something unique about the spirit of the people of the African Diaspora.

How does the African Diaspora raise its voice in praise when there is only lament? Can the difference in praise and lament be viewed through the lenses of hope and pessimism? In this sunken state the voice is present but not audible. It is the strange land of the Sunken Place where black bodies and minds have been dislocated from their native land and their voice. How can the people be anything but paralyzed and silenced in this state of being? When the conditions in the new land are too strange, the community cannot sing. Like the Israelites of this Psalm, "We wept when we remembered our native land." Dislocated and in exile, how do we sing when we only want to weep? It is a strange thing to ask a person in exile to sing. Singing while dislocated and moving from a place of abandonment and forsakenness. These are not normal conditions for singing. One might ask, how can we sing when we are in the Sunken Place? Yet this is exactly the place where the people of the African Diaspora begin their Exodus Song from the Middle Passage to the unknown. This state of pessimism—in its authenticity—allows the Spirit to transcend and also gives the world the gift of *The Spirituals*. Thus, in their suffering and their lowest state of being, the slaves resisted the strange land paradigm of their minds and allowed their spirits to transcend their circumstances, thus birthing *The Spirituals*. When the people of the African Diaspora began to sing in the "strange land" condition of exile, they created something out of the nothingness of their despair.

> How can we sing, African ancestors?
> Sacred spirits of the sea,
> Once chained in bondage,
> On an exodus journey,
> To the "strange land" of the free,
> Black holocaust victims of history's violent voyage,
> On unchartered waters journeying into the unknown,
> Searching for Spirit's holding place,
> In the balance of the middle space,
> Somewhere between death and life,
> Spirit rests beyond trauma of survival.

The sacred spaces change from generation to generation. Yet the Spirit of the lament remains the same. Eternal soul sounds that mark time with a mystic message from the Middle Passage sent to the future generations that the captured Africans in route to the Caribbean and the Americas—not even their descendants—would ever return home to their native land. African ancestral sound as familiar as a forgotten, fragmented refrain—like a distant memory of déjà vu—that wonders all the while, "Has my soul been here before?" The message urges future generations to continue to sing even while in a strange land.

African American music suggests something about where God is or isn't. Whether it's the hull of a slave ship, a plantation, or a ghetto, all African American original art forms—the spirituals, blues, jazz, rhythm and blues, soul, rap, and hip-hop—were born out of suffering and created within the time/space paradigm of the margins. It is within the creation of this sound quality characterized as soul that God can be seen as suffering with black musical bodies. But African American music is not just an expression of suffering. Our music has theological significance. Not only has music been our compass—our own Bible long before the King James version—music has also been the theological, cosmological, mystical, and spiritual source that connects the people of the African Diaspora to the divine.

From the depths of their wounded voices and their strong desire to escape slavery, the African ancestors first learned to defy, resist, and protest with the creation of *The Spirituals*. As examples of divine/human co-created works that demonstrate the interconnectedness of the human spirit with the Spirit of God and the relational context of suffering and creativity, *The Spirituals* are sacred texts originated by the people of the African Diaspora and co-created with God to express the spiritual pain of feeling abandoned by God. Present in the conditions of suffering that give rise to creativity we find *The Spirituals*. These sacred works compose an exodus narrative that chronicles the movement of Spirit throughout the African Diaspora over time, space, and eternity.

LORD, HOW COME ME HERE?

> Lord, how come me here?
> Lord, how come me here?
> Lord, how come me here?
> I wish I never was born
> There ain't no freedom here, Lord

There ain't no freedom here, Lord
There ain't no freedom here, Lord
I wish I never was born
They treat me so mean here, Lord
They treat me so mean here, Lord
They treat me so mean here, Lord
I wish I never was born
They sold my chillen away, Lord
They sold my chillen away, Lord
They sold my chillen away, Lord
I wish I never was born
Lord, how come me here?
Lord, how come me here?
I wish I never was born
I wish I never was born
I wish I never was born

Negro Spiritual

And the children of Israel said unto them, "Would to God we had died by the hand of the Lord in the land of Egypt, when we sat by the flesh pots, and when we did eat bread to the full; for ye have brought us forth into this wilderness."

Exodus 16:3

The lyric "Lord, How Come Me Here . . . I Wish I Never Was Born" interpreted inside the exodus wilderness narrative becomes a test for the hope and resilience of the human spirit. The existential question of being born just to suffer in a wilderness experience of exile offers a direct challenge for the people to hold Yahweh accountable for the conditions of the community. "Lord, How Come Me Here?" demands an answer from the creator for the unjust suffering of the people. For the people of the African Diaspora who suffer the horrors of racism the question to Yahweh becomes: Why would you create us to exist in this sunken state of being? Whether one frames the question from the point of view of afropessimism or not, the line of accountability must begin to be determined for the Africana world. If this spiritual of lament ends with "I wish I never was born," then God has an obligation to respond to the community about their suffering and to demonstrate justice and/or mercy. Why would Yahweh create us to be brought into the horrors of the Sunken Place—created to exist in an alternate reality—never to be fully actualized? Existence in the modality of afropessimism—much like the Sunken Place—puts the realism of the depths of transgenerational trauma into perspective for the African Diaspora. The memory of the forgotten that haunts future generations from the past makes it hard to stay in balance with hope. Pessimism as a response to the idea of being born that questions the motives of the creator is extreme to say the least. Yet it is in this place of authenticity that the honest assessment of the horror and terror of the existence transcends the spirit from the wilderness.

> The spiritual commentary on black suffering and its profane equivalent, the condition of being in pain, are of course sharply divided by the line that separates those who look for redemption to take place in this world and those who are content to anticipate its effects in the next.[2]

If you truly want to know the people of the African Diaspora, listen to their spiritual songs and you will know most everything there is to know about their exodus experience from Africa to the Caribbean to the Americas. There is an old African proverb that states, "The Spirit will not descend without song." One might ask why it is important for the Spirit to descend in the African Diaspora. Perhaps it's because grappling with suffering erases the black body and the black voice. Thus, the Spirit must descend so that the African Diaspora might sustain our voices to create new songs so that the Spirit will continue to descend into infinity for all generations.

These songs were born through the spiritual pain and forced labor from black bodies who—along with God—produced and introduced these songs as an alternative worldview—the Africana world's prophetic Good News that revealed the hidden truth about the stolen legacy of a people. Where would the people of the African Diaspora be without *The Spirituals*? Born out of trauma and baptized survivors, displaced black bodies possessing the ancestral spirit from the Middle Passage raised their voices in song to disrupt the patterns of genocide, and their souls survived.

The Africana Spirit in music is a revolutionary concept. As Spirit of truth and liberation, it serves as a disrupter to every form of racism, classism, sexism, oppression, and domination facing the Africana world. The oppressive sociopolitical and economic systems dominating the people of the African Diaspora need the kind of Spirit that can disrupt injustice and dispense justice. The African philosophy of Ubuntu teaches us to pass on the oral tradition of the sacred songs—as sacred texts—so they may continue as a living word with the transformative power to change the world as liberating forces for the times. This is why we must continue to identify the Africana spirit in music and culture.

CONCLUSION: LAMENT AIN'T NOTHING BUT THE SOUL ANSWERING AS GOD

(SPEAK LORD!) MAYBE GOD IS TRYIN' TO TELL YOU SOMETHIN'

> Yes,
> Yes,
> Yes,
> Yes, Lord!
> Oh oh,
> My soul, my soul says yes,
> Yes, Lord!
> If I were you I would say yes.
> Speak Lord, speak to me.
> Speak Lord!
> Speak to me,
> Oh, speak Lord!
> Want you speak to me,
> I was so blind,
> I was so lost,
> Until You spoke to me.
> Oh speak Lord,
> Speak Lord,
> And hear my mind,
> Oh with Your word,
> And in my soul,
> Oh speak Lord!
> Speak to me,
> Speak my Lord!

Yeah speak to me
Ooh oh,
I love you Lord,
Save my soul.

The Color Purple

Biblically, lament is a transition, like the Exodus, a tempted environment of murmuring and distrust, or a joyful anticipation of the Promised Land.

BRUCE WALTKE, *The Psalms as Christian Lament: A Historical Commentary*[3]

In the Spirit of Africana music is the relationship between liberation and lament. By giving voice to suffering as lament, God has a way to bear witness to our suffering. In the weeping and wailing of the soul—in its melancholy sound that dares to question injustices allowed by God—liberation can be found. This is how lament is likened to the soul answering as God. As the soul's liberating response to injustice, suffering is voiced through lament in the creation of sound. Lament connects us back to our ancestral memories through the creation of sound, which liberates us from oppression. And as long as lament helps the descendants of the African Diaspora to remember their Motherland while on their exodus journey, the Spirit will continue to descend and the people will live on to sing a new song in their strange land. Afrofuturism, fantasy, and hope that springs from transcendence will help the African Diaspora to "get out" of the Sunken Place because only then can the Spirit engage in the work of liberation despite an often afropessimistic worldview that can dislocate the African Diaspora from God.

NOTES

1. Paul Gilroy, *The Black Atlantic: Modernity and Double-Consciousness* (Cambridge, MA: Harvard University Press, 1993), 73.
2. Gilroy, *The Black Atlantic*, 211.
3. Bruce K. Waltke, James M. Houston, and Erika Moore, *The Psalms as Christian Lament: A Historical Commentary* (Grand Rapids, MI: Eerdmans, 2014), 4.

10. Must We Burn Isaac? A Four-Part Hermeneutical Fantasy for Africana Epistemology

MINENHLE NOMALUNGELO KHUMALO

PART I: AN OPPOSITIONAL AFRICANA HERMENEUTIC

As this essay has developed, I have been consistently compelled by Itumeleng Mosala's insistence that Black biblical hermeneutics needs to commit to epistemological starting points that reflect and recognize the sociopolitical locations of Black peoples.[1] Yet this starting point, in the theoretical framings of my approach to reading the biblical account of Hagar and Ishmael, has undergone multiple shifts. An initial commitment to Afrofuturism morphed into a messy defiance of archivism before landing in the oppositional hermeneutic I take on now.[2] Following the insights of bell hooks and TreAndrea W. Russworm, this essay offers a reading of the Hagar-Ishmael story through an *oppositional gaze* and *burning* desire for livable life of my South African, queer, immigrant, Black, female perspective. Thus, the Africana nature of this essay means that the epistemic pursuits of this work do not have the privilege of staying in place. Like Hagar and Ishmael, my reading of the Genesis text moves back and forth—between the known and unknown; between the possible and impossible; between the seen and unseen; between the heard and unheard; between past, present, and future; and between questions of resistance and of recognition. Still, what emerges commits to Black interpretive agency in a manner that prioritizes a narratological observation and exploration of the nonlinear arrangements and (con)figurations of Black existence over and against any excavations of "biblical truth."

"There is a power in looking."[3] In her essay, "The Oppositional Gaze: Black Female Spectators," bell hooks highlights the ways in which "the gaze" is often politicized in the lives of Black people.[4] Citing the example of the murder of Emmett Till, hooks notes that in the history of the racialized power dynamics of the United States, Black people have been "denied their right to gaze," and thus the act of looking, for the Black person, can be dangerous.[5] In relation to this, one might add to hooks's observation that Till's open-casket funeral also invokes the powers of looking in opposition to the violent suppression of the Black gaze. Indeed, in hooks's words, "Attempts to repress our Black people's right to gaze had produced in us an overwhelming longing to look, a rebellious desire, an oppositional gaze. By courageously looking, we defiantly declared, 'Not only will I stare. I want my look to change reality.'"[6] Additionally, hooks observes that the act of looking is also politicized by gender and points to "the white supremacist structure that murdered Emmett Till after interpreting his gaze of a white woman as an act of power and control of a white female body." Emmett Till's gaze is experienced by a white mob as the power of a Black male over a white female body.[7] Then hooks focuses the remainder of her essay on exploring and developing the idea(s) of Black female spectatorship of film. From hooks's discussion of Black female spectatorship, what has been most helpful to the work of this essay are the following two claims:

1. "Critical black female spectatorship emerges as a site of resistance only when individual black women actively resist the imposition of dominant ways of knowing and looking."[8]
2. "We do more than resist. We create alternative texts that are not solely reactions. As critical spectators, black women participate in a broad range of looking relations, contest, resist, revision, interrogate, and invent on multiple levels."[9]

In relation to the above, I would also add that "the gaze," as hooks identifies it, has an aural counterpart. To return to the example of the murder of Emmett Till, what motivates the fatal attack is not only claims that he was seen looking but also that of what he is allegedly heard saying and/or doing. Thus, my critical spectatorship of the Hagar-Ishmael story gives attention to the powers of looking and hearing in the Genesis text (as well as biblical scholarship). In this regard, listening to Mosala means that the theoretical arrangements of this essay pair the approaches built from hooks's idea of the oppositional gaze with Vincent Wimbush's notion of "reading darkness." Wimbush says, "Centering the study of the Bible upon African Americans would be a defiant intellectual and political act,"[10] which stands in opposition to the dominant trajectories of the academic guilds of biblical scholarship. He asserts that focusing biblical studies on Africana subjects presents a problematization of interpretation. The most pressing of which, according to Wimbush, involves "naming and dramatizing interpretation in relationship to socio-cultural power, indeed, interpretation itself as a form of social power."[11] In the words of Margaret Aymer:[12]

> The epistemological pretexts of biblical studies more often than not reflect the interests of the dominant culture. These pretexts include the presumption that the perspective of the guild-trained biblical scholar, who is often a member of the dominant culture, must be normative. And insofar as the dominant culture is proceeding as those in power believe it should, there is, therefore, no need for the guild-based biblical scholar to question status quo. Thus, readings of the guild are represented as objective, scientific and above all, a-political.

Said another way, the oppositional hermeneutics of this essay is entangled in the Black problematization of the power of interpretation as acts of looking at, hearing of, and speaking about biblical texts. From Wimbush, my engagement with the text is given an awareness of the allocations of "the power to speak and interpret on one's own terms, in one's own voice." With this awareness, I enter a reading of Hagar and Ishmael that moves toward identifying and engaging narrative visions of the sociopolitical construction of livable (Africana) lives.

In addition to its theoretical commitments, this essay moves with an anxious methodological pursuit of a single question, after which this work is titled: "Must we burn Isaac?" On the one hand, the question of burning and (burnt) sacrifice is directly influenced by the textual depictions of the Akedah in Genesis 22. Additionally, to the extent that dominant traditions of reading Genesis, as Katherine Doob Sakenfeld highlights in *Just Wives: Stories of Power and Survival in the Old Testament and Today* (2003), are forgetful of their story and subsequently erosive to recognitions of Hagar and Ishmael in favor of alignments to the status quo, the question "Must we burn Isaac?" is a questioning of dominant culture and the (literary) functions of figural representations of otherness.[13] Yet, on the other hand, it is also influenced by the theoretical work of TreAndrea M. Russworm's *Blackness Is Burning*. According to Russworm, "When blackness burns, it *signifies* phantastically because the representation of African American subjects is overloaded and *overdetermined* by so many things at once. As significations, the stories and images of black identity are inevitably ripe for cooptation, appropriation, and especially *transference*."[14] Russworm highlights the ways in which Africana/Black identity is "shifty" and "open." She asserts that "more than anything, when blackness burns, gesturing meaning multidirectionally, it also alerts us to the black identity's unstable and untenable relationship to the politics of recognition."[15] Here, I am making connections between Hagar-Ishmael and the Black (female) experience. As Nyasha Junior's monograph *Reimagining Hagar: Blackness and Bible* (2019) elaborately details, this is not unique. Delores S. Williams and Renita J. Weems, among many other womanist readers of the Hagar-Ishmael story, bear empathetic recognition of Blackness in the tale of Hagar and Ishmael. In the generative work, *Sisters in the Wilderness*, Williams highlights the "striking similarities" between Hagar's story and the experiences of African American women, claiming a shared heritage from both African and slave histories.[16] In *Just a Sister Away*, Weems notes that "for Black women, Hagar's story is peculiarly familiar. It is as if we know it by heart."[17] Yvonne Sherwood also notes that "the afterlives of Hagar and Ishmael lead us to dark alien spaces."[18] She states, "In Toni Morrison's *Song of Solomon*, and Maya Angelou's 'The Mothering Blackness,' Hagar is invoked as a name replete with cultural meaning—well beyond the biblical story—and it is taken for granted that Hagar is, by definition, black."[19] This assumption is not Morrison's or Angelou's alone. This is an assumption explicitly named by Williams and Weems that is later complicated by the assertions of readings like that of Vanessa Lovelace, where Blackness is allocated the racial identification of both Hagar and Sarah. The assumption of Blackness is also taken up in the biblical scholarship of Rosalyn F. T. Murphy[20] and Renee K. Harrison,[21] who although resisting womanist readings of Hagar read her as a Black woman in relation to another Black woman, Alice Walker's character of Celie. Moreover Dora R. Mbuyawesango, who does not directly name Hagar as Black, reads both Sarah and Hagar in relation to the Black female experience within Shona and Ndebele cultures of Southern Africa.[22] What I mean to point out with this is that, to Russworm's point, although the association of Hagar, and by extension, Ishmael's identity, with Blackness is familiar and common, the nature of the recognition of Blackness is changeable. It operates in trajectories that move in and out of Africa and its diasporas and across multiple space-time contexts. An attunement to Russworm's notion of *burning* is used to acknowledge the very open question of Africana identity. To consider what it means for the Africana subject, like the loaded representation of Hagar and Ishmael to "burns," is to be aware that the meaning and identity of the Africana subject is an open and shifting signification of Blackness, Africanness, and Diaspora. The shifting signification of the Africana subject should generate risky curiosity that imagines what it would mean if the dominant culture, its artifacts, and corresponding re/presentations were to burn instead of Blackness or as recompense for all the things that make Blackness *burn*.

This reading of Genesis is not contingent on a historical, physical Blackness of Hagar and Ishmael, although it is connected to the material realities of Black experience across time and space. Rather, this essay looks at the text as a site of in/sight to a *burning* Blackness. The biblical text is approached with an interrogative observation that is led by the question "Must we burn Isaac?" With this question, I couple the negotiation of the recognition of Blackness in the Genesis text with the politics of the evasive representation of Ishmael's sacrifice in the story. As I have suggested above, this questioning functions as interrogation of the ways in which those in dominant subject positions transfer their own "burnings" (literally and figuratively) onto othered bodies through ideological configuration of narrative that constructs their identity over and against oppressed individuals.[23]

Moreover, the line of questioning that grows out of "Must we burn Isaac?" gathers insight from hooks's reading of the documentary *Paris Is Burning*, where she discusses the fascination with the title of the film as "it evoked images of the real Paris on fire, of the death and destruction of a dominating white Western civilization and culture, an end to oppressive Eurocentricism and white supremacy."[24] While hooks points to the ways in which this fantasy is incomplete/inadequate in *Paris Is Burning*, my question hopes to conjure a similar fantastic imagination. To give a raw presentation of both the possibilities and desire for the death and destruction of the systems and ideologies that dominate and oppress. Nevertheless, it is a question that I, ultimately, leave open. In part because the creation of resistant fantasies of transformed worlds is arguably more dependent on the imaginative processes that question reality and fuel resilience than the (uncommonly occurring) resolutions to the concerns that lead us to questions. In this regard, my opinions are being led by the grim observations of an Afro-pessimism inherited from South African cultural memory. Finally, then, the question of burning, as a South African, must also be a question of trust and allyship.

During the anti-apartheid period of the 1980s, "necklacing" emerged as a form of public execution where perceived (Black) traitors to the resistance movements were bound with a car tire filled with petrol and burned for failed/false solidarity in the struggle against white supremacy.[25] As Solomuzi Mabuza notes in an essay in tribute to Desmond Tutu, during the struggle against apartheid, the accusation of selling out was punishable by death. Although this is an extreme treatment of the questions of loyalty and solidarity within resistance, I believe we must give serious consideration to the nature of the solidarity we seek to cultivate between each other as Africana people, particularly in a contemporary context where "cancel culture" rages against influential Black figures like Kanye West and Candace Owens. This is not an apology on behalf of Kanye or Candace, but a way to introduce a question about the costs we are willing to pay for solidarity among Black folk and the kinds of (potentially violent) demands our struggles make of each other. In a sense, it is a question that asks at what price do we advance Black life, Black culture, and even Black academia? What this means for this essay, then, is to question whether we, as Africana scholars, can trust our alignments and intersections—in suffering or privilege—with folks in dominant subject positions? Or are we, despite ideological, methodological, and material similarities to burn bridges with dominant (white) epistemological perspectives? Lest we crash and *burn* under the weight of trying to serve Black communities through writing and thinking that takes place within and is even curated by/for predominantly white institutions.

In the section that follows, I offer an overview of my critical spectatorship of the biblical text. As presented below, the spectatorship is an artificial re-creation of the readings that motivates my interpretation in this chapter. Arguably, that is the nature of interpretation within academia. As Michael Patrick Gillespie indicates, it is not an organic process.[26] Rather, it is one that is constructed specifically for someone else's gaze; so, the irony of an oppositional gaze as a form of interpretive hermeneutic is not lost on my reading of the Genesis text. In a way, the section below functions like a retelling of the text, but it is a selective retelling. Instead of summarizing the eventuation of Hagar and Ishmael's appearances in the biblical text, I focus on character exchanges that I believe mark the operation of the gaze (in its visual and aural capacities) in their story. As a reminder, this process, to be frank, is quite contrived in the sense that I am intentionally constructing an observation of the text that leads me to the interpretive spaces I believe I need to interrogate the larger question of burning.

PART II: LOOKING AND HEARING WITH HAGAR AND ISHMAEL

Let the people see what I've seen.

MAMIE TILL

I begin in Genesis, chapter 16, where we first meet Hagar and Ishmael. What is notable about the observation that will follow is that chapter 16 introduces most of the key terms that mark the gaze. The drama of this portion of the ancestral cycles begins with "You see that the lord has prevented me from bearing children" (16:2). This is not a question. It is an indication of an established recognition. The presumption is that this is already known to be true. The power of drawing attention to a presumably plain truth is that it sets up the premise for Sarai's request; making it seem obvious to Abraham that a solution, her solution, must be devised. Indeed, Sarai's utilization of "the gaze" in this portion of the text is effective because Abram listens to her voice (16:2).[27] Yet another appearance of "the gaze," in its aural nature. Abram then enters the Egyptian slave-girl named Hagar, with or without her consent, and she conceives. The narrator tells us that Hagar sees that she has conceived and looks upon her mistress, Sarai, with contempt. This textual observation is repeated by Sarai in an indictment of Abram. Phyllis Trible's insights on Abram's response are helpful here: "Abram said to Sarai, 'Since your maid is in your hand, do to her the good in your eyes' (16:6a); the idiom, 'good in your eyes,' plays upon the reference to Hagar's eyes: 'her mistress was slight in her eyes.' The vision of the mistress opposes the insight of the maid. What is good for the one is suffering for the other."[28] In turn, Sarai's response to Hagar's contemptuous look is to treat her harshly. So harshly

Hagar chooses to flee. When asked by the angel of the Lord, who finds Hagar in the wilderness, where she is going, she states that she is running from the face/presence of her mistress. That is, she wants to go to a place beyond Sarai's line of sight. This is a powerful depiction of the terror Africana folk experience under "the gaze." Yet Hagar finds no escape from watchful eyes in the wilderness. Instead, she is found by an angel of the Lord. The angel offers no refuge from the threatening exposure of being seen. In fact, he piles on. Not only is Hagar commanded to "return and submit" to the place where she can be seen (and oppressed) by her mistress, her child will be "god hears" (16: 9–12). I am aware that the conventional perception is that "god hears" is intended to be comforting. Yet as Trible explains, "Without doubt, these two imperatives, return and submit to suffering, bring a divine word of terror to an abused, yet courageous, woman."[29] Thus, in my reading, the message being sent here seems to be, "Sarai is watching you, and I am listening." Scary! For what comfort is a god-character who hears your affliction and sends you back into it?[30] What follows is the famous naming of the god-character. Much has been said about what Hagar means by her words in Genesis 16:13. According to Danna Nolan Fewell and R. Christopher Heard, "She utters a garbled response about seeing and being seen by God; she gives YHWH a new name *El-Roi* ('El who sees'); and, like Abram's erection of altars, her experience is inscribed on geographical space (*Beer-lahai-roi*, 'the well of a living one who sees me'), grounding (as it were) her identity in promised space."[31] In light of scholarly debate, Sakenfeld clarifies and insists that "Hagar here actually names God rather than the place of meeting. Ishmael, God hears, El-roi, God sees. These two verbs of hearing and seeing by which God is in touch with Hagar's affliction appear together again in the turning point of the exodus story."[32] In Trible's words, "The maid who, after seeing (r'h) the conception of a child, had a new vision of her mistress Sarai (16:4), now, after receiving a divine announcement of forthcoming birth, sees (r'h) God a in new vision. Hagar is a theologian. Her naming unites the divine and human encounter: the God who sees and the God who is seen."[33] Still, the god-character's vigilance is suspicious to Black female spectatorship because Ishmael is predestined to be "a wild ass of a man, with his hand against everyone, and everyone's hand against him" (16:12). Admittedly, the possibility of care is not precluded in the god-character's gaze, yet neither is the surveillance of a child who is being constructed as a potential threat before he is even born—which is a burden Africana folk are all too familiar with in our various historical contexts. Thus, this essay receives what is said in Genesis 16:13 in a way that feels as though Hagar is saying, *"I know you see me! On my life, I know I see you see me see you see me. Aren't you god with your looking ass?"* What is embedded in this *liberal* translation is the distress, confusion, and rage I imagine Hagar feels when she hears the words of the Lord's angel. What I attempt to take on here is an oppositional recognition of god that gives epistemic privilege to Hagar's affliction over the presumption of divine benevolence.

As the story progresses, we will be given various cycles of seeing and hearing. In chapter 17, the god character appears to Abram and says, "Look, this is my covenant with you . . ." (17:3), in which he establishes the unborn Isaac, and not Ishmael, as the heir to the covenant. Abram seems to mourn Ishmael's dismissal in the establishment of covenant lineage. "Oh that Ishmael might live in your sight/presence" (17:18). The god-character insists that Isaac is the one. But "as for Ishmael, I have heard you" (17:20), and Ishmael is given an alternate blessing that places him outside the covenant. Even in chapters 18 and 19, where Hagar and Ishmael are not the focus of the narrative's telling, the acts of looking and hearing mark accusations that lead to punitive action. The terminology is different, but the effects are similar. These effects are arguably most emphatically depicted through Lot's wife, who is condemned to be a pillar of salt after she looks back. Lot's wife was denied her gaze, and she is punished for making use of it after the angelic prohibition (19:24–26). Earlier in the Sodom saga, Abram is said to look up and see when the angelic guests arrive (18: 2). And his sighting of them sparks an urgent and generous hospitality. When the text returns to a telling of Hagar and Ishmael in chapter 21, we see the return of a distinct function of seeing and hearing. After we are told about the conception of Isaac, Sarah claims that hearing this news will bring laughter (21:5). But soon after, Sarah sees the son of Hagar the Egyptian. Why his name, "god hears," is not used here is unclear. Perhaps it is because god's hearing in chapter 16 sets up an expectation that the god-character is no longer upholding in chapter 21. God's hearing in chapter 16 is what keeps Hagar and Ishmael under Sarah's watch. It may be the case that the absence of explicit mention of "god hears" is an indication that what is being heard here is that which will drive Hagar and Ishmael out of her sight.

Indeed, the god-character insists that Abraham must listen to Sarah's voice and expel Hagar and her son. We are told that the matter is "displeasing in Abraham's sight" (21:11). Abraham's displeasure implies a recognition of the violence of Sarah's request. Yet Abraham's capacity for recognition in this portion of the text does not have the urgency or generosity that is seen in chapter 18, for if it did, he would have sent them off with more than the "astonishingly meager" serving of bread and a single skin of water.[34] After their deportation to the desert, Hagar does not want to "look on the death of the child." Yet again we are told god hears. Although it is Hagar who seems to be making pleas in this portion of the story, the text tells us that "god heard the voice of the boy" (21:16). This leaves one to wonder if god has given Hagar's voice any mind. Still, God opens her eyes, and she saw a well. Nevertheless, despite divine intervention, what can be deduced from the spectatorship above is that no matter who is wielding them, the visual and aural operations of "the gaze" in Genesis 16–21 almost always lead to the suppression of Hagar and Ishmael.

PART III: "BOY, BYE!"

Although mention of Hagar ends at chapter 21, and Ishmael will not reappear until we are given a genealogy of his descendants in chapter 25, to appropriate the words of R. Christopher Heard, as one reads chapter 22, "It is difficult to gaze at Isaac upon the altar without also seeing his older brother, Ishmael, just outside Moriah, somewhere off the side of the mountain of vision in one's peripheral vision perhaps."[35] According to Heard, "Genesis 21 and 22 exhibit parallel storylines."[36] He asserts, "To be sure, when Genesis 22 is read *alone*, it looks as though Abraham's sacrifice of Isaac is solely a response to God's command; it looks as though in giving death to Isaac, Abraham is giving Isaac's death to God." What Heard is recognizing here is that "Abraham, once God has endorsed Sarah's behest, effectively sacrifices Ishmael (and Hagar) for the sake of Isaac (and Sarah)." He continues to say, "To put it this way is accurate, but it leaves out one very important element in Genesis 21."[37] Abraham is initially upset about the demand for deportation and agrees to it only after the god-character assures him that he will live and thrive. "Yet, in the act of expulsion itself, Abraham in essence gives the exiles death by giving them insufficient food and water.[38] Informed by my critical spectatorship above and empowered with an oppositional gaze that seeks to counteract the suppressive effects of the textual function of "the gaze" on Hagar and Ishmael, this essay lingers on a reading of the Akedah.

It has become a near axiomatic presumption that the test given to Abraham in Genesis 22 is a test of Abraham's faith. That is, the god-character commands that Isaac is to be offered as a burnt sacrifice in order to present a divine test designed to gauge whether Abraham is willing to sacrifice his investment in the future.[39] By agreeing to sacrifice Isaac, as Mark G. Brett notes, Abraham's compliance to the command moves his faith "beyond any conventional sense of ethics."[40] In other words, *Abraham done lost his goddamn mind.* In isolation, Genesis 22 presents a tale of the arbitrary demand of an unbelievably cruel god-character that is met by an unbelievably silent compliance. In an oppositional stance, this essay insists that the Akedah should not be seen as the test of the existence of Abraham's faith or the limits of obedience. As Ronald R. Krebs points out in "The Binding of Isaac and the Arts of Resistance," Genesis 12–21 gives the god-character and the reader/hearer little reason to believe that Abraham's faith requires examination. He notes that the god-character's decision to test Abraham is puzzling and continues to highlight that "tradition has rightly seen in Abraham the exemplar of steadfast, disinterested loyalty to God."[41] Indeed, Abraham (and family) left his country when the god-character instructed them to (12:1–5). He has built an altar in the god-character's honor (12:7–8; 13:18). He is obedient to the command to circumcise the male members of his household. The reader/hearer is told that the god-character considers Abraham to be obedient and righteous (15:6). And Genesis 18:19 suggests that the god-character has chosen Abraham precisely because he already knows that Abraham "will charge his children and his household after him to keep the way of the Lord by doing justice and righteousness." In sum, as Sakenfeld also notes, "Although the story builds tension about how God's promise will be fulfilled, it is not necessary for readers of this story to suppose that either Sarah or Abraham showed lack of trust in God by turning to Hagar."[42]

Considering the above, Brett's observation that "the story in Genesis 22 defies domestication with any conventional code of obedience to [the] divine" becomes relevant. "God's demand to sacrifice Isaac is a chilling display of exclusivist ideology, tortuously trying to cover up the reality of the one[s] excluded."[43] That is, although the narrator would have reader/

hearers believe that those who occupy story world positions of socio-economic and political privilege in Genesis 16–22 face the direst threat to their existence and continued survival, a reading that is constructed through an oppositional gaze claims otherwise. Fewell and Heard assert that "death and near-death experience capture a sense of communal vulnerability" in the Genesis text.[44] And even though she highlights the contrasting power dynamics in the depiction of Hagar and Sarah, Julianna Claassens suggests that the two women are "equally marginalized."[45] I am skeptical of the leveling propensities in the implied mutuality these claims seem to connote. The preceding section of this essay has already shown that Sarah (along with Abraham and Isaac) is a privileged participant in the power of the textual operations of "the gaze." Additionally, Philip Yoo elaborately portrays in his philological engagement of the depiction and description of Hagar in Genesis 16 and 21 that the Hebrew text allows for multiple perspectives and gives conflicting indications of the status of Hagar—and by extension Ishmael.[46] Conversely, the text is consistent in its repeated reification of the privileged status of Abraham—and by extension Sarah and Isaac. To appropriate the words of Fewell, the god-character is, "the God of rich men" and their wives, who are promised land, offspring, and slaves, like Hagar.[47]

Abraham, Israel's proto-ancestor—whom the story shows to be a rich man who takes possession and occupies land in various territories—is commanded by the god-character to sacrifice his son, Isaac. The son, who, according to the divine covenantal promise, is chosen to be the first of many of Abraham's descendants destined to be a *great* nation. It is plausible to assume, as many have, that the textual manifestation of the god-character's sacrificial command is the product of the Israelite historical experience of imperial domination, exile, and return.[48] Yet the story world, nevertheless, by virtue of the repeated covenantal promise made to Abraham as embodied in Isaac, seems to already exclude the sacrifice of Isaac as a possibility. Following chapter 17, the god-character is seen and heard to be consistently and insistently clear that the covenantal promise is directly dependent on Abraham's son born by his wife, Sarah.

Moreover, the details surrounding the command made in Genesis 22 are dubious. The narrator gives an account of temporal-spatial activity that is seemingly ignorant of aspects of its own narrativized past. The god-character and the narrator refer to Isaac as Abraham's only son (22:2,

12, 16), as if reader/hearers have forgotten about Ishmael's existence. Yet how can those who have read/heard Genesis 21 forget? Especially after Sarah's crisis surrounding Ishmael's presence, as a son who stands to be heir to Abraham's inheritance, has been so dramatically laid out in Genesis 21. Along with the failure to name Ishmael in this portion of the story, Genesis 22 asserts that Isaac is the son whom Abraham loves (22:2); yet Abraham appears to have lost all capacity to distress over the loss of a son. His anxiety over Ishmael (21:11–12), the son facing possible death in Genesis 21, transforms into a silent compliance to the command to murder his younger son, Isaac.

Additionally, we are told that Isaac is spared on Mt. Moriah and replaced by a ram in the bush and that his offspring will multiply because Abraham did not withhold Isaac from a sacrificial fate (22:10–13, 15–18). We already know that in Genesis 21 Abraham did not withhold Ishmael from his arguably sacrificial fate either. The potentially threatening Ishmael, who Sarah sees as an obstacle to Isaac's claim to Abraham's inheritance (22:10), is seen by his mother Hagar and heard by the god-character as a child, a boy—near death—who cries in the bushes (22:15–17). Although the god-character intervenes, and Ishmael does not die, the boy is not returned to the custody of his father, like Isaac. Instead, the deportation of Ishmael, the will-be wild-ass-of-a-man predestined to a life of ambiguous relation in the wilderness, is seen to completion.[49] So much so, that when we are given an account of Isaac's life after the incident at Mt. Moriah, we are told in Genesis 25:11 that "Isaac settled at Beer-lahai-roi." Not only does Isaac displace Ishmael in the covenantal lineage, but he also goes on to occupy the very place of his divine annunciation, a move that seals Hagar and Ishmael's suppression in a strikingly colonial manner.

The narrative anxiety over Ishmael as a potential heir as well as the ritual demand made by the god-character is, then, actually brought into fulfillment through the Akedah's erasure of Ishmael. In this regard, I argue that the Akedah is and was always a phantasmatic *mocking* sacrifice that is used to validate the proposed future of the narrativized past. As Cheryl Exum notes, "The biblical narrators view the abjection of Hagar and Ishmael as necessary, since the Ishmaelites are a people separate from Israel and have no share in Israel's special covenant with God."[50] Thus Genesis 22 is seen as the construction of an ethno-nationalist fantasy that inscribes exclusivist ideologies through the phantasmatic tale of "the boy who lived": the chosen one who survives not only the threatening presence of he who is no longer named, the slave-born-boy-child-donkey-bowman but also the divinely inspired filicidal fires of Mt. Moriah. That is, the Akedah manipulates *alternative facts* in order to execute and complete the rejection and suppression of the Ishmaelite possibilities within the ethno-nationalist imagination of Israel.[51] By doing so, Genesis 22 reshapes the entire Genesis narrative, and its use of sacrificial devices is key to understanding the poetics of its ideologies of domination that have already been configured through the operations of "the gaze" in the preceding chapters. Genesis as a whole is then, in turn, seen as moving through nexuses of systematically making, consuming, and discharging othered multiplicities. In the words of Lovelace, "The politics of belonging and the political projects that drive them are constructed around boundaries that include some and exclude others. Hagar and Ishmael represent the 'Other,' who must be removed, as they posed a threat to the covenantal lineage that identified who was a member of Israel according to the ancestral narrative in Genesis 12–25."[52]

PART IV: "IF WE BURN, YOU BURN WITH US!"

The ethno-nationalist imagination of Israel's identity dominates the narrative before Israel even exists in the story world. It is the thing that the story world, past and present, must always make a possibility at all costs. Yet we know this thing must also exist within very particular ethno-religious parameters. Hagar and Ishmael are impermanent residents of the narrative space-time because they do not conform to the ethno-national identity of the proposed future of Israel. According to Tikva Frymer-Kensky, "Incomplete portrayals do in fact serve the purposes of the narrators, whose concern is the destiny of the people of Israel."[53] Indeed, although there *are* creative possibilities for them to avoid deportation, their continued stay in textual space-time is made impossible by the textual desire to distance the symbolic ethno-nationalist pseudo-genetic roots from that which is genealogically, and/or economically, other. Arguably, for the Yehud community, this ethno-nationalist fantasy is an establishment of what Lauren Berlant calls a *National Symbol* that conjures the ability to transform individual, private subjective identification into collective public identity that is seen as great.[54] A futurist fantasy that narrates the past, then, is made necessary because what is *great* about the past is promise for future greatness. In the event that past hopes for greatness are not achieved in the present, the authors must *return*, go back to the (narrated) past to regain access to the promised future that has been foreclosed by the present.

Moreover, rather than simply presenting the story of Abraham's family as exceptional personal experiences, Genesis 16–22 appears to suggest that they are also, always, necessarily a condition of the future identity of the Israelites. The text maintains multiple realities but only deploys them to work for an exclusively defined Israelite identity. The making and unmaking of heirs through socially driven and divinely sponsored sex acts (performed with or without consent, often at the expense of marginalized bodies) are not only representative of but literally configure national Israelite identity.[55] That is, while Genesis 16–22 presents "the experience of identity [as] personal and private, [the fantasy] forms are always 'collective' and political."[56] The narrator's presentation of the ethno-nationalist roots through the story of Abraham and his family function to personalize the constructed national identity for the reader/hearers. By repeatedly reporting to the reader/hearer that Abraham holds a divinely privileged ethical/moral position, it further reifies the fantasy of the past's future. Additionally, it contributes to the spread of a toxic masculinity modeled through a collaboration of personal and public violations enacted by and on the male ancestral progenitor. The narrator guides the reader/hearer through Abraham's life, in which the pursuit of covenantal promise made to him compels him to, on the one hand, occupy other people's land (12:1–9), deceive and endanger foreign leaders (12:10–17; 20:1–11), deny others the honor of performing cultural customs/duties (14:17–24), sexually exploit slaves (16:1–4), and disinherit and deport his second wife and son. On the other hand, the pursuit of covenantal promise also requires Abraham to move from his country, live as a foreigner, sexually mutilate the male members of his household (17:23–27), sacrifice his personal investment in the future (21–22), and replace personal honor/benefit with obedience to the divine character.

Ultimately, the textual operations of "the gaze" on Hagar and Ishmael as the Bible narrates what it intends to be Abraham's story allows for contradictions that in and of themselves do not result in the collapse of the progression of the literary world of Genesis.[57] Although Brett asserts that these contradictions are manifestations of a subtle resistance to the dominant ideologies of Genesis, the narrator—unaware, unaffected, or indifferent to this supposed subtle resistance— swaggers on with the pursuit of promise. He drags along with them the patrimonial heirs and leaves behind a long trail of disposed, dispossessed, and "dis-utopian" *expendables*. As Anne Michele Tapp emphasizes (in relation to Genesis 18 and Judges 19), the configurations and dynamics of biblical eventuation do not solely work to create mechanisms, motifs, and mediums of narration, but they also propagate an implicit or explicit ideology of who is expendable.[58] In this regard, for the narrator of the Genesis text, "the gaze," along with forgetful narrative activity, illegitimacy, and impossibility are opportunities to make possible ethno-nationalist exclusivist "zone[s] of potentiality."[59] These zones of potentiality are exploited through highly selective deployment of knowledge concerning the past, present, and future story world(s). The text moves backward and forward in space-time and across multiple borders and boundaries to construct Israelite national roots. That is, whoever is writing the Genesis narrative is seen to be writing a speculative fiction about the future of Israel's past that manifests itself as an ethno-national, exclusivist fantasy. This reading, then, insists that this text be read as such. Calling it historiography lends the narrative and its use of "the gaze" a bona fide status that allots it an undue authority over the understanding of history and marginalized peoples.[60] Naming the text as a retroactive construction re-opens the "burning" of the narrative that is continually transferred onto its expendable signifiers. Here, it is important to name the assumption that is implied by the lengthy detour into the discussion of Genesis and the constructions of Israelite national identity: that is the Euro-American co-optation of biblical epistemic apparatuses of re/constructing dominant ideology and exclusivist national identity. It is important because the above discussion, as Yvonne Sherwood points to in "Hagar and Ishmael: The Reception of Expulsion," has deep significance for the understandings of the reception history of this text. Sherwood states, "There is a tendency in academic biblical studies to channel reception studies into 'art and literature' or 'art, literature, and music' rather than say, land claims or 'politics.'"[61] Although reading the biblical text as fiction/fantasy may seem counter-intuitive to resisting this tendency, I find it helpful as a reminder of the ways in which dominant cultures possess and actively exercise the power to continually (re)imagine and (re)invent their claims to resources and traditions. That is, the power to artfully and dramatically narrate and (re)present themselves in positions of power and privilege, located and configured at the expense of others, in any time and space without the burden of fully accounting for the lived experiences that are affected by the narratives they construct. The question this raises, then, is What does this mean for the Africana bodies and epistemologies that the first part of this essay labors so intensely to prioritize?

In conclusion, then, this essay turns to the question it is most interested in: "Must we burn Isaac?" This question stands as a temporary substitute for the larger question of Africana subjectivity. A grave question that calls radical Africana minds to imagine beyond the limitations of (biblical studies') ideological apparatuses and pursue hospitable horizons even with the acute despair of our lived experience. One that takes on the difficult, creative thought that is required to address how the Africana subject, and in particular, the Africana scholar, can begin to work for constructing livable lives in the light of histories of the erasures, expulsions, and annihilations of people of African descent. In a way, this essay is a fantasy of its own. It takes great creative pains inspired by Octavia E. Butler to interrogate what it takes to change a (story) world narrative, where ethnically/racially/economically/socially othered bodies are continually constructed and recognized as alien and alienated in, between, and around literary space-times whose created boundaries and borders cut, erase, invade, and consume while (somewhat paradoxically) still embracing and appropriating foreignness, dislocation, and open-endedness as original possibilities for escape.[62] The uncomfortable question that is left entirely unanswered is *Must we burn Isaac*? That is a question that means to ask what it will take to escape and dismantle the operations of "the gaze" within story and lived world space-times that continually construct and impose the futuristic fantasies of power and privilege on Africana bodies. This question is asking whether we should continue the work of oppositional and retroactive fantasies for the reclamation of Africana subjectivities. Do we follow the lead of the comic series and film *Black Panther* and rewrite ourselves into existing (white) canons in a way that is redeeming and even superior? That is, do we participate in similar nexuses of futuristic ethno/racial reconstruction that reach from the present back into the past to re/write favorable futures? Do we continue in the existing trajectories of popular cultural Afrofuturism or do we dare to take on its grim darker, rough, counterpart, Afropessimism? As Africana biblical scholars, the question is Do we imagine a biblical text in which Isaac *does* burn so that the descendants of Africans and African slaves may have livable story worlds? Does centering the study of the Bible on the Africana subject mean centering our desires for the narrative of Hagar-Ishmael in a way that must surely ask how life is made livable for them without sacrificing them to the wilderness if we do not burn Isaac. Do we figuratively or literally burn that which is used to establish an unending claim to inheritances which is constructed through us and with the exploitation of our (re)productive capacities but fundamentally precludes us? Must we burn Isaac because the story world, and indeed the lived world, is not interested in change unless we assert it in the violent poetics it inscribes? Or must we burn Isaac for the dominant perspective to understand that we can no longer stand to be violated, exploited, entrapped, abused, and deported at their convenience? Or is there an alternate path to follow that will lead us to hospitable foreign places?[63] Is there hope that peoples inside and outside the text, who "are constantly on the move, migrating freely or under coercion, finding themselves exiles, wanderers, sojourners, and strangers with tenuous conceptions of 'home,'" can find a pragmatic manifestation of belonging?[64] How does the Africana subject find her way outside the context and contextual narration of her marginalization? The only response to these questions this essay can begin to offer, which is, by no stretch of the imagination, an answer, is to take up what Butler identifies as a monophobic response to challenge and even rough up against that which Chimamanda Ngozi Adichie points to in "The Danger of a Single Story."[65] What I aspire to when I resist singularly iterable disciplinary visions through an oppositional spectatorship of singularly iterable biblical narration and interpretation is pragmatic and flexible imagination that continually orients itself to the pursuit of hospitable belonging outside marginalizing boundaries through a hermeneutical search for a resistant power. As an Africana subject, I must, therefore, either begin to redefine for myself and my people what it means to be a biblical scholar, or I must hope against hope to survive biblical scholarship and its long-lasting impacts on Africana people somewhere outside of the existing academic guilds of biblical studies.

NOTES

1. Itumeleng J. Mosala, *Biblical Hermeneutics and Black Theology in South Africa* (Grand Rapids: Eerdmans, 1989), 123.
2. Both the pursuits of Afrofuturism and defiance of archivism grew out of the lingering intent to read biblical texts in order to identify, learn, and teach

counter-movements to the anti-Blackness of dominant culture, that is, identifying, learning, and teaching "lines of flight." My understanding of lines of flight is based on David Kline's use of Deleuze and Guattari's notion of "flight" here. The word translated as flight, *fuite*, is, according to Brian Massumi's translator's note in *A Thousand Plateaus: Capitalism and Schizophrenia* (1987), "covers not only the act of fleeing or eluding but also flowing, leaking, and disappearing into the distance (the vanishing point in a painting is a *point de fuite*). It has no relation to flying." (Gilles Deleuze and Félix Guattari, *A Thousand Plateaus* (Minneapolis: University of Minnesota Press, 1987), xvii).

3. bell hooks, "The Oppositional Gaze: Black Female Spectators," in *Reel to Real: Race, Sex, and Class at the Movies*, by bell hooks (New York: Routledge, 1996), 197.
4. Ibid., 197.
5. Ibid., 200.
6. Ibid., 198.
7. Ibid., 200.
8. Ibid., 210.
9. Ibid.
10. Vincent L. Wimbush, "Introduction: Reading Darkness, Reading Scriptures," in *African Americans and the Bible: Sacred Texts and Social Structures*, ed. Vincent L. Wimbush (New York: Continuum, 2000), 9.
11. Ibid., 5.
12. Margaret P. Aymer, *First Pure, Then Peaceful: Frederick Douglass Reads James* (London: T&T Clark, 2008), 2.
13. Katherine Doob Sakenfeld, *Just Wives: Stories of Survival and Power in the Old Testament and Today* (Louisville: Westminster John Knox Press, 2003), 9.
14. TreaAndrea M. Russworm, *Blackness Is Burning: Civil Rights, Pop Culture, and the Problem of Recognition* (Detroit: Wayne State University Press, 2016), 9.
15. Ibid., 10
16. Delores S. Williams, *Sisters in the Wilderness: The Challenge of Womanist God-Talk* (Maryknoll, NY: Orbis Books, 2013), 2.
17. Renita J. Weems, *Just a Sister Away: Understanding the Timeless Connection between Women of Today and Women in the Bible* (New York: Waner Nooks, 2005), 1.
18. Yvonne Sherwood, "Hagar and Ishmael: The Reception of Expulsion," *Interpretation* 68, no. 3 (2014): 287.
19. Ibid., 296.
20. Rosalyn F. T. Murphy, "Sista-Hood: Revealing the Meaning of Hagar's Narrative," *Black Theology: An International Journal* 10, no. 1 (2012): 77–92.

21. Renee K. Harrison, *Enslaved Women and the Art of Resistance* (New York: Palgrave Macmillan, 2009).
22. Dora R. Mbuwayesango, "Childlessness and Woman-to-Woman Relationships in Genesis and in African Patriarc(h)al Society: Sarah and Hagar from a Zimbabwean Woman's Perspective (Gen 16:1–16; 21:2–21)," *Semeia*, no. 78 (1997).
23. This phenomenon is described by Anne Anlin Cheng as relating to a kind of melancholia. According to Cheng, racial melancholia refers to "a complex process of racial rejection and desire on the parts of the white and non-whites that expresses itself in abject and manic forms. On the one side, white American identity and its authority is secured through the melancholic interjection of racial others that it can neither fully relinquish nor accommodate and whose ghostly presence nonetheless guarantees its centrality. On the other side, the racial other (the so-called melancholic object) also suffers from racial melancholia whereby his or her racial identity is imaginatively reinforced through the introjection of a lost, never-possible perfection, an inarticulable loss that comes to inform the individual's sense of his or her own subjectivity" (Anne Anlin Cheng, *The Melancholy of Race: Psychoanalysis, Assimilation, and Hidden Grief* [Princeton, NJ: Princeton University Press, 2001], xi).
24. bell hooks, "Is Paris Burning?" In *Reel to Real: Race, Sex, and Class at the Movies* (New York: London, 1996), 218.
25. Solomuzi Mabuza, "Still Speaking Truth to Power," *Church Times*, October 7, 2011.
26. Gillespie asserts: "For centuries, literary critics—like their counterparts in the sciences—have conformed to the expectations of a culture that has privileged linear, Cartesian logic as the most effective form of analysis. . . . In consequence, an exegesis often does not present a critic's full aesthetic experience with a work—a reading—but instead offers an abridged and adapted version emphasizing the validity of one or two impressions—an interpretation. A significant difference obtains between these two conditions. Interpretations follow an exclusionary impulse which domesticates responses, highlighting only a few ideas and constructing linear arguments from only portions of the material under consideration relevant to the support of that argument. This gesture parallels the reductivist thinking of Classical science. Readings, on the other hand, encompass the multiple responses that grow out of a creative engagement with words on the printed page. These impressions function like a series of directed explosions—imaginative bursts generated by the same source but with repercussions independent of that source and of one another. The nonlinear thinking that enhances comprehension of the physical world can

also facilitate a far more sophisticated understanding of the multiplicity and pluralism of this aesthetic" (Gillespie, "Reading on the Edge of Chaos: 'Finnegans Wake' and the Burden of Linearity," *Journal of Modern Literature* 22, no. 2 [1999]: 360).

27. Phyllis Trible's *Texts of Terror: Literary Feminist Readings of Biblical Narrative* (Philadelphia: Fortress Press, 1984) notes that Sarai is speaking in imperatives in this portion of the text. Not only does Sarai have the power to communicate observed concerns in a way that Hagar does not because, as Weems notes, Hagar is not consulted on the matter (Weems, *Just a Sister Away*, 4), Sarai's observations have a severe impact on Hagar's lived experience.
28. Trible, *Texts of Terror*, 13.
29. Ibid., 16.
30. Sakenfeld, *Just Wives*, 18.
31. Danna Nolan Fewell and R. Christopher Heard, "The Genesis of Identity in the Biblical World," in *The Oxford Handbook of Biblical Narrative*, ed. Danna Nolan Fewell (New York: Oxford University Press, 2016), 117.
32. Sakenfeld, *Just Wives*, 23
33. Trible, *Texts of Terror*, 18.
34. Fewell and Heard, "The Genesis of Identity in the Biblical World," 117.
35. R. Christopher Heard, "Triangulating Responsibility: How and Why Abraham, Isaac, and Ishmael Offer and Refuse the Gift of Death, and to/from Whom," in *Derrida's Bible: Reading a Page of Scripture with a Little Help from Derrida*, ed. Yvonne Sherwood (New York: Palgrave Macmillan, 2004), 152–53.
36. Ibid., 153.
37. Ibid.
38. Ibid., 154.
39. Mark G. Brett, "Abraham's 'Heretical' Imperative: A Response to Jacques Derrida," in *The Meaning We Choose: Hermeneutical Ethics, Indeterminacy, and the Conflict of Interpretation*, ed. Charles Cosgrove (Bloomsburg: T&T Clark, 2004), 166.
40. Ibid., 167.
41. Ronald R. Krebs, "The Binding of Isaac and the Arts of Resistance (Genesis 22)," in *Reading Genesis: Beginnings*, ed. Beth Kissileff (London: Bloomsbury, 2016), 133.
42. Sakenfeld, *Just Wives*, 10
43. Brett, "Abraham's 'Heretical' Imperative," 170.
44. Fewell and Heard, "The Genesis of Identity in the Biblical World," 110.
45. Juliana Claassens, "Laughter and Tears: Carnivalistic Overtones in the Stories of Sarah and Hagar," *Perspectives in Religious Studies* 3 (2005): 302.

46. Philip Yoo, "Hagar the Egyptian: Wife, Handmaid, and Concubine," *Catholic Biblical Quarterly* 78, no. 2 (2016): 227–31.
47. Danna Nolan Fewell, "Changing the Subject: Retelling the Story of Hagar the Egyptian," in *Genesis: A Feminist Companion to the Bible* (Second Series), ed. Athalya Brenner (Sheffield: Sheffield Academic Press, 1998), 183.
48. An experience, in part, which the narrative has already grimly predicted for the descendants of Abraham in chapter 15: "Know this for certain, that your offspring shall be aliens in a land that is not theirs, and shall be slaves there, and shall be oppressed for four hundred years; but I will bring judgement on the nation they serve, and afterward they shall come out with great possessions" (15:13).
49. R. Christopher Heard, "On the Road to Paran: Toward a Christian Perspective on Hagar and Ishmael," *Interpretation* 68 (2014): 277–78.
50. Cheryl Exum, "The Accusing Look: The Abjection of Hagar in Art," *Religion and the Arts* 11 (2007): 145.
51. To return briefly to the idea of melancholia introduced through Cheng earlier, Paul Gilroy's insights on post/imperial melancholy are helpful here. In a way the transference of both guilt and (divine) recognition at play as the biblical narrative progresses from the deportation of Hagar and Ishmael to the Binding of Isaac inscribes a "depressed reaction that inhibited any capacity for responsible reconstructive practice" (Paul Gilroy, *Postcolonial Melancholia* [New York: Columbia University Press, 2004], 98), and thus Genesis 22 functions as a narrative spectacle that suspends the horror of Hagar and Ishmael's abandonment and congests capacities for empathy and/or recognition of the violence that directly precedes that Akedah.
52. Vanessa Lovelace, "'This woman's son shall not inherit with my son,'" *Journal of the Interdenominational Theological Center* 41, no. 1 (2015): 77.
53. Tikva Frymer-Kensky, *Reading the Women of the Bible: A New Interpretation of Their Stories* (New York: Schocken Books, 2002), 333–34.
54. Lauren Berlant, *The Anatomy of National Fantasy: Hawthorne, Utopia, and Everyday Life* (Chicago: University of Chicago Press, 1991), 2.
55. For a detailed engagement on how Hagar's marginalized national status relates to the dynamics of identity and politics in Genesis, see Yvonne Sherwood's "Migration as Foundation: Hagar, 'the Resident Alien,' as Euro-America's Surrogate Self," *Biblical Interpretation* 26, no. 4/5 (2018): 439–68. For more on my perspective of sex acts and nation building in the biblical texts see "Judges 19 and Non-Con: Sado-Kantian Aesthetics of Violence in the Tale of an Unnamed Woman," in *Rape Culture and Religious Texts: Critical and Pedagogical Engagements*, ed. Rhiannon Graybill, Meredith Minister, and Beatrice Lawrence (New York: Lexington Books, 2019), 93–112.

56. Ibid., 2–3.
57. For more on the literary functions of contradiction and impossibility see Jan Alber, *Unnatural Narrative: Impossible Worlds in Fiction and Drama* (Lincoln: University of Nebraska Press, 2016).
58. Anne Michele Tapp, "An Ideology of Expendability: Virgin Daughter Sacrifice," in *Anti-Covenant: Counter-Reading Women's Lives in the Hebrew Bible*, ed. Mieke Bal (Sheffield: Almond Press, 1989), 157.
59. Jan Alber, "The Diachronic Development of Unnaturalness," in *Unnatural Narratives–Unnatural Narratology*, ed. Jan Alber and Rüdiger Heinze (Berlin: de Gruyter, 2011), 62.
60. Michael Patrick Gillespie, *The Aesthetics of Chaos: Nonlinear Thinking and Contemporary Literary Criticism* (Gainesville: University Press of Florida, 2003), 45.
61. Yvonne Sherwood, "Hagar and Ishmael: The Reception of Expulsion," *Interpretation* 68 (2014): 286.
62. Octavia E. Butler, "The Monophobic Response," in *Dark Matter: A Century of Speculative Fiction from the African Diaspora*, ed. Sheree R. Thomas (New York: Aspect-Warner Books, 2000), 415–16.
63. For an interesting poetic exploration of the possibility of reading Hagar as a figural representation of othered people whose journeys lead them to a hospitable foreign place see Itzik Manger's poem "Hagar on Her Journey," in Itzik Manger, *The World According to Itzik: Selected Poetry and Prose*, trans. and ed. Leonard Wolf (New Haven, CT: Yale University Press, 2002).
64. Fewell and Heard, "The Genesis of Identity," 109–10.
65. Butler, "The Monophobic Response," 415–16. Chimamanda Ngozi Adichie, "The Danger of a Single Story," TedGlobal 2009, https://www.ted.com/talks/chimamanda_adichie_the_danger_of_a_single_story/details?language=en.

PART III

❧ Africana Historiographies and Memories

TEMITOPE TEMITOPE

PAMELA MORDECAI

Yoruba, "enough to give thanks" or "give thanks to God." A name for both males and females, though more often females. igba: Many meanings including "rope," "two hundred," "time/season," "garden egg." Olorun: Creator, Supreme Being, one of many names for the Yoruba Sky God. My daughter tells me, "Mum, I don't have much more time, so I do not intend to read hundreds of baby books." She's thirty-eight. The girl child she is carrying is her first. I tell her, "Love, it isn't very kind of you to tell someone who's sixty-four about not having much more time!" But it is really fine. We say it is longer than rope, this time, this word that has no synonym, being itself or not itself, being, rather, liminal, an interstice between just then and a moment about to be. But we who come from islands know, crac-crlc, periphrastic, is so life go.

And as for baby books, we never read not one. We birthed you, named you, kept you clean, fed you, sent you to school, prayed God you would come to no harm. That cord of hours played out by tiefing hands so long ago to snare you on your way back home, water jar on your head, humming as your swift feet spat sand, slant eyes smiled at the spinning wheel of huts ahead, ears shut against the loud demanding threads of smoke from their cook fires, "Sapling, how come we wait the whole day and you don't reach home?" And then, "How come you fade like mist and nobody see you again?" How could we know a coffle choked your song air buckled in your throat as you grew thin down a rats' hole dug deep in watery dirt? How could we know they flayed your bark with whips rammed you between felled trees trussed end to end seasoned in vomit, blood and shit? Our tears spilled from closed eyes scoured pots of memory as fitful slumber tossed our heads, tumbled our dreams. We sought to conjure labyrinths crisscrossed by footprints shouting still, "Time you reach home!" We counted cowries hours, weeks, centuries. We prayed, day-clean and dark, "Olorun grant the stolen ones igba, a rope to climb out of fate's pit to eat sweet dates again, to see through green lashes of leaves your home of sky." Olorun heard. The infant came on a red string. Temitope.

11. From White Man's Magic to Black Folks' Wisdom

ALTHEA SPENCER MILLER

Africana, a word that conjures ideas of multiplicity, diversity, dispersion, home-making, the Black global, postcoloniality, history, loss, grief, betrayal, survival, oceans, creolizations, and so much more, wanders through my mind in a hungry search for the mechanisms of survival used by the descendants of enslaved peoples in an alien and self-alienating world of "White Man's Magic." In faces of the African hue, I search for a certain look. In each body of the African tinge I look for a certain swag, sway, rhythm. In each movement of the African tinge, I look for memory. Afro- is a root prefix that evokes African Americans and sometimes the wider Black experience in the United States. It is not a commonplace for it to evoke the peoples of the nations of the continent dubbed Africa, the Afro-Caribbean, Afro-LatinX, or the wider African Diaspora. The relationship between African Americans and the wider African Diaspora remains as fraught as it was in its predecessor, Pan-Africanism. That relationship interferes with cultural and political memory. Hints and innuendos of the U.S. imperial relations to the rest of the world haunt the African American/African Diaspora relationship wherever African Americans wittingly or unwittingly assumes a normative posture for global race and international relationships in which the African Diaspora participates. Given the monopoly of the U.S. on imperial relations in the twentieth and early twenty-first centuries, it would be easy to capitulate to the powerful normativities of any African American experience in the U.S. Thus, residence in the United States can cause African American national and cultural dominance and both complexify and simplify hue-based searches for familiarity and commonality. This quandary contextualizes my reading of Vincent Wimbush's *White Men's Magic: Scripturalization as Slavery*.[1]

Vincent Wimbush's analysis of Olaudah Equiano spawned a reactive impulse. Equiano's nomadic experience of slavery covered the British Commonwealth and the U.S.A. Yet in Wimbush, Equiano as a metonymic heuristic seemed more akin to an optic of U.S. racial and social class relationships. I am a citizen of Jamaica in the Caribbean. The analytical transposition of Equiano triggered a clash of empires fought over my islander body and psyche. The repetition of erasure roiled my Caribbean beingness. Admittedly, this essay is rooted in resistance to subsummation and the propulsive force of Caribbean visibility. It seemed an intolerable dispatch that marginalized the Caribbean Commonwealth experience that Equiano shared. There cannot be Africana Studies that participates in the ongoing neglect of less visible non-traditional contexts. Wimbush's later publication, *Theorizing Scriptures: New Critical Orientation to a Cultural Phenomenon*,[2] has a multicultural and global appeal. However, Wimbush does not participate in Africana discourse, and this essay could appear disingenuous if it engaged him in these terms. This essay, therefore, does not posit its analysis on the basis that Wimbush is doing Africana scholarship, although there is pertinence. The focus on Equiano as a metonymical African is the magnet that invokes a Diasporic conversation.

Contemplating the regions where the Atlantic Ocean meets the Caribbean Sea, it is possible to discern other cultural vernaculars that generated various experiences of transatlantic contact in different periods. Within the confidence of regional attunement, the desire for visibility focuses another hermeneutical posture with which to depict, for purposes of contextual and anti-colonial biblical interpretation, a resistant rather than accommodating colonial relational outcome. Ironically, the barely repressed, taut intraracial antagonisms of the Black Atlantic's diaspora peek out even in this introduction as the residue of colonialism. Its heritage resides in the present, governed by the musculature of a masked colonialism that maintains the divisiveness of classical colonialism. These strings invite us to perpetually relive the European conflicts of the fifteenth through the twenty-first centuries. This essay, then, is an effort to unveil a subterranean ancestral heroism, adaptations to a new land, and literary connections with a creolizing instinct. Yet this is not an anti-. It is an intratelluric shout for kinship and recognition, erupting with the heat of magmatic hope, the igneous strength of an amphictyonic plurality.

In that spirit of magmatic hope and igneous strength I engage Wimbush's analysis of Equiano as a signifier of the mechanisms of Black subjugation and seduction by the Christian book. Although Wimbush's analytical astuteness and percipience are formidable with respect to Equiano, there is an unanswered Diasporic question: What are the migratory possibilities in Wimbush's Equiano analysis? Can a sample from the African diaspora in the Caribbean add to the hermeneutical potential of Afrocentric anti-colonialism? Wimbush's reflections on the semiospheric role the Bible plays as mechanism, channel, legitimization, and reinforcer of the colonialist's rule and cultural arrogations stage the Bible's cultural web spinning. Erna Brodber,[3] a Jamaican novelist, is an interlocutor who exposes and argues for responses that counter the Euro-Christian semiosphere. Brodber offers a narrative of postcolonial Black/white and Afro-retentive/Christian co-habitation in *Myal*. Brodber does not declare this as the case she makes. However, it is unlikely that a reader of *Myal*, aware of the social and power differentials that each group occupies in Jamaica, would not marvel at the way the narrative divests and reinvests those social power differentials. Divestment and reinvestment are the mechanisms of a cultural imaginary that performs and offers a different hermeneutic.

These other narratives offer African Diasporic survival strategies that increase and elaborate Diasporic topoi within Africana Studies. They deflect the fragmenting impact of imperialism that occurs through national and racial mechanisms that fragment and hierarchize a U.S.-based Africana conversation. The magmatic, igneous potential is that other, abutting cultural narratives can lead the Africana conversation to other adaptations, resource sharing, recognitions of common ancestral resistance residues, and for the development of peoples of color. To that end, this essay introduces Myal religion from Jamaica as a diasporic, spiritual survival practice that is rooted in African memory, effective in post-Emancipation Jamaican society, and is still today a source of rooting, resistance, and intentional reorientation contra the order of established society.

Erna Brodber's book *Myal*, set in a fictional Jamaican countryside, introduces this religion as resistance or as a wonderful obduracy. Wonderful obduracy is the conversation partner to Equiano's survival acquiescence.

Myal, a Jamaican Revivalist tradition, offers its Afro-retentive practices and their perdurance against the faces of colonial ecclesial contact. This conversation is framed in terms of Wimbush's notion of scripturalization and Yuri Lotman's notion of semiosphere. With these I contend that Myalism, in its Jamaican manifestation, evidences resistance by, through, and for the necessity of Afro-centrism, not as liberative but as a vitalizing essential for existence in the Christo-political *Umwelt* of the postcolonial period. As a response to the colonial *Umwelt*, it distinctly differs from Equiano's, and as a resistant *Umwelt*, it is the Black folk's wisdom.

FROM WHITE MAN'S MAGIC TO BLACK FOLKS' WISDOM

Equiano was a focal signifier in Wimbush's *White Man's Magic*. Equiano's response to the Bible in European society discerned its function as the source of their power. Historically, the Bible has been foundational to the Christian religion. Christianity and European civilization were inextricably intertwined in the colonial period. To accept the Bible meant gaining access to and participation in European sociocultural and political acculturation. While Equiano in *White Man's Magic* is the signifier, in Wimbush's *Scripturalectics: The Management of Meaning* it is Chinua Achebe's *Things Fall Apart*. Both function as tropes in the purveyance of the power of the white man's magic. Equiano signifies its lure and power. *Things Fall Apart* is the overarching axiom of the devastating impact of the white man's magic in the "formation of the Black Atlantic."[4]

Wimbush addresses the normalizing of discourse around the Bible as scripture. He uncovers the invisible, silent, and materially effective functions that the Bible performs wherever it is invoked. It controls domains of meaning, social intercourse, politics, economics, and other spheres of social interaction. Wimbush's criticism is that the Bible is treated as an innocent book when it is the potent *de facto* mechanism of social control. Wimbush declares that "with the intensifications of religion-inflected ideological, civil, and geopolitical wars and their brutalities and genocide, nothing short of an orientation to *radical excavation* of the phenomenon of 'scriptures' is now required."[5] *Radical Excavation*, in Wimbush's thought, is the frontier of biblical studies. This is an idea that is not only "irritating, unpleasant, unbearable"[6] and provocative of "painful admissions, anxieties, and fears,"[7] it is also perplexing to persons who locate all biblical meaning as lexical and historical. What is this intangible function or mechanism that must be excavated?

The semiosphere, as a system of significations, was first developed by Yuri Lotman. It is a sphere of communication constituted by multiple interconnected *Umwelten*. According to Aleksei Semenenko, Lotman's semiosphere was the preexisting condition for the production of a culture, "the whole semiotic space of . . . culture."[8] "In that sense, a culture is a concrete manifestation of that semiosphere."[9] Four key premises of the semiosphere are particularly relevant:

> The semiosphere is the precondition of semiosis.
> The semiotic space can be depicted as a net of interconnected personal semiospheres. (I emphasize the interconnectedness within a network that constitutes or complexifies the semiosphere.)
> Any text translates and condenses its semiosphere in itself.
> The semiosphere is both an object and a metaconcept.[10]

These premises explicate the Bible's functionality within a Euro-Christian semiosphere. Wimbush's jettisoning of textual analysis is a critique of those approaches to Biblical interpretation as superstructural but not metaconceptual. Text-based Biblical interpreters tend to be oblivious to the ontological socio-political roles the Bible plays. So semiospheric functionality is not a matter pertinent to those enterprises. Rather, Wimbush attributes to his *sui generis* concept "scripturalization." "Scripturalization" is "a social-psychological-political structure establishing its own reality."[11] Scripturalization names and enacts a four-stage process.

Scripturalization as:

> a "socio-cultural matrix, within which ideological and discursive rules and practices are made evident and common;
> framework for nationalist polity and the politics of nationalization, in which the evident and common ideological and discursive practices are legitimized, encoded, and regulated;
> socio-psycho-logical carapace/overcoat, by which the evident, common, encoded, and regulated discursive practices are naturalized for the sake of social regulation; and

the translocal/transcendent field on which or regime in which power dynamics and strategies are played out or advanced as discursive coercion and sometimes negotiated and resisted on these terms."[12]

The amniotic sac surrounding the heart might, despite its metaconceptual limitations, provide a useful image. The semiosphere is omnipresent. Its existence and function are neither sequential nor linear. Simultaneity in functioning, dialogical processivity, and semiotic spiraling depict the logic of the semiosphere's efficacy. The semiosphere is the oxygen of a society. It is unavoidable. It is also dense. According to Wimbush, it sets the terms for negotiations and resistance. Wimbush derives these principles from his reading of Equiano's autobiography.[13] It seems inescapable that the inevitability of the Euro-Christian semiosphere's overwhelm is a projection of Equiano's subjective response to his own assessment of his environment. Even so, the evidence of that overwhelming coerciveness proliferates throughout "Christendom" even today.

Scripturalization is the metaconcept and the Bible its signifier within the semiosphere. As metaconcept, it is causative and generative. Its representational function is metonymical, articulative, and simultaneously dependent on heuristic *Umwelten*. *Umwelten* are particular epistemic, symbolic, linguistic, and legislative coercions that participate in the maintenance of the semiosphere while also sustaining the exertions and pressures of their semiosphere. The relationship is dynamic and dialogical. Epistemic dominance or epistemic colonialism permits the perpetuation of a semiosphere that can naturalize, normalize, and universalize its selected *Umwelten*. Scripturalization constituted a semiosphere that naturalized instructional norms, validated their effectiveness and impact with effects that have lasted for over seventeen hundred years. The Euro-Christian semiosphere has been the originary source of intellectual inquiry, the generative perspective that legitimizes and polices both questions to be asked and the acceptable methodologies for framing, experimentation, measurement, and assessment. It has set the life rules, demarcated the playing field, and situated any struggle for justice in its own propagandistic machine and has been the sac of predominantly Euro-Christian societies. Historically, subaltern self-assertiveness, perforce, strove within an *Umwelt* that was an alien and hostile atmosphere. Alien, hostile *Umwelten* host a restrictive system of significations reinforced by congruent and allied modes of governance.

The Euro-Christian semiosphere has proven to be formidable in its capacity to overwhelm the pre-conquest *Umwelten* of historically colonized and enslaved peoples, yet not all. An alternative response is available in Afro-retentive religions in the African Diaspora. One such is Myal.

OTHER SEMIOSPHERES

As a spiritual practice, Caribbean scholars usually rank Myal among earliest-stage Afro-Jamaican Revival religions dating back to the eighteenth century. Nathaniel Murrell describes African revivalism thus: "The story of the African fight for survival and dignity in colonial Jamaica is one of black resistance to a culture of negation and oppression in every aspect of life."[14] Myal's perdurance is remarkable, apparent reductions in census numbers in the twenty-first century notwithstanding. Yet census figures are notoriously unreliable for a very significant reason. The census figures would disallow this essay's confidence that these religions withstood the Euro-Christian semiosphere. Although the census figures may be cautionary for the purposes of this essay's claims, they are not deterrents. Practitioners have been reluctant, because of legal persecution and social stigmatization, to publicly declare their allegiance. Public declarations would happen in social situations, contemporary mass media publications, and the census. It is a truism to believe that many Christians are practitioners of Afro-Jamaican Revival religions. Myal practitioners declare themselves as Christian on the census forms, thus preventing accurate accounting. Myal and other historical Afro-Jamaican Revival religions are surviving into the twenty-first century and are very present aspects of Jamaica's religious landscape. The census figures remain unreliable partly for the reasons given but also because there is an element of inscrutability about Afro-Jamaican Revival religions historically and currently. Ironically, secrecy accounts in part for their perdurance.

Historically, it has been a bit difficult to differentiate between the theologies and practices of both Myal and Obeah, another Afro-Jamaican religion. Nathaniel Murrell writes that they complemented each other in equipping Afro-Jamaicans for psychological and spiritual survival in colonial society.[15] Dianne Stewart, according to Murrell, sees Myal as a subset of Obeah, although she nonetheless contends that the difference between them "was not moral but possibly structural."[16] However they were understood, in Jamaica, both were seen as the vehicle by which poor Black people, and some affluent ones, could survive the dehumanizing pressures of Euro-Christianity and the society that was constructed in colonial and postcolonial Jamaica. It is then reasonable to posit their semiospheric function, among some Afro-Jamaicans, as "withstanding."

That the origins of Myal are African is not disputed. It has proven difficult to specify its provenance geographically and in Afro-ethnicities, but there are general propositions. There is speculation that enslaved Ghanaian Akan peoples in North Central Jamaica were the first practitioners of Myal. Another contender for provenance is Central Africa and the Kongo peoples. At the eastern end of the island, many residents "commonly speak about 'catching Myal spirit' and being possessed by their ancestral spirits, who have Kongo characteristics."[17] Yet Murrell is unhesitant in affirming Myal as "the creole version of an ancestral West Central African traditional religion (ATR). It is a religious institution with a belief system, a dance ritual, an initiatory rite tradition, and a pharmacopeia for herbal and spiritual healing. Myal functioned as a fraternity modeled after a West African secret society and operated away from the watchful eyes of colonial authorities."[18] Akan and Kongo peoples were the largest African ethnicities among the enslaved persons in Jamaica.

Werner Zips notes this in his discussions on the origins of Maroon community organization; he attributes a special social organization to the Akan and Kongo peoples. Yet he decries an appeal to their religiosity as key to understanding their social organizing and arrangements. He argues that in Jamaica the term *Cromantee* or *Kromanti* was used to subsume multiple African ethnicities, notably, Akan, Ewe, Ga-Adangame Fante, Kongo, and others. Among the Maroons, the term *Kromanti* signified "the shared experience of their displacement from Africa."[19] It also signified the formation of new relationships and new social orders despite "old social and political differences."[20] So Zips claims that "like almost all former European colonies in Africa, Jamaica possesses at least two legal traditions: A European one and one that was born of the diaspora experience."[21] In Zips's modeling of Maroon life, *Kromanti* is not a preexisting African ethnicity. Rather, it is "a very broad category of reference, a conceptual framework that was developed in Jamaica to confer jural corporateness on 'a new community that we created out of former diversity,' and served as 'a kind of blueprint for all that it means to be Maroon and to live as a Maroon.'"[22] He adds that the *Kromanti* concept is inseparable from Maroon cosmology.[23] Myalism is the core religiosity, cosmology, and epistemology of the Trelawny Maroons. It is also important to the Charlestown Maroons of Portland. Myal then is to be associated with the preservation of the complete and holistic organization of a community that stands in parallel to dominant social systems that are based on a Euro-Christian semiosphere. Arguably, *Kromanti* was their semiosphere.

WITHSTANDING THE EURO-CHRISTIAN SEMIOSPHERE: SHAPING THE NARRATIVE

As overwhelming as the Euro-Christian semiosphere seems to be, it can be withstood. Withstanding the Euro-Christian semiosphere is here understood as perseverance in and practice of socially disparaged epistemologies and semiotic systems even when the very practitioners of the resistant cultural sphere must interact with the Euro-Christian semiosphere. It can be observed in Caribbean experience, but it requires focusing on the religious practices of groups such as Candomblé, Myal Pukumina, Santería, and Spiritual Baptists, among others. These traditions are eclectic, having adopted aspects of Christianity for integration into their Afro-retentive practices. The preceding sentence, at first glance, may not appear to offer any greater insight than the casual summation of all that we have ever known of their practitioners. To exceed that summation requires a number of strategic steps. These include dispensing with the optic of Christian religious supremacy, its myopic gaze on liturgical practices, and Christian evaluation of the above-named religious groups by their theological resonance with or distance from dominant Euro-Christianity. Neither semiospheric Euro-Christianity nor its varieties of national or ethnic *Umwelten* is paradigmatic for these practitioners. Writing from my position as a Christian thinker and pastor about groups with which I share racial and ethnic heritage but not a conscious religious history requires a rearranging of my priorities and preferences. This experience is itself an articulation of the strategies already named. It augurs requisite transformations in reckoning with, albeit from outside, the respectability and internal integrity of peoples against whom the Euro-Christian semiosphere militates. It requires a disaffected disposition toward my *Umwelt*, my semiosphere. Seeing this signals that they can withstand the Euro-Christian semiosphere and also dismantle it. The final requisite strategy is resistance against the reductionist gawker's gaze upon their ritual events. This strategy invokes the vulnerability that derives from divesting one's own power, at least enough, to overhear their perceptions of themselves and their others in their own *Umwelt*. *Myal* challenges these frontiers.

DR. ERNA BRODBER: THE CONNECTED NOVELIST

In Erna Brodber, we have a novelist whose primary locus of existence is among the rural people of Woodside District in the parish of St. Mary, Jamaica. Although a scholar of international acclaim, she lives in Woodside because it is her birth place and home. Her kinship and experiences with the living circumstances of Woodside residents is that of quotidian commonalties, shared heritage, and mutual respect. By dint of this enculturation her novel, *Myal*, can be regarded as fictional autoethnographic anthropology. Brodber's declaration is: "My work, fiction and non-fiction, is devoted to helping Africans of the diaspora to understand themselves and hopefully to consequently undertake with more clarity the job of social (re)construction which we have to do."[24] Her educative tools are folk songs, stories, and the novels she writes. These artifacts are of the living heritage, and she uses them "to inform a group often far from archival data. I inject information which I think this group needs to have, and which I arrive at from my investigations, into my novels."[25] Her novel, *Myal*, serves Brodber's purpose and aligns with the role of Myal, Obeah, as withstanding Christian semiospheres.

Brodber's anti-colonialist, pro Pan-Africanism stance substantiates her position as interlocutor for Wimbush/Equiano. She is emphatic in her rejection of standard Caribbean anti-colonialist intellectual postures. For example, she rejects "creole," as a Caribbean cultural characterization, the name Caribbean, the Jamaican motto, "Out of Many One People," but declares herself, "I'm 'African Diaspora.'"[26] Brodber is the embodiment, by her chosen residential community, her recourse to living archivists (oral history) as primary sources, and ideology, of withstanding the Euro-Christian semiosphere. This commitment is a searing anti-colonialism, anti-colonial residue by which she declares the following:

> Jamaica's relationship to the African continent and to the African diaspora needed affirmation *before* such a national vision [out of many one people] could be realized.

Caribbean is nice and creole and mixed and all that, but . . . I don't believe the point is reached yet, where what it is that we have of Africa has been honed and has been given to the world.[27]

As Petal Samuel points out as she interprets Brodber in the article "Erna Brodber and Pan-Africanism in Post-Independence Jamaica," "Brodber's suspicion, then, of the post-racial subtexts of 'Caribbean' and 'creole' signals how these terms can house a subtle strain of anti-blackness. The celebratory frame of hybridity and mixture often masked the reality that these constitutive elements (Europe, Asia, Africa) were not equally embraced."[28] This observation enables the deepening of Brodber's readers' insights into the intensities and constancy of Brodber's commitment to Blackness, Pan-Africanism (still), and to Africana. Her anthropological research is autoethnographic, based on shared alterities of living people, and with a profound commitment to honor the epistemologies and cosmologies which they activate and live by.

Brodber's novels may seem susceptible to the accusation of fantasy and therefore invalid for this essay's purpose. To the contrary, the seemingly fantastic characters and events ground her novels in her Woodside reality and the practice of Myal and other Afro-Diasporic religions. According to Petal Samuel, many of Brodber's writings "heavily emphasize spirituality and the psychic healing that results from a positive embrace of one's blackness."[29] And as Jennifer Harris observes, "Brodber weaves mythic and fantastical elements throughout, establishing non-rational events and happenings as just as crucially implicated in the psychology of her characters as their class, gender, education, or other more conventional factors."[30] The "mythic and fantastical" is the language of outsiders to this community. For Brodber's Myalists and Pukumina practitioners the so-called "mythic" and the fantastical are ineffables. The fantastic characters and events also indicate the connectedness between Brodber's person, her residential community, and her novels.[31] Brodber's connectedness determines that the novels are historical and existential fiction. That is to say, Brodber's novels derive from and represent a subaltern community that most clearly speaks within itself in the absence of gawkers. Her novels are not based in an idiosyncratic, individualistic, peculiar, or weird imagination. She writes about and from among those people who withstand Euro-Christian dominance. Brodber, in these novels writes about the efficacy of Black folks' wisdom, knowledge, and sacred powers. When the Euro-Christian semiosphere damages the psyche of her characters or invades their intellectual spaces and where that semiosphere wields a predatory grasp, then and there these Black people experience the efficacy of ancestral wisdom and ways. Beyond resistance this is "withstanding" the constant assault of that overwhelming Euro-Christian semiosphere.

This focus on Brodber arose from a methodological concern. The fundamental advocacy of this essay is to present another semiosphere that withstands the encroachments, incursions, and coercions of the Euro-Christian semiosphere. It posits, in withstanding, a narrative of the colonial encounter between Europeans and the peoples of Africa and their descendants in Diaspora other than acquiescence and assimilation. The narrative of withstanding is perceivable within the lived culture of communities that though living inside the Euro-Christian semiosphere have withstood its tendencies to stigmatize and demonize African epistemological and spiritual retentions. Indeed, these core aspects of their worldview are fundamental to their management of life. Unfortunately, this essay does not provide an anthropological report on these communities. I rely on Brodber's novels for access to the communities. It seemed necessary, then, to deflect Western literary criticism that scarcely has a genre for Brodber's novels. It would miss the important connectedness of auctorial contiguity with a psycho-spiritual epistemology that is of a particular context. Western literary criticism might assume that fiction must be a distorted representation that has enough plausibility to invoke credulity. The novels are not historical fiction, not autobiography, not autobiographical fiction, not biomythography,[32] and not fantasy. Rather, they are a mash-up of all those genres bound together by the wholistic pedagogical endeavor undertaken with the glue of auctorial connectedness with the kind of eventfulness of the stories. Auctorial connectedness is the guarantor of cultural community authenticity.

Auctorial connectedness is, I believe, an unaccustomed reliance in religious studies, and Brodber's methodological purpose had to be explained descriptively. Having introduced her and developed ideas about her, I can continue with the essay. My interest is a discernment process that seeks to perceive instances of withstanding Euro-Christian semiospheres and *Umwelten*. Equiano's assimilation and Myal's withstanding are the terms that shape their interlocution and discussion of their responses to the Euro-Christian semiosphere.

NARRATIVE OF ASSIMILATION: EQUIANO

In his introduction to *White Men's Magic* Vincent Wimbush indicated his interest in Equiano as a means of pressing "the matter of his uses of scripture into service for [biblical] criticism . . . including how they are made to function in a socio-political and discursive regime."[33] Olaudah Equiano as a Black man and former slave in his autobiography illuminated the circumstances that facilitated the Euro-Christian Bible in its transformation of a formerly "free African into a former slave, a Christian, an almost Englishman."[34] This transformation occurs through a process of assimilation, the term used in this essay. It is not assimilation into a cultureless religion. Rather, it is a religion whose good incarnational evaluation has been dependent on its cultural mimetic and articulative fidelity to the colonizing empire within which it flourished. Thus Euro-Christianity, by the late sixteenth century, when it arrived in Jamaica, provided the semiosphere that acculturated enslaved Africans into Europe in the New World. That Euro-Christian acculturation also attempted to coerce amnesia and eradication of the African cultural episteme. That, for Wimbush, is an insufficient observation and would be an inadequate, perhaps hackneyed, project. A more provocative question, taken seriously, might be: Why would any enslaved person engage with the imperial Christian project? Equiano[35] is an available figure by which to track the processes of that engagement as a "story about first contact and the resultant construction of the modern world."[36]

Olaudah Equiano is an ambivalent figure oscillating between his history as an African who was enslaved and then became European. As a somewhat European who wrote an autobiography, he is credited with influencing the passing of the British Slave Trade Act (1807), which abolished the Atlantic trade in Africans. His membership in the Sons of Africa aligned him with other prominent persons of African descent then living in Britain. In these ways Equiano (or Gustavus Vassa, as he was also known) participated in wielding influence within British politics and society. As substantial and significant as these actions were, arguably, they were as trace evidence, the collateral benefit of a process that left these efforts and results as artifactual residue of Olaudah's Africa and his people. Wimbush advances discussions that redefine the notion of fetish as a "state of critical consciousness. Fetish is an invitation to consider issues of power and agency as they are arranged around the fetish. Fetishism is the preservation by sanctification and taboo of an object that memorializes a past. According to Webb Keane, "Submitting to fixed discursive forms is not only an error or an affront to God; it threatens to undermine the agency proper to humans."[37] Fetishes, then, are objects and also texts that in themselves signify social proprieties, appropriate ritual actions, and taboos; therefore they are agents for controlling behavior. By Wimbush's accounting the Bible is the fetish.

Equiano demonstrates biblical fetishism's efficacy at the personal level when he highlights aspects of his relationship with Daniel Queen and then the betrayal of his master. Daniel Queen "taught me to shave, and dress hair a little, and also to read in the Bible, explaining many passages to me, which I did not comprehend"[38]—comportment and Bible. Equiano "was wonderfully surprised to see the laws and rules of my own country written almost exactly here; a circumstance which, I believe, tended to impress our manners and customs more deeply on my memory"[39]—familiarity with the Bible. However, Equiano saw in his master's kindness, moral teachings connected to the biblical God, and admonitions that protected him in God's love, augurs of freedom. Those kindly words and deeds converted to life threats when Equiano resisted being sent away by his master. Agency was not an option for Equiano. Equiano's options were to learn English, to acculturate, to encapsulate himself in this new world, and to survive as he could. By acculturation, "making do" with the fetish, Equiano thrived!

Wimbush's interest is in Equiano's making do with the fetish in order to elaborate the notion of scripturalization. The interest of this essay is in the elucidation of Equiano's response to the semiosphere shaped by the Bible in the culture, which Wimbush describes as "making do." The point of contact for an Africana conversation is marked by Wimbush's comment which I quote fully:

> Although Equiano was in many respects somewhat unusual in some of his experiences, his "making do" with the Bible (understood by him as nationalist cultural fetish) remains fairly typical of black folks' "making do" with the North Atlantic worlds they had been made to undergo, whether slave or "free" (the latter always and everywhere in

the eighteenth century throughout the Atlantic worlds understood in highly qualified terms on account of widely and contradictory codes and laws). Metonymic of the black inflected vernacularization of scriptures, Equiano's story provides the outline for a layered history of black North Atlantic representations, gestures, and mimetic practices as a history of scriptures.

It would perhaps be bellicose to dwell on the very direct connection between Equiano, Britain's colonial empire, and the Commonwealth countries to which Jamaica belongs. It would be cavalier to begin here an Africana internecine battle of rights to Equiano. Yet while respecting the North Atlantic location of the African American colonial experience and the association of Equiano with it, the very location of Equiano's semiosphere and its connection to the British Atlantic trade, it seems somewhat apropos to expropriate the heft of Wimbush's lifting, relocate it (even temporarily) within the British Commonwealth as a set of independent histories in which a dominant and hegemonic Euro-Christianity flourishes. Indisputably, the majority of these Commonwealth and North American peoples are represented by Equiano's "making do" with the fetish. It is also true that it is especially among the peoples of the Caribbean and Central America (i.e., not Northern Atlantic) that religious Afro-centrism dates back to colonial times. It is preserved in previously mentioned religious practices and in addition such as Convince, Macumba, Obeah, Orisha-Shango, Poco, Umbanda, Voodoo, Yoruba, and more lately Rastafarianism. Remembering Equiano as a man of the Commonwealth entrenches the interlocution with Caribbean Myalists within the very same semiosphere of which the North American experience is an isomorph.

The aforementioned religions have been studied with the weight of Western anthropology inflected by Euro-Christian semiospheric optics. These religions have not been addressed with respect, if at all, within biblical studies and core theological subjects. They responded to the same semiosphere in which Equiano thrived. Until recently, subaltern epistemic systems have not been granted respect as contributors to the current human project for constructive persons. Rather they are often regarded as the stubborn detritus of their more civilized and civilizable (European) societies, the debris of a best-forgotten past. How correct is Brodber then to say, when looking out from among the people of Woodside "from a political point of view, *creole* [hybridity] wants to forget where we're from and focus on what was made here in the Caribbean. . . . I think, first of all, especially for the Afro-people, you have to look at where you're coming from first."[40] That is the recognizable optic of the practice of Afro-retentive religions. They are the holders of memories, the artists of heritage, the prioritizers of Afro-centric survival, the Withstanders. Withstanding has not historically required distance from the practices of Euro-Christianity. It has meant strategic prioritization, and Euro-Christianity has not predominated. Brodber captures the non-predomination of Euro-Christianity in *Myal*.

MYAL AS A NARRATIVE OF WITHSTANDING

Myal is the *Umwelt* of the people of Grove Town in *Myal*. Myal is to be associated with the preservation of multiple African ethnicities learning to live in concert within the *Kromanti* system of community organization and governance. *Kromanti* signifies the Myal *Umwelt*. *Myal* moves the parallelism of the two semiospheres from coexistence to withstanding. This move is contingent on the cultural imaginary and purposiveness of Brodber. Brodber's contiguity with the cultures represented in her novels and her purpose in writing indicate another status arrangement within withstanding. That rearrangement occurs in two contexts in which the Euro-Christian semiosphere mingles with the *Kromanti* semiosphere and does not overcome it. In the rearrangement, the *Kromanti* styled semiosphere dominates or disrupts the epistemologies of the other.

MYAL

The general vicinity and topography of the novel's events are evoked by an early mention of the towns of Manchioneal, Kensington of Hope Bay, and Hector's River, in the parish of Portland. On a map of Jamaica, this locates the novel in a mountainous area of the island that has an aura of mystique. Manchioneal and Hope Bay define the longitudinal extremes of the region. The scope in terms of a small island associates Grove Town with hills and valleys, rivers, and the Marron towns of Cornwall Barracks and Moore Town—all lesser known and lesser explored parts of the island. They also describe the parish of Portland which along with the adjacent parish of St. Thomas in the eastern end of the island is renowned in hushed tones for dabbling in the deeply non/anti-Christian spiritual arts of Myal and Pukumina. The spread of the area locates the reader in an unsettling Afro-Jamaican religious mysteriousness but with a promise of unveiling. I highlight a sample of moments in the narrative that indicate the dynamics of Myal's *Umwelten*.

Similarly, the musings of Maydene Brassington, the mixed-race Methodist minister's white wife bears the narrative's contention which I demarcate. First she smilingly admires Miss Gatha's head-dress, "I wouldn't like to walk barefooted but I would like to wear that head-dress."[41] Then she laughingly self-deprecates, "My straight hair wouldn't give it half a chance to stay on."[42] She continues on to opine against her husband, who requires his members to replace their "colorful clothes" for "colourless white and those felt hats which people buy—buy you know—and wear only on Sundays."[43] The impact of the semiosphere is visibly personal at the level of dress and, particularly, women's dress. Of her husband's attitude, she reflects, "He would want Miss Gatha to give up her head-dress and put on my hat and be very grieved if she refused to. That is it. In church after church, the colourful clothes have gone, replaced by colour-less white and those felt hats."[44] The remainder of her musings reminisce on a conversation with William about the dress changes he imposes. His explanatory response indicates the purpose of religion—to convert "these people" to both Christianity and the English conventions. Tauntingly, he inquires, "Don't you wear a hat to church? Why should my people not wear hats? Isn't it nice that all of us in the fellowship behave in the same way? What do you do with that?"[45] Maydene remembers a warning question she put to him that inquired about his ability to replace what he has denied these people. He derides her concern. Her consequent accusation and his sneering reply constitute one core point of this novel. Mrs. Maydene Brassington declares of and to her husband, "William, you are a spirit thief. You keep taking away these people's spirit." That is the result of the Euro-Christian semiosphere—race- and ethnicity-based anthropological impoverishment.[46] Rev. William Brassington's reply reveals its dastardly intent. He responds, "That is the nature of this kind of ministry—to *exorcise and replace*."[47]

Predominantly, Western histories narrate the nonfictional success of the manifesto to *exorcise and replace*, as Brodber succinctly explicates through Rev. Brassington. With keen novelistic insight Brodber lays bare an entire project of Euro-Christianity's epic collusive, bamboozling cultural machinery and intent. Given the omnipresence of Euro-Christianity within Western histories and academics, *Myal* should be just another narrative of the struggle to survive, adjustments, accommodations, and acquiescence by the *exorcised* against the overwhelming *replacement*. Early on Brodber signals that this is not going to be the case. Maydene Brassington smiles and muses to herself, "at the thought of Miss Gatha, 'No way he could take away her head-dress' and congratulated her silently."[48] Maydene Brassington was convinced that the "Grove Town people would resist his efforts to separate them from their understanding of life."[49] That William Brassington would need a sledgehammer was her thought. The outcome would not be determined by the Christians.

The confrontation's drama unfolds around Ella's life. Ella is a mixed-race child born of an Irish police officer and a Black Jamaican peasant woman. Ella's brilliance in the recitation of Rudyard Kipling's poetry attracts the attention of Mrs. Brassington. Mrs. Brassington brings Ella to live in her household as a daughter and that leads to Ella's eventual migration to the U.S. with a white husband, Selwyn. Ella is already distraught because of the absence of her familiars, and Selwyn exacerbates Ella's distress when he uses her home stories to write and stage a Blackface minstrel show. Ella experiences a complete breakdown and returns to Jamaica with hope of healing. The migrant experience and Ella's encounter with a world of white people results in profound self-alienation. The symbolism of that experience, reflective of the economic, psychological, and cultural exploitation and abuse in the colonial encounter needs no elaboration in this compact narration of the experience. Ella's return heightens the intercultural tensions already expressed in *exorcise and replace*. What shall effect Ella's healing? What shall Ella's healing effect? Already in Ella's young life there has been an attempt to exorcise through assimilation and acculturation. The result for the metonymical Ella is a devastating, ego-disheveling, spirit theft.

A significant salvific character in *Myal* is "Ole African," a powerful Myalist whose name has eponymous force. He was a man of mysterious powers, an ancient. His "was no human hand. This was no young man. . . . For Ole African only went where there was a spirit to let loose needing to be cut and cleared."[50] Thus Ole African saved Mass[51] Levi using his shut-pan.[52] Ole African protected Euphemia's house from stone throwers. In that case there are reminiscences of Euro-Christian theology and biblical themes. As Ole African conducts his ritual with the house door wide open and he in front of it. Brodber describes the scene thus, "A scarecrow was hanging from top to bottom in the doorway, its arms stretched out so that it seemed as if he were a rugged cross. And the stones started to come like never before. They all landed on him. His blood was now sprinkling the steps. Then suddenly he left and the stones stopped."[53] Afterward, his blood remained on the step, and his cryptic, signature comment recalled from the scene, "The half has never been told." This is a salvific or healing episode. That signature statement sustains an aura of mystification about its circumstances and the mutterer. And as Ella narrated to Selwyn, according to Mrs. Brassington, "No child in Grove Town needed to see Ole African to know him. They had been hearing about him for centuries."[54] The children were not centuries old but the stories of centuries old Ole African added to his mystique and was a partial epiphany. Mrs. Brassington too had her brush with Ole African.[55] Mrs. Brassington's experience and other of the information provided about Ole African is given by Ella in conversation with Selwyn. All turned up in Selwyn's Blackface minstrel show. Selwyn listened so carefully that he transported Grove Town to the U.S., converting the town and its people into a farce. Selwyn's betrayal demonstrated that spirit thieves were not only in the church. Mrs. Brassington, reflecting on Selwyn, declared, "Spirit thieves come in so many forms."[56] This is why Ella fell apart. However, it was not Ole African that saved Ella.

Mrs. Brassington's understanding was rewarded by Miss Gatha after an experience that required the intervention by the Baptist pastor and which was connected to the stoning of Euphemia's house. The Baptist pastor was a Black man, and very familiar with the Myal arts. That experience had set the town agog. Mrs. Brassington took Ella with her to Miss Gatha, of whom she inquired the cause of the turbulence and the drumming. The goodly, godly Methodist Miss Gatha "dealt in drums and in spirits."[57] By insinuation Mrs. Brassington learns from Miss Gatha that the spirit thief is dead but inquires after Miss Gatha's well-being. Miss Gatha smiled her response and then re-christened Mrs. Brassington with the name "White Hen." She was the first Euro-Christian postulant for the power of Myal in *Myal*. Now she was an insider, capitulating her spirit and Miss Gatha's recognizing each other. And Pastor Simpson, the Baptist Myalist who was also Ole African's friend and interlocutor recognized White Hen.[58] Ole African, however, was the initiating counterforce to spirit thieves. His power was transmitted through the rituals and practices of Myal. The Euro-Christian semiosphere is moving toward Myal rather than overwhelming it.

Would Olaudah recognize these activities? Would they be as familiar to him as the peoples and laws of the Bible had seemed? He had a seemingly vague memory of the Eboe priests and rituals of his origins. The British were ignorant of those practices. Olaudah cannot tell those stories to reconstitute himself in England. Following Wimbush Equiano's early narration of their ways "was part of his interest in pointing out the compelling moral logic and cultural appropriateness of his integration into this world."[59] He recalls the knowledgeability of Eboe priests as comparable to British priests and learned men. They had powers of healing, expelling poisons, knowledge, discernment, and calculation. They knew how to make the world work. The British powers resided in books. Books made the difference between success and failure. True Brits were literate. There was every advantage to acquiring that skill. Wimbush surmises that "it is this observation of the British people's engagement with books that helped the historical Equiano over time to come to associate books, especially the Good Book, the Bible, with knowledge of the origins of things, with the ability to know or 'calculate' the times in the British world."[60] Equiano's Eboe priests were translators in the British Euro-Christian semiosphere. Because he could make a favorable comparison to British knowledge then that world was sufficient for his psyche and other needs. He transmorphed. His Eboe priests did not need to come with him.

READING THE SEMIOSPHERE

Reading skills, then, are an interlocutory contact. Olaudah should have affinity. How would he weigh his response to white people's reading against Ella's? If, as Wimbush assesses, scriptures for Equiano "captured not only the politics and practices of the colonials but also the terms around which the colonized and enslaved engaged in complex mimetics," then what of this intimate exchange of worldviews between Miss Gatha and Mrs. Brassington? And, what of Ole African and the commingling Baptist Pastor Simpson, practicing Myal, not as transactional but as the lived experience of real people surviving against a powerful *Umwelt* and its semiosphere. The vast majority of Equiano's interactions in his autobiography was with Europeans. He depended on them for goodwill, and they frequently failed him. Equiano, according to his autobiography either by preference or lack of opportunity did not avail himself of slave culture. His view was limited; his options completely defined by the *Umwelten* of his experiences. It would be premature to draw any conclusions about the semiospheric potency of Euro-Christianity sans the resistant epistemologies that emerge from cultural dissociation. Yet Equiano's and Myalists' types of dissociation, one from origins, the other from semiosphere, open to new hypotheses about religion and its escaping the effects of the colonial residue of anthropological impoverishment.

It would be remiss of this essay to avoid Wimbush's use of Equiano to explicate the role of the Bible in advancing the dominance of Europe through the Euro-Christian semiosphere. The Bible and the semiosphere are inextricably bound. Reading, associated with the Bible, that is biblical literacy. As Wimbush explained "Equiano seemed most adept and intelligent in his recognition of how much powerful officials . . . in British society were affected by what now may be termed the politics of the structure and media of knowledge and opinion. This would include the power of the press, which depended on the power of literacy."[61] À la Wimbush's Equiano the connection between power and literacy was causative and acculturative. This connection establishes education, literary canons, the curriculum as the most critical and uncontested means of incorporating conquered peoples of color into their conqueror's societies and ensuring our acquiescence. Wimbush is correct to see this. In contrast to the U.S. slave experience, English colonialists thought it important to ensure the education of their former enslaved. Their location in territories beyond the British Isles required that the formerly enslaved had the capacity to participate servilely in the governance of their territory. There was a need for a minimally educated Black populace. The Roman Catholics, Anglicans, and historical Protestants were foremost in that endeavor in the Caribbean. Despite varying degrees of loyalties to their home governments, throughout the British Commonwealth, churches undertook to educate the children of the formerly enslaved. Thus they provided for educated disciples and for a lower civil servant class initially. It is the power of literacy that provides the linchpin. The educated Black student would know William Shakespeare, Jane Austen, Charlotte and Emily Bronte, Elizabeth Barrett Browning, Charles Dickens, E. M. Forster, Thomas Hardy, Rudyard Kipling, Christina Rosetti, Robert Louis Stevenson, Alfred Lord Tennyson, Oscar Wilde, and others. Most importantly, we knew the Bible. Up until about the late 1990s biblical studies was an examination subject at the end of high school in the Caribbean. Of course that would be so. For over 100 years churches had been the sponsors of high schools. How percipient of Wimbush to discern that "Equiano figured out that one of the most important aspects of the structuring of authority and power in the Protestant British world was the facility for reading the book, *the* Book, the (English) Bible."[62] Yet Wimbush's painful recognition that despite Equiano's mastery of English in speech and literacy, despite his familiarity with the Bible, "Precisely because he could eventually come into (standard English) speech for himself—'read [English books] for myself'[63]—he made himself more powerful and potentially more embraceable, but also, paradoxically, he seems to be even more estranged from himself." The Bible is interwoven with Equiano's pain but not only his. With this, Wimbush, his Equiano, Brodber, and her Ella have contact but their responses to reading are opposites. For Brodber, the ignition point of self-alienation is in reading. The Euro-Christian semiosphere is its exacerbation, but the literacy acquisition complex as acculturating force facilitating survival and some kind of thriving within it is the canker.

In *Myal*, reading unravels. Ella, Mr. Dan, White Hen, Rev. Brassington unravel reading. The Bible is not centered in these closing scenes. The leaders of Myal in Grove Town analyze the discombobulation of those who learn and teach formal reading. If biblical literacy is White Man's magic, then reading is the sorcerer's wand. The list of Brodber's characters above includes names new to this essay and a previously decentered character. Mr. Dan is a new name but not a new character. He is also known as Rev. Simpson, the Baptist pastor.[64] Mr. Dan is his Myal name.[65] It is an Afro-cultural truism that Afro-Jamaicans would belong to both a church and an Afro-Jamaican religion. As a commonplace it does not extend to the clergy, although the possibility and likelihood are suspected. Rev. Simpson, the religious amphibian, is significant because, eventually, Rev. Brassington entrusts him with the propagation of the negative analysis of reading. Ella as a teacher of reading "excavates" the effects of reading. When she describes the work and effect of the book, it is possible to hear an echo effect that reverberates to the Bible, especially as she opines to Mr. Dan qua Rev. Simpson. Ella accuses the book of hiding alternatives.[66] The book contains ignorance.[67] The writer robs "his characters of their possibilities."[68]

The writer "dismissed the existence within them of that in-born guiding light—and left them to run around like half-wits, doing what the master has in store for them. . . . He has *Zombified* them."[69] She explains *Zombification*. The writer has "taken their knowledge of their original and natural world away from them and left them empty shells—duppies, zombies, living deads capable only of receiving orders from someone else and carrying them out."[70] Education is in question. She demands of Rev. Simpson, "Is that what I am to teach these children, Reverend Simpson? That most of the world is made up of zombies who cannot think for themselves or take care of themselves. . . . Must my voice tell that to children who trust me?"[71] Rev. Simpson remains in his pastoral persona. He challenges Ella to be an agent who is not coerced into self-alienation by the writer.

Wimbush's Equiano began his adjustments with insights similar to those of Brodber's Ella. He did not have Mr. Dan, Miss Gatha, White Hen, and certainly not Ole African. Where Equiano found connections between his old African practices and the Bible as reason to succumb to the Euro-Christian semiosphere, the Grove Town team vitalized the old African memories. Simpson, the Bapti-Myalist, challenges Ella to counter the writer, therefore to read and teach with her senses alive. Michael G. Cooke positions Brodber's approach to education within a Caribbean literary tradition. "Works such as Claude McKay's *Banana Bottom* and George Lamming's *Seasons of Adventure* favour the conclusion that the right route towards emancipation is frankly to turn your back on education."[72] Further, "Besides condemning or dismissing the conventional forms of education, [Brodber] furnishes at least the prospect of an alternative."[73] The alternative is the product of an epistemological alternative—Myal. The capitulation of the established order to this product is found in the final actions of Mr. Brassington. He attempted to persuade his wife, Mrs. Brassington, against her involvement with the Myalist. But, finally, the Methodist pastor whose plan was to "exorcise and replace" compromises. The exorcisms were of the spirit thieves, Mr. Levi, Selwyn, Ella's husband, and other establishment leaders of the community. Christianity and its mores were replaced. That replacement was most clear when Rev. Brassington visits Rev. Simpson to ask him about Zombification. Rev. Simpson explains in similar terms to Ella's but more expansively, including parts of Africa, Haiti, and Brazil. His explanation sounds suspiciously similar to Voodoo practices in Haiti. For his part, Rev. Brassington, attributes the word to Ella and requests Rev. Simpson to disseminate Ella's idea by giving her a wider audience.

Mr. Dan declares:

> My people have been separated from themselves . . . by several means, one of them being the printed word and the ideas it carries. Now we have two people who are about to see through that. And who are these people, White Hen? People who are familiar with the print and the language of the print. Our people are now beginning to see how it and they themselves, have been used against us. Now, White Hen, now, we have people who can and are willing to correct images from the inside, destroy what should be destroyed, replace it with what it should be replaced[74] and put us back together, give us back ourselves with which to chart our course to go where we want to go.[75]

It is commonsensical to assume that, within the novel, the "people who are familiar with the print and the language of the print . . . people who can and are willing to correct images from the inside" are Ella and Rev. Brassington, the two biracial characters. Their creole racialization reflects their hybrid position in relation to power, literacy, and the Euro-Christian semiosphere on the one hand and to active African memories, and Afro-Jamaicanisms on the other. Within themselves they demonstrate the conflicts between the two. Within themselves they resolve them. Mr. Dan/Rev. Simpson discerns, and invites the reader to discern, that Afro-Jamaicanisms with their African retentions have overwhelmed the Euro-Christian semiosphere and caused the capitulation of its representatives. Keshia Abraham, in an interview with Brodber, surmises the challenge to Diaspora Africans as "the failure to recognize the power that we had historically, the ability to connect with and utilize our power from within. It wasn't that people who were enslaved remained enslaved because they didn't know how to fight against slavery. What kept them alive was their ability to stay hidden, their shared knowledge of how to live, how to find spirit within themselves, how to transform themselves, how to manage."[76] Brodber does not verbalize any disagreement. Her response to Abrahams's further observation about her that, "as an educated, elevated person, you're supposed to be the one who advocates assimilation and openness" is core to the mission of Brodber's writing. "You can't assimilate until you are something. Then you have something to give other people." The challenge is to reject Zombification where and when the semiospheres intersect.

'Ow Wi Cum Ova, Weh Wi Reach, and Weh Wi fe Go
"'Ow we cum ova" and "weh we reach," written in Jamiekan (Jamaican English), begin with interrogatives but are declarative statements. They express this conclusion's intent. The first, translated "how did you manage," indicates that this essay is a methodical examination of two strategies, one dominant and the other overlooked, of responding to the colonial encounter and the role of religion. The second, translated, "where we are" reflects specifically on the essay's gain.

Semiospheres are posited as membranous matrices that affect the psycho-social, moral, spiritual, and juridical development of its inhabitants. There they are swayed by the systemic totalizing powers of the state or community. Within semiospheres symbols of success and sensations of thriving are undergirded by customs and conventions that require compliance and subordination. They contain presuppositions about the cohesive elements that definitions of good community, ethno-cultural mores and practices, roles, the status of roles, appropriate social locations for particular groups, and effective policing of its gateways supply. Religion can be the ultimate enforcer, education the devastating or stunning mechanism of conformity. By education one accepts enculturation into group histories, mythologies, philosophies, economies, symbols and their narratives, as well as the internal relativity of its mores and ethics. These are powerful tools of enculturation.

For Equiano, a man mostly alone in his race and in the strategies of survival and thriving that he had to deploy and the sociocultural circumstances he navigated, compliance was the route to survival, mastery, and integration. Ole African in Myal would say, "The half has never been told." *The Interesting Narrative of the Life of Olaudah Equiano* ought not to be above suspicion as to its incompleteness. It narrates his process of survival, mastery, and compliance. As a dweller of the Jamaican Diaspora in the midst of the larger African Diaspora, I know the tales that are told to ensure "comin' ova." There is much that remains unstated because it requires dense explanation and contains immigrant anxieties. The assumption that Equiano has been completely forthcoming cannot be assured.

Yet his *Narrative* is his legacy because the invisible is immaterial. But is it? The people of Grove Town in Brodber's *Myal* are akin to the Gramscian subaltern. As Joseph Parker observed, many of us in the academy, "carry considerable economic privilege well above anything resembling a subproletariat . . . and in this regard cannot be termed subaltern."[77] We cannot make the subalterns of our larger societies visible. The Grove Town people are mostly invisible to our work in the Western academy. They become material as objects of curiosity who practice curiosities. They are the way we left and they reveal our Zombification through Brodber's *Myal*. In her novel they materialize as communities of striving and thriving—but not on our terms. At best, we can be conduits. My contention is that knowing subalterns, hearing their speech, is essential to any Africana investigations.

Akin to but differing from Wimbush's concerns to distinguish biblical social functionality from textual interpretation, I aimed for a culture as the text to be read but interpreted on its own terms. Our focus in the encounter of cultures in which the Bible is a scripturalectical artifact requires a recalibrating of our optic for purposes of seeing. *Myal* characters will always be transacting their lives while we look on using the methodologies, preferred subjects, and viewpoint of our academic acculturation, that is wearing shades and blinders. Recalibrated optics make visible the invisible, uncover the places, ways, practices, communities where subalterns express agency but in coded discourses of particularity rather than in the vocabulary, grammar, and syntax of the dominant semiosphere.

In *Theorizing Scriptures* Wimbush's method intended to avoid rhetoric and argumentation about the subaltern. Rather, it was to use the "experiences of the historically and persistently subaltern, usually the darker peoples of the world" as the filter for his question, "'What is scripture?'"[78] The methodological intent is allowance of the experiential, and therefore, the existential culture of the subaltern to guide the response to the question. My concern in addressing the Euro-Christian semiospheric problem is that from the academic perch the subaltern experience can become a surface gloss, subject to a phenomenological approach. Hence, the significance of Parker's observations about the subaltern credentials of minority academics. It is difficult to actually divest ourselves of academic privilege without practicing interpretive anthropology or autoethnography. Many of us lack for immersion in or experience of the subalterns that we seek to represent. Our evaluation of their experiences is often affected by the academic audiences we address. This is a methodological issue. I share that limitation. The risk is that our analyses lack insight into religious coping mechanisms as responses to the various tsunamis of colonial encounters. Such groups are susceptible to misinterpretation, selective representation, skew(er)ed by the lens of a dominant religion or intellectual matrix that lacks experience in comprehending the utter otherness of the subaltern even where the subaltern has overlapping symbol systems, lore, mythologies, terms. The full authenticity of the subaltern is then unavailable for a number of reasons. Methodologically, Erna Brodber as an Indigenous novelist, with Pan-African commitments, and a philosophy that understands Afro-Jamaican religiosity as an anti-colonial, resistant, vitalizing force in subaltern lives satisfies the lack and mediates a particular subaltern group with the vivacity that derives from familiarity.

Myal and other Brodber novels of similar typology can be both antidotal to Equiano's metonymic dilemma and obviating of academic distance from its subject. It offers a frontier for hermeneutical gazes and analytical processes. It increases access to those places where the practices of the subaltern actually resist the co-opted academic subaltern and where the sociocultural subaltern vigorously maintain their own semiospheres and *Umwelten*. I also introduce this novel to offer another vignette for analyzing the potential of deep subalterns to navigate the colonial encounter and its heritage with a level of resistance that not only allows them to perpetuate their authentic traditions, cosmologies, and ideologies but which also can overpower and subjugate or incorporate the Euro-Christian heritage. That resistance is antidotal to the inevitability of acquiescence to the third-rate place that haunts Black Christianity in its tensive relationship with Euro-Christianity.

Myal is not about interpreting the Bible; neither does it excavate the sociopolitical and psycho-social function of the Bible in the Euro-Christian semiosphere. In a way it is a contest between the written/textual and the oral/performative text. It is so because although the Bible can be regarded as a locus of cross-cultural and trans-temporal encounter, this novel locates the encounter in the place where people live that encounter. It locates the encounter not as an act of textual embrace, text as subjugator arbiter mediator of power, cultural co-option, or dialectic. Rather it locates the encounter in the flux of life, in memory and adaptation, disidentification, re-identification, secret knowledge, body-spirit dialectic, esoteric power, terrain and camouflaging topography and demonstrates its own ability to migrate, influence, impact from the subliminal of the subaltern spheres. Grove Town, is an effective counter-semiosphere. It changes how we understand agency, in subaltern conditions. In a sphere in which rational epistemologies are disrupted by alternative cosmological epistemes, affective regimens, the reversal of credibilities, can argumentation also manifest differently? What would it mean for Africana conversations if *Myal* were the thesis of an existential conversation? That is where *Myal* takes us: to a question of magic and wisdom, exorcisms and replacements, and topsy-turvy.

Withstanding and assimilation might then be two topoi. This essay is a plea for the Africana conversation, a hope that the alliances of race and imperialism that occur by dint of citizenship/residency in the U.S. can be mitigated by a larger Africana conversation, which though nationalized, can be powered by diasporic interventions. In that way the Africana conversation can be enlarged, become more amenable to adaptations, resource sharing, and the ideo-epistemological development of peoples of color. As Nathaniel Murrell writes about Afro-Jamaican religions, "Africans sought to recreate and preserve a coherent worldview from the fragments of their home institutions, from their broken lives, and from the contradictions of the Jamaican colonial Christian culture." With that, the conversation between *The Interesting Narrative of the Life of Olaudo Equianah*, *Myal*, and others can begin with equity and not as an anti-. An anti- always has the other group resisted as the *raison d'être*. With equity, it is an intratelluric shout for kinship and recognition, erupting with the heat of magmatic hope for the igneous strength of an amphictyonic plurality—completely its own indigene.

NOTES

1. Vincent L. Wimbush, *White Men's Magic: Scripturalization as Slavery* (Oxford: Oxford University Press, 2012),
2. Vincent L. Wimbush, *Theorizing Scriptures: New Critical Orientation to a Cultural Phenomenon* (New Brunswick, NJ: Rutgers University Press, 2008),
3. Erna Brodber, based in Jamaica, is an award-winning novelist and sociologist. Her work and experience extend from the rural town of Woodside, St. Mary, Jamaica, to the University of the West Indies. She has won awards in Jamaica, the Netherlands, and Canada.

4. Vincent L. Wimbush, *Scripturalectics: The Management of Meaning* (New York: Oxford University Press, 2017), x.
5. Wimbush, *Theorizing Scriptures*, 3.
6. Wimbush, *Theorizing Scriptures*, 3.
7. Wimbush, *Theorizing Scriptures*, 3.
8. Aleksei Semenenko, *The Texture of Culture: An Introduction to Yuri Lotman's Semiotic Theory (Semiotics and Popular Culture)* (New York: Palgrave Macmillan, 2012), 112.
9. Semenenko, *The Texture of Culture*, 124.
10. Semenenko, *The Texture of Culture*, 124.
11. Wimbush, *White Men's Magic*.
12. Wimbush, *White Men's Magic*, 19.
13. See Wimbush, *White Men's Magic*, 19–20.
14. Nathaniel Samuel Murrell, *Afro-Caribbean Religions: An Introduction to Their Historical, Cultural, and Sacred Traditions* (Philadelphia: Temple University Press, 2010), 250.
15. Murrell, *Afro-Caribbean Religions*, 253.
16. Murrell, *Afro-Caribbean Religions*, 253.
17. For a fuller discussion see Murrell, *Afro-Caribbean Religions*, 253–55.
18. Murrell, *Afro-Caribbean Religions*, 251.
19. Werner Zips, *Nanny's Asafo Warriors: The Jamaican Maroons' African Experience*, loc. 533, Kindle (Kingston, Jamaica: Ian Randle Publishers, 2014).
20. Zips, *Nanny's Asafo Warriors*, loc. 540, Kindle.
21. Zips, *Nanny's Asafo Warriors*, loc. 541, Kindle.
22. Zips, *Nanny's Asafo Warriors*, loc. 166, Kindle.
23. Zips, *Nanny's Asafo Warriors*, loc. 169, Kindle.
24. Jennifer Harris, "Erna (May) Brodber Biography," https://biography.jrank.org/pages/4182/Brodber-Erna-May.html, accessed August 7, 2020.
25. Harris, "Erna (May) Brodber Biography."
26. Petal Samuel, "Erna Brodber and Pan-Africanism in Post-Independence Jamaica," https://www.aaihs.org/erna-brodber-and-pan-africanism-in-post-independence-jamaica/, October 12, 2016. Accessed August 9, 2020.
27. Both quotations are found in Samuel, "Erna Brodber and Pan-Africanism," an interview with Erna Brodber that explores her connection to Pan-Africanism and its presence in her work.
28. Samuel, "Erna Brodber and Pan-Africanism."
29. Samuel, "Erna Brodber and Pan-Africanism."
30. Harris, "Erna (May) Brodber Biography." Harris similarly describes Erna Brodber, *Louisiana: A Novel* (Jackson: University Press of Mississippi/New Beacon

Books, 1997), and Erna Brodber, *Jane and Louisa Will Soon Come Home* (Long Grove, IL: Waveland Press, 2014).

31. Oral history support for this statement derives from a conversation on August 13, 2020, with Ms. Caroline Allen, a friend and colleague of Dr. Brodber.
32. This is a term used by Audre Lorde as a subtitle to her autobiography, *Zami: A New Spelling of My Name* (Trumansburg, NY: Crossing Press, 1982), referred to in Heather Russell in *Legba's Crossing: Narratology in the African Atlantic* (Athens: University of Georgia Press, 1982). Russell describes Lorde's biomythography as a "project in other than traditional autobiographical ways" (59). Moreover, Russell writes, "The term biomythography unequivocally signifies on the Autobiographical form. If autobiography is traditionally believed to refer to accurate, chronological, and stable representation of the events of one's life . . . then for Lorde 'biomythography' refers to the self-conscious act of destabilizing such conventional dictates" (60). Destabilization occurs within a semiosphere and is an aspect of anti-colonial, decolonializing withstanding. Withstanding begins within an alien semiosphere but eventually forms its own.
33. Wimbush, *White Men's Magic*, 9.
34. Wimbush, *White Men's Magic*, 10.
35. See Olaudah Equiano, *The Life of Olaudah Equiano or Gustavus Vassa, the African* (New York: Dover Publications, 1999),
36. Wimbush, *White Men's Magic*, 15.
37. Webb Keane, *Christian Moderns: Freedom and Fetish in the Missionary Encounter* (Berkeley: University of California Press, 2007), 2.
38. Equiano, *Life of Olaudah Equiano*
39. Equiano, *Life of Olaudah Equiano*, 63.
40. Samuel, "Erna Brodber and Pan-Africanism."
41. There are two cultural signifiers in this sentence. The name Gatha in Jamaica even as recently as the 1970s indicated a low-class status and indicated someone belonging to the servant class. In upper social echelons it functioned as an insult and character or behavioral derogation. "Head-dress" insinuates a market woman, that is, one who makes a living selling in the market. The wrap is usually colorful and likely to hold the bandana colors that are now part of the national costume. In colonial times the bandana was associated with Quadrille dancing. Even this dancing reflected social class associations. In popular and tourist literature the Quadrille is described as having three styles——the Ballroom, the Camp, and the Contra. Camp-style Quadrille, in particular, contains African elements. See "Jamaica's Heritage in Dance," https://jis.gov.jm/information/jamaicas-heritage-dance-music/jamaicas-heritage-dance/, accessed August 14, 2020.

42. Erna Brodber, *Myal* (Long Grove, IL: Waveland, 1988), 18 Kindle edition.
43. Brodber, *Myal*, 18.
44. Brodber, *Myal*, 18.
45. "My people" is his reference to the members of his Methodist congregation.
46. Englebert Mveng, a Cameroonian theologian introduced the term "anthropological poverty" to refocus ideas of poverty in Africa as a solely material or economic reality. Mveng writes, "When persons are bereft of their identity, their dignity, their freedom, their thought, their history, their language, their faith universe, and their basic creativity, deprived of all their rights, their hopes, their ambitions . . . they sink into a kind of [that] strikes at the very being, essence, and dignity of the human person. It is this poverty that we call anthropological poverty." Englebert Mveng, "Impoverishment and Liberation: A Theological Approach for Africa and the Third World," in *Paths of African Theology*, ed. Rosino Gibellini (New York: Orbis Books, 1994), 156.
47. Brodber, *Myal*, 18. The emphasis is mine.
48. Brodber, *Myal*, 19.
49. Brodber, *Myal*, 19.
50. Brodber, *Myal*, 34.
51. Mass, pronounced *mawhs*, means Mr.
52. The shut-pan was also known as the shet pan. Shet is likely a spelling of shut based in the Jamaican English pronunciation of "shut." The pan was known by both names. Conventionally, farmers used it to carry food to their farms and workplaces. A *Gleaner* article referring to the linguist and lexicographer Frederic G. Cassidy explains the use of the shet pan in *Myal*. It was used in shadow-catching rituals. It was filled with water to capture the shadow. Later that water was dabbed on the patient's head in order to return the shadow. The shadow was integral to the functional well-being of the human. Presumably the shadow was that which spirit thieves stole. Assuredly it is not co-terminous with Jung's shadow. See "Celebration of Jamaica's Heritage," in *The Gleaner*, November 17, 2017 accessed August 16, 2020. See also "Shet Pan" in *Dictionary of Jamaican English*, ed. F. G. Cassidy and R. B. Le Page (Barbados: University of the West Indies Press, 2002).
53. Brodber, *Myal*, 40.
54. Brodber, *Myal*, 55.
55. Brodber, *Myal*, 54–57.
56. Brodber, *Myal*, 83.
57. Brodber, *Myal*, 77.
58. Brodber, *Myal*, 77.
59. Wimbush, *White Men's Magic*, 31.

60. For the full discussion see Wimbush, *White Men's Magic*, 30–32.
61. Wimbush, *Theorizing Scriptures*, 25.
62. Wimbush, *Theorizing Scriptures*, 26.
63. Olaudah Equiano, *Olaudah Equiano: The Interesting Narrative and Other Writings*, edited with an introduction by Vincent Carreta (New York: Penguin Books, 2003), 191, as cited in Wimbush, *Theorizing Scriptures*, 26.
64. It matters that Mr. Dan is a Baptist pastor. As such, he signifies in two ways. He signifies for the impact of Euro-Christianity on African descendants. The Baptist church in Jamaica was founded by two African Americans. George Liele had been emancipated and left the U.S. to preach in Jamaica. He founded the Ethiopian Baptist Church. Moses Baker, also of the U.S., joined Liele in this effort. Pastor Simpson, as a Baptist, invokes this history.
65. Brodber, *Myal*, 105.
66. Brodber, *Myal*, 105.
67. Brodber, *Myal*, 106.
68. Brodber, *Myal*, 106.
69. Brodber, *Myal*, 107.
70. Brodber, *Myal*, 107.
71. Brodber, *Myal*, 107.
72. Michael G. Cooke, "Myal, Erna Brodber, London: New Beacon Books,. Review," in *Jamaica Journal* 23, no. 2, 56 (1988).
73. Cooke, "Myal, Erna Brodber," 56.
74. The phrase, "replace it with what it should be replaced" functions as a nominal phrase and is an indeterminate specification. It may seem oxymoronic to name it an "indeterminate specification," but in Jamaican English the indeterminacy leaves room for content that is agreed upon by both the community and its individuals. It connotes insider knowledge to be decoded by those who are Jamaican English speakers and understand that the phrasing as presented is more than an innuendo. Speakers of U.S. or British English might expect a specific replacement to be named. The phrase is tautological and the tautological nominal phrase provides the anticipated specification.
75. Brodber, *Myal*, 109–10.
76. Keshia Abraham, "Erna Brodber," in *BOMB*, January 1, 2004, https://bomb magazine.org/articles/erna-brodber/, accessed August 18, 2020.
77. Joseph Parker, "Racial and Colonial Politics of the Modern Object of Knowledge: Cautionary Notes on Scripture," in Wimbush, *Theorizing Scriptures*, 273.
78. Vincent L. Wimbush. "Introduction: TEXTures, Gestures, Power: Orientation to Radical Excavation," in Wimbush, *Theorizing Scriptures*, 11.

12. Solidarity by Sharing Power: An Inculturated Organic Storytelling of Jonah and Mami Wata

'SHOLA D. ADEGBITE

The writing of this article is time-stamped by the COVID-19 pandemic, and New York City where I live is one of the hotspots of the virus. As the world tried to recover from the pandemic, in Minneapolis, Black George Floyd died needlessly, crushed by the knees of a white police officer. Protests against this unfortunate circumstance, as well as the long list of racially motivated deaths, are happening all over the United States. People in New York City are participating in these protests. In my home country, Nigeria, the pandemic worsened living conditions. On top of that, Uwavera Omozuwa, a young twenty-two-year-old lady, was raped in a church and died on May 30, 2020. Unfortunately, she was not the first publicized rape case in the country, and Nigerians took to the streets to protest sexual violence and the long list of rape cases for which perpetrators have not been brought to justice. Government officials in Nigeria and the United States, people all around the world on social media, and the Nigerian and U.S. police made promises of reform and stated their commitment to justice. I can only hope that these promises are not empty.

The oppression of people of African descent is a global reality that is rooted in the colonial agenda that dates as far back as the fifteenth century. African-focused studies have many forms in African biblical studies, Pan-African studies, African theology, and so on. These African-focused studies are a response to Western/white Christian imperial readings that have dominated the academic discourse. David Adamo explains the reality of this denigration, saying that "unfortunately, whenever we [African scholars] submit academic articles that reflect African biblical hermeneutical methodology, our articles are often dismissed as fetish, magical, barbarous and unscholarly."[1] Yet, Adamo continues, "Eurocentric ideology presented Western history, philosophy, theories, methods, texts, stories, cultures and structures as the epitome of knowledge production and all that is best."[2] This Eurocentric ideology was also ingrained in Christian missionary activity and in formal education in Africa. In my Yoruba-Nigerian context, as Aladesanmi Agnes notes, "Formal education is synonymous with Christianity. . . . As a result of the new Christian faith, many people of Yoruba society who showed interest in sending their children to school had to convert from African Traditional Religion (ATR) to Christianity for them to enjoy the benefit of getting formal education."[3] In other words, the adoption of Christianity is inseparable from formal education which simultaneously meant a rejection and demonization of traditional belief and practices.

Africa-focused studies, therefore, seek to reclaim Africanness, to empower the people, and undo Western hegemony. That said, Africa-focused studies are formally a relatively new field of study. As it is evolving, Africana scholars take seriously the dynamics of power that are ingrained in the academia from which Africana studies are not immune. As noted in the foregoing, formal education, also called "academia," is intrinsically linked to imperialism; hence there is the toxic ideology that the educated person is superior to, more exposed than, better than, and civilized unlike the "illiterate" person. Unfortunately, the accompanying reality is that socioeconomic privilege comes with being in academia unlike for "illiterates" whose lack of formal education condemns them to poverty.[4]

Bearing the above in mind, this essay is within the sub-division of African biblical studies and would be a storytelling of Jonah and his encounter with Mami Wata. However, this essay acknowledges or, better put, is empowered by the reading of an untrained clergyman from whom I first learned the possibility that Jonah's story can be read as an encounter with Mami Wata. By presenting my rendition of Jonah's encounter with Mami Wata within the context of academia, I hope that this reading exhibits a way in which a trained African Bible reader can silence denigrating voices of Western imperialism and rather empower and be empowered by untrained readers, standing in solidarity with them in the pursuit of liberation for all.

A NOTE ON METHODOLOGY

A major diverging point of an African biblical reading from Eurocentric modes is its connection to the real-life everyday experiences of the average African person and the African worldview. African ways of reading the Bible prioritize pragmatic and existential concerns over abstract intellectual musings.[5] Taking this fact seriously, we now make sure to clarify the relationship between trained readers of African descent and untrained readers of African descent who also read the Bible. Without this clarification, there is a real threat and danger that trained African readers would produce readings that perpetuate oppressive structures and ideas that denigrate untrained African people.

Alpheus Masoga, in the article "Redefining Power: Reading the Bible in Africa from the Peripheral and Central Positions," addresses the relationship between the center, trained readers, and the periphery, untrained readers of the Bible.[6] Masoga discusses Gerald West's famous approach of "reading with ordinary people." In this reading, academic critical tools are used to guide untrained (ordinary) readers in reading the biblical text. This engagement produces unique readings that cannot be found in academic circles or in communities of ordinary readers. More so, quoting Gerald West, Masoga highlights the "ongoing tension between avoiding the insult of speaking for the oppressed and attempting to respond to their voices by challenging and engaging in social and political endeavours."[7] This is a tension between a critical reading of the Bible and one's commitment to ordinary people, both of which have different concerns and approaches to reading the Bible.

Masoga's critique of West is that some privilege and power is still given to the center and to (Western) academic modes of reading. Masoga challenges trained African readers to let the periphery (communities of ordinary readers) remain the periphery without the center trying to help or correct it or attempting to make it a copycat of the center. Masoga calls this hermeneutic "a conversational biblical hermeneutic and theology" in which one levels the field for the center and periphery and makes them conversation partners. In this way, for Masoga, the tension between trained and untrained readers dissipates.

It is within this context that Masoga suggests the need for organic readers. The organic reader originates from the periphery, has advanced toward the center, and has learned skills from the center, but trained readers in the center use their skills in service of those on the periphery. Organic readers are meant to be empowered by the periphery and their commitment is to the periphery to help the periphery be *itself*. Masoga states this more forcefully by adding "if necessary commit academic treason when there is time to do so."[8]

A methodological kink in Masoga's article is that in describing organic readings, the scales tilt in favor of the periphery and the center is meant to use its skills *only* in service of the periphery. This seems to contradict Masoga's explication of a conversational biblical hermeneutic and theology that aims to give equal prominence to trained and untrained readers/ readings.

While Masoga's methodology can use more fine-tuning, I take seriously his vision for organic readings. For me, an organic reading emphasizes the mutuality that must exist between the center and the periphery. Each is to mutually empower and be empowered by the other. To state it more concretely, the center needs to let go of the imperial ideology that the periphery is inferior and is made of uncritical readers of the Bible, and that their readings should be confined to their fellow illiterate circles. One needs to let go of the need to "standardize" readings of untrained people with academic critical tools. As conversation partners, the periphery and center can learn from each other, share ideas, appreciate their similarities and differences.

To my mind, an organic reading is more of a reading lens or a reading standpoint than an actual methodology. Yet this reading lens is crucial to ensure shared power between trained and untrained readers.

The methodology inherent in this essay is primarily an inculturation methodology that takes seriously the African worldview and reads the Bible in dialogue with that worldview. Justin Ukpong, a proponent of inculturation hermeneutics, defines it as a "contextual hermeneutic that seeks to make any community of ordinary people and their social-cultural context the *subject* of interpretation of the Bible through the use of the conceptual frame of reference of the people and the involvement of the ordinary people in the interpretation process" (italics original).[9] In other words, an inculturation hermeneutic is one in which an African reads the Bible *as an African* using their African worldview to engage with the biblical text and doing so in relationship to a wider community. Ukpong delineates the five-step process of an inculturation hermeneutics.[10] First, one must identify the context of the interpreter that dynamically corresponds to the historical context of the text. Second, one must analyze the interpreter's context of interpretation, which would form the background against which the Bible would be read. Third, one must explicate the historical context of the text. Fourth, one must analyze the text in light of the interpreter's context. Fifth, one gathers the fruits of the discussion.

This essay does not follow that five-step process exactly but takes seriously that an inculturation hermeneutic includes an interaction between the historical context and interpreter's context and that the former context is in service of the latter.[11] In using inculturation broadly as a lens that takes seriously the African worldview, this essay uses storytelling to present an inculturated reading of Jonah's story as an encounter with Mami Wata.

Storytelling as a hermeneutic is an acknowledged mode of reading, at least in African circles. Culturally, storytelling is a life force of the Yoruba/African community. As Funlola Olojede writes, "If we take Africa as a case in point, the timeless mode of imparting ethical teachings in traditional societies is through storytelling throughout the continent."[12] Many of these stories are set in a world where animals can talk, and eyes were at the knees. Some popular stories include those of the Tortoise *Ijapa oko Yanibo* and Anase the Spider. For these stories and even stories featuring human characters, the question is never about whether these characters are real or imagined or whether the "facts and figures" are accurate. One might even use the literary genre of "myth" to describe storytelling.[13]

Furthermore, as Adamo notes, storytelling, as is true for other African modes of biblical interpretation, is about "break[ing] the hermeneutical hegemony and ideological stranglehold that Eurocentric biblical scholars have long enjoyed." It is about "seek[ing] to acquire and celebrate their [African] God-giving [sic] identity by delving into their indigenous resources."[14] To reframe this for my purposes, the use of storytelling as a hermeneutic is not a rejection of Western modes of hermeneutics per se but a rejection of the hegemony and oppressive stances that come with Western hermeneutical modes that tend to view (African) storytelling as primitive. In rejecting such hegemony, African modes of hermeneutics are to be used and acknowledged equally alongside non-African modes of hermeneutics.

Madipoane Masenya (Ngwan'a Mphahlele) has used a storytelling hermeneutic in reading Ruth and Esther.[15] In using storytelling as a hermeneutical tool, Adamo writes, "Biblical stories are seen as divine stories to be told not because of their aesthetic value, but because of the divine power inherent in them which can deliver poor, weak and oppressed Black people, as it is depicted in the stories themselves."[16] In other words, storytelling in an African biblical sense is done because of the engagement and transformative experience that readers can have with Bible characters.

For any kind of inculturation hermeneutic even if storytelling informs its presentation, one must take Musa Dube's warnings seriously.[17] "Inculturation from above" does not acknowledge African religions as a set of traditions in their own right and uses African religions only as a prop to serve evangelistic purposes. "Inculturation from below" acknowledges the autonomy of African religions and takes seriously the reading perspectives of ordinary people. Dube's explication of "inculturation from below" echoes Masoga's desires for a shared power relationship between trained and untrained readers of the Bible and also balanced use of African traditional religion as a resource.

Taking all these insights together, I, as a trained reader of the Bible, take seriously the call to place the center and periphery on a leveled field, to acknowledge the perspectives of untrained readers of the Bible, to empower and be empowered by those readers/readings, to take seriously African cultural worldviews and read/tell the Bible in ways that can be empowering and liberating to an African person.

My training in Western Christian modes of reading provides useful Westernized/Christianized tools. These tools are all in my toolbox alongside tools rooted in African Indigenous cultures and even Jewish Midrashic modes of reading. The reading of Jonah offered in this essay draws primarily from the African "compartment" of my toolbox, not to the exclusion of other modes of reading. After all, a true African would look to the baobab tree and learn. Wisdom is like the baobab tree which no one individual, and, dare I say, no one culture or mode of reading can fully embrace.

As we turn now to read Jonah as a Mami Wata story, I first explicate who/what the Mami Wata is.

MAMI WATA

Mami Wata, Mami for short, is pidgin English for "mummy water" or "mummy in/of the water." Micah Issitt notes that the name Mami Wata "does not precisely refer to a single deity or mythological figure but more accurately refers to a family of water spirits, collectively known as mami wata."[18] Although this is true on the one hand, on the other hand, folklore reports of Mami as well as art depictions of Mami conceive of a single feminine water spirit/deity. She is singular and/or plural. As a result, grammatically, I take liberties to use either singular or plural verb forms. In the capital form, Mami Wata, I mean the spirit(s), and in the small letter form, mami wata, I refer to the human(s) who are possessed by Mami. Mami Wata is often depicted as having an upper human half and a lower fish-like body. She can possess other people, and they can take up a human form and live as humans.

Since I grew up in Nigeria, my understanding of Mami Wata did not come from faithful adherents of Mami who often inform academic reports on her. In my upbringing in church circles, Mami Wata is most notorious for her seductive powers. When I was much younger, around ten years old, I was suspected of and warned about being mami-wata. One man told me that because I was light-skinned and beautiful, I needed to take prayers seriously and make sure I do not eat in my dreams so that I would not be lured into Mami Wata's cult. Another man expressly told me that out of fear he could never marry someone like me because I was "too light-skinned" and therefore dangerous to his ministry—he was a pastor in training.[19] At that time, the irony for my young mind was that these two men who told me these things were light-skinned too. It was much later that I would learn that Mami Wata is quintessentially feminine and possesses women.[20] When Mami possesses women, Mami enables those women to seduce and tame men. One deliverance pastor had said that he learned from a girl he exorcised that if necessary, the Mami-Wata-possessed woman can alter her body shape to match the features her target-man would find most attractive.[21] To conclude my personal experience, people stopped suspecting me of being a mami as I grew into my late teenage and early adult years. Here is why. Mami is not only seductive but also has high tastes in fashion. She uses makeup, wears jewelry, dresses exotically, loves to make beautiful hairstyles, and loves looking at herself in the mirror. I did none of these things due to my very poor fashion tastes, so I was no longer suspected of being a mami wata but of being "too spiritual."[22]

Mami as a seductress might be the most prevalent imagery in churches, particularly Pentecostal ones. Henry Drewal, who has studied Mami extensively, notes that "her dangerous and seductive attributes align her with the forces of Satan. Mami has thus become a primary target of a widespread and growing religious movement led by evangelical (Pentecostal) Christians and fundamentalist Muslims who seek to denigrate and demonize indigenous African faiths."[23] Traditional beliefs about Mami Wata, particularly from Mami's adherents, are more nuanced and hold that Mami, like all other beings in the seen and unseen world, have the capacity for both evil and good.[24] As Issitt notes, "Mami Wata's dual role as saviour and siren . . . is an important concept regarding the duality of nature."[25] Mami is associated with wealth, sex (fertility), prosperity, art, creativity, and beauty.

Sir Victor Uwaifo, a popular Nigerian musician, wrote the famous song "Guitar Boy" in 1967 as a reflection on his positive encounter with Mami Wata. In a live concert around 2000, Uwaifo briefly explained that forty years earlier, while he was lounging at Bar Beach, a popular beach resort in Lagos, he met Mami Wata, whom he said "was glittering, silverish in colour, almost blinding."[26] Uwaifo said that if anyone sees Mami Wata, they should never run away but instead listen to the melody. This experience inspired and informed the lyrics of the song which simply say that "Guitar boy . . . if you see Mami Wata . . . never never run away . . . sing a song of love, sweet melody." This song, at the time of its release, became so popular that the name Guitar Boy replaced Victor Uwaifo's real name.[27]

A less favorable experience with Mami is depicted by the Ghanaian artist Kwame Akoko, also known as Almighty God. Kwame Akoko drew a portrait of himself being watched closely by the forest spirit Tata Buta, Saint Anthony (believed to be a disguise for the devil), and Mami Wata.[28] In the image Mami is on the farthest right. She is portrayed as bare-breasted with a lower fish-like body. She is light-skinned with straight long black and brown hair. She is reclining on the shore, and her hands are crossed across her waist. Mami's eyes are haunting in terms of seduction but also as a tormentor. Doran Ross, who has studied Almighty's artwork closely, notes that Akoko has frequently referred to Mami as a tormentor.[29] Ross also notes how Almighty depicts Mami's underwater mansion as "complete with a classical column and staircase. She is, as always, entwined with a serpent and here is feasting on her 'favorite meal banana, orange, pineapple, and milk.'"

Finally, Mami can take on the role of a judge. As Issitt notes, "Mami Wata abducts individuals for the purposes of passing judgment on their relative moral or social merit. Those she deems worthy may then be returned to the surface and undergo a kind of spiritual enlightenment that can lead their lives in new directions, helping them to achieve wealth or increased status within their society."[30]

To summarize this brief overview of Mami, here are things to keep in mind. First is the gender dynamic that Mami represents. Mami Wata is feminine; her power to tame and torment men is not to be toyed with. Second is Mami's sexuality. While she is a seductress, her seductive power is not about wild sexual encounters or orgies. Her seductive power is her preference of using sex as a means to tame and torment her prey/men. Third, Mami is a judge, punisher, and rewarder. Finally, Mami has the capacity for both evil and good—as all beings in the Yoruba/Nigerian cultural ideological framework. She is not simply an evil force.

With this understanding about the Mami Wata, we turn now to read Jonah's story as a Mami Wata story. First, we shall look at an untrained clergyman's reading of Jonah, the clergyman from whom I first learned that Jonah's story can be read as an encounter with Mami.

A CLERGYMAN'S READING OF JONAH AS A MAMI WATA STORY

It was the second week of a seven-week revival program of a church. Every evening from 6 pm to 9 pm, a revivalist would lead sessions that included prayers and some Bible expositions. This day, I was in the pews and the revivalist[31] for the week did some Bible expositions and led prayers. His working topic for this day was "Powers at the Gate."

He explained the gate as the point at which someone is about to make a breakthrough in life or hit a new milestone. The powers at the gate are those forces or people that prevent people from achieving that new goal or having that breakthrough. He referred to the famine incident during Elisha's time, emphasizing the captain's death *at the gate* as opposing Elisha's prediction (2 Kings 7). The captain was a power at the gate that wanted to oppose and challenge God's plan for food provision for the people. He then talked about powers that existed in various places that oppose a person's success or well-being.

On this note, he talked about marine powers that are colloquially called Mami Wata. He referred to Jesus calming the storm, and his interpretation was that the marine powers were seeking to kill Jesus before it was his time and Jesus silenced them. Also, in the time of Moses, it was marine powers that were fighting. This was why Pharaoh said all the baby boys should be thrown into the river.

The story of Jonah was his other example. He specifically premised this story by saying, "What we are doing today is not Bible study. This is prophetic revelation." After a dramatic pause, he said, "Do you know it was marine powers that wanted to kill Jonah?" The marine powers were eager to take Jonah's life when the sailors had thrown him overboard. The marine powers almost killed him, but God saved Jonah's life by sending the fish to rescue him (Jonah 1).

He explained that the marine powers were very powerful, and the way to counteract them would be to bring a sachet of water on which the pastor would pray. When people drink or bathe with the water, it would counteract any marine powers affecting the people.

On this note, he concluded his exposition and led several prayers. The prayers he led were along the following lines.

> Call God and say
> My father, my father,
> Every power trying to kill me, die by fire.
> Call Jesus three times
> Call Holy Spirit one time
> then say
> every marine power standing in the way of my success in life,
> die by fire.
> Call Jesus three times
> Call the Holy Spirit three times
> Then say
> Wherever I am
> In this situation I am going through
> God, have mercy on me.

REACTIONS TO THIS MESSAGE

The book of Jonah is my favorite book in the Bible, so my strongest reactions arose when the pastor spoke about Jonah. My Western-trained historical-critical mind protested. We shall look at some of these questions I had raised as a means of also exploring some of the problems with the sermon *according to Western critical ways of reading*.

The first contestation I raised was: What do marine powers have to do with Jonah or Jesus or anyone in the Bible? The notion of marine powers, in colloquial terms Mami-Wata, belongs to Indigenous African cultures. It is anachronistic and a-cultural to read them into the biblical text that belongs to a different cultural worldview and time in history. This is eisegesis rather than exegesis, and eisegesis is an unacceptable practice in academic circles. Not to mention, when a contemporary community reads the Bible, priority should be given to the original author/audience and message.[32]

My second issue was the claim that marine powers were trying to kill Jonah. My question was how one might ascertain that it was *really* Mami Wata. Does the presence of any water body automatically signify the presence of Mami Wata? More so, the text says God sent the storm, and storms are inanimate.

Third, the claim to esoterism was bothersome. When the pastor said that this was "prophetic revelation," I sighed because the claim to revelation to me was an excuse to irresponsibly interpret scripture and also to reject academic approaches to a text.

I sighed and felt sorry for all the people in the church. There were at least one thousand. For the reasons my Western-trained historical-critical mind suggested, this pastor's interpretation was simply wrong, and he was teaching the congregation "wrong" things about the Bible.

Something changed for me as soon as the pastor started calling prayers. These prayers were asking people to pray over themselves and families that they should start seeing the progress that has been long delayed in their lives, that every oppressive power should be made powerless over them. I acknowledged that whether or not I agreed with his interpretation of the biblical text, the reality of oppression cannot be denied and that the Bible, the church, and prayers are important coping and life-giving practices for the people in that congregation. The importance of praying and having faith is far beyond whether or not those prayers would be answered. As the Yoruba proverb goes, people strongly believe that "whether or not God hears or answers prayers, prayers are still better than curses."[33]

Little wonder that when I looked around, I saw that people prayed fervently. The fans were on and meant to keep us cool, but they were no match for the heat that came from all the moving bodies around me. Many were stomping their feet on the floor as they were throwing their hands up in the air; some held up pictures of their loved ones screaming their names and shouting their prayers, pleading with God to have mercy on them, to help them overcome their challenges and destroy the oppressive spirits tormenting them.

In the face of such realities, I had to revisit my historical-critical Western-influenced reactions to the message. Mixed emotions of shame, confusion, responsibility, disappointment, care, love, and concern swept over me as I thought about my (predominantly) Western-trained critical-reading training, African scholars' attempts at producing African-centric/appropriate modes of reading, non-academic faithful readers of the Bible and their modes of using the Bible, and the reality of people's desperation to survive in the world and their reliance on the Bible to help them. I thought about the gaps among these spheres and what kind of relationship should exist among them. Thankfully, I am not the first to ponder on these things. As we have noted in the methodological section, much work has been done and more work still needs to be done in clarifying the relationship trained readers need to have with untrained readers of the Bible and how both parties can mutually nourish one another. A major goal of any African-focused reading should be to attend to the needs of its people even if this means deconstructing Western hegemonic interpretations.

To the African, inculturation is important. Reading the Bible must happen in the context of the African worldview. In that worldview, spirits are real and part of the African reality. Water is not an inanimate chemical component of the material world. Water is life and spirit and Mami is the queen of the sea. Spirits, including the Holy Spirit, can communicate to people. If the pastor claimed he had a revelation, it is not my place to confirm its factuality. However, I affirm that for the African receiving revelations is a real phenomenon.

Exploring this pastor's sermon on Jonah and my reactions to it are crucial in light of the earlier considerations on methodology. If Africana studies is to do what it is meant to do, it must resist notions of the inferiority of Africans and their reading of the Bible even if denigrations are in the name of academia, "standard," Western, historical-critical, or whatever else. Readings that take seriously Africans and their worldview need to have their place side by side with readings that are rooted in Western worldviews. As African readers of the Bible receive training, they have a role to bridge the gaps between Western modes and African modes of reading, undo the hegemony in Western-centric readings, and most importantly to perform their task without re-inscribing hierarchies or oppressive ideologies.

In the remainder of this essay, I attempt a reading of Jonah as a Mami Wata story, acknowledging that I was first introduced to the possibility of this reading during my encounter with this pastor's preaching during that revival. That said, my reading is not an attempt to help, buttress, or correct the pastor's reading. What I am doing is correcting the error of *my* Western-trained historical-critical mind that raised inappropriate concerns about the clergyman's preaching. In offering my own reading of Jonah as a Mami Wata story, I am taking my own Africanness seriously as well as the call to empower and be empowered by African readers of the Bible, trained and untrained alike.

AN INCULTURATED STORYTELLING OF JONAH'S ENCOUNTER WITH MAMI WATA

Jonah did not go to Nineveh as God instructed. Presumably, he was somewhere in Israel, so instead of heading eastward toward Nineveh, he boarded a ship that would take him westward to Tarshish.[34] God noticed this and sent Wind as a messenger to Mami to inform her of Jonah's passing through her territory and to ask for her help in teaching Jonah a lesson.

Mami, of course, is all too familiar with men like Jonah. She seduces them, tames them, rewards them, punishes those who steal from her. Sometimes, she grants the desires of men who come seeking wealth; other times punishes men who are too money-hungry. Mami judges each one that comes her way and decides what each deserves from her. Mami gladly accepted to teach Jonah a lesson, and the first step was to get Jonah into her waters. With God's approval, Mami and Wind collaborated, causing a storm that almost broke the ship Jonah was on. The only solution was that Jonah must be thrown overboard. The ship's crew without any other choice reluctantly threw Jonah overboard.

From the start, Jonah's case was different. He had not come seeking her. He was passing through the waters with a different destination in mind. Nor was Mami particularly attracted to Jonah. Mami's encounter with Jonah was orchestrated specially by God, who had intervened in Jonah's escape plans. As a result, Jonah was not to be treated like all the other men. God wanted special exemptions for Jonah. Instead of letting Jonah drown in the water until he got to the Mami's palace in its depth, God appointed a special service animal *Dag* to provide transport for Jonah.[35] Mami did not complain about this arrangement. Jonah would be protected in *Dag* only for a while.

Dag took Jonah into the depths of the sea and stopped when *Dag* reached the innermost gates of Mami's territories. Beyond Mami's innermost gates, time did not exist and male fishes were not allowed there. At the other side of the gate was *Dagah*, Mami's appointed female fish, waiting to receive Jonah. Mami sent *Dag* away, saying she would inform him when Jonah's fate was decided.

Dag spewed Jonah, and Mami watched as Jonah crossed into her most sacred territories, descending further into the sea toward *Dagah*, who waited at the roots of the mountains. The weeds were excited to receive Jonah as a guest, they wrapped around his head hoping to tie him down and keep him with them forever. Just before Jonah would stop breathing, *Dagah* swallowed him and in her womb, she provided space for Jonah to breathe again.

For the timeless period Jonah spent in Mami's territory, Mami allowed her waters to provide a mirror for Jonah to see himself and process his experience. Mami watched Jonah as he despaired when he realized how deep in the seas he was, trapped at the bottom of the ocean never to see the land of the living again. Mami heard as Jonah cried out to God lamenting that he was cast away from God's presence. Mami felt Jonah's desires to see God's Temple. She was bothered that in his prayers, Jonah did not reflect on his role as a prophet or his mission to the Ninevites. Jonah did not seem to regret his disobedience; instead, he was making vows to sacrifice to God and was asking for deliverance. Instead of reflecting on his shortcomings as a prophet and making promises to amend, Jonah was castigating idol worshippers, saying that they had forsaken their true loyalty. At that moment, Mami knew that Jonah should never return to the land of the living.

However, God too heard Jonah's prayer and being so merciful decided to return Jonah to dry land. Mami protested, saying that Jonah needed to spend more time in her palace to learn the errors of his ways. Jonah needed to spend more time looking at the mirror. Mami was all too familiar with men like Jonah. If she had made him her slave, he would have quickly learned obedience. But God did not allow. Mami protested again that even if Jonah would be let back into the land of the living, she needed to mark him as she loved to mark all those she encounters.[36] But God did not allow. Mami asked again if Jonah could at least be initiated into her cult so that she can visit him in his dreams to monitor, torment, and remind him of his encounter with her. Still God did not allow. Jonah was to be released from Mami's grip with no strings attached. God also instructed *Dag* to release Jonah back to dry land. Mami knew that she could not challenge the sovereign God; she had no choice but to ask *Dagah* to hand Jonah back to *Dag*. As Jonah crossed over to *Dag*, time resumed for him, and he spent a total of three days and three nights in *Dag* before he returned to dry land.

Mami would find out later that Jonah's prayer became a poem and chapter in the Bible. She was amused that his prayer highlighted his experience being in her waters much more than being in a fish. She learned that he had haphazardly carried out his assignment in Nineveh. Jonah preached for only one day when the city was a three-day walk across. She heard that Jonah may have even changed God's message for the Ninevites making it harsher and making their destruction more certain. God had told him to preach against the city because of their wickedness, but Jonah said gave them a forty-day ultimatum before they were to be completely destroyed. When the Ninevites quickly repented, God chose to be merciful to them just as God had been merciful to Jonah when he was in Mami's territory. Mami learned that Jonah was so outraged that he wanted to die. Jonah lacked introspection, and Mami already knew this.

Mami was least surprised that after preaching, Jonah went eastward further away from the Mediterranean where he had encountered her. Jonah had, in fact, gone to an arid area lacking in Mami's essence where the sun scorched him and where he remained forgetful of his experience of receiving mercy and forgiveness while he was a prisoner of Mami. Mami remained convinced that Jonah was undeserving of the life and mercy that God granted him. Yet Mami knew that such were the ways of God. Those whom God chooses to be merciful to are most blessed and highly favored.

So I pray, God, please have mercy on me.

FINAL OBSERVATIONS ABOUT JONAH'S ENCOUNTER WITH MAMI WATA

The reading of Jonah offered above intersects with other non-African readings in interesting ways. First, we consider a feminist reading of Jonah. Niveen Sarras notes that the book of Jonah is patriarchal because it has no female presence in the book.³⁷ From this standpoint, Sarras takes on a feminist reading of Jonah by connecting Jonah's experience as a disadvantaged person in lieu of the powerful Assyrians (Ninevites). Such an analogy allows Sarras to read Jonah's story through the eyes of a minority reader. While Sarras's minority reading is well done in its own context, Sarras's initial premise that the book of Jonah is lacking in female presence is immediately disrupted by a Mami Wata reading of the story. Mami as the quintessential powerful feminine spirit played a significant role in Jonah's journey. Even if one were to disregard the notion of Mami Wata because she belongs to an African worldview, the Hebrew text makes clear that Jonah prayed to God while he was in the belly of the *dagah*, the female fish.³⁸ This is a strong feminine presence, albeit through a fish, that marks a crucial junction in Jonah's story.

Second, we consider Jewish Midrashic interpretations of Jonah. These readings are abundant, and they bear striking similarities to some of the ideas presented in my reading of Jonah as a Mami Wata story. In fact, Africans have always indicated strong similarities between their cultures and the Jewish culture.³⁹ Igbos in Eastern Nigeria claim to be part of the lost tribes of Israel. Among the Yorubas who are predominantly located in Western Nigeria and the ethnic group to which I belong, one myth of origin traces us back to Lamurudu, Oduduwa's father, an Arabian migrant who fled persecution in the Middle East. Hence it is not a surprise, to me at least, that the Mami Wata reading presented here shares some similarities with some of the midrashic interpretations of Jonah's story. One of these midrashic interpretations is by Pirkei DeRabbi Eliezer 10.⁴⁰ In this interpretation, the fish that swallowed Jonah had glass eyes, and Jonah could see the depths of the sea through its eyes. Jonah had an in-water mission that involved defeating Leviathan the sea monster by using the seal of the Abrahamic covenant.

Finally, but by no means least, this reading of Jonah's story as an encounter with Mami not only maintains a more nuanced understanding of Mami Wata but also maintains God's supremacy over the world. This is a basic Nigerian/African belief. The liberational characteristic of this reading is evident in that God uses God's sovereign power to grant life and mercy to Jonah even when Mami did not deem him worthy nor was Jonah particularly qualified to receive such favor. In other words, even when we are at our lowest and worst, God is able to have mercy on us to help us and grant second chances.

CONCLUSION

To conclude, this essay has explored a number of things. This essay utilized methodologies that privilege African modes of reading the Bible. This multi-method Africa-centric approach is necessary to break the Western imperial hegemony present in scholarship and to produce a reading that attends to needs of the African by taking the African worldview seriously. This approach also maintains a mutual, not hegemonic, relationship, between me as a trained African Bible reader to untrained African readers of the Bible. As a result, I reveal the true source of my story, a clergyman who preached on Jonah's encounter with Mami Wata.[41] In doing so, I affirm his reading as a valid reading not necessarily because I agree with him but because his reading spoke to the present existential realities of his African congregation in encouraging them to call on God and ask for help and mercy. In offering my own rendition of Jonah's story as a Mami Wata story, I affirm all Africans that exist in the world, and I affirm the African worldview. Most of all, I affirm my own Africanness as one formerly suspected of being a mami wata.

Finally, I had started this essay by naming George Floyd and Uwavera Omozuwa, people of African descent who died under unfortunate circumstances powered by the hegemony of racism and sexism. In keeping with traditional beliefs, I do not invoke the dead in vain. On June 30, 2020, I remember them and celebrate their transitioning with a dish of tasty Jollof and a malt drink. I set aside a portion for them and pour some drink into the earth. I pray to the God of the living and the living dead who grants mercy to even the most undeserving, please, have mercy on us and help us.

NOTES

1. David T. Adamo, "What Is African Biblical Hermeneutics?," *Black Theology* 12, no. 1 (2015): 63.
2. Adamo, "What Is African Biblical Hermeneutics?," 63.
3. Aladesanmi Omobola Agnes, "Yoruba Primary School Songs: Issues and Lessons for the Younger Generation," *Theory and Practice in Language* Studies 10, no. 3 (2020): 291.

4. It is beyond our present scope to explain how poverty in African villages is the product of imperialism and globalization. This poverty is not because illiterate farmers are inferior in anyway. Justin Ukpong explains it thus: "Economically, modernity was structured on the center periphery configuration whereby the periphery (the colonies) produced raw materials imported cheaply to feed the industries at the center, and the finished products were exported to the periphery in a commercial venture that fueled the economy of the center to the detriment of the periphery." Justin Ukpong, "Reading the Bible in the Global Village," in *Reading the Bible in the Global Village: Cape Town*, ed. Justin Ukpong et al. (Atlanta: Society of Biblical Literature, 2002), 31.
5. Justin Ukpong, "Rereading the Bible with African Eyes," *Journal of Theology for Southern Africa* 6, no. 91 (1995): 19.
6. Alpheus Masoga, "Redefining Power: Reading the Bible in Africa from the Peripheral and Central Positions," in *Reading the Bible in the Global Village: Cape Town*, ed. Justin S. Ukpong et al. (Atlanta: Society of Biblical Literature, 2002), 95–110.
7. Masoga, "Redefining Power," 97.
8. Masoga, "Redefining Power," 109.
9. Ukpong, "Reading the Bible in the Global Village," 12.
10. Ukpong, "Rereading the Bible with African Eyes," 10–13.
11. Ukpong, "Rereading the Bible with African Eyes," 9–10.
12. Funlola Olojede, "Storytelling as an Indigenous Resource in the Interpretation of Old Testament Ethics and Religion," *Scriptura* 113, no. 1 (2014): 7.
13. To borrow from Joseph Blenkinsopp, in talking about myths, "we are thinking of myth not as the opposite of factuality or history but as a way of addressing and exploring matters of concern for the life of the individual in any society, at any period of history, and in the first place of our own lives at this point in history" (Joseph Blenkinsopp, *Creation, Un-Creation, Re-creation: A Discursive Commentary on Genesis 1–11* [London: T&T Clark, 2011], 16).
14. Adamo, "What Is African Biblical Hermeneutics?," 63.
15. Madipoane (Ngwan'a Mphahlele) Masenya, "Engaging with the Book of Ruth as Single, African Christian Women: One African Woman's Reflection," *Verbum et Ecclesia* 34, no 1. (2013): 1–9, and Madipoane (Ngwan'a Mphahlele) Masenya, "Esther and Northern Sotho Stories: An African-South-African Woman's Commentary," in *Other Ways of Reading: African Women and the Bible*, ed. Musa W. Dube (Atlanta: Society of Biblical Literature, 2001), 27–48.
16. Adamo, "What Is African Biblical Hermeneutics?," 65.
17. Musa W. Dube, "Villagizing, Globalizing, and Biblical Studies," in *Reading the Bible in the Global Village: Cape Town*, ed. Justin Ukpong et al. (Atlanta: Society of Biblical Literature, 2002), 51–53.

18. Micah Issitt, "Mami Wata," in *Critical Survey of Mythology and Folklore: Love, Sexuality, and Desire*, ed. Thomas J. Sienkewicz; vol. 1 of *Critical Survey of Mythology and Folklore*, ed. Thomas J. Sienkewicz (Ipswich: Salem Press, 2013), 141–50.
19. Skin color in the context of Nigeria functions in a different cultural framework than skin color in America and association with race. In America, I would be considered a Black woman not only because of my literal skin color but also because of African body features and origins in Africa. In Nigeria, I grew up with nicknames like white or yellow because I am light-skinned compared to the general darker skin tone of Nigerians.
20. Mami is quintessentially feminine, but this does not mean that men cannot be initiated into her cult. These men may be called papi wata.
21. One deliverance pastor shared his experience with one young lady who was delivered from Mami Wata spirits. After her deliverance, the lady explained how she can alter her body features to seduce spiritual men. She said she would first study whether the man had preference for plump or slim, light- or dark-skinned women. Once she knows, she could alter her body features to match the man's desires.
22. The Deeper Life Christian Fellowship is a popular church denomination in Nigeria known for their rejection of technology, exotic lifestyles, artificial hair products, trendy fashion. They emphasized holiness in their preachings and evangelicisms, and their women dressed very conservatively, obscuring their womanly features so as not to seduce men. I was not part of this Christian group, nor did I necessarily agree with their extreme conservatism. (In fairness, since their beginnings in the 1970s, they have since evolved and relaxed some of their rules. At least, many members now watch TV to listen to news and wholesome channels when earlier watching TV was a sin because the devil used it to show immorality.) Due to my poor fashion tastes, I was associated with this spiritually conservative group.
23. Henry John Drewal, "Mami Wata: Arts for Water Spirits in Africa and Its Diasporas," *African Arts* 41, no. 2 (2008): 72.
24. God may be the only exception who has no evil side. As popular Yoruba sayings go, "God does [whatever] and no one can question God, yet God does no evil"; "Those who are ignorant may say that God does evil, but God is the just avenger and does no evil"; and "God is full of mercy and does no evil."
25. Issitt, "Mami Wata," 146.
26. Victor Uwaifo, "Guitar Boy," YouTube video, uploaded by Premier Records Limited, uploaded August 23, 2016, https://youtu.be/W6wsGVUdwgk. Accessed May 20, 2020.

27. Osakue S. Omoera and Daniel E. Omoruan, "The River Goddess and Melody-Makers in Nigeria: A Cultural View on Majek Fashek and Victor Uwaifo," *Modern Africa: Politics, History and Society* 7, no. 2 (2019): 49.
28. Drewal, "Mami Wata: Arts for Water Spirits in Africa and Its Diasporas," 72.
29. Doran H. Ross, "The Art of Almighty God: In His Own Words," *African Arts* 47, no. 2 (2014): 25.
30. Issitt, "Mami Wata," 1:142.
31. Although I know this clergyman's name, I have chosen to keep the name confidential.
32. As noted in the methodology section, inculturation, Africana readings, takes seriously the worldview of the contemporary reader, and the original context is placed in service of the contemporary reader. For Western readings, original contexts take priority; hence, the dissatisfaction Africans have with Eurocentric methods.
33. O gba abi ko gba, adura san ju epe lo.
34. The book of Jonah does not say where Jonah was before he got to Joppa to board the ship toward Tarshish. If this Jonah son of Amittai is the same as Jonah son of Amittai named in 2 Kings 14:25, Jonah was probably based in his hometown Gath Hepher in Northern Israel, about two miles north of Nazareth.
35. An interesting detail in the Hebrew is about the fish(es) that swallowed Jonah. The gender of the fish changes from masculine fish 2:1 (דג), to feminine fish 2:2 (דגה) and back to masculine fish 2:11(דג). The text goes thus: "But the Lord provided a large fish (masculine) to swallow up Jonah and Jonah was in the belly of the fish (masculine) three days and three nights. Then Jonah prayed to the Lord his God from the belly of the fish (feminine). . . .Then the Lord spoke to the fish (masculine), and it spewed Jonah out upon the dry land." Rabbi Rashi comments on this detail saying that while Jonah was in the male fish, Jonah had much room in its belly and did not think to pray. When the male fish spit Jonah out into a female fish, Jonah had little room as he was pressed upon by the many embryo in the female fish, then Jonah prayed to God (Rabbi Rashi, "Commentary Jonah Chapter 2," n.p. https://www.chabad.org/library/bible_cdo/aid/16184/showrashi/true).
36. Henry J. Drewal ("Performing the Other: Mami Wata Worship in Africa," *TDR* 32, no. 2 [1988]: 169) notes how in a conversation with Mami Wata adherents that "Mami Wata 'marks' her people."
37. Niveen Sarras, "A Palestinian Feminist Reading of the Book of Jonah," *Journal of Lutheran Ethics* 15, no. 8 (2015): n.p. Accessed May 30, 2020, https://www.elca.org/JLE/Articles/1112.

38. Mami Wata is actually known all over the world under different names. She is known in other places with other names such as Lasìren, Yemanja, Santa Marta la Dominadora, and Oxum (Drewal, "Mami Wata: Arts for Water Spirits," 61).
39. For instance, Andrew Mbuvi summarizes John Mbiti's Kenyan New Testament Eschatology noting that one of the major outcomes is "exposing a closer affinity of African religious outlook to the first-century biblical worldview in contrast to the Enlightenment-driven western methodologies" ("African Biblical Studies," *Currents in Biblical Research* 15, no. 2 [2017]: 150). In addition, the Igbos of Eastern Nigeria have often referred to themselves as one of the lost tribes of Israel. The Yorubas of the South-West region have their origins in the Middle East.
40. Pirkei DeRabbi Eliezer, "The History of Jonah," n.p. Accessed May 28, 2020, https://www.sefaria.org/Pirkei_DeRabbi_Eliezer.10?lang=bi.
41. Masoga ("Redefining Power," 95) quoting Cone notes, "Theologians do not normally reveal the true source of their theological reflections. They often tell us about the books that are similar and not so similar to their perspectives, but seldom do they tell us about the non-intellectual factors that are decisive for the arguments advanced on a particular issue" (James H. Cone, *God of the Oppressed* [Maryknoll, NY: Orbis Books, 1977], vi).

13. Envisioning Africana Religions: Seeking a Distinctive Voice for the Study of Religions in Africa and the African Diaspora

SALIM FARAJI

Akan spirituality as with most other African Traditional Religions is experiential, practical, and mystical. There is no body versus spirit conflict, and neither is religion simply a rational exercise based on the acceptance of creeds and doctrines. Akan spirituality engages the whole human being through supersensory immersion—that is, the body and the senses are the ground and vehicle through which to explore the inner dimensions of the spiritual and ancestral worlds. This is possible because the human being does not exist independent of the cosmos, creation, and ancestors, but as a member within the Divine Collective.[1]

I want to theorize and reflect on Africana religious studies as co-constitutive of four fundamental premises—a conceptual framework that prioritizes the epistemological, hermeneutical, and existential primacy of African traditional religions as the core cosmological framework for all Africana religious traditions and practices:[2] (1) the preeminence of African traditional religions (ATR) as the foundation for a transhistorical paradigm that presupposes an Africana history of religions, (2) the centrality and agency of Africana religious categories in the interpretative enterprise, (3) the ongoing dialogue with Africana religions and cultures as a source for addressing the existential realities that shape the mundane and metaphysical experiences of African-descended people and the global community,[3] (4) transgressive transdisciplinarity that encompasses various disciplinary approaches to the study of Africana religious expressions, for example, anthropology, archaeology, linguistics, African Studies, African American Studies, African philosophy and religions, and the theological disciplines of Black and Womanist theology. Africana religious studies can possibly serve as a meeting ground or canopy for this diverse and complex topic. Africana religious studies may serve as a synthesis of the scholarship of those in the religion academy and other scholars in the humanities and social sciences.

Yet Africana religious studies also provides a distinct and new orientation to the study of religion in Africa and the African Diaspora by epistemologically privileging African traditional religions and cultures as the beginning point for the numerous permutations of Africana religious diversity throughout the world. Such an approach calls into the question methods that elevate the priority of the so-called world religions such as Christianity, Islam, and Buddhism as "macro-traditions" that are universal and absolute vis-à-vis the "local," "parochial," "contextual," and "tribal" religions of Africa and the African Diaspora. The imperative of Africana religious studies is to excavate what Kofi Asare Opoku calls the "enduring heritage" of African traditional religions as a transhistorical, transnational, multicultural, multiethnic, and multilingual phenomenon indigenous to Africa and the diaspora, equipped with its own categorical and existential prerogatives about the world and human existence.

BETWIXT AND BETWEEN: THE MAKING OF AN AFRICANA RELIGIOUS STUDIES SCHOLAR

As an Africana studies scholar who is also a trained religion and theological scholar, I am situated in two of the most prominent intellectual traditions in African American and Africana thought in American academia. My intellectual formation in Africana Studies began in the late 1980s when as a student at Penn State University I attended my first African American studies conference at the First Annual Cheik Anta Diop Conference in Philadelphia. This experience was enhanced by informal, but very substantial, ties with the Department of African American Studies at Temple University, which occurred soon after. Although never a formal student at Temple University, I participated and taught in their Pan African Studies Community Education Program through the mentorship of one of the inaugural doctoral students in the new PhD program in African American Studies, Rev. Dr. Cecil Gray. There are now according to the National Council of Black Studies nineteen universities across the United States that offer doctoral degrees in Africana/African American/African Diaspora studies, and

Temple University was the first in 1987 to launch this innovative field of transdisciplinary research and scholarship.

Dr. Molefi Kete Asante, the founder and architect of Temple's PhD program, now known as the Department of Africology and African American Studies, also proposed a theoretical paradigm called Afrocentricity as a method of positioning Africa and people of African descent as subjects, agents, and actors in history as opposed to objects on the periphery of European intellectual culture and experience.[4] Asante's theoretical formulation of Afrocentricity, although a unique contribution, was built on earlier traditions of Africana historiography, epistemology, cosmology, and hermeneutics in the works of W. E. B. Du Bois, Carter G. Woodson, Drusilla Dunjee Houston, William Leo Hansberry, John Henrik Clarke, Cheik Anta Diop, and Kwame Nkrumah, among others. Kwame Nkrumah in his presidential address to the International Congress of Africanists in Accra, Ghana, in December 1962, heralded that a regeneration of learning was emerging in the African world where Africans were being treated as subjects and not objects and African scholars were utilizing a "new African-centred approach" to the study of African history and societies.[5] Nkrumah's remarks foreshadowed Asante's theory of Afrocentricity. Notwithstanding genealogical considerations, the department as well as the theoretical lens of Afrocentricity have attracted a great number of advocates and detractors over the past forty years. Yet it is this school of thought that provided my earliest introduction to Africana Studies and equipped me as a scholar to navigate the plethora of theoretical, ideological, and methodological perspectives that have come to define not only Africana Studies broadly, but also Africana religious and theological scholarship, specifically.

My venture into religious and theological scholarship began in 1994 at Howard University School of Divinity, where I was guided and mentored by Cain Hope Felder, Cheryl Sanders, and Elias Farajaje-Jones. During these years HUSD was leading a national discussion regarding Afrocentric theory and biblical studies through Felder's publications, *The Original African Heritage Study Bible, Stony the Road We Trod: African American Biblical Interpretation* and *Troubling Biblical Waters*. Cheryl Sanders's work, *Living the Intersection: Womanism and Afrocentrism in Theology*, represented at the time the only critical, theological appraisal of both Womanist thought and Afrocentricity's relevance for constructing an empowering "post-Black Theology" centered in Black women's experience and African and African Diaspora epistemologies. Ibrahim Farajajé (formerly known as Elias Farajaje-Jones) modeled for me the most superb example of radical transdisciplinarity and intersectionality that I had witnessed during my graduate theological studies. Both his theory and praxis were informed and shaped by his practice of multiple religious traditions, including Eastern Orthodox Christianity, Santeria, and Islam while also existing as a bisexual, LGBTQ-identified African American male.[6] His predilection for African and African Diaspora religions was reflected in the book he co-edited with Davis Kortright, *African Creative Expressions of the Divine*, and in his single-author book, *In Search of Zion: The Spiritual Significance of Africa for Three Black Religious Movements*. These experiences at Penn State, Temple, and Howard provided the intellectual frameworks and theoretical language I needed to begin to synthesize and integrate the disciplinary aims of both Africana Studies and Black religious and theological scholarship into emerging conceptualizations of first, Pan African religious studies, and ultimately Africana religious studies.

My quest to formulate a theory of Africana religions evolved and expanded during my graduate theological studies at Claremont School of Theology and Claremont Graduate University. I was able to employ my bourgeoning interdisciplinary vision of Africana religions and theory in such varied disciplines as history of Christianity and Early Christian Studies, Coptic and Nubian Studies, process theology, and African and African diaspora religions. In the autumn of 1993 Professors Karen and Garth Kasimu Baker-Fletcher established the Center for Pan African Religious Studies at the Claremont School of Theology. The uniqueness of the center was that it represented at the time the only institute in North America, if not all the African Diaspora, to create the discipline of Pan African Religious Studies at an Association of Theological Schools graduate theological institution.

The goal of the center was to provide ministers, scholars, and community members with a forum to discuss social and religious issues affecting the African American and African Diaspora communities. From 1995 to 2000, the center hosted a wide range of scholarly symposia, representing diverse disciplinary interests on the topic of Africana religious studies. Contributors to these forums were Christian ministers, Africanists, and Africana Studies scholars, process and Womanist theologians, and practitioners of West African traditional religions and ancient Egyptian religion.

The center also hosted a delegation of Claremont School of Theology students to South Africa to study the intersection between religion and society in newly post-apartheid South Africa, as well as a forum and book on the significance and meaning of the Million Man March for Black Religion. *Black Religion after the Million Man March*, edited by Garth Kasimu Baker Fletcher, assembled a group of Black theological scholars representing disparate voices to assess the value of this historic event for the future of Black religion as we approached the twenty-first century.

My contribution to this volume titled, "Walking Back to Go Forward," was my first scholarly essay in which I initially proposed a theological synthesis of liberation theology and theology of religions perspectives in order to situate African American churches within the matrix of African American religions—and account for the reality of religious pluralism and non-Christian religions among African-descended people.[7] My contribution represented an original and distinctive theological perspective that positioned me as the first academically trained Black theologian and religious thinker in the history of African American religious thought to utilize ancient Egyptian narratives, symbols, and metaphors to interpret the African American religious experience and proffer a pluralist, non-Christian African American theology.[8] I utilized the ancient Egyptian deity *Heru* (Horus), patron "god" of pharaonic kingship and resistance to injustice as a theological archetype to interpret the tradition of liberation spirituality in African American religions.[9] I was responding to what I thought was an overemphasis of the oppressed-oppressor dichotomy in the analysis of African American religions, and instead I argued that in sovereign cultures such as ancient Egypt and Nubia the triumph of injustice is not executed by the oppressor over the oppressed, but by an equal contending opponent who can ultimately be overcome.

I was attempting to delineate a shift in hermeneutical approaches to the study and practice of Black Religion. This is important because some Black theologians and religious practitioners have exclusively relied on biblical narratives and symbols to interpret the African American religious experience. Although some biblical motifs have proved to be useful and even emancipatory, the biblical world also placed ideological constraints and limitations on the ways in which people of African descent viewed their unique history and the overall human saga, which began on the African continent. Sole reliance on the biblical tradition, I argued, tended to alienate African-descended people from more ancient, indigenous, and relevant Africana sources.

My academic training was also producing a theory of Africana religious studies—one that begins with re-prioritizing the centrality of Africana spiritual traditions and sources from antiquity to the present—traditions that included but also exceeded the textual canons of the major monotheistic religions and their symbols and ideologies. In fact, this stance represents the initial step in the shift from Black religion and Black theology to Africana religions and Africana theology. Such were the conversations, ruminations, and dialogues during my seminary and graduate school days, and the Center for Pan African Religious Studies provided a welcoming and safe theological space to creatively explore these "new" and what otherwise seemed as off-the-cuff ideas about a field that was coming into existence. The Million Man March project included various conferences and programs that were successful, and the center was influential in affecting public discourse on social, political, and theological issues in the Los Angeles metropolitan region and southern California. Notwithstanding these positive contributions, there was still an outstanding and fundamental inquiry, "What is Africana Religious Studies?" The center went defunct in the early 2000s, but its epistemological and theoretical questions and concerns remained vital, necessary, and urgent for the work of African-descended peoples and the world—and so, the charge to define the discipline of Africana religious studies has been left for our current era of scholars and theologians

IN THE BEGINNING WAS AFRICANA STUDIES: RETHINKING THE FOUNDATIONS OF RADICAL TRANSDISCIPLINARITY

Africana studies, Africanist studies, and religious and theological scholarship have provided a transdisciplinary methodology that encompasses the U.S. regional context, African diaspora, and the African continent. An intersectional analysis of these three disciplines in the development of Africana religious studies not only underlines diasporic forms of religious expression that have been shaped by resistance to slavery, imperialism, racism, capitalist exploitation, and colonialism, but also the flourishing of Africana religions in antiquity when they thrived unencumbered in the sovereign societies of classical and traditional Africa. Fundamentally this is a matter of distinguishing between Africana religions as "religion of the oppressed" in juxtaposition with African religions as "sovereign religion." The former refers to religions that emerge in the context of hegemonic domination where adherents are marginalized and viewed as a minority group unsanctioned by the status quo. Sovereign religion is the religion of politically autonomous, self-governing societies where the reservoir for religious ideals is indigenous to the historic, cultural norms of their civilization. It is imperative that the disciplinary scope of Africana religious studies include these parallel foci—and that this emerging discipline incorporate the transdisciplinary insights that the social sciences, humanities, environmental, physical, and biological sciences as well as the arena of foreign affairs, international studies, business, and security and strategic studies can provide.

I have sought to maintain an intellectual rapport among the three disciplines, and throughout my career I have attended conferences hosted by the American Academy of Religion, the National Council for Black Studies, and the African Studies Association. Yet what I have observed is that there is very little transdisciplinary engagement between Africana Studies scholars, Africanists, and Black religion and theological scholars. There is an association of Africanist scholars who focus on religion called the African Association for the Study of Religions, but much of this scholarship has been divorced from the study of religion among Africana Studies scholars and Black religion scholars and theologians. The African and Diasporic Religious Studies Association founded at Harvard University in 2012 is on the cutting edge of connecting scholarly research on African and African diaspora religions with the practitioners of these religions. Yet scholars in Africana Studies, particularly the member institutions of the National Council for Black Studies, are rarely part of these conversations. The principal challenge is how we construct the discipline of Africana religious studies if religion and theological scholars are not in dialogue with Africana Studies and Africana Studies scholars often minimize the importance of religion relative to the social sciences and other humanities such as literature, philosophy, and the musical and performing arts.

Dianne M. Stewart and Tracey E. Hucks's essay, "Africana Religious Studies: Toward a Transdisciplinary Agenda in an Emerging Field," provides an in-depth and extensive analysis of the intellectual lineages that have informed the study of African American and African diaspora religions. Their essay positions the classic debate between E. Franklin Frazier and Melville J. Herskovits regarding the extent to which "African cultural survivals" continued to influence the development of African American culture as instructional for how contemporary Africana religious studies scholars develop theoretical and methodological approaches to the diaspora. Herskovits emphasized the continuity between African cultural traditions and African American culture, and E. Franklin Frazier was far more tentative and cautious in attributing explanatory value to supposed "Africanisms" underlying African American culture. Although the Frazier/Herskovits debate provides a window into the foundational debates that framed the study of religion and culture in the African diaspora, I suspect that Stewart and Hucks although critical of Frazier and Herskovits also overestimate the utility of this debate for our present conceptualizations of Africana religions as integrally related to, although not limited by, African cultural traditions and sensibilities.

Stewart and Hucks attempt to salvage E. Franklin Frazier's views on African cultural continuities in the Americas by emphasizing his research and travels in Brazil and throughout Africa and the synergistic insights he shared with Herskovits. They privilege the African continent as the source of Africana religions in the diaspora while also challenging and deconstructing "the quest for an 'original Africa' where Africa and its diaspora exist in stasis and remain uncomplicated by the vicissitudes of time and history."[10] What is needed, they argue, are "serious studies of Africa as 'originary space' that interrogate the problem of immanent primordialism and the uncontestable question of historical origins."[11] Consequently, Stewart and Hucks do not view Africa as "originary space" as ultimately problematic, but call into question faulty methods that may be employed to render Africa as a static construct suspended in notions of historical primevalism. To guard against invalid claims of historicity and primitivistic notions of archaic origins, Stewart and Hucks recommend a reassessing of Africa as:

1. a continent and diaspora of diversity, encounter, and transition;
2. a proliferation of "Africas" that have emerged in global milieus; and
3. a series of "unfinished migrations" and continuous diasporas of African peoples and their religious traditions worldwide.[12]

Stewart and Hucks also critique Albert Raboteau's landmark work *Slave Religion: The "Invisible Institution" in the Antebellum South* for prematurely concluding that "African gods, theology, and ritual 'did not survive' in the United States."[13] Furthermore, even more contemporary scholars such as Eddie Glaude and Cornel West are taken to task for suggesting that African American religious history begins with the revivals of the Great Awakening in the mid-eighteenth century in their anthology, *African American Religious Thought*. Stewart and Hucks argue that considering the preponderance of scholarship on the presence of African Islam and African indigenous religions in early African American culture prior to the mid-eighteenth century and throughout the nineteenth century, it is curious as to why Glaude and West wish to make African American religious history synonymous with Christianity. It is for this reason that Stewart and Hucks propose that Africana religions studies be "able to engage the 'geo-politics of knowledge' ... and subvert normative understandings of Africans represented in intellectual discourses of coloniality."[14] To assert African agency in the theoretical and hermeneutical dimension of Africana religions they use language reminiscent of Afrocentric theoretical imperatives by averring that Africans should function as "knowledge producers," "creators of meaning structures," and "self-authorized specialists."[15] Such a posture establishes Africana religious studies upon its own epistemological ground undiminished by the colonial assault on African and African Diaspora religions, which assault pursued an unrelenting agenda of Christianization, demonization, and criminalization of African cosmology, philosophy, and ritual traditions.

In recounting the intellectual lineages of Africana religious studies by reviewing the scholarship of what Stewart and Hucks describe as the two primary camps of scholars, "religionists" and "secular historians," it is evident why the two scholars continually underscore the necessity for transdisciplinary research and dialogue in the construction of Africana religious studies. Yet Stewart and Hucks fail to provide an analytical review of scholarship produced by the Black Studies/Africana Studies tradition, specifically the intellectual trajectory that emerged from the Black Power and Black Student Movements of the 1960s. This is not a criticism as much as an observation to fill a major lacuna in how we relate the disciplinary, theoretical, and methodological imperatives of the term "Africana" to the study of the religions of Africa and the African Diaspora. Unquestionably, Africana religious studies cannot be conceived independent of the discipline that created the conceptual framework of Africana Studies in the

United States. Neither can Africana religious studies establish a distinctive space within American academia separate from the historical exigencies that gave rise to the need for Africana studies as an autonomous intellectual enterprise.

Africana Studies also known as Black Studies during its inception emerged out of the Civil Rights, Black Power, and Black Studies Movements of the late 1960s.[16] The first Black Studies department was approved at San Francisco State University in 1967 in the wake of Black student activists and Black Panther party members pressing the university administration to create a distinctive academic program centered on the social, cultural, and political realities of Black people in the United States. The Black Studies Department at San Francisco State University would become fully functional in 1969 after the launch of a historic student strike organized by SFSU's Black Student Union and Third World Liberation Front. The students were not only successful in negotiating for a Black Studies Department, but also the establishment of a College of Ethnic Studies. The founding chair of the Black Studies Department at SFSU, Dr. Nathan Hare, was a sociologist who had obtained his PhD from the University of Chicago studying under E. Franklin Frazier.

The first academic unit in an American university to use the nomenclature "Africana Studies" as a disciplinary approach to study people of African descent in both the diaspora and Africa was the Africana Studies & Research Center (ASRC) at Cornell University in 1969. The ASRC like the Black Studies Department at San Francisco State University came into existence as a result of student protests. At Cornell it was a student-led takeover of Willard Straight Hall. The founding director of the Africana Studies & Research Center was James Turner, an activist-scholar and intellectual leader in the development of Africana Studies and Black social and political movements.[17] He was a member of the African Studies Association and the second president of the African Heritage Studies Association after his mentor, John Henrik Clarke, one of the premier architects of Africana Studies and Pan Africanist historiography. Indeed, James Turner and John Henrik Clarke led a delegation of African American scholars in 1973 to the Third International Congress of Africanists in Addis Ababa, Ethiopia.[18] Their conceptualization of Africana Studies was rooted in Pan Africanist politics and the history of both Africa and the African Diaspora. The Africana Studies & Research Center conceptually emerged out of a long tradition of Africana historiography forged through the works of such scholars as W. E. B. Du Bois, Drusilla Dunjee Houston, Carter G. Woodson, Arthur A. Schomburg, J. A. Rogers and William Leo Hansberry. John Henrik Clarke was the intermediary of this tradition for Cornell University, and his name was bestowed upon the John Henrik Clarke Africana Library at this same institution. He also served as the founding chair of Black and Puerto Rican Studies at Hunter College, and his conceptualization of "Africana" influenced the founding of countless other Africana Studies departments in the United States.

Hansberry was also a founding scholar of Africana scholarship and, like W. E. B. Du Bois and Carter G. Woodson, was one of the first African Diaspora scholars to utilize the term "Africana" as a descriptive designation and methodological approach for the study of people of African descent in both Africa and the diaspora. Hansberry's two posthumously published works, *Pillars in Ethiopian History Vol. I: William Leo Hansberry African History Notebook* and *Africa and Africans as Seen by Classical Writers: African History Notebook Vol. 2* provided a foundation for the exploration of ancient and medieval African history. Hansberry was also among a group of Harvard scholars that under the tutelage of Professor Earnest A. Hooten and the Peabody Museum of Anthropology and Ethnology, participated in launching the publication *Varia Africana*, a Harvard journal that focused on "African anthropology in its widest sense" and "papers of a non-controversial character dealing with the American Negro."[19] Hansberry in his essay "The Material Culture of Ancient Nigeria," referred to the first volume of *Varia Africana* as "timely but unsuccessful" and therefore may have seen Howard University as the more appropriate institution to fulfill the goals of this new journal.[20] Hansberry's understanding of the significance of the *Varia Africana* was quite similar to Du Bois's and Woodson's concept of the encyclopedia Africana, and along with these two preeminent historians he paved the way for institutionalization of Africana Studies in the late 1960s.[21]

The Africana historiographical tradition presupposes a particular social, cultural, and intellectual history that is essential in situating Africana religious studies within a transhistorical paradigm, an Africana history of religions that incorporates the totality of African history from antiquity to the present. In my book, *The Roots of Nubian Christianity Uncovered: The Triumph of the Last Pharaoh—Religious Encounters in Late Antique Africa*, I devote attention to defining an "Africana Transdisciplinary Theory of History," which includes Egyptology, Nubiology, Coptology, Africanist scholarship, ancient Greek and Roman Studies, Early Christianity, Byzantine Studies, and Islamic Studies. Each of these disciplines represents unlimited possibilities for the exploration of Africana religious studies spanning the ancient world to our contemporary era.

The early pioneers of both African American Religious Studies and Black Church Studies acknowledged that these two strands within Black religious and theological scholarship originated in the Black Studies Movement of the late 1960s. James H. Evans Jr., in an essay titled "Black Church Studies and the Theological Curriculum," asserts that "the ferment of the 1960s, which gave rise to Black Studies programs in colleges and universities, also spawned Black Church Studies programs in predominantly white seminaries and divinity schools. . . . Unfortunately no comprehensive dialogue has taken place between both types of programs."[22] Not much progress has been made in that regard in the nearly thirty years since Evans wrote this essay for *African American Religious Studies: An Interdisciplinary Anthology* in 1989. Evans also argued that the primary task for Black Church Studies was the recovery of African American religious history. He described this as a reclamation project for Black Church Studies, which should begin with the revalorization of Africa. Evans intimated that "Africa must be reclaimed as a place where three of the great world religions met: Judaism, Islam, and Christianity. . . . Moreover it must be seen as the appropriate place to begin study of African American religion."[23] Evans provided recommendations that can be adapted and applied to the development of Africana religious studies: (1) recognize the common origin of Africana Studies/Africana religious studies programs and the significance of this relationship for methodological, theoretical, and historical orientation; (2) maintain ongoing transdisciplinary dialogue between Africana religious studies and Africana Studies scholars; (3) position African history and religions as the foundation of the Abrahamic religions and African diaspora religions.

Gayraud Wilmore, the prolific scholar of African American religious history and Black Theology, also affirmed the connection of African American Religious Studies and Black Studies when he commented, "African American Religious Studies, as we understand it today, evolved from the Black Studies movement of the 1960s."[24] Wilmore also suggested that the scope of African American Religious Studies should include Black

Judaism, Islam, neo-African Religions, and the new urban sects and cults in the African American community. He characterized African American Religious Studies as an interdisciplinary enterprise that also must engage in intellectual exchange with research in Black Studies, African Studies, and "Hispanic, Asian, native American and other Third World Religions."[25] Both Wilmore's and Evans's prescriptions for the construction of Black Church Studies and African American Religious Studies were not only instrumental for the disciplinary development of these two fields of study but also prescient in anticipation of how Black religious and theological scholarship would evolve into Africana religious studies. Yet just as Black religion and theological scholars should strive to resist a colonial legacy of intellectual amnesia regarding the significance of Africana studies and historiography for the formation of what is now Africana religious studies, likewise there is a need to seek to disrupt the intellectual provincialism and academic protectionism that potentially obstruct opportunities for transdisciplinary collaboration between the various scholars and fields committed to establishing Africana religious studies as a premier discipline in its own right.

Gayraud Wilmore in *Black Theology: A Documentary History Volume 2* reminisced about the potential for transdisciplinary cooperation between Black Studies scholars and Black Religion scholars as well as the missed opportunities in the 1960s:

> I remember talking with Black Professors from several of the New York colleges and universities .... during the early 1960s about the theories .... of ancient Nile Valley civilizations, on Egyptology and cultural anthropology, the rediscovery of the writings of early twentieth-century Afrocentric historians, such as Edward Wilmot Blyden, W. E. B. Du Bois, Willis N. Huggins, John G. Jackson, John W. Cromwell, Joel A. Rogers, and Arthur Schomburg. There was an air of excitement for me about those conversations at Frank's Restaurant on 125th Street and other places, that later brought me into contact with the writings of J. C. deGraft-Johnson, John Henrik Clarke, G. G. M. James, Yosef ben-Jochannan, and Maulana Karenga. Among my contemporaries, these men, who were outside the traditional Black Church, were the real pioneers of Black Studies and serious investigations into African origins.[26]

Wilmore's reflections convey the relative ease of intellectual rapport between Black scholars from distinct disciplines within informal Black spaces. Yet he also went on to say that theologians like James Cone and J. Deotis Roberts were not greatly influenced by the pioneers of Black Studies in the 1960s beyond the political context of Black Power's meaning for Black Theology. Missed opportunities have also fallen on the side of Black Studies/ Africana Studies scholars who have often not focused on religion or minimized its importance in constructing the discipline of Africana Studies. Religious studies is often viewed as tangential to socio-cultural and sociopolitical analyses in Africana Studies, and many Africana Studies scholars are cynical about the perceived Christocentric bias and exclusivism inherent in some trajectories of Black religious and theological scholarship. Yet James Cone often exclaimed, "How do we construct Black Studies without taking seriously the continuous legacy of Black Religion?" in response to Africana Studies' curricula devoid of Black religion and theological content.[27] In some instances, a few of my colleagues in Africana Studies were unaware of the critical, systematic, and transdisciplinary rigor that drives religious and theological scholarship. I have often reminded my faculty-peers from the social sciences and other disciplines in the humanities that it was philosophy, religion, and theology that founded universities in the Western intellectual tradition and even in classical African civilizations. Considering that religion is a synthesizing element of all aspects of culture in African and the African Diaspora, the study of Africana religions would be an integral component of Black and Africana Studies as well as Black religious and theological scholarship.

RELIGION WITHOUT AFRICANA STUDIES AND AFRICANA STUDIES WITHOUT RELIGION

The conundrum facing our conceptualizations and integration of the field of Africana religions within the realm of graduate theological studies and religious studies in Western academia is the failure to provide disciplinary space for religious expressions centered on the heterogeneous and multi-faceted cultures of Africa and the Africa Diaspora. Undoubtedly my observations may at first appear counterintuitive considering the plethora of scholarship produced in African American religions, African diaspora religions, Black Theology, Womanist and Black Feminist religious scholarship, and African traditional religions. Also, the study of Africana religions and the utilization of Africana cultural epistemologies and theoretical foci seemed to have made significant headway in the field of biblical studies with the publication of *The Africana Bible: Reading Israel's Scriptures from Africa and the African Diaspora* in 2009 and the launch of the *Journal of Africana Religions* in 2013. The numerous essays in this volume are representative of Drew Theological Seminary's 16th Transdisciplinary Theological Colloquium on "Africana Religious Studies," and signify the mounting importance and relevance of examining the cultural worlds and religious experiences of nearly 1.5 billion people, representing almost 20 percent of the world's population—Africana religions is indeed transhistorical, transnational, and global.[28]

Yet religious and theological studies and the discipline of Africana studies often relegate the study of religious phenomena pertaining to African-descended people to the periphery of what is considered "core" and "foundational" in their respective disciplines. For Africana studies especially, departments and programs situated in public universities and non-theological environments, religion is often considered secondary to the social sciences or simply a part of the broader arena of the humanities. In religious and theological studies Africana religions are situated as subordinate to the Abrahamic religions of Judaism, Christianity, and Islam or viewed as "minor traditions" when compared to other world religions such as Hinduism and Buddhism. Although people of African descent practice the Abrahamic religious traditions and the religions of Hinduism and Buddhism, their distinctive histories and practices within these traditions are approached as contextualized replicas, subsidiaries that function in an ancillary role to the established conventions of what is deemed "normative" and "canonical."

Recent social scientific research conducted by the Pew Research Center's Forum on Religion & Public Life found that African Americans are the "most religious ethnic group" in the United States.[29] A similar Pew Study on African religiosity ascertained that Africa is the "most religious continent" in the world.[30] Such data appears to confirm John Mbiti's observation that religion represents the totality of culture in Africa and Kofi Asare Opoku's insight that religion is the determining principle of life in Africa and the African Diaspora—and equally so Dwight Hopkins's admonition that African Americans practice faith as a total way of life.[31]

The population of the African continent is substantially made up of women, and the African Union has declared the years 2010–2020 as the African Women's Decade. Mercy Amba Oduyoye clearly demonstrates that it is the "Daughters of Anowa," African women, who are the driving force of agriculture, trade, and religious activities on the African continent.[32] In terms of African American religiosity in general and Black Church culture in particular it is African American women who form the critical mass of congregants and devotees who sustain African American religious organizations. In fact they represent what Cheryl Townsend Gilkes calls the "Indispensable Black Women."[33] Hence religion functions as a primary guiding orientation for African-descended people worldwide, and women are at the heart of the diverse spiritual expressions that shape the cultures and societies of Africa and the African Diaspora. The demographics of religious adherents in Africa and the African Diaspora accompanied with the centrality of religion suggest that within Africana Studies and Religious Studies, Africana religions should be elevated from an often marginalized subfield to a theoretical paradigm that defines the core of both disciplines—that is, provides a primary lens through which to approach and interpret human experience in Africa and the African Diaspora.

I envision as a distinct discipline the historical contours of Africana religions as encompassing classical antiquity to the present. Consequently, this range of study should include minimally the ancient African religious traditions of the Nile Valley and Sudanic-Sahelian Africa, including the "Western Sudan," Egypt, Nubia, Axum, and the Khoisan of southern Africa as well as the other indigenous religious of East and West Africa, and the myriad expressions of African American and African Diaspora religious traditions. Africana religious studies also comprise the emergence and unique character of the various Christianities and Islamic traditions in both Africa and the African Diaspora. Despite the variegated nature of Africana religions, I argue that the epistemological foundation of all Africana religious expressions begins with classical and traditional African cultures as the starting point for evaluating and assessing the varied religious traditions in Africa and the Atlantic diaspora. In other words, African indigenous religions are the font and cultural matrix out of which the religious logic, philosophy, and ethos of Africana religions were born. It informs the diversity of Africana religions in all their plurality and numerous manifestations.

AFRICAN TRADITIONAL RELIGIONS: FORGING A TRANSHISTORICAL AND TRANS-REGIONAL THEORY OF AFRICANA RELIGIONS

I readily acknowledge that the construction of a unified schema for the study of religions in Africa and the African Diaspora is a gargantuan task. These religious traditions represent diverse cultures, languages, customs, ethnic identities, and practices. Often Africana religious identities also represent congruent and conflicting legacies that may manifest in various syncretic forms of religious expression. Yet the conceptual framework proposed in this essay provides a model that positions African traditional religion and culture as a transhistorical, transdisciplinary enterprise capable of functioning as the epistemological ground as well as the primary hermeneutical lens to assess Africana religious studies. Africana religious studies therefore may begin with the assertion that the human is the agent and pivot of culture and religious experience. Consequently, the human in Africa represents the oldest endeavor in the history of civilization to construct cosmogonical, cosmological, mythical, religious, and scientific explanations of our world and reality. Classical and traditional African culture represents not only African-descended people's religious heritage but also serves as humanity's most ancient and indigenous spiritual traditions. How would a consideration of KhoeSan shamanism, a tradition indigenous to the San people of southern Africa, inform Africana cosmologies, healing and medicinal practices, aesthetics and performative practices? The San according to recent genetic studies represent the cradle of anatomically modern humans, and therefore San religion may serve as a paradigmatic culture for Africana religions.[34] San culture represents 200,000 years of human evolutionary history and suggests by their continued existence that the basis of Africana religions is not only "primordial" but also novel due to its ability to adapt, thrive, and motivate future innovation. The South African astrophysicist Thebe Medupe, who is also from the San people, says he was inspired to become a physicist by the cosmic stories of his indigenous KhoeSan roots. His story illustrates not only the transhistorical elasticity of Africana religions but also the possibility or forging links in the arena of science, technology, engineering, and mathematics (STEM). Our concern, therefore, is the study and evaluation, assessment and appraisal of how Africana peoples construct, define, and practice the multitudinous phenomena of religious thought and practice. The basic epistemological stance of Africana religious studies is the assertion that the African Traditional Worldview is the foundational and guiding cultural orientation of the diverse religious manifestations present in Africa and the African diaspora.

For Peter Paris it is the African worldview that provides hermeneutical clarity in the explication of Africana religions. Peter Paris argues that the "African Worldview" is the interpretative frame of reference which enslaved Africans in the United States utilized to negotiate the horrifying trauma of their encounter with their Western captors.[35] This "interpretative frame of reference" is also the primary cultural and religious orientation for the plethora of religious traditions in Africa and the African diaspora. Scholars of African American religions and Afro-Latin-Caribbean religions substantiate that the religious experience of African diasporic peoples in the Western Hemisphere is based primarily on the encounter between historical and historicized African Traditional Worldviews and Euro-Christian traditions and indigenous American religious traditions.[36] In the Caribbean and South America the African Traditional Worldview can be observed as a vital tradition in such religions as Vodun, Santeria, and Candomblé. These traditions are usually interpreted as distinct from African religious expression in North America because of their preservation of African deities, rituals, and cosmological structures. Nonetheless, despite the varied interpretations of the impact and perpetual influence of the African Traditional Worldview in the African Diaspora it remains the common denominator upon which our questions, research, and differing perspectives cannot avoid. The African Traditional Worldview is the starting place, the primary orienting location in which to comprehend the uniqueness of religions in the African diaspora. Ontologically, we ask questions, "What is the descriptive context of the African Traditional Worldview?" and "What is the quintessence, or essentials of the African Traditional Worldview?" Jacob Olupona readily acknowledges that is difficult to characterize an African indigenous spiritual tradition because of its diversity and complexity. Nonetheless, he proposes that there are essential features that can be enumerated and systematically ascertained.[37] Olupona asserts that the key constitutive elements of the African Traditional Worldview are the prominence of myths about the origins of the world, the existence of a multiplicity of deities, ritual and ceremonies, religious functionaries, divination, and ancestral veneration.

Cosmologically, myths about the origin of the world, or what we may also identify as cosmogony and cosmology, are the foundational narratives that sustain and perpetuate the worldviews of African cultures. They are the blueprints for a culture's philosophical, theological, anthropological, social, political, and economic self-understanding. Olupona states that the African proclivity toward conceptualizing Ultimate Reality of the Divine as consisting of a multiplicity of deities and divinities, gods and lesser gods, is an essential and common feature among African cultures. Olupona posits the role of ritual as fundamental to understanding how relationships between humans, and between the human and divine are established, organized, and negotiated in African cultures. Olupona stresses the importance of ritual for the stability and cohesion of African cultures. For Olupona rituals are primarily "modes of communication between humans and the extra-human agents." They also serve as "rituals of transition" in that they demarcate specific periods of social transition in African cultures such as birth, puberty, marriage, elder-hood, and death. Olupona also identifies the role of "religious functionaries" as characteristic of African cultures. These various offices may encompass the realms of spirituality and communalism as governed by the priesthood, the social and political as governed by kings, queens, and chiefs, and agricultural and health practices as governed by the custodians and practitioners of African medicine. In many instances these various roles overlap and intersect with various individuals or specialized groups within traditional culture.

Olupona suggests, "Perhaps no feature is more revealing of the traditional religious systems than the method of divination that each religious tradition employs." It is through divination that cosmic processes are ascertained for the benefit of humanity. Olupona defines the purpose and process of divination:

> Divination is a way of knowing the views and intentions of the supernatural world. Through the divination process, the feelings and messages of the deities are revealed to humans. From the perspective

of individuals or groups of people who see divination, it is a way of discerning past, present, and future occurrences that have meaningful consequences in life.[38]

Olupona discusses the various forms of divination prevalent throughout African traditional cultures. One of the most common features of divination is the interpretation of diverse signs or omens. Signs can range from occurrences in natural phenomena to the experiences of dreams. Building upon the work of Evan Zuesse, Olupona elaborates on three primary forms of divination: intuitive, possessional, and instrumental. Intuitive divination requires an exceptional perspicacity or "spiritual insight" into the nature of the events that occur in the mundane and spiritual worlds. Possessional divination is the most complex and popular mode of divination in African traditional cultures. This form of divination consists of the diviner being possessed by a spiritual entity, deity, or ancestor. In the state of possession, the diviner receives knowledge on how to address the needs of the inquirer. Instrumental divination consists of a three-tier process that involves consultation, diagnosis, and prescription. Instrumental divination utilizes a wide range of tools and sacred texts that are most often memorized and rehearsed through orality. The Ifa system of the Yoruba-speaking people of Southwest Nigeria is the most popular form of this mode of divination, particularly to people in the Americas. Ifa divination is widely used in the United States, Cuba, and Brazil due to the dispersal of Yoruba cultural traditions through slavery and migrations.

Laura Grillo reported on her research in "Divination in Contemporary Urban West Africa." Through extensive field study in Abidjan, Ivory Coast, she has substantiated a common West African Traditional Worldview through the practice of divination among diverse West African peoples.[39] The city of Abidjan is a cosmopolitan center consisting of diverse African ethnicities from throughout West Africa. Grillo has observed that the common acceptance of divination by diverse African peoples is an indicator of a common epistemological stance in West African cultures. The various individual sacred stories, myths, and traditions that make up specific divination systems of cultures are superseded and transcended in the actual practice and consulting that takes place during a divining inquiry. Through the processes of adaptation and innovation the practitioners and adherents of different systems of divination find common ground in a way that is only possible by the existence of a prior shared worldview.

Olupona identifies ancestral veneration as one of the most distinguishing features of African Traditional cultures, although the practice varies throughout continental Africa and the African diaspora. Olupona summarizes the importance of ancestors in African Traditional cultures:

> Ancestor belief and veneration is an extension of the cosmology of African people. Ancestors, male and female, are generally deceased elders who have passed through the transition from the realm of the living to that of the super-human without necessarily losing their membership in the community of their family, clans, and kin group. As in the structure of the African pantheon of gods, beliefs, and practices regarding ancestors vary greatly in African societies and religious traditions. But despite the variation almost everywhere, ancestor traditions, wherever they are found, are "well situated in the large context of the cosmological thought" and in the social institutions of the people, especially the kinship system.[33]

Ancestors in the African Traditional Worldview occupy both mundane and metaphysical dimensions. Their influence and power begins and is rooted in the familial structures from which they emerge, thereby sanctioning and legitimizing kinship, moral values, and standards of excellence. The ancestral sphere of influence also extends into the realm of the cosmic, thus serving as intermediaries between the physical and spiritual worlds. Ancestral veneration is also fundamentally interrelated with the other characteristics that Olupona identifies as distinctive about African Traditional Religions. Ancestors are often the subjects of myths about the origin of a people. They may function as deities in the pantheon of "gods" and be invoked and supplicated during important rituals and ceremonies. Ancestors and ancestral wisdom are also important for the legitimization of religious functions and the transmission of traditions concerning a specific religious office. The ancestors are of fundamental importance in terms of possessional divination because of their expected ability to convey information and insight from the spirit world to the individual or community seeking guidance and solutions. Anthony Ephirim-Donkor reiterates this common ancestral view among African people in his discussion of the ancestors,

Nananom Nsamanfo, among the Akan of Ghana, West Africa. Upon "death" the Nsamanfo become resurrected spiritual personalities "joining the collective body of apotheosized agencies so that they influence the affairs of their posterity on earth."[40]

Similarly to Olupona, Kofi Asare Opoku posits a unifying thread among the diversity of African Traditional Religious:

> Africa is so vast and has such a large number of societies which differ from each other considerably that one runs the risk of generalization when one speaks of traditional African religion. And yet there is a common thread in indigenous values, views, and experiences which shows a large measure of uniformity. Out of this emerges the African concept of the supernatural, ideas about man, society, and nature. All these ideas form a system which gives meaning and significance to African life.[41]

Opoku identifies such features as the belief in God, ancestral spirits, supernatural entities or lesser deities, mystical powers, and talismanic magic as essential to the African Traditional Worldview. Laurenti Magesa asserts that African Traditional Religion can be interpreted as a unified cultural orientation while simultaneously acknowledging the variegated nature of distinct cultures and ethnicities.[42] He opts in favor of the nomenclature "African Traditional Religion" as opposed to "African Traditional Religions." Magesa argues that Western and Western-oriented scholars emphasized the diversity and disconnectedness of African Traditional Cultures. Anthropologists, missionaries, and many Africanists compartmentalized African traditional cultures based on the uniqueness of specific cultural customs, traditions, ritual practices, and deity conceptualizations. Colonialism and missionary activity in Africa are the major forces responsible for the artificial fragmentation of African Spirituality and religious practices. Magesa also proposes that African Traditional Religion be viewed as a world religion. Its presence on the continent of Africa and throughout the Americas constitutes it as an international force on par with the other prominent world religions. The adaptability of African Traditional Religion is an added asset that enables the essential tenets of this worldview to be integrated and synthesized with other religious traditions. The African Traditional Worldview is not stagnant, and it is because of its dynamism that this worldview re-creates itself in new forms, as it emerges in new contexts and interacts with other cultural and religious traditions.

ENVISIONING THE FUTURE OF AFRICANA RELIGIOUS STUDIES

Africana Religious Studies is the study of Religions in Africa and the Africa Diaspora. The nomenclature "Africana" refers not to an explicit political category, but to a global cultural phenomenon, an African World Community. Africana represents all African people and African-descended people throughout the world who designate themselves and their religion, culture, and language as derivative or influenced by Africa. Africana religious studies asserts the African Traditional Worldview as the fundamental guiding orientation for the study of religions in Africa and the African Diaspora. However, Africana religious studies is not solely the study of African Traditional Religions per se or the African Traditional Worldview. Africana religious studies is also concerned with the various encounters, permutations, and manifestations of Africana religious experience as they are embodied in other religions.

Africana religious studies understands religion as a cultural system composed of a repertoire of interconnected practices that elicit affective and psycho-emotional responses in human beings. This culture is concretized in the thought-world of a culture's organizational apparatus, social structures, and institutions. The concretization of culture via "religious practices" fulfills the existential aim in African traditional religion and Africana religious studies in ways that do not simply reduce religion to the ideational. Hence, it not only guarantees the cognitive and mental allegiance of its constituents, but it also ensures the generational transmission of cultural practices in order to sustain meaningful existence. If there are "essential" tenets and beliefs in the diversity of Africana religious expression, they are not to be found exclusively on the level of "critical race theory," "philosophy," "ideology," or "theology." The interpretation and assessment of Africana religions and cultural identities should not always be based on what people say or think; on the contrary, culture is best observed by what people do, how they understand what they do, and how they symbolize what they do. It is within the praxis of culture that scholars and practitioners are best equipped to assess how particular peoples and communities shape and make sense of existence. Africana religious studies minimally seeks to establish an ongoing dialogue with Africana religions and cultures as a source for addressing the existential realities that shape the mundane and metaphysical experiences of African-descended people and the global community. What is at stake is the re-assertion of the dignity and humanity of African-descended people after centuries of being rendered irrelevant and inconsequential by the hegemonic posturing of European modernity.

NOTES

1. I am an ordained minister in the African Methodist Episcopal Church who has been initiated in ancient Egyptian spiritual traditions and, more recently, Akan traditional religion of Ghana, West Africa. In October 2009 I was initiated as an Okomfowaa (priest-initiate), to prepare for the sacred priesthood of the Okomfo. I was given the name Kweku Amen Nkrumah. Similar to Tracey E. Hucks's characterization of the "Yoruba-Baptist" in her book *Yoruba Traditions and African American Religious Nationalism* (Albuquerque: University of New Mexico Press, 2012). I suppose that I am "Kemetic-Akan Methodist." The prefatory quote comes from my personal reflections on Akan spirituality.
2. I understand the word "traditional" in the sense explicated by Kofi Asare Opoku. See Kofi Asare Opoku, "African Traditional Religion: An Enduring Heritage," in *Religious Plurality in Africa: Essays in Honour of John S. Mbiti*, ed. Jacob K. Olupona and Sulayman S. Nyang (Berlin: Mouton de Gruyter, 1993), 78. Opoku argues that the term does not denote "changelessness." He states it is only to indicate that it is undergirded by a fundamentally Indigenous African value system and that it has its own pattern with its own historical inheritance. I utilize the term "classical" in the same sense that Opoku uses the word "traditional," but I also mean it to refer to those traditions of remote antiquity such as the cultures of ancient Kemet (Egypt), ancient Kush (Nubia), and the ancient spiritual traditions of the present-day Kung (San) people of modern-day Namibia and Botswana.
3. See Maulana Karengam, *Kawaida: A Communitarian African Philosophy* (Los Angeles: University of Sankore Press, 1998). Dr. Maulana Karenga with his construction of Kawaida theory has influenced and framed my conceptualization of this particular premise. Kawaida as defined by Dr. Karenga is the "ongoing synthesis of the best of African thought and practice in constant exchange with the world." It is a dialogue with Africana cultures, worldviews, and values as a resource and not merely as a reference.
4. Molefi Kete Asante introduced the theory of Afrocentricity in the landmark works, *Kemet, Afrocentricity, and Knowledge* (Trenton, NJ: Africa World Press, 1990), and *The Afrocentric Idea* (Philadelphia: Temple University Press, 1987).

5. Kwame Nkrumah, *Revolutionary Path* (London: PANAF, 1973), 208–9.
6. Elias Farajaje-Jones, "Breaking Silence: Toward an In-The-Life Theology," in *Black Theology: A Documentary History*, vol. 2: *1980–1992*, ed., James H. Cone and Gayraud S. Wilmore (Maryknoll, NY: Orbis Books, 1993), 139–59.
7. Salim Faraji, "Walking Back to Go Forward," in *Black Religion after the Million Man March*, ed., Garth Baker-Fletcher (Maryknoll, NY: Orbis Books, 1998), 68–78.
8. Tracey Hucks and Dianne Stewart, "Religious Pluralism and African American Theology," in *The Oxford Handbook of African American Theology*, ed. Katie Cannon and Anthony Pinn (New York: Oxford University Press, 2014), 331–50. Hucks and Stewart assert that Salim Faraji's work on Kemetic sources of Neo-African religious cultures offers original perspectives on how religion is improvised in contemporary African U.S. American contexts and supports non-Christian constructions of African American theology.
9. Faraji, "Walking Back to Go Forward," 70.
10. Dianne M. Stewart Diakité and Tracey E. Hucks, "Africana Religious Studies: Toward a Transdisciplinary Agenda in an Emerging Field," *Journal of Africana Religions* 1, no. 1 (2013): 28–77.
11. Ibid., 30.
12. Ibid.
13. Ibid., 38.
14. Ibid., 41.
15. Ibid.
16. Fabio Rojas, *From Black Power to Black Studies: How a Radical Social Movement Became an Academic Discipline* (Baltimore: Johns Hopkins University Press, 2010); Ibram X. Kendi, *The Black Campus Movement: Black Students and the Racial Reconstitution of Higher Education, 1965–1972* (New York: Palgrave Macmillan, 2012).
17. Scot Brown, ed., *Discourse on Africana Studies: James Turner and Paradigms of Knowledge* (New York: Diasporic Africa Press, 2016).
18. John Henrik Clarke, "Towards Pan-Africanism: Report from Addis Ababa, Ethiopia December 1973—The Third International Congress of Africanists," *Black World/Negro Digest* 23, no. 5 (1974): 71–76.
19. Kwame Wes Alford, "The Early Intellectual Growth and Development of William Leo Hansberry and the Birth of African Studies," *Journal of Black Studies* 30, no. 3 (2000): 269–93.
20. William Leo Hansberry, "The Material Culture of Ancient Nigeria," *Journal of Negro History* 6, no. 3 (July 1921): 261–95.
21. Meghan Keita, *Race and the Writing of History: Riddling the Sphinx* (Oxford: Oxford University Press, 2000), 100.

22. James H. Evans Jr., "Black Church Studies and the Theological Curriculum," in *African American Religious Studies: An Interdisciplinary Anthology*, ed. Gayraud S. Wilmore (Durham, NC: Duke University Press, 1989), 29.
23. Ibid., 27.
24. Ibid., xiii.
25. Ibid.
26. James H. Cone and Gayraud S. Wilmore, eds., *Black Theology: A Documentary History*, vol. 2: *1980–1992* (Maryknoll, NY: Orbis Books, 1993), 179–80.
27. James Cone, *Risks of Faith: The Emergence of a Black Theology of Liberation, 1968–1998* (Boston: Beacon Press, 1990), 121–29.
28. Gustavo López and Ana Gonzalez-Barrera, "Afro-Latino: A Deeply Rooted Identity among U.S. Hispanics," Pew Research Center (March 2016); "Black Europeans and People of African Descent in Europe," European Network Against Racism (August 2012); *World Population Prospects: The 2017 Revision Key Findings and Advance Tables* (New York: United Nations, Department of Economic and Social Affairs, Population Division, 2017); *World Population Prospects: The 2017 Revision* (New York: United Nations). The demographic reports listed above indicate that the U.S., Caribbean, and Latin African Diaspora consists of approximately 175 million people, and the African Diaspora in Europe's population is approximately 7 million people. The African continent's population is estimated to be 1.3 billion, which amounts to just slightly fewer than 1.5 billion for Africa and the Atlantic diaspora. These figures do not include people of African descent in Oceania, Asia, and the Indian Ocean diaspora.
29. Neha Sahgal and Greg Smith, "A Religious Portrait of African-Americans," Pew Research Center's Forum on Religion & Public Life (2009).
30. "Tolerance and Tension: Islam and Christianity in Sub-Saharan Africa," Pew Research Center's Forum on Religion & Public Life (2010).
31. John S. Mbiti, *African Religions and Philosophy* (Oxford: Heinemann, 1990), 1–2; Kofi Asare Opoku, *West African Traditional Religion* (Accra, Ghana: FEP International Private Limited, 1978), 1; Dwight N. Hopkins, ed., *Black Faith and Public Talk: Critical Essays on James H. Cone's Black Theology and Black Power* (Waco, TX: Baylor University Press, 2007), 1.
32. Mercy Amba Oduyoye, *Daughters of Anowa: African Women and Patriarchy* (Maryknoll, NY: Orbis Books, 1995).
33. Cheryl Townsend Gilkes, *If It Wasn't for the Women . . . Black Women's Experience and Womanist Culture in Church and Community* (Maryknoll, NY: Orbis Books, 2000).
34. E. K. F. Chan, A. Timmermann, B. F. Baldi, et al., "Human origins in a Southern African Palaeo-Wetland and First Migrations," *Nature* 575 (2019): 185–89.

35. Peter J. Paris, *The Spirituality of African Peoples: The Search for Common Moral Discourse* (Minneapolis: Fortress Press, 1994), 162.
36. Timothy E. Fulop and Albert J. Raboteau, *African-American Religion: Interpretive Essays in History and Culture* (New York : Routledge Press, 1997); See also Mechal Sobel, *Trabelin' On: The Slave Journey to an Afro-Baptist Faith* (Princeton, NJ: Princeton University Press, 1988). Sobel describes the African Traditional Worldview as the "African Sacred Cosmos."
37. Jacob K. Olupona, ed., *African Spirituality: Forms, Meanings, and Expressions*, vol. 3: *World Spirituality: An Encyclopedic History of the Religious Quest* (New York: Crossroad, 2000); Jacob K. Olupona, "Sacred Cosmos: An Ethnography of African Indigenous Religious Traditions," in *African Americans and the Bible: Sacred Texts and Social Textures*, ed. Vincent L. Wimbush (New York: Continuum, 2000), 163–78.
38. Jacob K. Olupona, "Sacred Cosmos: An Ethnography of African Indigenous Religious Traditions," 172.
39. See Laura S. Grillo's photo-essay, "Divination in Contemporary Urban West Africa, "*Religious Studies News* 3, no. 3 (1998), In March 2000 I organized a lecture presentation for Dr. Grillo to present her research at the Claremont School of Theology Center for Pan African Religious Studies. For more recent research see, Laura S. Grillo, "Divination: Epistemology, Agency, and Identity in Contemporary Urban West Africa," *Religion Compass* 3, no. 6 (2009): 921–32.
40. Anthony Ephirim-Donkor, *African Personality and Spirituality: The Role of the Abosom and Human Essence* (Lanham, MD: Lexington Books, 2016), 2.
41. Opoku, *West African Traditional Religion*, 8.
42. Laurenti Magesa, *African Religion: The Moral Tradition of Abundant Life* (Maryknoll, NY: Orbis Books, 1997), 14–28.

14. Interpreting from the Back/Black-Side: Exodus through the Shawl of Memory

KENNETH N. NGWA

STANDING IN THE ROCKY PLACE:
HERMENEUTICS FROM THE BACK-SIDE

> And the Lord said to Moses, "I will also do this thing that you have asked; for you have found favor in my sight and I know you by name." He said, "Let me see your glory." But he said, "I will cause all my goodness to pass before you, and I will pronounce the name LORD before you, and I will show favor to whoever I show favor and be merciful to whomever I am merciful. And he said, "You cannot see my face; for no human can see me and live." Then the Lord said, "See, there is a place by me where you shall stand on the rock; and while my glory passes by I will put you in a cleft of the rock, and I will cover you with my hand until I have passed by; then I will take away my hand, and you shall see my back; but my face shall not be seen."
>
> Exodus 33:17–23

This encounter and dialogue between Moses and Yahweh stands in a rocky place within the mountain narratives—those narratives that simultaneously bodily (physically) remove Moses from the community he co-leads, put him in difficult conversation with a supreme power, and then return him to a community that is hard at work formulating its future. It is in these mountain areas and their discourses that particular forms of communal myths of survival are born and/or revalorized.

Moses and the exodus/exile community have barely survived a series of events associated with textualizing the Exodus story—through a golden calf and its associated ritual activity that extends and uses human bodies as custodians of history and memory, or through stone tablets and their associated legal activity that regulates and valorizes human behavior. In the unfolding narrative, these events have resulted in multiple forms of brokenness: bodily, textual, and environmental. Along with that fracturing, and concurrent with it, many migrant bodies are killed and the divine image melted and ingested. In this political and ritual act of trauma and loss, the community internalizes and carries its deity inside its body, very much like the exilic prophet, Ezekiel, consumed the divine scroll (Ezek. 3:3) and Jeremiah felt the burning of the divine word in his heart, shut in his bones (Jer. 20:9). The unfolding story of exodus has been exiled and erased—dispersed, fragmented, shattered, killed—but also ironically internalized and digested into the very fabric of the human body. Communal death converges with narrative death; but so too, communal survival is etched to bodily survival.

Life in the shadow of the mountain—the site of divine abode and revelation—has also become life made possible as custody of Exodus-Israel's textual and bodily brokenness. It is from within this spatial, textual, and communal lacuna that Moses begins to make specific demands of the deity about the future. Moses asks for a form of healthy (Hebrew: good, pleasing) memory that would transition and transform the migrant, perhaps weary, divine leader into a permanent resident within a community. Such a transition and transformation in the divine social and spatial residence contributes to new forms of collective identity for a community that has experienced conquest and destruction (Exod. 33:12–17).

The deity approves of Moses's demand.[1] Moses has found favor in the sight of the deity, who also knows Moses by name and has spoken to Moses face-to-face (Exod. 33:11). The embodied and epistemological proximity of the exodus deity to Moses and his demands puts the deity within the textual and geographical lacuna of the unfolding story; the deity, much like the exodus community, is located in the textual, bodily, and environmental lacunae of the unfolding story. Moses's appeal to the deity uses memory as a narrative shawl to gather the endangered and dispersed people into a nation that will survive existential fractures and uncertain futures (Exod. 33:12). Through physical and epistemological proximity (memory), the deity and the migrant share more than the same living space; they have also opened up an ideological space around a darkened (folded) history and an unfolding future (Exod. 33:12–13).

In this dark and darkly place, where exodus narration about a promissory land intersects with exodus narration about fractured community and embodied trauma (e.g., the people are called "stiff-necked"—Exod. 33:1–6), fragmented visions of survival and ultimate thriving unfold in clouded "tents of meetings," that are partially separated from the community, which must stand at a distance. The future, to quote a New Testament Jewish writer, folds and unfolds "through a glass, darkly" (1 Cor. 13:12).[2] At this intersection between memory and imagination, where communal face-to-face is fractured or unavailable, Moses makes a demand that retains the embodied character of the communal text: "show me your weightiness" (Exod. 33:19). It is a moment of textual body-reading that requires a certain amount of unveiling and self-disclosure. But it is also a moment of communal formation—communal folding. The demand is weighty and catalytic; it prompts the divine being into activity. Still located within the material and textual lacuna, a boundary marker is set and, in setting that boundary, the divine body becomes very active: The divine body places Moses in an in-between spot, between rocks; as its weightiness passes by the place where Moses stands, the deity covers Moses, preventing him from seeing the divine face; the deity then removes the divine hand, allowing Moses to see the divine back-side (Exod. 33:21–23). There is no unveiling of the divine face, and this is—the deity says—to avert very ominous outcomes: "man cannot see me and live" (Exod. 33:20). For the community to which Moses belongs—the community that tells this story—Moses's death is averted, because he stands/lives in the shadows; he has become a survivor! And so too the community to which his story belongs; the community that weaves the narrative shawl holds Moses within that shawl, until he is able to weave new laws (Exod. 34).

To live is to be a survivor, attached to the literary or material body of another. The story has turned from a promissory story of a future formed from a convergence of divine-human vision at Horeb (Exod. 3) to a story of a future formed on the memory (the back-side) of the divine—or that of a generation which has just gone before, a generation that experienced and endured rupture and deadly encounters. To be on the back-side of such a deity or generation is to be gathered around epistemological and hermeneutical space-time where the catalyst for, and the shape of, the community is borne—not by the imaginary and unknown face (future) but by the rhythmic movement of the fully formed back. The story's future depends on its ability to develop powerful bonds of memory that can gather its endangered and fragile bodies into a community. Through the rhythms of the moving body and the repositioned body, the future folds into community.

UN/FOLDING FUTURES AND EXODUS SHAWLS:
THE FUTURE OF THE PAST: BODY-CARRYING BODIES

The image of an African woman (perhaps a mother, surrogate mother, nanny, aunt, or elder sister) carrying a child on her back, supported by a sling or shawl, is iconic. This social and cultural deployment of the mother's body is accompanied by—and indeed intended to capture—forms of routine and non-routine mental and physical tasks: walking with a basket on her head, very likely engaged in educational and entertaining conversations about generational and intergenerational community building. It is motherly supremacy which, in Chinua Achebe's *Things Fall Apart*, is explored and described as the time-space-body where communal bonding happens even in the wake of violence and diaspora. Culture, economics, parenting, and education are all a part of this moving community. That is the cultural lesson that Okonkwo learns when he is exiled from his village and must return to the motherland. The image of a mother carrying her baby on her back is astonishing because of the way it depicts an adult body multitasking, but also because it depicts the social and affective connective tissue—the shawl—that binds the mother-baby body in the production of routine and non-routine tasks of communal nurture, protection, discipline, and bonding; and the impact that such baby-carrying has on the shape of the mother's body—how she has to "carry" her own body in order to carry another.

The baby is tightly wrapped on the mother's back, securely fastened to mimic the movement of her body. It is a position of safety and security—regulated for body temperature, age of child, alignment between the two bodies, firmness of the grip, and sociocultural purpose (including veiling the body to keep it from harm). It is one of the ways the adult body manipulates the infant body and gets it to relax, to experience the rhythmic movement of the adult body, and perhaps to sleep. Whether asleep, partially awake, or fully awake, the child navigates the world through the rhythm of the mother's body. It is a position of highly affective subjectivity, where two bodies are linked together. Participation in the future does not require individual abilities to see that future, but rather the communal ability to "carry" bodies into that future. Future is not avoidance of exile; it is the transformation of exile into exodus.

The mother—biological or adoptive mother—carries the child on her back, and the child can only see her back; or, more specifically, the child can only hear and feel the movement of her back. Detached from the land (or unable to navigate its terrain), yet attached to the mother's body (which navigates the land), the child can imagine and dream and see in different ways—ways that are burdened, but not confined, by the fracturing of environmental space; ways that feel and enter the future through the rhythmic movements of the adult body. Attached by a shawl to the moving body, whose hands have placed it on their back, the child is able to engage the rough terrains of geography and patriarchy and economics and culture through the body and embodied movement of its mother. Life is attached to that formative space where exile is experienced in the shadowy and darkened place mediated by the mother. The child's inability to see its mother's face is not obstructionist or obscurantist action. Though deprived of the ability to see "face to face," the child is able to see the backside, and so can imagine futures with real bodies queued up and linked up, future as a function of real bodies queued up.

In her study of the relation between baby-carrying practices, music, and rhythm, Barbara Ayres speaks of "socially shared personality processes."[3] Moses's initial demand that the deity should engage in pleasant memory has received a divine response that also compels and positions Moses in a space of experiencing the divine back-side as memory. The poetic character of the divine-human body synchronized around memory is captured in these words: "You shall see my back-side, but my face shall not be seen." It is the space-time that engages the trailblazing divine and liberating body as also simultaneously a co-resident, or fellow migrant, navigating the fractured textual, geographical, and political terrains that must now be turned into residential places for the liberated body. In the context and the wake of violence that has wrecked the community, the future depends on the narrative capacity of the endangered body or community to demand that its trailblazing leaders be transformed into co-residents. Placed on the divine back-side, in a primordial and historical space-time of memory and sovereignty that precede and perpetually resist fragmentation, the exodus story produces a death-defying body: of Moses in a rocky place, in a shadowy place, partially veiled and darkened, surrounded by rocks and a divine body, capable of using its memory shawls to link its broken histories and intergenerational bodies together, and restructure the lacunae of communal belonging. The "socially shared personality process" understands the future as a form of binding together, being held together by textual, material, or cognitive fabric (shawls).

EXODUS MEMORY AS A SHAWL

The narrative of exodus is partially premised on a promissory—even utopian—land to which the exodus people are taken. The story originates in a lacuna, in a highly consequential discrepancy between history and memory, represented by a Pharaoh who did not know Joseph. Because that discrepancy fuels Pharaoh's political machinations—his erasure of Hebrew life and attempt to transform Hebrew existence into a subsidy for the preservation of the nation—the exodus story's emergence from that lacuna becomes an attempt to transform erasure into fullness of life. As postcolonial and cultural hermeneutics have shown, the exodus narrative cannot—and does not—unfold without facing the *ambiveilence*[4] of its colonial and postcolonial weightiness: the weightiness of living and forging life in the shadow of nations and empires, the weightiness of living and forging life in shadowy and fragmented places and texts, with darkened and endangered bodies, all seeking to become a nation that is like and unlike the one they reject. The beckoning weightiness of history to which Moses invites the divine ("show me your glory") is matched by the beckoning weightiness of memory to which the divine invites Moses ("you will see my back-side"). Communally, it is the weightiness of encountering memory as the material transformation of promise, where the community exhumes and carries Joseph's body with them (Exod. 13:19) as part of exodus-becoming that is soon described as divine carrying of the body analogous to being carried on eagle's wings (Exod. 19:4).

The irony of this weighty mirroring and unveiling process is dark but also transforming: What unfolds before (in front of, in the face of) Moses is not sight, but sound. That is, the future unfolds not as an enlightenment moment—a flash in the dark that suddenly makes the invisible fracture visible—but as a darkened movement, captured and articulated not by the prophetic vision but by the prophetic utterance. Moses's body—and by necessity the exodus-community body—is situated between seeing the future and hearing that future through the voice of history's rhythmic movement. What secures Moses's life and prevents him from becoming a perpetual migrant and a permanently disposed body—perhaps transformed into an object of voyeurism—is his ability to be placed on, and to see, the back-side, of history and story as embodied memory—that is, memory attached to the promissory and imaginative power of story and becoming, but also to the movement and rhythm and spaces of survival: the divine hand and divine back-side in the dark; the beauty that is protected and shielded and comforted and perhaps even rocked to sleep on the mother's back; the cultural, economic, narrative, and religious resources held together by the shawl of communal identity formation en marche.

From that in-between space of momentary and momentous folding and unfolding—in the cleft of rocks, a rocky history held by the warmth of memory—Moses sees the back-side of a potentially deadly force, whose passing-by (much like the Passover angel) causes or requires an eclipsing (a covering) of the endangered body. Moses's endangered body—his life—is held together and contained in the fragmented place where he stands, and by a deity that is willing to use its own body as a protective shield for Moses. Memory becomes the crucial narrative and interpretive shawl that holds the divine and human bodies together. The passing presence does not completely leave the scene—in fact, the deity's body dis/places the endangered body, but also maneuvers its own body to protect the endangered body. The divine and the human bodies are tethered together, as both seek to create a new future that is formed and lively, rather than promissory and deadly. The endangered body's survival depends, in part, on its need to stand in (solidarity with) the broken space, and develop a darkened view of the divine body to which it is now intimately attached.

Survival in the shadows is hermeneutically significant; it is exodus hermeneutics from the back-side, from a partially occluded place and by a partially occluded body. From this darkened space-time of the weightiness of endangered existence, and informed by the foregoing analyses of the African mother bearing the child on her back, I want to explore how future consciousness manifests itself in two intersecting ways: first, as a form of negritudian riposte,[5] a claim to a form of sovereignty that escapes the temporality and spatiality, though not the effects, of erasure and attempted erasure; and second, as internalized trauma of diasporic and homely existence in the shadow of empire. In the weightiness of darkened and displaced existence, Moses's face undergoes veiling and unveiling (Exod. 34:28–30); and in the weightiness of darkened and homely existence, Moses is barred access to the face-to-face encounter because that space is filled by all-encompassing divine weightiness (Exod. 40:34–35). In the shadow of that history and its narrative power, memory functions as a shawl that knits generations together.

The view from black/back-side responds to both realities by creating and using narrative shawls to link up migrant existence that is tethered to the human and environmental body. The view from behind—the view by the darkened body from a darkened place—means that there is no real exodus future for Moses—or for the marginalized—if his/their body is erased: if the exodus community is destroyed, or if their bodies simply become subsidies to the production of a future reserved for a select chosen few, or if post-liberation institutions do not have the capacity or commitment to protecting vulnerable bodies, or expanding their space-time continuum beyond generational accomplishments. Black/back-side hermeneutics is homeostatic future-making that unfolds from the darkened places and histories, but that also folds fragile bodies together and folds into song by those who dwell in the shadow of the highest deity (Psalm 91). Thus, although Moses dies outside of the land, back-side/black-side hermeneutics insists that his body—not just his spirit—survives (unfolds) into the world of the honorable and honored ancestors, and becomes a folded body around which divine and human characters gather in their discussions about futures (Jude v.9).

The story and consciousness of survival is textually and physically embodied in the community to which Moses belongs, but also in material spaces where sight and sound form modes and nodes of communal belonging tethered together in defiant resistance to ongoing national and imperial attempts to erase and to own erased bodies. From this embodied shadowy place-time of wreckage and shadowed subjectivity, Africana biblical interpretation of exodus insists that liberation must mean more than personnel changes atop pyramid-like master narratives and their machinery. Departure from such machineries and accompanying narratives is only a first step in negritudian riposte as an elaborate production of processes, conditions, spaces, and discourses that do not simply develop into, or replicate, oppressive governments.[6] To put it in the words of Masiiwa Gunda, Moses must not become Pharaoh;[7] and exodus must not become conquest. In back-side/black-side hermeneutics, the community must not allow Moses to become a pharaoh, or allow the exodus story to become a conquest narrative.

And in fact, Moses does not become Pharaoh; he dies in the shadowy mountain, before the story becomes a conquest narrative. But must he die outside of the promised land, outside of the community that he produced, the community that—through narration and tradition—places him on their back, reproduces him and gives him a history and a geography? What does it mean to occlude Moses's vision in Exodus—in Deuteronomy he is described as a man with amazing vision even in old age—but increasingly give him powerful speech (in Horeb, he is granted muffled individual speech, but he is becoming a more influential speaker)? And what does it mean to give him a chirographic text about a future but not an embodied place in that future; to give him tradition and history, perhaps mnemohistory, as Jan Assmann argues,[8] but not concrete land, not even mnemogeography (in the biblical account, no one knows where Moses was buried)? Why are Moses and his exodus community severed from Egypt and launched into perpetual diaspora, orbiting a seemingly time- and-space-defying exodus universe?

In the face of daunting fractures that produce death, the story needs to be recast. The story, or its embodied form in Moses, must be placed on the black-side of the divine, if it is to develop sustainable and credible futures. The story needs shawls to gather its broken pieces and displaced migrants and fractured ecosystems. It is a weighty task that falls on the back of the divine mother. Unable to see her child's face, but nevertheless fully capable of speaking to her baby on her back, the griot deploys her literary craft to give narrative form to the physical body she is carrying. This story of an endangered body's survival in-between fractured spaces, is also the story of surviving in textual and narrative lacunae. The story of Moses's survival between cleft rocks is itself placed in-between, and on the back of, a larger concentric narrative, defined by the fracturing (Exod. 32) and reconstruction (Exod. 34) of texts and narrative. It is a story of the endangered body's relation to a particular mode of divine and communal representation.

Moses and his community find and develop survival modes of being, not in a clear and clean story line, but in the fragments, in the lacunae of an unfolding story that is subjected to fracturing and dispersal. The power of liberation as back/darkened-side hermeneutics—the power to transform broken histories into imagined futures, and then into formed futures—depends on making sure that narrative lacunae speak, and that they speak not as subsidies to perfectly designed stories, with only occasional detours, but as themselves resilient selves carried on the backs of resilient stories that regenerate and produce new life and life forms. Back-side hermeneutics seeks to explore how the surviving community understands its identity and survival by intentionally gathering around and gathering its broken or vulnerable bodies and attempting to carry those bodies into their futures.

Because narrative survival intersects with bodily survival, the story places its characters in temporalities and spaces where textual survival and bodily survival are negotiated. For Africana hermeneutics this means exploring the dynamics of life and survival in the colony and the postcolony, where imperial and state powers produce broken bodies and spaces as subsidies to their very existence and future-making. As a response to gathering around the ideologies and machineries of body-breaking, the distinctive markers of back/darkened-side hermeneutics are, through ideological and epistemological gathering around the broken body/space, back/darkened-side hermeneutics constructs sovereignty by repositioning itself *before* the arrival of brokenness as a modus operando, and therefore not completely subject to the originating concept of brokenness. Temporal and spatial repositioning functions as a mode of establishing sovereignty outside of and beyond the totalizing category of erasure and permanent dispersal.

The shawls of memory as repositioning are powerful enough to create new space-time structures and modes of being and becoming. Second, through its refusal to "move on" from broken bodies and spaces and through its refusal to leave broken bodies in the custody of the state or empire that broke them, black/back-side hermeneutics create futures that include real bodies. By insisting on having custody of the broken body—

historical, human, environmental—and moving it into a future of life (cf. Joseph's body), back-side hermeneutics resist voyeuristic appropriations of broken bodies and histories as subsidies for the production and power of the state or empire. The broken body survives and lives in the custody of the community that nursed and continues to nurse it, not the one that broke and continues to haunt or commodify its existence.

BODIES IN ROCKY PLACES: BODIES IN THE BLACK/ BACK-SIDE: IDENTITY, BELONGING, AND NON-BELONGING IN THE CAMEROONIAN POSTCOLONY

The Berlin conference of 1884–85 did not inaugurate violent territorial mapping of Africa into colonies; it codified such fracturing for "effective occupation."[9] The conference gave "legal" structure to the political and narrative lacunae that defined colonized nations, and to theorizing Africa itself as a lacuna. The conference constitutes a particularly traumatizing moment in modern African history, geography, and memory because—beyond its relatively brief episodic duration in relation to African history—effective occupation underwrote and was underwritten by more elaborate productions of African fissures and identities to serve as subsidies for the colonial enterprise. The process was as sinister as it was grotesque. After creating the lacuna (the colonial wound), the colonizer then pointed to the wound/lacuna as reason for setting up a formal process of occupation and extraction. In a process that erased any distinctions between means and ends, the bleeding colonized body became the ontological subsidy for the colonial project.[10] Supposedly civilizing enlightenment created and enriched European futures on the backs of the bleeding darkened bodies. It is from these darkened places and through these darkened bodies that anticolonial movements and communities will emerge.

German aspirations, for example, included a grand vision of *Mittelafrika*, a colony extending from the Atlantic to the Indian Ocean, linking German Kamerun to German East Africa. As colonial patronage evolved and increasingly stepped in to buttress and then consume the fractured bodies it had produced, France agreed to exercise power over Morocco while Germany would take a sizeable portion of French-controlled Congo, creating Neukamerun.[11] After World War I (hypocritically, or maybe not so hypocritically, termed the war to end all wars), the remapping of Cameroon's geography, history, and identity continued: France reclaimed Neukamerun and reasserted plans to align Cameroun with Equatorial Africa, in opposition to Germany's goal of a new African empire.[12]

Colluding with this colonial maneuvering and remapping was a period that Cheikh Babou calls "the internationalization of the colonial problem," namely, "the founding of the League of Nations after the First World War, the creation of the mandate system, and the introduction of the language of trusteeship in the language of international politics."[13] In fact, "the establishment of the international community as legal custodian of the Ottoman and German colonies, in the Middle East and Africa, respectively, created a juridical precedent that undermined the rights of conquest, which, since the Berlin conference in 1885, had served as legal framework for colonial rule."[14] Placed under French and British rule as part of the League of Nations trusteeship program, Cameroon's identity and governing structure changed, again: British Cameroons, administered in two parts, Northern and Southern; and French Cameroun. It is not just that cultures and religions and geographies and histories were fractured; it is also that colonial fracturing was—to employ a farming metaphor—colonial sowing that produced colonial harvesting, as articulated by F. Kange Ewane in *Semence et Moisson Coloniales*.[15]

Interwar debates included the possibility of Cameroon being reoffered to Germany to appease the Third Reich, but the outbreak of World War II ended this option, and Cameroon's regional and political identity would be "settled" on the battlefield,[16] and later, through a plebiscite in which part of British Cameroons joined Nigeria. This violent history and its geopolitics of territorial and political patronage resulted in post–World War II Cameroonians negotiating multiple colonial lacunae and legacies held together by enforceable but moveable lines on the changing maps of belonging from 1884 through 1919 and to 1961. The relation of "nationality" to territorial boundaries was not only fluid, but boundaries and narratives changed in the wake or anticipation of war. Whose Cameroon was it? Which colonial faces needed to be examined and unveiled? What memories of Kamerun/Cameroun/Cameroon would become canonical, heretical, suppressed, or transformed into promise? And what governing ideologies and processes would provide structure to these fluid identities?

The decades-long independence movements that developed across the continent after the Second World War created "national" consciousness which enjoyed its highest popularity by being anti-colonial in its discourse and (sometimes forceful) actions. But these national identities and consciousnesses developed not just as postwar spaces and identities, but more precisely as "Cold War" spaces: The Cold War might have been cold in the northern hemisphere, but it was very hot in the southern hemisphere, where African independence movements were gathering momentum, repurposing or building memory shawls to reconstitute accountable processes where colonialism had collapsed distinctions between the means, the forms, and the ends of citizenship and governance.[17]

In Cameroon, there is regional consciousness articulated in the notion of "Anglophone consciousness." This consciousness has its roots in post–World War I colonial politics when the (former German) colony, Kamerun, was partitioned into (British) Southern Cameroons and (French) République du Cameroun. A complex process of nation-formation would later bring these two regions with different colonial legacies together, following political wrangling, anti-colonial upheavals in French Cameroons, and a unification plebiscite in Southern Cameroons.[18] This consciousness is one of geopolitical minority, which has taken on violent manifestations in recent years, with some members demanding complete separation and independence from the francophone part of Cameroon. Because of its cultural diversity and biodiversity and its "unnatural" political makeup from colonial mapping and governance, Cameroon has been described as "Africa in miniature," as a "paradise of paradoxes," prompting Francis Nyamnjoh, one of the country's leading sociologists and anthropologists, to speak of a country held together by its ethnic ambition and diversity.[19] Underneath this shawl of national identity, memory provides the space and time for critical examination.

Elias Bongmba has proposed four hermeneutical approaches to understanding Africa: (1) the privatization of power; (2) the pauperization of the state, in the form of major declines in economic infrastructure and productivity as well as in intellectual and political ideas and environmental degradation; (3) the prodigalization of the state, where ruling elites consolidate power and resources to their exclusive benefit and that of their clientele, resulting in waste, abuse, and destruction of resources; and (4) the proliferation of violence, both in the forms of civil war and nation-state wars.[20] Using the examples of Cameroon and Côte d'Ivoire, Bongmba argues that privatization occurred as a function of political leaders using rhetoric to persuade their audiences of a need to reclaim a traditional mode of existence that predates the colonial encounter. In other words, the loosening of the colonial grip coincided with the emergence of the Cold War in ways that largely framed colonial ills and devastations as essentially a problem between outsiders and insiders, not a problem of power and governing relations. Power was deployed to the extent that it served to create a boundary between "we" and "them."

Ahidjo's government was de facto perceived as "foreign" by the masses and, needing to legitimize itself, became obsessed with remaking the country in its image. Branded and portrayed as a unifier, the president was given many political names: "Father of the Nation," "Great Comrade," "Apostle of Peace," "Providential Guide," and so on.[21] Political, economic, and moral patronage set in; or rather, the political, economic, and moral patronage that underwrote and subsidized colonial governance was localized. To privatize power, Ahidjo referenced traditional rulership to advocate a single ruler, in blatant avoidance of traditional setups and processes in which governing councils worked to appoint, regulate, and even depose kings who arrogated all power to themselves. Furthermore, privatization worked through a process of centralization of bureaucracy; then through the elimination of political competition and restriction of access to electoral process; and through monopolizing narration (the press).

In 1982, Ahidjo, a practicing Muslim, was coaxed by France into resigning his presidency. In his place, Paul Biya, a Christian, was installed, again with support from the French government. This led to Ahidjo's attempted coup d'état in 1984, which failed and resulted in civilian deaths, deep anxieties over issues of religious, ethnic, and political identities, and the emergence of a repressive single-party government, the Rassemblement Démocratique du Peuple Camerounais (RDPC). For critics of this regime defined by fracture, the acronym RDPC was metaphorized, playing on its phonetic sound, to brand the party, *redépécer*, meaning "cut it out and dole it"—reflecting the economic nepotism that funded political patronage and the colonial notion of the capture and re-distribution of spoils.[22]

As mentioned above, most other African nations got "independence" not immediately following the Second World War, but at the beginning of the Cold War. After the official "end" of that war and the advent of heightened discourse about political liberalism, Achille Mbembe started theorizing on the political, epistemological, and cultural constructions and manifestations of governance in the postcolony.[23] Mbembe began formulating his theories at a time of deadly crackdown on political dissidents in Cameroon, crystallized in violent clashes between "law enforcement" and citizens after the launching of a major political opposition party in 1990. The political climate was defined by massive popular demands for multiparty democracy, anti-government sit-ins, protests, and stay-at-home boycotts of public activity and business (government or private) popularly known as "ghost towns"—an apt, yet dreadful, haunting metaphor for the public sensibilities about postcolonial subjectivity plagued by endangered existence and profound alienation from official governance.

Mbembe theorized necropolitics in relation to the power and technology of life and death: "The ultimate expression of sovereignty resides, to a large degree, in the power and capacity to dictate who may live and who must die."[24] He explored a sense of "intimate tyranny" between the ruled and the rulers, following the rubrics of the state of siege and state of exception that Carl Schmitt, Hannah Arendt, and Giorgio Agamben had formulated in the wake of World War II and the totalitarianism of Nazism and the concentrations camps.[25] For Mbembe, the story of Cameroon, a postcolony produced and contested through a mix of fantastic ideology and violent mapping and remapping of "national" identity between 1884 and the 1990s, and embroiled in postcolonial political violence under so-called "states of emergency," provided a useful test case for the theory of sovereignty and the state of exception. Building on Michel Foucault's notion of biopower, Mbembe focused on the relationship between colonial and postcolonial governance, paying attention to the power or right to govern, which he called Sovereignty or *Commandement*. He argued that "to exercise sovereignty is to exercise control over mortality and to define life as the deployment and manifestation of power." Moving away from questions of ontology (personal, institutional, and national) to questions of praxis, Mbembe asked: "Under what practical conditions is the right to kill, to allow to live, or to expose to death exercised? Who is the subject of this right? What does the implementation of such a right tell us about the person who is thus put to death and about the relation of enmity that sets that person against his or her murderer?"[26]

The state of exception, otherwise stated, did not simply stand outside of the norms of acceptable, routine behavior, but was also a feeder for more substantive questions about identity formation and the use of violent power. Necropolitics was as useful for understanding social behavior as was Foucault's concept of biopower. Both forms of power and politics converged in the emergence of the nation-state. Colonial Sovereignty, Mbembe argued, rested on three sorts of violence: (a) founding violence, which underpinned the right to conquest and the prerogatives flowing from that right. Founding violence created "the space over which it is exercised; one might say it presupposed its own existence," regarding itself as "the sole power to judge its laws"; (b) legitimizing violence, which functioned to give the founding order meaning, to justify the "universalizing mission" of the colonial enterprise, and to convert "founding violence into authorizing authority"; and (c) a third form of violence that fell short of what is properly called war, and that sought to ensure the "maintenance, spread, and permanence" of legitimizing authority.[27] Mbembe then concludes:

> Colonial sovereignty only existed in areas where these three forms of violence were deployed, forming a seamless web. This violence was of a very particular sort, immediately tangible, and it gave natives a clear notion of themselves in proportion to the power that they had lost. Its distinctive feature was to act as both authority and morality. . . . Thus, in regard to colonial sovereignty, right was on *one* side. And it was seized in the very act of occurring. In face of it, there could only be "wrong" and infraction. Anything that did not recognize this violence as authority, that contested its protocols, was savage and outlaw.[28]

Later modern criticism favored reason as the standard marker for the moral subject and their public life, making reason and unreason the dividing line between modern and traditional subjectivity and making the individual person the subject of autonomy and sovereignty. Mbembe did not focus on struggles for self-autonomy, but on *"the generalized instrumentalization of human existence and the material destruction of human bodies and populations,"* and thus on "less abstract and more tactile" categories of life and death.[29]

Drawing on Freudian psychology, Mbembe interpreted violent governance as libidinal desire that ultimately manifests itself in a peculiar space, *fantasm*,[30] which Mbembe analyzed in terms of monotheism. He argued that monotheism "implies organization of some arrangement that is presented as legitimate and that resolves the conflicts between a plurality of divinities such that one is endowed with a monopoly on truth. How this arrangement is produced is clearly a political *travail*."[31] This political travail with its "narcissistic self-definition" as distinct from all others may find its impulse in the divine being, making the "biblical god a tribal god," who, in contrast to pagan gods, had a "distinctive" trait of "relative solitude." This god "had no relatives, was neither the son nor the cousin of any other god, had neither wife nor children. His claim to power was thus total, unchallenged by any member of a possible lineage."[32]

Although Mbembe's depictions of the divine in the Hebrew Bible are incomplete and do not address the ways in which the notion of divine "solitude" has its narrative fault lines (Exod. 4:22–23—Israel as Yahweh's endangered "son"; Ezek. 16: 4–7—Yahweh as an adopting parent; Hos. 2: 4–7—Israel as Yahweh's "wife," sometimes abused), his insights into the monotheistic impulse as religious, political, ethnic, and gendered *fantasm* is relevant to understanding the biblical text as a postwar story addressing the role of violence in constructing and defining notions of distinctiveness and multiplicity, but more importantly, processes of absolute othering.

To address these issues, Mbembe sought to appropriate the notions of the grotesque and obscene (which Mikhail Bakhtin located with the general populace) and deploy them to understand their roles and functions in structuring power (or sovereignty) in the postcolony. Mbembe sought to understand "the banality of power" and its ability to use symbols, vocabularies, and narratives to create a particular form of political consciousness and make it effective, including through the systematic use of pain.[33] When the grotesque and obscene are examined not just for their power and function in the lives of ordinary persons but also in the way state power deploys them to create a sense of time (memory, perhaps even history), of place (geography and non/belonging), and of self-aggrandizement (the prestige and privilege of not being subject to violence), then "we can come to understand that the postcolonial relationship to power is not primarily a relationship of resistance or collaboration but can best be characterized as illicit cohabitation, a relationship made fraught by the very fact of the *commandement* and its subjects having to share the same living space."[34] This reality of the postcolony as shared space—public and private space—by the dominant and the dominated results in a particular kind of logic: "mutual zombification of both the dominant and those whom they apparently dominate. This zombification meant that each robbed the other of their vitality and has left them both impotent (*impouvoir*)."[35]

Subjects in the postcolony learn to navigate multiple public spaces, each with its own internal logic but nevertheless enmeshed with others in different contexts. On the one hand, there is the convergence or intersection of the state power or *Commandement*'s ratification of its institutionalized (and hegemonic) identity as a fetish to which the subject is bound; and on the other, the subject's deployment of the talent for play and fun which make such a subject a *homo ludens par excellence*, capable of performing a form of mitosis of identity to negotiate public or private spaces.[36] And yet those who laugh and participate in laughter are not just the ordinary people but also officialdom. And from this, Mbembe makes a claim:

> Those who laugh, whether they do so in the public arena or in the private domain, are not necessarily bringing about the collapse of power or even resisting it. Confronted by the state's eagerness to cover up its actual origins, people are simply bearing witness, often unconsciously, to the fact that the grotesque is no more foreign to officialdom than the common man is impervious to the charms of majesty. Indeed, in its desire for majesty the popular world burrows the whole ideological repertoire of officialdom, along with its idioms and forms. Conversely the official world mimics popular vulgarity, inserting it at the very core of the procedures by which it takes on grandeur.[37]

Accordingly, it is not just the excesses of power and power abuse that distinguish the postcolony from other forms of governance; it is also the nature of the relationship between rulers and the ruled, crystallized around a specific form of practice: simulacrum (*le simulacre*). This simulacrum becomes the very basis for unpredictable and predictable political activity; and people whose identities have been partly confiscated are able "to glue back together the bits and pieces of their fragmented identities. By taking over the signs and language of officialdom," people are able to "remythologise their own conceptual universe while in the process turning the *commandement* into a sort of zombie. Strictly speaking this process does not increase either the depth of people's subordination or their levels of resistance; it simply produces a situation of disempowerment (*impouvoir*) for both the ruled and the rulers."³⁸ The relation of power between rulers and the ruled is not just one of control, but also of conviviality and even connivance; it goes beyond political entanglement to one of intimacy, and thus defines the identity of the postcolonial subject beyond its relation to the state's abilities of surveillance or coercion; and defines the agency of the postcolonial subject beyond acts of resistance or deconstruction of power or disengagement. That is why political liberation or deconstruction alone is not enough; one must also deal with the trauma of oppression, which lasts beyond political transitions. One ought then to consider the reality that "an intimate tyranny links the rulers with the ruled. . . . If subjection appears more intense than it might be, it is because the subjects of the *commandement* have internalized the authoritarian epistemology to the point where they reproduce it themselves in all the minor circumstances of daily life."³⁹ In these intimate settings, where the daily routines of life and death—eating, working, drinking, dancing, sleeping, clothing, singing, farming, funerals, etc.—take on biological, cultural and political meanings, notions of material surplus and scarcity unfold as manifestations of power or disempowerment, but also as markers of collective identity and moral capacity.

BEARING HOPE-FULL FUTURES ON THE BLACK-BACK-SIDE: HERMENEUTICAL SHAWLS

After the turn of the twentieth century, in the midst of World War I—a devastating and deadly war that remapped global geopolitics; that entrenched economic exploitation of populations through ongoing colonization; and that compelled the creation of new global structures and legal processes of governance (e.g., the League of Nations)—W. E. B. Du Bois wrote a short essay examining the cause and impact of war—which he called "our chiefest industry."⁴⁰ This was decades before Dwight Eisenhower, in the middle of the Cold War, warned of the spiritual, economic, and political impact of the rise of the military industrial complex, in which "our toil, resources, and livelihood are all involved."⁴¹ Bringing history, race, religion, ethnicity, economics, and psychology to bear on his analyses of colonial oppression, Du Bois diagnosed humankind's propensity to conquer and dominate others, and linked that propensity to an ideological thrust that he called "the world-wide mark of meanness—color."⁴² From this analysis of the fusion of violent "industry" and colonial ideology, Du

Bois expounded one of the most salient claims of his essay: "The cause of war is preparation for war."[43] This preparation for war was evident in the acts of colonization and exploitation, and thus necessarily raised the question whether war—precisely World War I—could also function to usher in the end of war?

> This world war is primarily the jealous and avaricious struggle for the largest share in exploiting darker races. As such it is and must be but prelude to the armed and indignant protest of these despised and raped peoples. . . . Is then this the end of war? Can it be so long as its prime cause, the despising and robbery of darker people sits enthroned even in the souls of those who cry peace? So if Europe hugs this delusion then this is not the end of world war—it is the beginning.[44]

This diagnosis of the souls of white folk came just over a decade after Du Bois had diagnosed and talked about the strivings of the souls of black folk, the hermeneutical overlap between the two diagnoses unfolding around color; the worldwide mark of meanness articulated in 1917 was only the latest articulation of the "the color line" found in the *Souls of Black Folk* initially published in 1903. "The problem of the twentieth century," Du Bois had written, "is the problem of the color-line—the relation of the darker and lighter races of men in Asia and Africa, in America and the Islands of the sea."[45] When Du Bois wrote those words, effective colonialism was in full force, so his 1917 essay and its critique of Europe's apparent search for peace in Europe without attention to Europe's own warring and colonizing madness was as much about the hypocrisy of "self-contained" and unaccountable meaning-making in Eurocentric discourse about global distributions and regulations of citizenships, as it was about the starting point of interpretation, and the multi-positional interpretive stance that colonized and marginalized persons adopt, by necessity.

The question, as Brian Blount has diagnosed and posed it in relation to biblical studies, is about the "meaning line"—the tension between standardized meaning and meaning potential, the methodologies that are granted power and prestige, and the troubling of the interpretive soul that reads otherwise. Working from Du Bois's description of the color line, Blount writes:

Instead of a color line, biblical operations proceed about a meaning line. Simplistically put, text meaning is determined through historical and literary engagement that uncovers text intent, or text meaning is ascertained through an engagement between the reader, reading out of her place, and the text as it is engaged in that space. There develops an interpretive veil behind which cultural interpreters are positioned and from which they must operate frequently in the shadows. . . . The meaning line is destructive to readers on both sides of it. All are Othered from each Other by its very existence. It is because interpretive power rests on the historical, literary scientific side that cultural hermeneuts are required to become at the very least bi-cultural, knowing their own space and its influence on text meaning as well as they know the historical and literary principles that allegedly unearth static text meaning. But this prescience comes with a cost. The necessity to acquire it threatens the very soul of the cultural hermeneut, who must occupy and absorb the space of the objective Other without losing hold of the spiritual mooring of his own space. This bicultural, two-Other-ness has now expanded exponentially. Scores of readers vie for the opportunity to read rightly from their particular space and have the meaning derived from that cultural reading be received and engaged rather than Othered. Scores of souls are thereby troubled.

The troubling, though, can also be efficacious. Du Bois recognized that wherever Others operated with sincerity across the color line, particularly when Whites engaged empathetically out of the black space, there dawned the potential for just societal transformation. *Reading from an Other's space transforms not only how one reads but how one lives.*[46]

This troubling of the historical and interpretive soul means, in part, that in methodology and subject matter, Africana biblical hermeneutics often travels a richly contested and varied road, sometimes survives improbably, but always seeks to transition from survival to thriving. In the face of colonial, racist, ethnocentric, and patriarchal ideologies and structures, it has emerged and forged its identity and subject matter from the margins of interpretive alienation and erasure; but it is also taking shape in centers of cosmopolitan, academic, and governing power in universities, research centers, and theological institutions on the African continent and in the Diaspora—using a variety of methodologies to look both inward and outward. Andrew Mbuvi has charted the *reactionary* methods that have characterized African biblical hermeneutics, in response to punctual and persistent acts of racism, colonialism, sexism, economic exploitation, cultural imperialism, environmental disaster, and apartheid; but also the *innovative* methodological and thematic frameworks around which Africana subjects seek to diagnose their existence and forge healthy, holistic and thriving approaches to life.[47]

By placing the Bible and its varied interpretations within the unfolding history of Africa, questions of interpretive methodology, of political and cultural power, of gender inequality and patriarchy, and of economic exploitation and disparity continue to inform *why* and *how* Africana readers relate to the Bible. Why? In part because a significant part of the Bible's origins and ideological map resides in, and addresses, portions of Africa;[48] in part because, despite becoming an imperial tool, the Bible has also become an African document, even an African contested icon[49] that, nevertheless, must not become an idol. And how? Through foregrounding both the creative and the burdensome experiences of gendered, ethnic, racial, religious, cultural, and political sensibilities and cosmologies that have shaped the histories of African-descended persons in their majority world engagements with the Bible, as well as in their minority and minoritized worlds of erasure upon encountering the Bible as a text of trauma.

In *Hebrewisms of West Africa: From the Nile to the Niger with the Jews*,[50] Joseph Williams examined—in comparative fashion—resonances between ancient Hebrew and west African language and culture. Similarly, in *The Sons of the Gods and the Daughters of Men: An Afro-Asiatic Interpretation of Genesis 1–11*, Modupe A. Oduyoye deploys philological tools and mythological analyses to explore the spiritual worlds of the biblical texts (e.g., the language of the "sons of gods" in Genesis 6) and African languages and cosmologies (e.g., "the wide scope of Niger-Congo Languages of Africa from Senegal to Cape Town") to argue that African biblical interpretation, and biblical interpretation in general, cannot ignore the reality of the spirit world and its impact on everyday life.[51] And John Chijioke Madubuko's *The "Pauline" Spirit World in Eph. 3:10 in the Context of Igbo World View: A Psychological-Hermeneutical Appraisal* explores notions of Pauline spirituality in Ephesians and in Igbo cosmologies that attend to the deeply religious worldview, the role of spirits, the dualisms that govern existence, and the understanding of human existence in close relation to these cosmologies. For Madubuko, African biblical interpretation needs to engage the oral cultures of Africa, which prompt a sense of vibrancy and ongoing engagement with the Bible and its prime author, the divine.[52] Finally, within this spectrum of analyses, a lengthy and detailed exploration of divination ideas and practices in the ancient Near East, in Europe, and in Africa (DRC), and in the biblical text about the woman of Endor brings Kabamba Kiboko to affirm that biblical interpretation has for a long time had contact points with divination practices. The practical implications of this research are articulated as follows:

> I apply, each and every day, a fixed canon of religious texts, the Bible, written in an alien tongue, translated into another alien tongue, to real life situations of my predominantly African American Texan parishioners and all others with whom I come in contact. I read the Bible with them in a way that reveals the will of God, brings answers to people and helps them make difficult decisions, cast out demons, confront evil, brings comfort to the suffering and courage to the anxious, heals the many wounds that life brings whether via supernatural or natural forces, and always, always hears the voices of our long gone ancestors of both Africa and Israel. I divine.[53]

This divining work unfolds at the intersection of the sacred and the secular; but it also unfolds especially at the intersection of broken and whole bodies. That is, it is as much a result of conjuring as it is the result of historical experiences and analyses of loss and diaspora. It is analyses that develop around broken bodies—textual, environmental, human, and divine—that populate the exilic spaces of ancient Israel (Isa. 52:13–53:12; Ezek. 37) and the crucifixion spaces of the New Testament gospel narratives (Matt. 27; Mark 15; Luke 23; John 19). Under imperial regimes, these texts become especially infused with meaning and survival as resistance to political and religious necropolitics. Reading texts and reading bodies fuse in interesting methodological formulations.

These formulations require reflection on hermeneutics as cluster-storytelling. It is a method not unfamiliar to readers of the exodus story. When strategizing with Moses about what Moses and Aaron must say to Pharaoh, Yahweh proposes cluster narrative as a method: "You Shall speak to him and put the words in his mouth; and I will be with your mouth and with his mouth and will teach you what you should do. He indeed shall speak for you to the people; he shall serve as a mouth for you" (Exod. 4:15–16). Bodies and stories are linked up. David T. Adamo's edited volume, *Biblical Interpretation in African Perspective*[54] represents a textual form of communal interpretation, a form of cluster storytelling that intentionally represents the interpretive force and character of multiplicity variously framed. So too is the edited volume by Jione Havea, Margaret Aymer, and Steed Davidson, *Islands, Islanders, and the Bible: RumInations*,[55] which explores the possibility of reading biblical texts as islands, in fact, as archipelagic, and thus inviting reflection on hermeneutics as *talanoa*, story that is both fiercely independent and yet interdependent on other stories: "Biblical texts are like islands, and readers are like islanders. At the underside of our invitation is a double affirmation: islands are like biblical texts and islanders are (like) readers."[56] These similarities between readers and texts and spaces is not simply metaphoric; they have interpretive significance: interpretation itself is experienced and performed as "waves"—movements that have direction but also depth, and that produce the reader even as they are produced by the reader.

Ron Eyerman has argued that "as opposed to psychological or physical trauma, which involves a wound and the experience of great emotional anguish by the individual, cultural trauma refers to a dramatic loss of identity and meaning, a tear in the social fabric, affecting a group of people that has achieved some measure of cohesion."[57] Thus, personal experience of the traumatic event is not necessary for participation in cultural trauma, which is transmitted through mediation—artistic representations and interpretations, through ritual practices and symbols, through stories, tales, fables, and even riddles, through monuments, and so on. Cultural trauma develops and sustains its presence and power through ongoing narration, not just through the initial act or wound. For Eyerman, this cultural trauma coalesced for African Americans particularly in the aftermath of the civil war, when the promises of emancipation and citizenship for former slaves were rejected in the systems of segregation that followed.[58] Through policy, the cultural body of the marginalized community is repeatedly subjected to distress and stress; it remains fractured.

Writing about the role of the body (human and social) in understanding the effects of the Chinese Cultural Revolution (1966–1976), Arthur Kleinman and Joan Kleinman argue that the process of cultural and political transformation included a period when there was focus on the stories of trauma, "literature of wounds or scars." In the process, "bodily memory, biography, and social history merged." Kleinman and Kleinman identify three "paradigmatic symbols"—dizziness, exhaustion, and pain—that "created an interpersonal space of suffering in which bodily complaint indirectly expressed (remembered, directly experienced) social distress and shared criticism."[59] Dizziness represented not just a medical condition of dis-ease (or lack) related to health and well-being but also a cultural signal of imbalance. Exhaustion represented vital signs of having reached the end of a tough process of political revolution; the life force (qi) had been drained. And pain—represented in muscle, back aches, headaches, and cramps—signaled the turmoil of revolution, linking personal anatomy to the social body. Accordingly, "the exhausted, painful, and vertiginous body—the body that had lost its social force and moral face—became the grounds for negotiations over jobs, time, responsibilities, and resources."[60]

Memory work is social and political and ecological in its capacity and task of piecing together fragments of identity and life for hopeful futures. Exodus is thus read as "a vocation to survive" that must "devote itself to the task of sustaining what can be called the *reservoirs of life*. The refusal to perish may yet turn us into historical beings and make it possible for the world to be a world."[61] Such work includes deploying the exile-exodus modes of seeing (facing the wreckage of oppression), hearing (amplifying the articulations of communal distress), remembering (repositioning oneself alongside the broken bodies), and coming down (committing oneself to transforming systems of erasure into systems of life and creativity). To see, hear, remember, and act in this epistemology and praxis is to create living hermeneutics that include conjuring the possibility and enacting the reality of relegating endangered existence to the dustbin of a past—a past that need not return, but nevertheless a past that the survivor always returns to (remembers), in an effort to create epistemological, structural, and ethical guardrails that mitigate constructing futures that simply reenact erasure. A claim of such hermeneutic is that memory must be accountable, not just sacred; imagination must be qualitatively expansive, not just different; and liberation means more than a change in governing personnel atop a system of extraction and patronage.

AFRICANA THEORIZING: BODIES, TEXTS, AND BACK/BLACK-SIDE HERMENEUTICS

Theorizing Africana biblical interpretation within these vectors includes engagement with the intersection of biblical interpretation and the materiality of existence and meaning-making in habitable spaces and places, but also in inhabitable spaces and places; it is to inquire, also, in ideological and methodological terms, what makes Africana narratives and historical spaces and places habitable or uninhabitable; to inquire what happens to bodies and cultures and peoples that inhabit uninhabitable spaces (colony, postcolony, prison, enslavement, apartheid, displacement) and the inherent struggles to transform such spaces into habitable ones. The question about the possibility and modality of transforming uninhabitable places and spaces into habitable ones is itself a key element of the analyses: Can the uninhabitable conditions in the colony become habitable in the postcolony? Can a racist system be inherently transformed to become postracist and antiracist? Can ethnocentric forms of governance become inherently transformed? How might such transformation fit into larger narratives and systems of global productions?

The starting point of back-side/darkened hermeneutic is not singularity but multiplicity, which means that historical and cultural (or contextual) hermeneutics are not secondary acts of meaning-making, but rather primary and essential. Time, space, and place are theorized and deployed in terms of linear movement and relationality, but also in terms of epistemological and cultural depth. History as well as literature and cultural praxis aid in this process of seeing and hearing and belonging across time and horizontal displacement, but also seeing and hearing and belonging and rising from below—from underneath a history and structure of oppression and erasure that does not easily go away. These multi-formed and multiply-located Africana methods demystify the sovereignty of colonial and postcolonial oppressive systems, historicize and critique foundational oppressive ideologies and traditions, and open up new and/or renewed vectors of social existence and covenanting commitments. Akin to hermeneutics that have defined the work of other historically marginalized communities, Africana's attention to cluster-storytelling de-centers interpretive emphases on singular and/or inaugural authorial intent, and rather amplifies voices that have been muted, silenced, displaced, or erased. Such voices speak, as we find in Akiki Nyabongo's *The Story of an African Chief* or in Zora Neale Hurston's *Moses, Man of the Mountain*, and require as much interpretive excavation as analyses of their apparent departures from single-hero narrative modalities, toward explorations of multiple—and thus communal—dimensions of the issues at hand: power and its uses; layers of authority and associated infrastructure; multiple interpretive perspectives linked up together; and above all, striving to survive.

For Africana hermeneutics, the text itself—of exodus, of diaspora, of exile, and of interpretation—cannot be sufficiently probed and understood without exploration of its episodic and semantic materialities: the spaces it creates, imagines, navigates, and exits; the bodies (human, material, and institutional) it produces and/or erases; and the narrative and historical touch points it uses to do this work. The text and its materiality function as modes and methods of existence, but also simultaneously as artifacts of endangered existence, of survival, and of (imagined) flourishing; and the story represents these experiences and aspirations as markers of identity that escape singular narration. The question is not simply whether one can permanently escape exile, permanently forge liberation out of survival, permanently rest/return from the launch of a past that threatens to make perpetual migrants of its subjects. The question is also, principally, whether the survivor, the escapee, and the exiled self can securely live, and forge futures that are formed and no longer simply promissory (unformed) or trapped in an always looming threat of being erased.

The Africana reader and interpreter of this story does not have the luxury of exegesis and its propensity toward prioritizing textual production; instead, we also interrogate our encounters with the text (and story) and what it has made of us; we register and protest the story's nagging silences to our inquiries about its productions and regulations of identity; we excavate the un/shared histories of our struggles as a people, resist productions of futures in which our full existence is either partial or unformed, and conjure or create modes and methods of collective belonging and living that enrich sacred, communal, and accountable memory.

This Africana reading-read body, as a trans body (divine, spatial, and human) engages a story that is attuned to, and valorizes, *seeing* ongoing communal affliction, *hearing* the voices of a groaning people, *remembering* covenantal commitments that summon ancestral life, and *coming down* to partner with new generations of actors to effect major religious, social, and geopolitical transformations (Exod. 2:23–25; 3:7–8). The metaphor itself is liquid and trans: the imagined land is described as flowing with milk and honey. To explore that narrative and political shift using the metric and metaphor of travel—"let my people go"—is not to assume that temporary or permanent departures of bodies and histories and cultures from oppressive boundaries are inherently liberating. The watery places in the story are also places of death and destruction and ecological destruction. Thus, a shift in exodus imagination from Pharaoh's (as ethnocentric retraction in the face of transnational forces) to Yahweh's (as programmatic embrace of transnational identity) does not necessarily assume that inserting methods of survival and liberation into violent systems of confinement and dispersal will permanently enshrine the survival and flourishing of the endangered community. The exile-exodus story cautions against such assumptions by indicating that human and narrative migration, and the calls for radical changes to political and religious institutions of erasure resulting from such movements of populations, are often met by, and co-existent with, corresponding narrative motifs of hardened hearts and deployment of governing infrastructures to entrench and solidify social boundaries and stringently regulate the theory and praxis of migration and migrant bodies. To inquire about the exile-exodus story's capacity to identify, create, interpret, and/or respond to local and global productions of in/habitable spaces and narratives is to historicize endangered existence as well as its opposite—privileged, protected, and healthy existence—and subject both to the accounting of memory and the durability of hope.

The theology of reconstruction, the brainchild of André Karamaga, emerged in the wake of the Rwanda genocide, making "reconstruction" a postwar interpretive paradigm. In contrast to such postwar rituals as praise songs to the victorious (divine) warrior or even the distribution of spoils and prisoners, Karamaga's reconstruction theology emphasized such ritual activities as honorable reburials of victims (who had been hurriedly covered) and debates about theological concepts of forgiveness and wholeness, *ubuntu*.[62] The content of this non-celebratory postwar hermeneutic is important, not just because it ultimately required assessment of internecine violence, but also because it required imagining a future space-time in which the broken bodies of colonial and postcolonial violence were present.⁶³ Victims were local, and the war was fought on home soil, which meant reengagement with the shared space of violence and hope through mourning. To mourn is to embrace and internalize loss of a part of one's selfhood. The relation between trauma, mourning, and survival has been explored and theorized in great depth.⁶⁴

In *Theology, Liberation, and Genocide*, Mario Aguilar examines the failure of high Christianity in Rwanda to engage in liberation hermeneutics, leading up to the genocide. For Aguilar, moments of human suffering in history can become moments of grace only through a process of re-reading history "within God's actions and God's plan."⁶⁵ This interpretive endeavor ultimately involves "the reconstruction of social memories through a Christian theology and political practice that avoids the dichotomy between contemplation and political activity."⁶⁶ Although it is often repeated that the Rwanda genocide represented an example of the saying that "blood is thicker than water"⁶⁷—that family and ethnic ties proved stronger than the ritual waters of baptism—and therefore that Christianity proved too feeble to provide social and cultural structures strong enough to fend off violent ideologies, it is also the case that the genocidal violence in Rwanda cut across ethnic groups: Tutsis and moderate Hutus were victims. The collapse of social and cultural bonds and the resulting violence is indicative of a different truism: that the nerves that supply communal identity and healthy social interaction are as nourished by ideology as by genealogy. To state the obvious, the human as well as the cultural body is more than its blood; it is also a powerful tool of water/food supply (economy); a typology and creator of habitat (cosmology); and the executioner of power (governance).⁶⁸ These arteries of human and social existence become explicitly evident in the theater and debates about war and violence.

These nerves converged anew post genocide, as families summoned the courage to assemble in churches and around the bones of loved ones:

> On a daily basis some relatives go to talk to their loved ones and the cohesion between a physical and a metaphysical world is ever strengthened. This communion between living human beings and their ancestors who live in another world is not unusual; what becomes unusual is the centrality of a hermeneutics of presence that dictates readings and interpretations of memory through silence and the memories of silence.⁶⁹

Hermeneutics becomes a "second act" of theological reflection, preceded by a hermeneutic of "presence and empathy with the human and divine in a place of bones."[70] To contemplate and attempt to interpret the artifacts of war or genocide, or more precisely, to take the interpretive posture that "bones are not only texts to be interpreted, but represent the presence of God,"[71] is to engage in disjunctive memory that prioritizes silent and discarded bodies and spaces as the starting and primal places for postwar hermeneutics. To prioritize otherwise is to make a mockery of the power of disjunctive memory as the basis for a reconstructive hermeneutic. "Bones theology," as Aguilar calls it, is similar to forensic work: "Bones and skeletons tell a story because by examining them it is possible to know what happened. Bones show age, sickness, brokenness, strength, variety and ultimately they are a forensic extension of a human being who died."[72] The forensic body is also a cultural, narrative, and religious body.

BACK TO EXODUS: NARRATIVE SHAWLS FOR MOUNTAINSIDE LIFE

In *God on the Mountain*, Thomas Dozeman sets out the premise that the interweaving of biblical narrative in Exodus 19–34 as well as the priestly material in Exodus 35–Numbers 10 constitute part of "the Sinai Complex" rooted primarily in law, yet derived from a central event at Sinai, namely, the divine revelation of God on the mountain in Exodus 19–24.[73] Israel's arrival at the mountain, along with divine instructions for communal purification, theophany, and ritual activity all constitute the narrative around the mountain. This narrative is "structured in a vertical hierarchy" in which the deity is located at the top of the mountain while the people are camped at the bottom of the mountain and even restricted from coming close. The mountain thus provides narrative structure to the Sinai complex; the physical structure of the mountain itself contributes to the symbolism of that narrative structure. In this vertical hierarchical structure, there is a sense that divine presence is identified with the mountain where the people see and hear God speak.[74]

This understanding feeds the Zion theology of fixity of divine presence at the mountain. However, the canonical structure of the text reveals layers of traditions and revisions, which Dozeman associates with Deuteronomic and Priestly traditions. The first, developed as part of the so-called Name Theology of Deuteronomy, critiques Zion tradition and insists on Moses as an intermediary between God and the people; Moses literally scales the heights of the mountain, moving back and forth between the top and the bottom, and communicating God's word to the people through speech.[75] The second, developed as part of the so-called Kabod Theology, modifies or qualifies the nature of divine presence, insisting that that presence is impermanent. The very symbols of this presence (the cloud, the tabernacle) constitute a break from previous notions of permanent divine presence in the mountain.[76] Both traditions permanently dislodge the divine from the physical and symbolic mountain, and, in the process of insisting on divine transcendent and cosmic presence, create an overarching narrative framework around ongoing story, legislation, covenants, and rituals.

Dozeman presents his analyses under a temporal frame: "When it is anchored in the past, Zion unifies the canonical Sinai Complex as an ideal archetype that makes Horeb and Sinai possible; in the present Zion provides a critical point of unity between Horeb and Sinai, by representing what a theology of divine presence cannot be; and finally, as a future hope Zion once again becomes an ideal."[77] The result is "undergrounded doubling" in which "fundamentally different symbols of Sinai and Horeb are presented to the reader as being the one revelation of God on the mountain."[78] A critically important element of Dozeman's work is his description of the narrative and symbolic function of the mountain "as a signifier of something that is absent—the signified—which in this case is the cultic presence of God."[79] Indeed, the mountain is the creation of God (Ps. 95:4) and the divine dwelling place (Ps. 74:2).

Within this narrative corpus, Exodus 32 is intriguing. In the Priestly tradition, arrival at the mountain of God (cf. Exod. 19:2–3) fulfills exodus pilgrimage from Egypt (cf. Exod. 3:12). Exodus-Israel's association with this (divine) space is marked by arrival (*bā'āh*) and departure (*'ālāh*) for the land of Promise (19:1; 33:1), both movements echoing Israel's arrival (*bā'āh*) and departure (*'ālāh*) from Egypt (1:1; 12:38). In the unfolding story of Exodus, the liberated and migrant community reaches a mountain area, a place shrouded in clouds and smoke and fiery earthquakes, a place that functions as a literary and symbolic representation of the divine abode[80]—in fact, as the "seat" of divine governance.[81] But it is also the place where they receive, destroy, and reconstruct the textual representation of their experience of exodus. Within the ongoing and unfinished narrative, Exodus 32 bears the task of repurposing memory to effect a new form of exodus; it is exodus inside/after exodus.

It is an un-natural scene in the mountain narratives. Not only is Moses's ascent to the mountain sudden and his return delayed, the apparent reason for his departure is to secure laws, even though the community that trails him—the community that responded to his clarion call for the creation of an anti-Pharaonic world—is already hard at work establishing apodictic and case laws that anchor their communal identity and hold them accountable, one to another, to their ecosystem, and to their deity (Exod. 20–31). Moses's departure inserts a break in the unfolding narrative and its ongoing work of transforming a formerly enslaved people into a flourishing people, whose identity is tied as much to land/space as to religious belief. To remove Moses from the scene is to remove the story that makes material presence meaningful and purposeful. In response, the people build a golden calf and proclaim a festival unto the Lord.

The narrative and interpretive power of the story of the golden calf is not only enormous, but perhaps one of the most hotly and divergently contested parts of its legacy. From text-critical and historical-critical to narrative and form-critical analyses, from literary to cultural studies, and from theological and political analyses, the story of the calf in Exodus 32, along with other calf stories in the canonical text, continues to animate scholarly research and hermeneutics around questions of apostasy, idolatry, orality, ritual practice, and covenant, among others; and how these thorny issues are related to the histories of ancient Israel and Judah, pre- and postexilic, and into the Second Temple period.[82]

The story is often regarded as one of the most infamous passages of Exodus; in its memory of exodus, it tries to hold together a community that is broken—separated from their own bodily experiences and from the divine body. Avigdor Shinan and Yair Zakovitch describe the story of the golden calf as "the worst of all the sins that the Israelites commit in the wilderness."[83] It is a sin so outrageous and insidious that it provokes divine wrath, prompting the deity to contemplate erasing an entire generation of people. Yet the story also portrays the sin as a one of leadership failure on the part of Aaron, not of moral failure on the part of the people; the sin is brought upon the people, as opposed to being committed by the people (Exod. 32:21). This sin of leadership—failed leadership, precisely—finds resonance with the building of the golden calves by Jeroboam as an act of liberation from the oppressive policies of Solomon and Rehoboam in Jerusalem (1 Kings 12:26–30) and the resulting condemnation of that separation as a cardinal sin (2 Kings 17:16). Shinan and Zakovitch rightly point out that this condemnation originates from, and seeks to enhance, the southern kingdom and Jerusalem's temple: "Jeroboam was reinstating an ancient tradition when he erected the calves. Wanting to defame the northern kingdom, however, the Pentateuch fashioned the tale of the calf in Exodus 32 as a story about sin of idolatry."[84]

The story is retold, in Deuteronomy 9 and Psalm 106. In the Deuteronomic rendering of this incident, the blame largely falls on the people. Moses not only intercedes for them, sparing their life from the threatening deity, but the intercession takes as much time as Moses needed to receive the stone tablets: forty days and forty nights, without food or drink (Deut. 9:18). If Moses's acquisition of, and engagement with, the text was supposed to ensure the survival of the people, the ritual act of prostrating his body before God also functions as a credible guarantor of communal survival. Moses's body, gripped with fear, presumably lying on the ground—giving itself up to the custody of the ground—prostrates before the Lord to secure communal survival. Furthermore, after Moses burned and crushed the calf into dust, he did not compel the people to drink it; instead, he threw the dust "into the stream that runs down the mountain" (Deut. 9:21). The trauma and residue of legislative and cultural death is captured and launched into the ecosystem where the people reside. The community no longer reads the text in order to survive; it reads Moses's prostrating body and its fractured ecosystem. It is the voices from this prostrating body/fragmented land—along with ancestral memories/voices—that Moses channels to Yahweh to secure the people's future (Deut. 9:27–28).

In Psalm 106, the calf story functions as one of the catalogues of unapproved actions by the wilderness community. The episode is portrayed as an unacceptable transactional act in which the people exchange the immaterial glory of God for an ox (that eats grass). The retelling of the calf story in Psalm 106 is intended to highlight and emphasize divine forgiveness.[85] But the community's survival is linked to divine acts of self-honor (Ps. 106:7–8) or to Moses's remarkable abilities to effectively secure their survival by "standing in the breach" (Ps. 106:23), or to Phinehas's righteous intercession (Ps. 106:30–31). The metaphor of standing in the breach is military language and signals the struggle to survive.

The narrative is something of a puzzle. When Aaron proclaims and thus defines the celebrations at the bottom of the mountain as a festival of the Lord, what kind of festival is it and what is its function? Earlier in the exodus story, we hear Moses and Aaron speaking to Pharaoh, saying: "Thus says the Lord, the God of Israel: Let my people go that they may celebrate a festival for me in the wilderness" (5:1). Is Aaron reappropriating the words he and Moses spoke to Pharaoh? The puzzle is expressed at the bottom of the mountain, in Moses's question to Aaron: "What did this people do to you that you have brought such a great sin upon them." Here, the people are not the moral culprits, the feckless unbelieving community, prone to acts of idolatry. Instead, they are portrayed as victims of a great sin of leadership. Aaron's response, in ironic allusion to the burning flames of the festival, pushes back against Moses's burning anger (that accompanies the descent of the law from above) and then makes generalizing statements about the people being bent on evil. It is here in this moment of moralizing political narration—Aaron narrating what the people said—that we encounter the most intriguing aspects of this religious puzzle: "They said to me, 'make us gods, who shall go before us; as for this Moses, the man who brought us up out of the land of Egypt, we do not know what has become of him.' So I said to them, 'whoever has gold, take it off'; so they gave it to me and I threw it into the fire, and out came this calf!" (Exod. 32:23–24).

The story of victims of political leadership takes a turn toward self-determination in which they are portrayed as partially responsible for the production of a magical object in a carnival-like event that includes transforming their bodies into custodians of exodus memory. Here's the magic of storytelling, at once enigmatic and captivating in its attempts to convey and communicate the lived experience and anguish of abandonment. This response to political abandonment and resulting acts of self-determination includes a political puzzle, represented by Moses's and Joshua's interpretations of the sounds (voices) of communal self-production. Joshua thinks they are sounds of war. Moses thinks they are sounds of song. Both responses, developed en route to the community from the mountain, and inconsistent with Yahweh's proclamation that the people had sinned and deserved erasure, raise questions about the relation between the rhythms and sounds of war and the rhythms and sounds of song. This reference to war and song recalls the sounds of Miriam, the political strategist who secured Moses's survival by wrapping him in the nursing arms of his mother (Exod. 2), the prophet and poet who enunciated the significance of understanding exodus survival as centrally communal rather than focused on individual heroes, and profoundly healing (Exod. 15:21–27).

Although Israel is spatially removed from the house of Pharaoh (Israel is now in the symbolic residence of Yahweh), Egypt returns, not as a trope or commemorative historical reference, but as a protective shawl of memory that shapes ongoing exodus narration. Faced with threats of communal extinction, Moses will pose a quintessential question of postcolonial subjectivity—subjectivity deprived of the privilege of telling linear stories or single-subject (single-people) stories; and that appropriates the vocal power of the darkened place: "Why should the Egyptians say, 'it was with ill intent that he brought them out of Egypt to destroy them in the mountains and wipe them from the face of the earth'?" (Exod. 32:12).

To simultaneously remember the place of initial violent departure and the place of new residence, and to remember these places as co-extensive experiences, is to claim an embodied form of adjunctive memory: memory that bears the scars of violent erasure, celebrates the particularity of new space and experience, but also reengages (even critically so) shared communal identities handed down from generation to generation and linked from region to region. This communal endeavor is evident in the fact that the mountainside community's new stone tablets are like the former (broken) ones, but not quite; divine presence with Israel is like of old (a warring deity), but not quite (an angel, a messenger leads the community); the tabernacle construction is like the (shattered) golden calf construction, but not quite. In the end, Israel's life and movement is coordinated to divine life and movement. The work of survival-liberation is partial and incremental, always endangered but capable of enduring beyond generational fragmentation and regional alienation.

The clash for the meaning line is the clash between the power of singular and multiple meanings. The clash itself is multilayered, though organized around two major categories: textual (produced by the deity, atop the mountain) and ritual (produced by the community at the bottom of the mountain). Both are concerned with how to understand exodus, and the story depicts how the bodies and voices that fill that contested space—the ruptured human, textual, and ritual bodies—also transition from being objects of exodus (characters in a story world) to becoming analyzing subjects (characters producing the story world). The ruptured space becomes simultaneously a folded and a creative (an unfolding) space, where the people at the bottom—feeling and filling the rupture with narrative and material form—begin to reproduce their historicized identity as migrants facing unknown futures. These unknown futures include risks of being erased from the divine book, and thus from their ecological space and their ancestral memory. But the generative work from below—the construction of a deity that goes before, and thus on whose back they stand—also means the creation of futures that include the material extensions of their bodies and generative work into the future.

The rupture signaled by Moses's absent body becomes part of the narrative. Moses's delayed return *is read and narrated* by the community as experience with unknowability. This unknowability is not so much an epistemological category as it is the experience of political powerlessness. The removal of Moses from the scene is not the removal of the architect or the trope of exodus from Egypt; the removal signals the community's anxiety about the process of entrenching power and authority in a single hero. This process of single-hero making from above causes shame and distress for the exodus community, which now sets us its cluster narration ("us") in contradistinction to the singularity of Moses (referred to as "this man"). In the face of imperial removal of cluster narration, the community's *interpretation* or *reading* of that removal as unknowability begins to shape identity, to summon memory, and to regenerate communal creativity beyond single-hero-narration. That communal narration is internalized and given shape in the form of the calf (which, according to priestly expert, Aaron, is as much a production of the people as it is a sudden, almost magical, emergence from the fires).

The building of the calf functions hermeneutically as a response to rupture. By locating this break in the mountain area—at the seat of divine power and governance—the narrative signals that idolatry is as much political as it is religious; precisely, it is about political and religious power. Within the grand movement of exodus imagination, the story also functions differently: the narrative scene—along with its political and religious manifestations and discourse—risks becoming idolatrous because it potentially deviates from understanding exodus as a story that distributes rather than consolidates power. That is, the narrative is attempting to represent the empire's failed but costly attempt to co-opt Moses and the exodus story—an attempt that, if successful, would transform exodus into a story of imperial gift that engenders communal commemoration, rather than as a story of repurposed memory that mobilizes and galvanizes a marginalized community in its liberative and transformative work. As if a narrative performance of postcolonial subjectivity, the people gathered around the mountain (the symbol of stability and security) ironically don't seem to have a secure sense of spatial and communal belonging. Whose people are these? Moses's? Yahweh's? The ancestors' and ancestresses'? Do they belong to an actual land or to a promissory one? Are their futures yet undetermined?

Given that communal productions of freedom and accountable power are quintessential antipathies of historical modes of dehumanizing confinement (enslavement and colonization), the Africana biblical interpreter rigorously examines the deployment of power, not just through liberation ("I am the Lord who brought you out of Egypt"), not just through expulsion ("I will cause Pharaoh to drive you out"), but also through re-examinations and re-articulations of the story of migration/liberation/exile ("*These* are your Gods who brought you out of Egypt"). Because this story of exodus always runs the risk of being co-opted by and for imperial purposes, such reexamination and rearticulations become the artistic and narrative "golden calves" that emerge from the places of rupture. The narrative builds and deploys political and ethical power not only because its rhetorical and interpretive crown jewel—its goal of enacting liberation out of exile/oppression and conjuring new futures out of foreclosed or erased histories—is broken and unfinished, but also because its engagement with unformed (or partially formed) futures—futures built on promissory notes—signals more than an inherent deficit in liberation ideology, or a nagging tendency for such endeavors to be derailed. The narrative of exodus continues to garner power across generations and across its multiple landscapes—Egypt, the wilderness, the mountain area, and Canaan—because the story addresses, again and again, a perennial question about the in/habitability of places of origins, the in/habitability of origins stories, and the in/habitability of its future places and futures stories: if places of origins are permanently lost and future places are already cognitively and materially inhabited or restricted or unavailable or co-opted into imperial stories, the story runs the risk of being perpetually trapped in a peculiar form of trauma—the haunting of an erased singularized past and the ruthless austerity of a future linked to the productions of global placelessness (unrelenting diaspora).

As an exilic and postexilic text, the nomadic story of Exodus is not inherently bold or transformative. Its boldness as a communal (or "national") story resides in its shadowy attempt to transform a text of trauma into a text of trauma-hope, its attempt to transform exile into exodus by using the shawl of memory to place exile on the back of exodus. The story attempts to transform the traumas of social, political, and geographical displacement, erasure, and internal alienation into survival; and to create new futures from the ashes and the depths of cultural, political, and religious erasure. The task is more than a generation's to diagnose and resolve. The need to adequately respond to overt and covert demands for the protection of vulnerable bodies within nations and vulnerable bodies at the crossroads of multiple national boundaries is more than a single leader, no matter how heroic, can sufficiently provide. The story's deep memories of survival and loss and rebellion and fleeting flourishing—stretched out across multiple landscapes and generations—are more than any single ancestral deity, no matter how powerful and wise, can permanently interpret and translate for healthy communal futures. The story's movements across gendered places and spaces generate new identities that require more than a single methodology to fully render accessible. And the subjection of the story's ecosystem to massive violence and destruction requires formulations of return as reengagement with the earth's trauma and liquidity (that is, to the land's capacity to function as a subject and custodian of communal memories). Exodus is compelling because it is at once proximate and fragile, but also elusive and enduring. Its liberation work produces multiple heroic characters, gathers around multiple voices, navigates multiple violent ecosystems, and engages in cluster-storytelling that confronts and overturns structural and systemic oppression.

As Charles Villa-Vicencio argues, liberation theology emerges not just on the basis that *"event precedes word and interpretation"* but also on the premise that there is a "residue of oppression" that continues to influence religious traditions.[86] That this residue of oppression also morphs into new structures of oppression is precisely the reason why exodus cannot be singularly defined or associated with the work of any individual. Precise questions unfold: Will the endangered community survive? And, if it does, how? Will the violently displaced community find new space? And if so, where? Does a new space emerge from the wreckage of violent conquest? If so, what happens to the wreckage? Does the empire co-opt the liberation movement? And if so, what happens to the movement? These issues are explored not simply as by-products of the exodus story but as elements of the afterlife of exodus's first act: liberation. What does communal return look like? And what experiences and infrastructures provide assessment mechanisms for such communal returns? These questions constitute the narrative and cultural "archives" to which the story of exodus returns, and from where the story provides interpretive options and choices at the margins of the story's struggle to create life and a healthy society.

CONCLUSION

Exodus is a story of intergenerational and interregional embodiment. This embodiment is marked with the scars of oppressed, embittered, endangered, and displaced lives. Reactive against such forms of fractured embodiment, the story develops a deep sense of, and commitment to, episodic and systemic resistance against forces and infrastructures of erasure. Exodus's intergenerational and interregional embodiment is also marked and informed by an enduring sense and praxis of the vibrancy, beauty/health/goodness, and creativity of its target and primary community. Proactive toward these values, the story depicts a community hard at work developing its religious, cultural, legal, and political systems to respond to the changing circumstances of its existence. In its reactive and proactive dimensions, the story is culturally and politically deep and spacious; tellers and hearers of this story are nurtured to embody and perform multiple roles as creators of narratives and counternarratives of communal belonging: (a) to challenge deadly oppression and its technologies of sudden and/or systematic erasure and elimination of life and life forms. The insistence is that ethnocentrism cannot become the foundational premise for healthy communal identity formation and covenantal relation; (b) to engage and reengage the vagaries of violent political changes, and insist that communal memory, variously construed, is necessary for ensuring that history does not become an abstract monstrosity; and (c) to envision and embody the ethics of social (not just spatial) hospitality, understood not as acts of magnanimity or patronage toward others, human or divine, but as an indispensable, though constantly endangered, justice virtue that builds and sustains healthy communities.

The story's encounter with state and imperial power has left its brutal mark on the community and its environment; there is no escaping that reality, and no escaping the manipulation of bodies and spaces to protect the face of the state or empire. The existence and life of the marginalized community has been used to subsidize the privilege of the state/empire and its religious underpinnings. It is from this space and perspective that back-side/black-side subjectivity develops its hermeneutics. The maneuvering required to secure bodily survival is the same maneuvering that locates interpretive perspective. The reproduction of texts (Exod. 34) is back-side maneuvering and interpretation that connects bodily survival to textual production; the community writes and speaks itself back to life. This existential and hermeneutical move is not developed as an explanation of the original text, but as a process of re-scribing and re-inscribing the broken text; it is hermeneutical shawling that produces a future with real bodies. In order to survive in spatial lacuna, with an outer layer of textual lacuna, Moses's endangered body is aligned with the broken text—a text initially written on stones produced exclusively by the divine (Exod. 32:16) and later partially produced by Moses (Exod. 34:1). The work of human and textual survival unfolds as the work of re-inscription, even conjuring, rather than simply reinterpretation; that is, Moses survives not in the textual and technological world of the divine monarch, but in the modified broken text and space wrapped up in the shawl of communal memory and bonding. The power of survival is not in mutual revelation of face-to-face or face-to-text exploration and duplication, but in the double encounters with unformed futures and accountable re-imaginations of the pasts.

One tells this story in order to chart survival paths and create sacred memories from broken bodies and places; but one interprets the story and revisits those memories in order to give purpose to survival, to make meaning of the wreckage that trails the story of survival, and to create accountable processes that resist continued erasure, or the deployment of such erasure as subsidies for the construction of national and transnational identities.

NOTES

1. This divine approval is only the latest version of divine embodiment that Moses has secured. To ensure the survival of the community, the deity has promised to send a messenger in front of the people (Exod. 33:2, 3) and Moses has built a tent of meeting where the divine cloud descends and Moses speaks face to face with God (Exod. 33:7–11). The movement of the divine body—through

the descending and lifting cloud around the tent—mirrors the movement of the communal body that bows and rises each in their tents. For discussions on the divine presence and pathos within the human experience, see Terence E. Freitheim, *The Suffering of God: An Old Testament Perspective* (Philadelphia: Fortress, 1984).

2. For more on this Pauline text, see Dorota Hartman, "'Through a Glass, Darkly' (1 Cor 13, 12) in Paul's Literary Imagination," *Vetera Christianorum* 54 (2017): 59–91.

3. Barbara Ayres, "Effects of Infant Carrying Practices on Rhythm in Music," *Ethos* 1, no. 4 (1973): 388.

4. The term *ambiveilence* is Shanell Smith's in *The Woman Babylon and the Marks of Empire: Reading Revelation with a Postcolonial Womanist Hermeneutic of Ambiveilence* (Minneapolis: Fortress Press, 2014).

5. For more on Négritude, see Aliou Niang's piece in this volume.

6. On the importance of processes, spaces, conditions, and discourses in diaspora theorizing, see Paul Tiyambe Zeleza, "Rewriting the African Diaspora: Beyond the Black Atlantic," *African Affairs* 104, no. 414 (2005): 41.

7. Masiiwa R. Gunda, "African Theology of Reconstruction: The Painful Realities and Practical Options," *Exchange* 38 (2009): 90.

8. Jan Assmann, *Moses the Egyptian: The Memory of Egypt in Western Monotheism* (Cambridge, MA: Harvard University Press, 1997).

9. Jane Burbank and Frederick Cooper, *Empires in World History: Power and the Politics of Difference* (Princeton, NJ: Princeton University Press, 2010), 312–20.

10. On the erasure of the distinction between means and ends in the colonial project, see Achille Mbembe, *Critique of Black Reason* (Durham, NC: Duke University Press, 2017).

11. Richard A. Joseph, "The German Question in French Cameroun, 1919–1939," *Comparative Studies in Society and History* 17, no. 1 (1975): 67.

12. Joseph, "Question," 68.

13. Cheikh Anta Babou, "Decolonization or National Liberation: Debating the End of British Colonial Rule in Africa," *AAAPSS* 632; Perspectives on Africa and the World (2010): 43.

14. Babou, "Decolonization," 43.

15. F. Kange Ewane, *Semence et Moisson Coloniales: Un Regard d'Africain sur l'Histoire de la Colonisation* (Yaoundé, Cameroon: Editions CLE, 1985).

16. Joseph, "Question," 69.

17. See Milton Krieger, "Building the Republic through Letters: 'Abbia: Cameroon Cultural Review,' 1963–82 and Its Legacy," *Research in African Literatures* 27, no. 2 (1996): 155–77. Some of these nation-states have fractured (such as Sudan).

18. See Victor Julius Ngoh, *Origins of the Anglophone Problem: Southern Cameroons, 1922–1961: A Constitutional History* (Aldershot: Ashgate, 2001); Paul Nugent, *Africa since Independence: A Comparative History* (New York: Palgrave Macmillan, 2004). 71–77; Piet Konings, "The Anglophone Cameroon-Nigeria Boundary: Opportunities and Conflicts," *African Affairs* 104, no. 415 (2005), 275–301; Piet Konings and Francis Nyamnjoh, "The Anglophone Problem in Cameroon," *Journal of Modern African Studies* 35, no. 2 (1997): 207–29. The plebiscite of 1972 brought together "Southern Cameroons" and "La République" to create the United Republic of Cameroon. A decade later in 1982, President Paul Biya unilaterally renamed the country "The Republic of Cameroon," reverting to and nationalizing the ideology of pre-unification French-speaking Cameroon and causing political anxiety for English-speaking Cameroon.
19. Francis B. Nyamnjoh, "Commentary: Cameroon: A Country United by Ethnic Ambition and Diversity," *African Affairs* 98, no. 390 (1999): 101–18.
20. Elias K. Bongmba, *The Dialectics of Transformation in Africa* (New York: Palgrave, 2006), 9–37.
21. Achille Mbembe, "Provisional Notes on the Postcolony," *AJIAI* 62, no. 1 (1992): 17–18.
22. Mbembe, "Provisional Notes," 6. See also Bruce J. Berman, "Ethnicity, Patronage and the African State: The Politics of Uncivil Nationalism," *African Affairs* 97, no. 388 (1998): 305–34; Nubohiro Mizuno and Ryosuke Okazawa, "Colonial Experience and Postcolonial Underdevelopment in Africa," *Public Choice* 141, no. 3–4 (2009): 405–19.
23. For example: Mbembe, "Provisional Notes on the Postcolony," 3–37; *On the Postcolony* (Stanford CA: Stanford University Press, 2001); "On the Postcolony: A Brief Response to Critics," *Qui Parle* 15, no. 2 (2005): 1–49; "On Politics as a Form of Expenditure," in *Law and Disorder in the Postcolony*, ed. Jean Comaroff and John Comaroff (Chicago: University of Chicago Press, 2006), 299–335.
24. Achille Mbembe, *Necropolitics* (Durham, NC: Duke University Press, 2019), 11.
25. Giorgio Agamben, *State of Exception*, trans. Kevin Attell (Chicago: University of Chicago Press, 2005); Paul W. Kahn, *Political Theology: Four New Chapters on Sovereignty* (New York: Columbia University Press, 2011).
26. Mbembe, *Necropolitics*, 12.
27. Mbembe, *On the Postcolony* (Berkeley: University of California Press, 2001), 25. Italics original.
28. Mbembe, *On the Postcolony*, 26. Italics original.
29. Mbembe, *Necropolitics*, 14. Italics original.
30. Mbembe, *On the Postcolony*, 212–13. Italics original.

31. Mbembe, *On the Postcolony*, 215. Italics original.
32. Mbembe, *On the Postcolony*, 219.
33. Mbembe, "Provisional Notes," 3–4
34. Mbembe, "Provisional Notes," 4. Italics original.
35. Mbembe, "Provisional Notes," 4. Italics original.
36. Mbembe, "Provisional Notes," 5. Italics original.
37. Mbembe, "Provisional Notes," 10.
38. Mbembe, "Provisional Notes," 10. Italics original.
39. Mbembe, "Provisional Notes," 25. Italics original.
40. W. E. Burghardt du Bois, "Of the Culture of White Folk," *Journal of Race Development* 7, no. 4 (1917): 436.
41. Dwight D. Eisenhower, "The Military-Industrial Complex," *American Journal of Economics and Sociology* 46, no. 2 (1987): 150.
42. Du Bois, "White Folk," 439.
43. Du Bois, "White Folk," 442, 446.
44. Du Bois, "White Folk," 444–45.
45. W. E. B. Du Bois, *The Souls of Black Folk* (Atlanta, GA: A. C. McClurg & Co., 1903), 7.
46. Brian K. Blount, "The Souls of Biblical Folk and the Potential for Meaning," *Journal of Biblical Literature* 138, no. 1 (2019): 9. Emphases original.
47. Andrew M. Mbuvi, "African Biblical Studies: An Introduction to an Emerging Field," *Currents in Biblical Research* 15, no. 2 (2017): 149–78.
48. See, for example, James K. Hoffmeier, Alan R. Millard, and Gary A. Rendsburg, eds., *Did I Not Bring Israel Out of Egypt?: Biblical, Archaeological and Egyptological Perspectives on the Exodus Narratives* (Winona Lake, IN: Eisenbrauns, 2016).
49. Gerald O. West, *The Stolen Bible: From Tool of Imperialism to African Icon* (Pietermaritzburg: Cluster Publications, 2016).
50. Joseph Williams, *Hebrewisms of West Africa: From the Nile to the Niger with the Jews* (Baltimore: Black Classic Press, 1931).
51. Modupe A. Oduyoye, *The Sons of the Gods and the Daughters of Men: An Afro-Asiatic Interpretation of Genesis 1–11* (Eugene, OR: Wipf and Stock, 1984).
52. John Chijioke Madubuko, *The "Pauline" Spirit World in Eph. 3:10 in the Context of Igbo World View: A Psychological-Hermeneutical Appraisal* (New York: Peter Lang, 2015), 407. See also essays in Craig S. Keener and M. Daniel Carroll R., eds., *Global Voices: Reading the Bible in the Majority World* (Peabody, MA: Hendrickson Publishers, 2013).
53. Kabamba J. Kiboko, *Divining the Woman of Endor: African Culture, Postcolonial Hermeneutics and the Politics of Biblical Translation* (New York: Bloomsbury and T&T Clark, 2017), 231–32.

54. David T. Adamo, *Biblical Interpretation in African Perspective* (Lanham, MD: University Press of America, 2006).
55. Jione Havea, Margaret Aymer, and Steed Davidson, eds., *Islands, Islanders, and the Bible: RumInations* (Atlanta: Society of Biblical Literature Press, 2015).
56. Havea, Aymer, and Davidson, eds., *Islands*, 1.
57. Ron Eyerman, *Cultural Trauma: Slavery and the Formation of African American Identity* (New York: Cambridge University Press, 2001), 2
58. Eyerman, *Cultural Trauma*, 24.
59. Arthur Kleinman and Joan Kleinman, "How Bodies Remember: Social Memory and Bodily Experience of Criticism, Resistance, and Delegitimation Following China's Cultural Revolution," *New Literary History* 25, no. 3 (1994): 714–75.
60. Kleinman and Kleinman, "How Bodies Remember," 176.
61. Mbembe, *Critique of Black Reason*, 181. Emphasis original.
62. André Karamaga, "Memories and Experiences of Violence," in *Worlds of Memory and Wisdom: Encounters of Jews and African Christians* ed. Jean Hapérin and Hans Ucko (Geneva: World Council of Churches Publications), 141–47.
63. Karamaga, "Memories," identifies three conditions that could lead to such violence anywhere: "a population living mostly in poverty, a dictatorship afraid of being overthrown and the identification of some group or other as its emissary" (147).
64. See, for example, Vamik Volkan, *Killing in the Name of Identity: A Study of Blood Conflicts* (Chicago: Pitchstone Publishing, 2006).
65. Mario I. Aguilar, *Theology, Liberation, and Genocide: A Theology of the Periphery* (London: SCM, 2009), 17.
66. Aguilar, *Theology, Liberation, and Genocide*, 19.
67. Referenced in Aguilar, *Theology, Liberation, and Genocide*, 23; Philip Gourevitch, *We Wish to Inform You That Tomorrow We Will Be Killed with Our Families: Stories from Rwanda* (New York: Farrar, Straus and Giroux, 1999).
68. Aguilar, *Theology*, 15–32.
69. Aguilar, *Theology*, 35.
70. Aguilar, *Theology*, 35.
71. Aguilar, *Theology*, 35.
72. Aguilar, *Theology*, 45.
73. Thomas B. Dozeman, *God on the Mountain: A Study of Redaction, Theology and Canon in Exodus 19–24*, SBL Monograph Series 37 (Atlanta: Scholars Press, 1989), 2. Included in this "Sinai Complex" is deuteronomic legislation.
74. Dozeman, *God on the Mountain*, 19–35. Dozeman attributes this understanding of the mountain to pre-deuteronomic tradition.

75. Dozeman, *God on the Mountain*, 37–86.
76. Dozeman, *God on the Mountain*, 87–143.
77. Dozeman, *God on the Mountain*, 174.
78. Dozeman, *God on the Mountain*, 175.
79. Dozeman, *God on the Mountain*, 30.
80. Dozeman, *God on the Mountain*, 30.
81. It is in the mountain area that Yahweh gives legal and statutory instructions for Israel's covenantal relation with God and one another (Exod. 20–24), as well as instructions for the construction of a sanctuary where the Lord will tabernacle among the people (Exod. 25:8).
82. Pekka Lindqvist, *Sin at Sinai: Early Judaism Encounters Exodus 32* (Winona Lake, IN: Eisenbrauns, 2008); Youn Ho Chung, *The Sin of the Calf: The Rise of the Bible's Negative Attitude toward the Golden Calf* (New York: T&T Clark, 2010); Jan Assmann, *The Invention of Religion: Faith and Covenant in the Book of Exodus*, trans. Robert Savage (Princeton, NJ: Princeton University Press, 2018), 302–22; Jörg Jeremias, "The Wrath of God at Mount Sinai (Exod 32; Deut 9–10)," in *The Bible as Christian Scripture: The Work of Brevard S. Childs*, ed. Christopher R. Seitz and Kent Harold Richards (Atlanta: SBL Press, 2013), 21–35; James Watts, "Aaron and the Golden Calf in the Rhetoric of the Pentateuch," *Journal of Biblical Literature* 130, no. 3 (2011): 417–30; Carola Hilfrich, "'Making Writing Readable Again': Sign Praxis between the Discourse on Idolatry and Cultural Criticism," *Journal of Religion* 85, no. 2 (2005): 267–92; Uri Rubin, "Traditions in Transformation: The Ark of the Covenant and the Golden Calf in Biblical and Islamic Historiography," *Oriens* 36 (2001): 196–214.
83. Avidgor Shinan and Yair Zakovitch, *From Gods to God: How the Bible Debunked, Suppressed, or Changed Ancient Myths and Legends*, trans. Valerie Zakovitch (Philadelphia: Jewish Publication Society, 2012), 101.
84. Shinan and Zakovitch, *From Gods to God*, 106.
85. Gordon J. Wenham, "The Golden Calf in the Psalms," in Jamie A. Grant, Alison Lo, and Gordon J. Wenham, eds., *A God of Faithfulness: Essays in Honour of J. Gordon McConville on His 60th Birthday* (New York: T&T Clark, 2011), 170–75.
86. Charles Villa Vicencio, *A Theology of Reconstruction: Nation-Building and Human Rights* (Cambridge: Cambridge University Press, 1992), 26.

15. Conjuring Lost Books: (Re-)membering Fragmented Litanies at the Intersection of Africana and Biblical Studies

(THE REV. CANON) HUGH R. PAGE JR.

I am both delighted and honored to be included in the proceedings of this trans-disciplinary *colloquy*. In the spirit of full disclosure, when I began doctoral studies more than three decades ago, the idea that mine would be a voice with anything meaningful to contribute to a conversation of this kind was unimaginable. Hebrew Bible scholars trained in programs that focused on Semitic philology, text criticism, and the comparative study of the ancient Near East in the 1980s learned early on that the parameters for research are narrowly inscribed and heavily policed. Moreover, the group of partners with whom collaboration across disciplines was allowed rarely included, at least during my formation, African, African American, African Diaspora, or Africana Studies.

Nonetheless, the current trans-disciplinary conversation has brought me full circle and given me a chance to ponder three fateful encounters, each of which has shaped in some way my understanding of the intersection of Africana and biblical studies and the dynamics of what Vincent Wimbush has termed "scripturalization."[1] The first occurred in the spring of 1989, when I was interviewed for a Fund for Theological Education fellowship by the late William R. Jones, author of *Is God a White Racist?* (1973) and Robert Hood, author of *Must God Remain Greek?* (1990) just a few miles from Drew University's campus at a hotel on the grounds of the Newark Airport. In that conversation, Jones shed light on why, in the latter stages of his career, he had elected to become an academic administrator. He did so in seven words that have challenged me to this day. "Someone," he said, "has to hold open the door." The second encounter came, if memory serves, during that same year when a mentor warned me that at some point, as an African American Bible scholar, I would likely be asked to run a Black studies program. The third occurred in the mid 1990s. Not long before his passing, one of my senior colleagues at the University of Notre Dame, the late Erskine Peters (1948–1998),[2] invited me into his office for a brief chat. The topic was our university's ongoing diversity efforts. I remember quite vividly the weariness in his eyes and, in particular, the fatigue in his voice when he exclaimed, at one point, "I'm tired."

With each advancing year my appreciation of these moments deepens, as does my recognition of their role as guideposts on what has been an unusual professional journey: one that has taken me from the narrow confines of source criticism and reception history to the disciplinary *crossroads* where the theoretical, spiritual, pragmatic, and political dimensions of scholarship meet. Black bodies and ideas in academe have long been, and indeed remain, in peril. Opening the door so that others like us may enter involves positioning oneself at those thresholds where entry can be barred and full participation limited—e.g., admissions offices, classrooms, review panels, dissertation committees, administrative positions, etc.—and helping to ensure that People-of-Color and others marginalized in the academy are guaranteed access. It may require that those of us at institutions where faculty diversity remains a challenge be prepared to become curricular innovators and catalysts for *trans-disciplinary* program planning and publishing. It may also necessitate facing squarely the likelihood of further exclusion, fatigue, and burnout.

Such cannot help but have a profound impact on the kinds of research we undertake, the questions we ask, and the methodologies we employ. It will help decide the conversation partners we cultivate and the publics we seek to engage. This certainly appears to have been the case with Jones, Hood, Peters, and many others I have come to know. It has also been true of my own career. After, in fact, becoming director of an African and African American Studies Program in the late 1990s, my research began to veer from narrowly defined philological projects to others that asked what Marcella Althaus-Reid (2000) might term "indecent" theological questions.[3] I think of these now as discomfiting queries that challenge established orthodoxies. For example, in what ways is disciplinary meta-narration akin to mythmaking? Why *has* there been such resistance to research on the Bible that explores how exclusionary practices have shaped the discipline dedicated to its critical examination? Why has there *not* been a translation and critical edition of the Bible—produced *by Africana* scholars *for Africana* readers in the Anglophone world or the Francophone and Lusophone worlds? Why was there lacking an Africana commentary on the First and Second Testaments, however one chooses to delimit that problematic genre, until the 2000s?[4] Why are African and African Diasporan hermeneutical theories ofttimes classified as non-rigorous and outside of the scholarly mainstream? What might the benefit be of allowing research on the so-called Christian Scriptures to use the lived realities of Black life, in all of their complexity, as its points of departure? What if every biblical studies project began with, or incorporated, an evocative cultural inventory like those in Kevin Young's "Overture" to *The Grey Album*[5] and Ishmael Reed's "Neo-Hoodoo Manifesto"[6]; or the vignettes in bell hooks's *Bone Black: Memories of Girlhood* (1996) and Claudia Rankine's *Citizen: An American Lyric* (2014)?

Posing *queries* of this kind and allowing them to help us reshape the contours of research and teaching—a standard practice within Africana studies—is a way of planting the seeds of the Baobab tree in the at times arid terrain of biblical and theological studies. Such a simple act of resistance can create the possibility of *transmuting* scholarship by, about, and for the Africana World into *materia medica* for empowerment, healing, and restoration. It is also a means of engaging in the imaginative and curatorial enterprise advocated by Kevin Young.[7] Such involves identifying our own discipline-specific "shadow books"—i.e., those *"unwritten," "removed,"* or *"lost."*[8] Such would also entail reappropriating cultural *realia* now considered non-mainstream, or, in Young's own words:

> Forget reparations—we need to rescue aspects of black culture abandoned even by black folks, whether it is the blues or home cookin' or broader forms of not just survival, but triumph.[9]

On the whole, at least one goal of this process would be to, engage in, as Young notes, "the willed recovery of what's been lost."[10] To this, I would add that the means for so doing can and should be inclusive of corporeal epistemologies and lore at home in the larger realm of Africana Esotericism(s).[11]

An illustrative case-in-point is the biblical narrative describing Saul's encounter with an unnamed woman at the city of Endor, who "calls up" for him the spirit of the old judge and seer Samuel (1 Samuel 28). I've been perplexed by this text since the late 1980s and have written two iterations of an as yet unpublished paper on it. Both were relatively straightforward examinations that utilized ancient Near Eastern comparative data to illumine the structure of the divinatory inquiry made by Saul and the taxonomy of purportedly non-Yahwistic Canaanite and Israelite religious practitioners. The first was a doctoral seminar paper written in the late 1980s when I was a graduate student. It incorporated a mild probing of how the episode at Endor deconstructs the harsh sentiment toward cultural and religious outsiders that is so pervasive in the Deuteronomistic History (DH). It also mused as to why a tale that appears to cast this figure in such a favorable light—e.g., she displays compassion for Saul and prepares what would be one of his final meals before he died in battle—was not excluded from such a tendentious work. The second version[12] was a *little* more daring in arguing that a text of this kind should *not* be used to justify modern opposition to religious practices considered aberrant, in particular by fundamentalist Christian communities. It was decidedly social scientific in tone.

It is helpful to note three salient factors affecting these interpretive forays. First, I was in a fundamentally vulnerable position professionally as a doctoral student (1980s) and untenured assistant professor (1990s). Second, in order for the aforementioned projects to be judged as credible, both had to be in dialogue with the work of other scholars in my intellectual lineage. Third, given the tenor of my subfield, which focuses on early Israelite literature and its congeners, it was important to affirm my core identity as a philologist with *nuanced* ethnological sensibilities. Thus, certain kinds of hermeneutical "play" were off limits. This is no doubt one of the reasons I set this work aside and have *not* returned to it until now.[13]

The translations of the Hebrew designation given to this woman *baʿalat ʾôb*— (1 Samuel 28:7)—in the Old Greek, the Vulgate, the King James Version (KJV), Jewish Publication Society (JPS), the Revised Standard Version (RSV), New Revised Standard Version (NRSV), and others vary quite widely. They include: "a ventriloquist" (LXX) "a woman possessing a spirit of divination" (Vulgate); "a woman that hath a familiar spirit" (KJV); "a medium" (NRSV); and "a woman who consults ghosts" (JPS). In each of these instances, translators appear to have drawn on points of reference from their own milieu in defining who and what they consider her to be.

None of these sufficiently do justice to the semantic range of ba ʾalat ʾôb, which is suggestive of someone that serves as a guardian of Indigenous epistemologies and that can, literally, *make ancestors present.*

Within the North American Diaspora, such individuals—many of whom are women—are well known but often operate "off the grid" in a religious economy where conservative Christian values and norms of social acceptability marginalize those who are stewards of older non-mainstream knowledge systems. Some are what might be termed *church-going people* who might have been born with the veil, or gifted with what is popularly known as "the sight." A few may operate as readers of cards or *folk* to whom one goes when in need of prayer or special counsel.[14] Several may even be guardians of apothecary traditions that have been passed down for multiple generations. Some might simply say that they possess *àshe*, the innate ability to get things done or, in the words of Robert Farris Thompson, "the power-to-make-things-happen."[15] Implicit in such an identity is the capacity to protect themselves and others under siege. Almost never are they recipients of the public accolades that physicians and pastors receive. In fact, their names are often mentioned in hushed terms, if at all. In some quarters, their mention is reduced to what they can do, or have done, and why one must remain wary of them. Their stories are part of the corpus of "removed" and "lost" books to which Kevin Young refers.[16] We owe a great debt to scholars like Yvonne Chireau (2003) and Stephanie Mitchem (2007) for helping us understand more clearly, appreciate more deeply, and re-embrace more fully these individuals and their traditions. What Bible scholars have to do is challenge those impulses within both the text and our interpretive communities that *instrumentalize* and erase them. This is the place where a conscious decision to take biblical studies to the *crossroads* so that it can commune with the Blues tradition may have a positive impact. A creative encounter of this kind is made possible only when those of us in the field are at liberty to broker conversations with Africana studies and its various subfields. Only then might we be able lovingly to recognize the *ba ʾalat ʾôb* as part of the honorable lineage of *conjurers*, wise women, and folk healers on whom many within Africana communities around the world have long relied for solace and empowerment.

The mechanics and predisposing circumstances that make such encounters possible, however, must also be subject to critical reflection. They tend not simply to happen on their own. Our institutional structures, particularly in an era of shrinking, rather than expanding, educational resources tend to privilege investment in disciplines that promise concrete outcomes for students on the job front. Those of us in the humanities and theological disciplines have to compete for "air time" in a market of ideas where science, technology, engineering, and mathematics hold sway. Freestanding seminaries and some schools of divinity are struggling in this environment and are undergoing their own reconfigurations. As for Africana studies, an uninvited guest to the great disciplinary banquet in the academy since the late 1960s, many of its centers, departments, institutes, and programs continue to fight for recognition, resources, and survival. Given these factors, can we be in any way assured that *trans-disciplinary* conversations such as those taking place in this ongoing series of *colloquies* at Drew will occur elsewhere and with greater frequency?

Furthermore, in light of escalating expectations for discipline-*specific* research productivity, how do we ensure that work growing out of the encounter between Africana and biblical studies is published, deemed of equal importance, and reviewed by those capable of fairly assessing its merit? Who will the next generation of "door opening" administrators be—i.e., those in a position to head the academic units in which this kind of groundbreaking work can be done? Who will "fight" this "good" and exhausting "fight" in an academy that has shattered more than its share of dreams and broken no small number of *Black bodies*? These too are questions to be pondered at the *crossroads* and under the Baobab tree. The stories of those who were or are currently engaged in these endeavors are among the "unwritten" and "lost" corpus of "shadow books"[17] we must also honor and cherish. Their strategies and accomplishments are among the fragmentary litanies we must, "re-member," as it were.

In sum, a pivotal dimension of scholarship done at the intersection of biblical and Africana studies, particularly in our current era of political turmoil and transition, should have a self-reflexive dimension that allows us to consider how our scholarly identities have been formed and to ponder those experiences most influential in shaping the questions we ask and the methods we employ. Work in this vein should include, at least in part, *searching for and listening to* the *heterodox* voices in the texts we engage as well as the fields and subfields dedicated to their study.

Those comfortable taking on the rather old-fashioned and some would say *passé* identity of the philologist[18] would do well to reimagine that odd vocation as an improvisational performance,[19] indeed, to see one of its core tasks as that of calling attention to the unpredictable contours of language and the cultural artifacts utilizing this medium (apud Gumbrecht).[20] They might also engage in interventions that *descripturalize*—i.e., that reinscribe what has been *erased* or *muted* and that seek to "break up" those parts of authoritative texts that have been artificially joined so as to reify manifestations of the religio-political *status quo* and *orthodoxies of exclusion*. Scholarly efforts that embrace such a paradigm may be judged pejoratively to have, as a result, an activist dimension. What we, and all others engaged in this work, must remember is that *all* academic disciplines have activist dimensions. What is distinctive about the *trans-disciplinary* alliance between Africana and biblical studies is that the focus thereof is unapologetically on the African-descended peoples within or affected in any way by applications of Scripture, as well as those who read or whose academic pursuits are focused on the Bible. What is also true is that this endeavor, which might be termed *Africana Biblical Studies,* affirms that the lives of such persons—within and beyond both the church and the academy—matter.

NOTES

1. Vincent Wimbush, *White Men's Magic: Scripturalization as Slavery* (New York: Oxford University Press, 2012), 9, 19, 105, 111.
2. For a brief profile on Erskine Peters and the fellowship established in his honor, see the webpage maintained by the Africana Studies Department at the University of Notre Dame: https://africana.nd.edu/about/peters-fellows-network/ (accessed April 23, 2018).
3. See especially the prefatory section of the monograph titled "Indecent Theology." Marcella Althaus-Reid calls us to scrutinize "the dialectics of decency and indecency" in this one-page summary and to bring into mainstream theological discourse issues of sexuality—indeed, to appreciate the sexual dimensions of the theological enterprise. Such a disciplinary intervention implies, in my mind, deconstructing altogether the disciplinary "politics of respectability" that govern not only the ways we talk about the body, but the norms that determine those methodologies theologians often consider unassailable as well.
4. A strong claim can be made that The Africana Bible (2010) was the first such project.
5. Kevin Young, "Overture" to *The Grey Album: On the Blackness of Blackness* (Minneapolis, MN: Graywolf, 2012), 3–5.

6. Ishmael Reed, "Neo-Hoodoo Manifesto," in *Conjure: Selected Poems, 1963–1970* (Amherst: University of Massachusetts Press, 1972), 20–25.
7. Young, *The Grey Album*, 14, 15, 19.
8. Young, *The Grey Album*, 11–13.
9. Young, *The Grey Album*, 15.
10. Young, *The Grey Album*, 14.
11. On which, see S. Finley, M. Guillory, and H. R. Page Jr., eds., *Esotericism in African American Religious Experience: "There is a Mystery"* (Leiden: E. J. Brill, 2014), and H. R. Page Jr., "The Bible and Africana Esotericism—Toward an Architectonic for Interdisciplinary Study," in *Hidden Truths from Eden: Esoteric Readings of Genesis 1–3*, ed. S. Scholz and V. Stichele (Atlanta, GA: Society of Biblical Literature, 2014), 213–28.
12. Hugh Page Jr., "Studies in Applied Ethnology and Afrodiasporic Exegesis—The Case of the Medium at Endor," for the African-American Theology and Biblical Hermeneutics Group, 1994 AAR/SBL Annual Meeting, Chicago, IL.
13. I am choosing at this point neither to reproduce nor to share these earlier papers, and to treat them as what I would call intentionally misplaced "shadow books," to extend Young's taxonomy (Young, 11)—i.e., works that I choose as an author selectively to disclose. In so doing, I honor an old family dictum: "Tell some. Keep some. You'll always have some."
14. One might think of these as individuals comfortable negotiating the various "Modes of Being" identified by L. LeShan in *Alternate Realities: The Search for the Full Human Being* (New York: M. Evans, 1976), 86–119—i.e., the "Sensory," "Clairvoyant," "Transpsychic," and "Mythic."
15. Robert Farris Thompson, "the power-to-make-things-happen," in *Flash of the Spirit: African and Afro-American Art and Philosophy*, 1st ed. (New York: Random House, 1983), 5.
16. Young, *The Grey Album*, 11–13.
17. Young, *The Grey Album*, 11–14.
18. I would place myself in this cohort.
19. Here, I am applying Murray's contention that "improvisation is the ultimate human (i.e., heroic) endowment" (A. Murray, *The Hero and the Blues* [New York: Vintage Books, 1973], 107) to the work of philologists seeking to break free from narrow strictures defining their scholarly endeavors.
20. H. U. Gumbrecht, *The Powers of Philology: Dynamics of Textual Scholarship* (Urbana: University of Illinois Press, 2003), 84–85.

∽ Afterword

CATHERINE KELLER

This Afterword can offer no last word. No final wrap, no closure. The book might close, but its subject, its world of subjects, will not. They do not and will not come to a stopping point in time, space, or resolution. As these essays so magnificently demonstrate, the embodiments, the interpretations, the hyphenations of "African" do not stop moving, gathering, proliferating. The diaspora—from *diasperein,* to scatter or to sow—does not cease in its dispersion to root and survive, across a globe of diversely inhospitable social soils. As the Introduction puts it, "This global mapping from the back/black-side is the phenomenon of study and analysis that gathers around broken spaces, broken bodies, and broken stories." So this conversation has gathered around the brokenness of people, peoples, denied even their humanity, let alone native soil.

Life Under the Baobab Tree undulates between a work of memory and of new creation—while never losing the cadence of its cultural complexity or the pathway of its liberating epistemology. "This is a hermeneutics," the editors wrote, "that examines the 'trans' of transatlantic and trans-Sahara as a form of narrative and spatial lacuna" (not "narrative and spatial transition"). In that interval, that pause, the essays work back, from the blackside—and all the more powerfully, poetically, pry open worthy futures.

It is an honor for our Transdisciplinary Theological Colloquium to host this conversation. Blackness has been voiced amid the many tones and colors of these twenty years of colloquia. But only now has it taken center stage. And so finally the "trans" of transdisciplinarity, not without its own transgressive manifolds, here rediscovers itself in that transatlantic, trans-

Saharan interval. These essays therefore have been mindfully multiple in their disciplinarity, within, between, beyond the areas of theology, religion, the Bible, and so on. Refusing the divide-and-conquer discipline of the modern academy—religious, secular, or postsecular—the conceptualizations here practiced hold themselves accountable, hold us all accountable, to the greater multiplicity that is at stake in this volume. It not an abstract multiplicity, with a plurality of separable units, nor a manifold that captures its many in an overarching unity. What we might in the language of other TTC's call its plurisingularity reveals a dynamism that is "quintessentially 'Africana' in its centering of multiplicity." No single national or continental form of Blackness commands the terms of this conversation. Arguments about which limb of the Africana tree is most endangered, or most radical, or most essential do not occupy these thinkers. Yet its multiplicity is for that reason all the more disclosive, indeed coherent. Indeed, it is its framing as quintessentially Africana that demonstrates a nonhierarchical coherence at work within and through its complexity.

No doubt you have begun to imagine a splendid earth-toned trunk reaching out through numerous branches, which grow into a great nonlinearity of intersections. So there unfolds in this volume not just a prose of multiple voices, skins, methods, styles, actions. For as the Introduction makes clear: Unfolding across the essays we read a poetics, indeed specifically a "poetics of trees" framed as a "relationality of simultaneous multiplicity." So, the density of poetry and fiction twined through these essays performs an alternative discourse. It models a creativity that intensifies resistance to the myriad forms of white supremacism. And it refuses reduction to opposition alone. At the end we find ourselves where this collection has gathered all along: under the Baobab Tree. This African "tree of life" that can survive, indeed thrive, in tough, dry, and rocky landscapes itself offers nourishment and shade. In its wide adaptability and variation, its tough and grounded expansiveness, it has provided metaphorical cover for this conversation and for the possibility of new and spreading versions of Africana solidarity. In this the baobab's sheer size matters: The diameter of its trunk runs seven to eleven meters, far wider than any other tree. Facing conditions of local oppression, of regional colonialism, communities of African descent may gather courage and force from the immense width of the Africana diaspora. That this is no top-down power, no matter of sheer arboreal height, is key to the metaphor. This book delights in the designation of the baobab as "the upside-down tree," as its branches, when bare, look like roots. It troubles normal parameters of breadth and height, as does the down-to-earth and yet towering scope of the present conversation. Between the voices of this conversation is echoing the African Ewe proverb, "Wisdom is like a Baobab tree; no individual can grasp it." And so this Africana thinking never comes down to mere individual capacity or lone authorship—it roots and grows in the ethics, the politics, and the poetry of its solidarity. The relationality this wisdom—this very conversation— expresses is already more than one can get one's arms or mind around—and so it fosters a solidarity adequate to the task, the nearly impossible task, of racial justice across the diasporic globe.

Yet for all the massive strength of the ancient baobab, these essays never convey mere optimism. This is a powerful expression of "hope draped in black" in the face of great vulnerability. And I am sad to add, the literal baobab shares this vulnerability. It is one of the species susceptible to the extremes of climate change. (Racially marked populations are of course far more vulnerable to and far less responsible for climate change than white and wealthy ones. This anthology is mindful of the ecological dimension of colonialism and neocolonialism.) One in seven of the varieties of baobab is now threatened with extinction. At the same time that leaves still plenty of upside-down tree power—metaphorical and material—to gather with, under, and through. In the mattering of Black lives, in the renewed and renewing vitality of African roots and planetary branchings, multiplicity becomes a formidable force of solidarity. Its world-rich manifold of spirits, theologies, and religions twist and branch with its most worldly critiques.

White supremacism overt and hidden may bring down the tree of earthly life. But that outcome is unnecessary. A transition beyond its hegemonic pattern of pale destruction is also underway. So the voluminous strength and shade of *Life Under the Baobab Tree* provides a space, a lacuna, for the transdisciplinary poetics and practices of this postcolonial transit.

CONTRIBUTORS

'SHOLA D. ADEGBITE is a PhD candidate at Union Theological Seminary, NY. She engages the Bible using storytelling as well as her Yoruba-African background and socio-historical and ideology criticisms. She also has interests in gender, embodied, and earth-centered approaches with a goal of liberation, justice, healing, and diversity. She is a teaching fellow for introductory level classes on the Bible, New Testament, and church history.

AN YOUNTAE is an associate professor of religious studies at California State University, Northridge. Dr. An specializes in religions of the Americas with a particular focus on Latin America and the Caribbean. His research focuses on the construction of religion, race, and political identity in colonial and postcolonial Americas. He is author of *The Decolonial Abyss* (Fordham University Press, 2016), and *The Coloniality of the Secular: Race, Religion, and Poetics of World-Making* (forthcoming 2023, Duke University Press). He is co-editor with Eleanor Craig of *Beyond Man: Race, Coloniality, and Philosophy of Religion* (Duke University Press, 2021).

DESMOND COLEMAN, PhD, is a humanities teaching fellow in philosophy at Alvernia University. His current interests lie at the intersections of critical philosophy of race, Black critical philosophy of film, and the uses of alchemy within Western histories of science, art, theology, and philosophy. He's currently in the process of rewriting his dissertation, for which he received a Ford Foundation Fellowship award, into a book (provisionally titled: "Ruminations on Alchemy and Blackness").

SALIM FARAJI is a professor and former chair of Africana Studies at California State University, Dominguez Hills. He is also the founding executive director of the Master of Arts in International Studies (MAIS) Africa Program at Concordia University Irvine in Ghana, West Africa. He is a member of the International Society for Nubian Studies and a founding member of the William Leo Hansberry Society. He specializes in early Christian history, Africana and Africanist historiography, Coptic studies, and the Kerma, Napatan, Meroitic and Medieval periods of Nubian history. Professor Faraji is a contributor to *Albert Cleage Jr. and the Black Madonna Child*, the *Encyclopedia of African Religion*, the *Oxford Dictionary of African Biography*, and more recently, *Origins and Afterlives of Kush: Proceedings of the University of California at Santa Barbara Conference in Nubian Studies, July 25–27 2019*. He is the author of *The Roots of Nubian Christianity Uncovered: The Triumph of the Last Pharaoh*. Professor Faraji is an ordained minister in the African Methodist Episcopal Church and a practicing African Traditional Priest who has been initiated in both the Akan traditions of Ghana, West Africa, and ancient Egyptian and Nubian religious practice. He is an adjunct faculty member of the University of La Verne's Ecumenical Center for Black Church Studies, Payne Theological Seminary, and is currently president of the Amen-Ra Community Assembly of California-Amen Ra Theological Seminary.

RACHEL ELIZABETH HARDING is a poet, historian, and scholar of religions of the Afro-Atlantic diaspora. A native of Atlanta, Georgia, Dr. Harding teaches in the Ethnic Studies department of the University of Colorado Denver and writes about religion, creativity, and social justice in the experience of communities of African descent in the U.S. and Brazil. Dr. Harding is author of two books: *A Refuge in Thunder*, a history of the Afro-Brazilian religion, Candomblé; and more recently, *Remnants: A Memoir of Spirit, Activism and Mothering*, co-written with her mother, Rosemarie Freeney Harding, on the role of compassion and mysticism in African American social justice organizing. Dr. Harding is also an ebômi (ritual elder) in the Terreiro do Cobre Candomblé community in Salvador, Bahia, Brazil. She co-directs the Veterans of Hope Project—an interdisciplinary initiative on religion, grassroots democracy, and healing, that was founded by her parents, Vincent and Rosemarie Freeney Harding. (www.veteransofhope.org).

CATHERINE KELLER is a professor of constructive theology at the Theological School of Drew University. In her teaching, lecturing, and writing, she develops the relational potential of a theology of becoming. Her books reconfigure ancient symbols of divinity for the sake of a planetary conviviality—a life together across vast webs of difference. Thriving in the interplay of ecological and gender politics, of process cosmology, poststructuralist philosophy and religious pluralism, her work is both deconstructive and constructive in strategy. She is author of several books, including *Facing Apocalypse: Climate, Democracy and Other Last Chances* (2021); *Cloud of the Impossible: Negative Theology and Planetary Entanglements* (2014); *Face of the Deep: A Theology of Becoming* (2003), and many other essays and articles.

MINENHLE NOMALUNGELO KHUMALO is a South African biblical scholar who focuses on reading sacred texts with understandings of popular cultural production of narrative. Her work makes use of ancestral, sociocultural, and academic practices toward constructing pedagogies for collective psychosocial resistance.

ALTHEA SPENCER MILLER is an assistant professor of New Testament, Drew Theological School. Spencer Miller's recent research and work in progress under the heading "Reading with Island Eyes, Speaking in Island Tongues: A Postcolonial, Autoethnographic Approach to Orality" focuses on the development of an oral hermeneutic for decolonizing biblical interpretation. This research includes a teaching interest in Africana studies and religion and the development of oral and Africana pedagogies. Spencer Miller is co-editor of *Feminist New Testament Studies: Global and Future Perspectives* with Kathleen O'Brien Wicker and Musa Dube (2005) and has contributed essays as chapters in many publications since then. One essay that introduces her thinking on orality as a cultural phenomenon is "Creolizing Hermeneutics: A Caribbean Invitation," in *Islands, Islanders, and the Bible: Ruminations* (2015).

PAMELA MORDECAI writes poetry, plays, and long and short fiction. Born and raised in Jamaica, she and her family immigrated to Canada in 1994. A former teacher and teacher-trainer with a PhD in English, Mordecai has authored and co-authored numerous textbooks and edited and co-edited groundbreaking anthologies, especially of Caribbean women's writing. Her poetry has been translated into Spanish, French, Romanian, and Serbian. With her late husband, Martin, she wrote a reference work, *Culture and Customs of Jamaica*. She has published a novel, a short story collection, five children's books, and nine poetry collections, the latest of which are *de book of Joseph*, which completes her New Testament trilogy in Jamaican patwa, and *A Fierce Green Place: New and Collected Poems*. Her poetry is archived at https://mordecai.citl.mun.ca/.

KENNETH N. NGWA is a professor of Hebrew Bible at Drew Theological School. Ngwa's current research interests are in the fields of African/a biblical hermeneutics. He is also the founder and director of the Religion and Global Health Forum at Drew Theological School, an interdisciplinary forum that examines the relation between religion and health, healthy disparities, and collaborative work for health equity. Ngwa is the author of *The Hermeneutics of the 'Happy' Ending in Job 42:7–17* (2005); co-editor of *Navigating African Biblical Hermeneutics: Trends and Themes from Our Pots and Calabashes* (2018); and *Let My People Live: An Africana Reading of Exodus* (2022).

ALIOU CISSÉ NIANG is an associate professor of biblical interpretation—New Testament—at Union Theological Seminary in New York. Niang is the author of *Faith and Freedom in Galatia and Senegal* (2009); co-author of *Text, Image, and Christians in the Graeco-Roman World* (2012); *A Poetics of Postcolonial Biblical Criticism: God, Human-Nature Relationship, and Negritude* (Cascade Books, 2019); "Catholic Epistles," in *Anselm Companion to the New Testament* (Anselm Academic, 2014); "Space and Human Agency in the Making of the Story of Gershom through a Senegalese Christian Lens," *Forum-Journal of Biblical Literature* (2015); "Islandedness, Translation, and Creolization," in *Islands, Islanders, and Bible: RumInations* (2015); "Christianity in Senegal," and "Diola Religion," both in *Encyclopedia of Christianity in the Global South*, ed. Mark A. Lamport and Philip Jenkins (2018).

(THE REV. CANON) HUGH R. PAGE JR. is a professor of theology and Africana studies at the University of Notre Dame, where he also serves as vice president for Institutional Transformation and advisor to the president. He is author, editor, or co-editor of several books, including most recently: *Israel's Poetry of Resistance: Africana Perspectives on Early Hebrew Verse* (2013—as author), *The Fortress Commentary on the Old Testament* (2014—as co-editor), and *Esotericism in African American Religious Experience: "There Is a Mystery"* (2014—as co-editor).

ARTHUR PRESSLEY is an associate professor of psychology and religion at Drew University, where he has also served as academic dean. Pressley is also a clinical psychologist, a past president of the New Jersey Association of Black Psychologists and has worked on numerous international issues, most notably the Childhood Chernobyl Childhood Illness Project. He currently teaches a course titled "Fanon and Psychoanalysis of Black Novels." Some of his published articles include "Using Novels of Resistance to Teach Intercultural Analysis and Empathy"; "Teaching Black: God Talk and Black Thinkers," in *Being Black, Teaching Black: Politics and Pedagogy in Religious Studies*, ed. Nancy Lynne Westfield (2007), and "The Story of Nimrod: A Struggle with Otherness and the Search for Identity," in *African American Religious Life and the Story of Nimrod*, ed. Anthony Pinn and Allen Dwight Callahan (2008).

A. PAIGE RAWSON is an interdisciplinary scholar-practitioner, who spent almost a decade in the ministry before obtaining a PhD in order to study and teach the Bible and theology through feminist, queer, and poststructuralist lenses. Paige's work eschews traditional Western European individualism and its methodologies, and is animated by their commitment to social justice, antiracist epistemological activism, and embodied cognition. Having recently made an exodus out of academia into coaching and consulting, Paige is now happier and more fulfilled than ever.

NIMI WARIBOKO is the Walter G. Muelder Professor of Social Ethics at Boston University. He is one of the most original and provocative economic ethicists, theological theorists, and philosophers in the world today. His original, transdisciplinary oeuvre combines social sciences, philosophy, radical theology, literary, and cultural studies to create new ideas and theories, disrupt conventional wisdom, and promote human flourishing. He is the author of twenty-four monographs, co-editor of six volumes, and multiple journal articles, book reviews, and book chapters. The six pillars of his scholarship are economic ethics, Christian social ethics, African social traditions/political theology, Pentecostal studies, philosophical theology, and literary studies. In 2020 a group of scholars from multiple continents honored Wariboko with a book on his thoughts, *The Philosophy of Nimi Wariboko: Social Ethics, Economy, and Religion*. In the same year, another group organized an international conference on his ideas and their impact on the global academy. Over forty papers were presented at this conference. Some of the papers presented at the 2020 conference will be published as *Public Righteousness: The Performative Ethics of Human Flourishing* (forthcoming). He is also the co-editor of *Pneuma: The Journal of the Society for Pentecostal Study*.

SHARON KIMBERLY WILLIAMS is a clinical lecturer in religion and cultures in the Department of Religion at Iona University. She is a part-time faculty member for the Faith, Health, and Social Equity cohort in the Doctor of Ministry program at Drew University Theological School. Her clinical research training was completed at Brigham and Women's Hospital at Harvard Medical School through a partnership with the Religion and Global Health Forum at Drew. Sharon's research explores music, spirituality, healing, and social activism through the sociocultural lenses of Africana, Black church, Global South, and peace and justice studies. A former justice artist for the Social Justice Leadership Project at Drew, Sharon has performed sacred music and poetry all around the world. She is currently finishing up her first book manuscript, a collection of creative nonfiction essays titled *Breath | Voice | Fire*.

INDEX OF MODERN AUTHORS

'Ali, 'Abdullah Yūsuf, 217
Abble, A., 169
Abraham, Keshia, 298, 306
Adadevoh, Delanyo, 108
Adamo, David T., 18, 307–8, 311–12, 323–24, 378, 398
Adichie, Chimamanda Ngozi, 267, 272
Adogame, Afe, 20
Agamben, Giorgio, 57–58, 62, 72, 369, 396
Agnes, Aladesanmi Omobola, 308, 323
Aguilar, Mario I., 383–84, 398
Akoto-Abutiate, Dorothy, 14, 92–96, 106–9, 113
Alber, Jan, 272
Alford, Kwame Wes, 352
Althaus-Reid, Marcella, 401, 406
Angoula, Jean-Claude, 222
Arendt, Hannah, 36, 185, 193, 369
Asad, Muhammad, 202–3, 217–18
Asante, Emmanuel, 222
Asante, Molefi Kete, 330, 351
Assmann, Jan, 363, 395, 399
Aymer, Margaret P., 252, 268, 378, 398
Ayres, Barbara, 359, 395

Ba, Silvia, 160
Babou, Cheikh Anta, 366, 395
Baldi, B. F., 353
Baldwin, James, 48, 53, 56, 139–41, 164
Barker, P. A., 218
Baum, Robert, 220
Bergson, Henri, 165, 209
Berlant, Lauren, 263, 271
Berthelot, Marcellin, 84, 91
Berti, Anna, 80, 90
Bhabha, Homi, 14, 114, 129–31, 142, 161, 163
bin Muhammad, Ghazi, 216, 222
Biondi, Jean-Pierre, 162
Bird, Phyllis A., 112
Blenkinsopp, Joseph, 324
Blount, Brian K., 374, 397
Bongmba, Elias K., 367, 396
Borg, Marcus, 219
Brand, Dionne, 5, 21
Brett, Mark G., 260, 264, 270
Brodber, Erna, 277, 284–86, 289–93, 296, 302–6
Brown, Scot, 352
Brueggemann, Walter, 204, 219

Brydon, Diana, 161
Bulhan, Hussein Abdilahi, 162
Burbank, Jane, 395
Butler, Judith, 13, 58, 69, 71–72, 74, 97, 111
Butler, Octavia E., 266–67, 272

Caputo, John D., 120
Carby, Hazel V., 29, 31, 34, 44, 55–56
Carroll R., M. Daniel, 397
Carter, J. Kameron, 67, 74
Caruth, Cathy, 40, 55
Cassidy, Frederic G., 305
Césaire, Aimé, 10, 20, 59, 125–26, 131–32, 134, 143, 162–63, 166
Chalmers, David, 82–83
Chan, E. K. F., 353
Cheng, Anne Anlin, 12, 49–50, 56, 269, 271
Chidester, David, 73
Chireau, Yvonne, 3, 20, 231, 234, 404
Christensen, Thomas G., 108
Chung, Youn Ho, 399
Claassens, Juliana, 261, 271
Clark, Andy, 76, 78–83, 87, 90
Clark-Bekederemo, John P., 186, 190, 192–94
Clarke, John Henrik, 330, 337–38, 340, 352
Clements, Ronald, 216
Cone, James H., 156–57, 168–69, 327, 341, 352–53
Cooke, Michael G., 297, 306
Cooper, Frederick, 395
Cooper-White, Pamela, 37, 55
Crossan, John Dominic, 217
Crow, Captain Hugh, 193
Dalfovo, A. T., 109
Davidson, Steed, 378, 398

de Benoist, Joseph Roger, 162, 221
de Chardin, Pierre Teilhard, 146, 151–53, 155, 167, 209
Deacon, Terrence William, 76–78, 82–83, 87, 90
Dekar, Paul, 222
Deleuze, Gilles, 96, 103, 109, 116–21, 124, 268
Depestre, René, 163
Diagne, Souleymane Bachir, 162, 165–66, 209, 220
Diatta, Christian Sina, 222
Diatta, Nazaire N., 158, 169
Diédhiou, Paul, 221
Dieng, Bassirou, 169
Diop, Alioune, 141, 164
Diop, Mamadou, 166, 220–21
Diouf, Léon, 212, 214, 221–22
Dioum, Baidy, 147, 166
Doob Sakenfeld, Katherine, 252, 268
Dozeman, Thomas B., 384–85, 398–99
Drewal, Henry John, 313, 325–27
Du Bois, W. E. B., 238, 330, 338, 340, 373–75, 397
Dube, Musa W., 129, 161, 167, 312, 324, 413
Dupuy, Jean-Pierre, 188, 194
Dussel, Enrique, 71, 74
Dzobo, Noah K., 108–9

Eco, Umberto, 117
Eisenhower, Dwight D., 373, 397
Eliezer, Pirkei DeRabbi, 322, 327
Ellison, Ralph, 140–41, 164
Ephirim-Donkor, Anthony, 348, 354
Equiano, Olaudah, 276–78, 280, 284, 286–89, 294–97, 299, 301, 304, 306
Estes, Steve, 168
Eudell, Demetrius, 68, 74

Evans, Craig, 219
Evans Jr., James H., 339–40, 353
Ewane, F. Kange, 366, 395
Exum, Cheryl, 262, 271
Eyerman, Ron, 378, 398

Fabre, Michael, 164
Fanon, Frantz, 12–13, 41, 49–51, 57, 59, 68, 70–72, 74–75, 82–84, 87–88, 90, 125, 134, 141, 143, 156–57, 162–63, 165–66, 168–69
Farajaje-Jones, Elias, 330–31, 352
Faraji, Salim, 18–19, 352, 412
Ferreira dos Reis, Isabel Cristina, 234
Fewell, Danna Nolan, 257, 261, 270–72
Fields, Barbara Jeanne, 91
Fields, Karen E., 89, 91
Finley, S., 407
Floyd-Thomas, Stacy M., 20
Foucault, Michel, 61–62, 72, 83, 111, 369–70
Frassinetti, Francesca, 80, 90
Freitheim, Terence E., 395
Frymer-Kensky, Tikva, 263, 271
Fulop, Timothy E., 354
Furnish, Paul, 112, 217

Gadjigo, Samba, 163
Gates, Henry Louis (Skip), 38, 40, 55
Geismar, Peter, 162
Gillespie, Michael Patrick, 255, 269–70, 272
Gilroy, Paul, 2, 12, 49, 236, 238, 240, 243, 249, 271
Ginés de Sepúlveda, Juan, 64, 73
Glissant, Édouard, 14, 92–96, 98–107, 109, 113–25, 224
Gonzalez-Barrera, Ana, 353
Gordon, Lewis, 59, 72

Goss, Robert E., 111
Gourevitch, Philip, 398
Gourgouris, Stathis, 192
Grillo, Laura S., 347, 354
Guattari, Félix, 96, 103, 109, 116, 118–21, 124, 268
Gugelberger, Georg M., 161
Guillory, M., 407
Gumbrecht, H. U., 406–7
Gunda, Masiiwa R., 363, 395

Hamidou Sall, Elhadj Abdoul, 208, 220
Hanke, Lewis, 73
Hansberry, William Leo, 330, 338, 352
Harris, Jennifer, 285, 303
Harrison, Renee K., 253, 269
Hartman, Dorota, 395
Hartman, Saidiya, 44, 56
Havea, Jione, 378, 398
Heard, R. Christopher, 257, 259, 261, 270–72
Hilfrich, Carola, 399
Hoffmeier, James K., 397
Honig, Bonnie, 193
Hood, Robert, 400–1
hooks, bell, 11, 17, 21, 132, 161, 250–51, 254, 268–69, 402
Hopkins, Dwight N., 342, 353
Horsley, Richard A., 217
Horton, Robin, 176, 182–83, 192–93
Houston, James M., 249
Hucks, Tracey E., 3, 20, 334–36, 351–52
Humez, Jean, 232, 234
Hutchinson, George, 30, 55

Iriki, Atsushi, 79–80, 90
Issitt, Micah, 312, 314, 325–26

Jeremias, Jörg, 399
Jones, G. I., 176, 191, 193
Jones, William R., 400–1
Joseph, Richard A., 395
Joyce, James, 117
Juergensmeyer, Mark, 201, 214, 218, 220

Kaltner, John, 218
Kane, Abdoulaye, 21
Kane, Cheikh Hamidou, 127, 129–30, 132, 142, 160, 165
Kane, Ousmane Oumar, 164
Karamaga, André, 382, 398
Karengam, Maulana, 351
Keane, Webb, 288, 304
Keener, Craig S., 397
Keita, Meghan, 352
Keizer, Garret, 201, 218
Kellogg, Catherine, 74
Kendi, Ibram X., 352
Kesteloot, Lilyan, 160, 162–64, 166
Kiboko, Kabamba J., 377, 397
Kincaid, Jamaica, 43, 55
King Jr., Martin Luther, 218
Kirszenberg, John, 109
Klassen, William, 216, 219
Kleinman, Arthur, 379, 398
Kleinman, Joan, 379, 398
Kline, David, 268
Konings, Piet, 396
Koskenniemi, Marti, 73
Krebs, Ronald R., 260, 270
Krieger, Milton, 395

Laburthe-Tolra, Philippe, 168
Le Page, R. B., 305
Lebron, Christopher J., 168
Lecourt, Jean, 221

Leedy, Todd H., 21
Legun, Colin, 20–21
Leichtman, Mara, 221
LeShan, L., 407
Lindqvist, Pekka, 399
Locke, Alain, 163
López, Gustavo, 353
Lorde, Audre, 304
Lovelace, Vanessa, 253, 263, 271

M'Baye, Babacar, 140, 164
Mabuza, Solomuzi, 255, 269
Madubuko, John Chijioke, 376–77, 397
Magesa, Laurenti, 349, 354
Malabou, Catherine, 74
Manga, Mohamed Lamine, 221
Manger, Itzik, 272
Manning, Patrick, 21
Maravita, Angelo, 79–80, 90
Marut, Jean-Claude, 221
Masenya, Madipoane (Ngwan'a Mphahlele), 311, 324
Masoga, Alpheus, 324
Massumi, Brian, 268
Matory, J. Lorand, 20
Mbembe, Achille, 62, 73, 368–72, 395–98
Mbiti, John S., 165, 327, 342, 353
Mbuvi, Andrew, 327, 376, 397
Mbuwayesango, Dora R., 269
McKittrick, Katherine, 73–74
Mettinger, Tryggve N. D., 110
Meyers, Carol, 112
Mignolo, Walter, 68, 74
Milgrom, Jacob, 198–99, 216–17
Millard, Alan R., 397
Miller, Patrick D., 199, 217
Mizuno, Nubohiro, 396
Monson, Ingrid, 21

Moore, Erika, 249
Moore, Stephen D., 167, 417–18
Moreau, Abou Bakr, 205, 219
Mosala, Itumeleng J., 251, 267
Mphahlele, Ezekiel, 163
Murphy, Rosalyn F. T., 253, 268
Murray, A., 407
Murrell, Nathaniel Samuel, 281–82, 302–3
Muslim, Imam Abdul-Husain, 216
Mveng, Englebert, 305

N'Diaye-Corréard, Geneviéve, 169
N'Diaye, Papa Gueye, 166
N'Dong, Henri Biram, 166
Nagel, Thomas, 82–83
Nahum, Sana, 167, 217–18
Nardal, Paulette, 164
Nayar, Pramod, 72
Ndao, Papa Alioune, 220
Neale Hurston, Zora, 7, 21, 31, 35
Nelson, Richard D., 216
Némo, Geneviève Lecuir, 221
Ngoh, Victor Julius, 396
Niang, Aliou Cissé, 14–16, 159–61, 169, 216, 220, 395
Nkrumah, Kwame, 97, 111–13, 330, 351–52
Nora, Pierre, 9–11, 21
Nugent, Paul, 396
Nyamnjoh, Francis, 367, 396

Oates, William, 176, 191–92
Ochshorn, Judith, 112
Oduyoye, Mercy Amba, 343, 353
Oduyoye, Modupe A., 376, 397
Okazawa, Ryosuke, 396
Okpewho, Isidore, 174, 187, 192, 194
Olojede, Funlola, 311, 324

Olupona, Jacob K., 3, 20, 345–49, 351, 354
Omoera, Osakue S., 326
Omoruan, Daniel E., 326
Opoku, Kofi Asare, 329, 342, 349, 351, 353–54

Pagden, Anthony, 73
Page Jr., Hugh R., 407
Palmié, Stephan, 16, 223–24, 234
Paris, Peter J., 345, 354
Parker, Joseph, 300, 306
Phillips, Layli, 227, 228, 234

Rabaka, Reiland, 138, 163
Raboteau, Albert J., 335, 354
Ramose, Mogobe B., 169
Rancière, Jacques, 180, 184, 186, 193–94
Rawson, A. Paige, 13–14, 107–8, 110, 113, 116, 122
Reed, Ishmael, 402, 407
Rendsburg, Gary A., 397
Rey, Philippe, 169
Rimbaud, Arthur, 157, 168
Rivera, Mayra, 68, 74, 122
Robinson Waldman, Marilyn, 220
Ross, Doran H., 314, 326
Ross, Eric, 221
Rubin, Uri, 399
Ruelle, Charles-Émile, 84, 91
Russell, Heather, 3/, 44, 55, 304
Russworm, TreaAndrea M., 250, 253–54, 268

Saayman, Willem, 106–7, 109
Sahgal, Neha, 353
Said, Edward, 14, 129–31, 138, 142–43, 161, 164
Samuel, Petal, 285, 303–4

Sanneh, Lamin, 215, 220, 222
Santner, Eric L., 193
Sarras, Niveen, 321–22, 326
Sartre, Jean-Paul, 137, 138, 141–42, 163
Schaeffer, Francis August, 146, 166
Schmitt, Carl, 62, 192, 369
Scott, David, 60, 72
Segovia, Fernando F., 160, 167
Sellers, Robert, 222
Sembène, Ousmane, 136, 163
Semenenko, Aleksei, 279, 303
Senghor, Léopold Sédar, 10, 14–15, 126–60, 195, 197, 204–13, 216, 219–21
Serequeberhan, Tsenay, 169
Sharpley-Whiting, T. Denean, 164
Sherwood, Yvonne, 253, 265, 268, 270–72
Sheth, Falguni A., 55
Shinan, Avigdor, 386–87, 399
Smith, Greg, 353
Smith, Shanell, 395
Sobel, Mechal, 354
Soyinka, Wole, 163, 207–8, 220
Spickard, Jim, 20
Spivak, Gayatri Chakravorty, 14, 129, 131, 142, 161
Spohn, William C., 201, 217
Staley, Jeffery L., 167
Stewart Diakité, Dianne, 281, 334–36, 352
Stone, Ken, 97–98, 111–12
Sugirtharajah, R. S., 142–43, 147, 165, 167
Swartley, Willard M., 204, 218–19, 222

Talbot, P. Amaury, 176, 192
Tamba, Moustapha, 212, 221
Tapp, Anne Michele, 265, 272
Tatum, Beverly, 52, 56

Thandeka, 46, 50, 56
Thioune, Birahim, 206, 219
Thomas, Dominic, 164
Thomas, Douglas H., 221
Thompson, Robert Farris, 404, 407
Timmermann, A., 353
Tiyambe Zeleza, Paul, 20, 395
Townsend Gilkes, Cheryl, 228, 343, 353
Trible, Phyllis, 112, 256–57, 270
Tutu, Desmond, 159, 169, 255

Ukpong, Justin, 18, 310, 324
Umozurike, U. O., 20

Vaillant, Janet, 127, 135, 160–63, 166, 216, 219
Van Ausdale, Debra, 52, 56
Vásquez, Manuel A., 13, 75, 89
Villa-Vicencio, Charles, 392, 399
Volf, Miroslav, 216–17, 222
Volkan, Vamik, 398

Wallace, Michelle M., 56
Waltke, Bruce K., 249
Ware III, Rudolph T., 221
Wariboko, Nimi, 14–15, 192–93
Washington, Mary Helen, 29, 34, 55
Watts, James, 399
Wayne White, Carol, 74
Weems, Renita J., 253, 268, 270
Weheliye, Alexander, 36, 58, 60, 68, 72
Wengst, Klaus, 222
Wenham, Gordon J., 399
West, Gerald O., 18, 309, 397
West, Mona, 111
Westermann, Claus, 217
Wierdorn, Michael, 125
Wilder, Gary, 162
Williams, Delores S., 253, 268

Williams, Joseph, 376, 397
Wilmore, Gayraud S., 339–41, 352–53
Wimbush, Vincent L., 17, 252, 268, 276–80, 287–89, 294–97, 300, 302–6, 354, 400, 406
Win, Adam, 167
Wintz, Le R. P. Edouard, 20
Wlodarczyk, Nathalie, 218
Wolf, Hans Walter, 217, 221
Wolfe, Cary, 72
Wright, Michelle, 3, 20, 37, 49, 51
Wright, N. T., 219
Wright, Richard, 139–41, 163–64

Wynter, Sylvia, 13, 57–61, 63, 69, 72–76, 82–83, 87, 90, 224

Yarrington, Melissa, 216, 222
Yoder, Perry B., 222
Yoo, Philip, 261, 271
Young, Kevin, 402, 404, 406–7
Young, Robert J. C., 129, 161

Zakovitch, Yair, 386–87, 399
Zeleza, Paul Tiyambe, 2, 20, 395
Zips, Werner, 282, 303
Žižek, Slavoj, 192, 194

INDEX OF ANCIENT DOCUMENTS

Genesis, 7, 13, 93–96, 99, 110, 250–52,
    254, 256, 261, 263–65, 271
  1, 98
  1–2, 198
  1–2:4, 97, 112nn44 and 48
  1:1–2, 206, 219n59
  1:2, 153
  1:3, 153
  1:6, 153
  1:9, 153
  1:11, 153
  1:14–15, 153
  1:20, 153
  1:24, 153
  1:26, 153
  1:26–28, 202
  1:27, 198
  1:28, 154
  1:30, 167n111, 217n17
  2–3, 96, 107n4, 110
  2:7, 154, 157, 197, 199, 202, 215
  2:9–3:24, 110n30
  2:16b–17, 112n42
  2:22, 111n36, 112n47
  2:23, 111n36–37, 112n47
  3, 98
  3:1–5, 112n44
  3:6, 110nn33 and 34, 111n36, 112n47
  3:7, 111n35, 112n47
  3:9, 120
  3:9–10, 112n46
  3:11–12, 112n46
  3:16–20, 97, 111n36
  3:24, 113n53, 122n120
  6, 376
  9:11–17, 202
  9:13–14, 202
  9:13–17, 202, 203
  12–21, 260
  12–25, 263
  12:1–5, 260
  12:1–9, 264
  12:7–8, 260
  12:10–17, 264
  13:18, 260
  14:17–24, 264
  15:6, 260
  15:13, 271n48
  16, 256, 258, 261
  16–21, 259

Genesis (continued)
   16–22, 261, 264
   16:1–4, 264
   16:2, 256
   16:4, 257
   16:6a, 256
   16:9–12, 257
   16:12, 257
   16:13, 257–58
   17, 258, 261
   17:3, 258
   17:18, 258
   17:20, 258
   17:23–27, 264
   18, 265
   18:2, 258
   18–19, 258
   18:19, 260
   19:24–26, 258
   20:1–11, 264
   21, 258–59, 261–62
   21–22, 264
   21:5, 258
   21:11, 259
   21:11–12, 262
   21:16, 259
   22, 252, 259–63, 271
   22:2, 12, 16, 261–62
   22:10–13, 15–18, 262
   25, 259
   25:11, 262

Exodus, 249, 363, 379
   1:1, 385
   2, 388
   2:23–25, 382
   3, 357
   3:7–8, 382
   3:12, 385
   3:14, 123n123
   4:15–16, 378
   4:22–23, 371
   5:1, 388
   6:9, 6
   8:1, 240
   12:38, 385
   13:19, 360
   15:21–27, 389
   16:3, 246
   19:1, 385
   19:2–3, 385
   19–24, 384
   19–34, 384
   19:4, 360
   20–24, 399n81
   20–31, 386
   20:3–17, 198
   20:10, 198
   22:21, 198
   23:9–12, 198
   25:8, 399n81
   32, 364, 385–87
   32:12, 389
   32:16, 394
   32:21, 386
   32:23–24, 388
   33:1, 385
   33:1–6, 357
   33:2, 3, 394n1
   33:7–11, 394n1
   33:11, 356
   33:12, 356
   33:12–13, 357
   33:12–17, 356
   33:17–23, 355
   33:19, 357
   33:20, 357
   33:21–23, 357

34, 357, 364, 394
34:1, 394
34:28–30, 362
35–Num 10, 384
40:34–35, 362

Leviticus
16:29, 198
19:10, 33–34, 198
19:17–18, 198
19:18, 197, 199–200, 217n26
19:18, 34, 198

Numbers
15:14, 198

Deuteronomy, 363, 384
5:7–21, 198
5:14, 198
6:4–5, 198
6:4–9, 198
6:4–19, 199
6:5, 197–200, 202, 217n26
9, 387
9:18, 387
9:21, 387
9:27–28, 387
10:12, 198
11:13, 22, 198
19:9, 198
24:17–21, 198
27:19, 198
30:6, 16, 19–20, 198

Judges
19, 265
311
Ruth

1 Samuel
28, 403
28:7, 403

1 Kings
12:26–30, 386

2 Kings
7, 315
14:25, 326n34
17:16, 387

Esther, 311

Psalms, 239
72:7, 203
74:2, 385
91, 362
95:4, 385
106, 387
106:7–8, 387
106:23, 387
106:30–31, 387
137:1–4, 243

Proverbs, 13, 93–96, 99, 105, 108–10, 122n117, 124n127
1, 107n4, 122n117
1:20–21, 122n119
1:27–33, 122n118
3, 107n4, 110n33, 122nn117 and 123
3:14–17, 122n117
3:18, 92, 101, 116n79
3:19, 104, 121n112
4, 107n4
4:7a, 104, 121n113
6:20–22, 199
8, 107n4, 121n109, 122nn117,119–20 and 123

Proverbs (*continued*)
  8:4, 108n15
  8:7, 123n123
  8:12, 14, 17, 27, 123n123
  8:17, 122n123
  8:22–31, 123n123
  8:35, 36, 123n124
  8:36, 121n107
  9, 107n4, 122n117, 123n125
  9:5–6, 123n125
  25:1–29, 108n20

Isaiah
  48:18, 203
  52:13–53:12, 377
  54:13–14, 203
  59:8, 203
  60:17, 203

Jeremiah
  20:9, 356
  29:13, 122n123, 123n123

Ezekiel
  3:3, 356
  16:4–7, 371
  34:25, 218n41
  37, 377
  37:26, 218n41

Hosea
  2:4–7, 371

Jonah, 312, 315–16, 326n34
  1, 316
  2:1, 326n34
  2:2, 326n34
  2:11, 326n34

4 Maccabees, 110n29

2 Esdras, 110n29

Matthew
  1:20–21, 206
  1:21–23, 219n59
  5:9, 204
  5:45–48, 199
  6:2–3, 217n30
  6:10, 169n136, 216n2
  6:33, 211
  7:12, 199, 215
  7:21, 195
  8:26, 219n50
  10:13, 204
  18:20, 219n59
  22:37–39, 199
  26–28, 219n59
  26:52, 157
  27, 377
  28:18–20, 219n59

Mark
  4:39, 219n50
  5:34, 204
  9:50, 204
  10:5–6, 200
  10:45, 146
  12:28, 217n27
  12:30–31, 199
  15, 377

Luke
  1:26–35, 219n59
  1:78–79, 204
  2:10, 199
  2:14, 204

4:18–19, 146, 200
5:34, 204
6:21, 215
6:31, 199–200
6:46, 216n1
8:24, 219n50
8:48, 204
10:5–6, 204
10:17–24, 200
10:23–37, 200
10:25, 200
10:25–33, 200
10:27, 199
10:30–37, 200
10:33, 200
10:33–37, 197, 200
17:16, 200
22:19–20, 219n59
23, 377
23:34, 158
24:13–37, 219n59

John
1:1, 14, 154
1:1–4, 123n123
1:1–5, 206, 219n59
1:1–14, 153
1:14, 206, 219n59
3:16, 154
4:7, 9, 22, 200
4:39–40, 200
6:35, 48, 123n123
8:12, 123n123
8:48, 200
8:58, 123n123
9:5, 123n123
10:9, 11, 123n123
11:25, 123n123
13:34–35, 152
14:6, 123n123
14:27, 204
15:1, 123n123
19, 377
20:10–27, 219n59

Acts, 147
1:1–9, 219n59
2:1–20, 206
2:1–23, 219n59
8:25, 200

Romans
1:7, 204
5–8, 204
8:19–23, 207
11:17, 109n26

1 Corinthians
1:3, 204
1:10, 152
11:23–26, 206, 219n59
13:12, 357
15:35–44, 160n8
15:37–44, 128

2 Corinthians
1:2, 204
5:17, 207

Galatians
1:3, 204
2:20, 153
3:1, 206–7
5:14, 151, 199
5:22–23, 152
6:14–16, 207

Ephesians, 376
    1:2, 204

Philippians
    1:2, 204
    4:7–9, 204

Colossians
    1:2, 204

1 Thessalonians
    1:1, 204
    5:23, 204

2 Thessalonians
    1:2, 204

1 Timothy
    1:2, 204

2 Timothy
    1:2, 204

Titus
    1:4, 204

Philemon
    3, 204

James
    2:8, 167, 199
    4:7–10, 199
    4:20–21, 199

1 Peter
    1:2, 204

2 Peter
    1:2, 204

2 John
    3, 204

Jude
    2, 204
    9, 362

Revelation
    1:4, 204
    1:8, 152
    21:6, 152
    22:13, 152

Al-Qur'an
    Al-ʿAhzāb 33:4, 199
    Al-Baqarah 2:165, 199
    Al-Hijr 15:28–29, 197
    Al-N¯' 4.114n625, 217n30
    An-N¯ a, 4.114, 195, 201, 211
    An-N¯a' 4.114n138, 217n30
    Az-Zumar 39:23, 199
    b. Sabb. 31.a, 199
    Hûd 11:25–49, 197, 203
    Hûd 11:37, 45–46, 203
    Hûd 11:47–48, 218n39
    Hûd 11:48, 203, 218n40

Hadiths
    Hadith 13, 216n2
    Hadith 15, 216n2

TRANSDISCIPLINARY THEOLOGICAL COLLOQUIA

Laurel Kearns and Catherine Keller, eds., *Ecospirit: Religions and Philosophies for the Earth.*

Virginia Burrus and Catherine Keller, eds., *Toward a Theology of Eros: Transfiguring Passion at the Limits of Discipline.*

Ada María Isasi-Díaz and Eduardo Mendieta, eds., *Decolonizing Epistemologies: Latina/o Theology and Philosophy.*

Stephen D. Moore and Mayra Rivera, eds., *Planetary Loves: Spivak, Postcoloniality, and Theology.*

Chris Boesel and Catherine Keller, eds., *Apophatic Bodies: Negative Theology, Incarnation, and Relationality.*

Chris Boesel and S. Wesley Ariarajah, eds., *Divine Multiplicity: Trinities, Diversities, and the Nature of Relation.*

Stephen D. Moore, ed., *Divinanimality: Animal Theory, Creaturely Theology.* Foreword by Laurel Kearns.

Melanie Johnson-DeBaufre, Catherine Keller, and Elias Ortega-Aponte, eds., *Common Goods: Economy, Ecology, and Political Theology.*

Catherine Keller and Mary-Jane Rubenstein, eds., *Entangled Worlds: Religion, Science, and New Materialisms*.

Kent L. Brintnall, Joseph A. Marchal, and Stephen D. Moore, eds., *Sexual Disorientations: Queer Temporalities, Affects, Theologies*.

Karen Bray and Stephen D. Moore, eds., *Religion, Emotion, Sensation: Affect Theories and Theologies*.

Clayton Crockett and Catherine Keller, eds., *Political Theology on Edge: Ruptures of Justice and Belief in the Anthropocene*.

Kenneth N. Ngwa, Aliou Cissé Niang, and Arthur Pressley, eds., *Life Under the Baobab Tree: Africana Studies and Religion in a Transitional Age*.

www.ingramcontent.com/pod-product-compliance
Lightning Source LLC
Chambersburg PA
CBHW020348080526
44584CB00014B/935